After America

Narratives for the Next Global Age

Paul Starobin

VIKING

VIKING
Published by the Penguin Group
Penguin Group (USA) Inc., 375 Hudson Street,
New York, New York 10014, U.S.A.
Penguin Group (Canada), 90 Eglinton Avenue East, Suite 700,
Toronto, Ontario, Canada M4P 2Y3
(a division of Pearson Penguin Canada Inc.)
Penguin Books Ltd, 80 Strand, London WC2R 0RL, England
Penguin Ireland, 25 St Stephen's Green, Dublin 2, Ireland
(a division of Penguin Books Ltd)
Penguin Books Australia Ltd, 250 Camberwell Road, Camberwell,
Victoria 3124, Australia
(a division of Pearson Australia Group Pty Ltd)
Penguin Books India Pvt Ltd, 11 Community Centre, Panchsheel Park,
New Delhi — 110 017, India
Penguin Group (NZ), 67 Apollo Drive, Rosedale, North Shore 0632,
New Zealand (a division of Pearson New Zealand Ltd)
Penguin Books (South Africa) (Pty) Ltd, 24 Sturdee Avenue,
Rosebank, Johannesburg 2196, South Africa

Penguin Books Ltd, Registered Offices:
80 Strand, London WC2R 0RL, England

First published in 2009 by Viking Penguin,
a member of Penguin Group (USA) Inc.

1   3   5   7   9   10   8   6   4   2

Grateful acknowledgment is made for permission to reprint an excerpt from "Musée des Beaux Arts" from *Collected Poems* by W. H. Auden. Copyright 1940 and renewed 1968 by W. H. Auden. Used by permission of Random House, Inc.

While the author has made every effort to provide accurate telephone numbers and Internet addresses at the time of publication, neither the publisher nor the author assumes any responsibility for errors, or for changes that occur after publication. Further, the publisher does not have any control over and does not assume any responsibility for author or third-party Web sites or their content.

Library of Congress Cataloging-in-Publication Data

Starobin, Paul.
After America: life after the American century / by Paul Starobin.
p. cm.
Includes index.
ISBN 978-0-670-02094-2
1. United States—Civilization—1945–   2. United States—Foreign relations—2001–
3. International relations—21st century.   I. Title.

E169.12.S737 2009
973.91—dc22
2008046685

Printed in the United States of America

Set in Warnock Pro • Designed by Alissa Amell

For Samuel and Deora: "Seek Truth Always."

And indeed there is a serious criticism here, to any one who knows history; since the things that grow are not always the things that remain; and pumpkins of that expansiveness have a tendency to burst. I was always told that Americans were harsh, hustling, rather rude and perhaps vulgar; but they were very practical and the future belonged to them. I confess I felt a fine shade of difference; I liked the Americans; I thought they were sympathetic, imaginative, and full of fine enthusiasms; the one thing I could not always feel clear about was their future. I believe they were happier in their frame-houses than most people in most houses; having democracy, good education, and a hobby of work; the one doubt that did float across me was something like, "Will all this be here at all in two hundred years?"

—A visitor from England, G. K. Chesterton,
in *What I Saw in America*, 1922

Contents

Prologue

High Tide: August 1991, Moscow

The crowd flooded onto Lubyanka Ploshad, one of central Moscow's immense public squares, named for the fortresslike building that served as the headquarters of the KGB. It was a spontaneous gathering of at least ten thousand, perhaps as many as fifteen thousand, and it included rowdy, drunken young men as well as elderly pensioners. Night was falling and the mood was celebratory. A desperate attempt by leaders of the KGB to take power in a coup had ended in failure, and everyone could sense that the Soviet Union itself might not have much longer to live. Soviet monuments all around Moscow were under physical assault, and this group had gathered at one of the most infamous of them all: "Iron Felix," a giant fifteen-ton bronze statue of Felix Dzerzhinsky, the founder of the Cheka, the original Soviet secret police. Iron Felix stood upright in an unbuttoned military overcoat, hands in pockets and head uncovered, and he gazed away from the Lubyanka and down the boulevard leading to the Bolshoi Theatre. Beyond the Bolshoi lay Red Square, containing Lenin's Tomb, and the massive brick walls and tall towers of the Kremlin. Iron Felix had been a fixture of Moscow for more than thirty years. He was unveiled on an afternoon in December of 1958, in a formal ceremony led by then Soviet premier Nikita Khrushchev. The Kremlin's advance team had arranged for a representative selection of scientists, doctors, artists, manual workers, and schoolchildren to be on hand, and the assemblage placed flowers on Iron Felix's granite pedestal. "The twilight descended on the city, but the people stay," *Pravda* duly reported, "bringing in their hearts' great love" to the "fearless knight of the proletarian revolution."

This was at the height of the cold war, one year after the Soviets had launched Sputnik, the world's first satellite. "Whether you like it or not, history is on our side. We will bury you!—*My vas pokhoronim!*" So Khrushchev told a group of Western ambassadors at a reception in Moscow.

Now, on a summer evening thirty-three years later, a crowd had come to bury Iron Felix. His pedestal had already been defaced with inscriptions like "antichrist" and "bloody executioner," and the crowd shouted epithets like "hangman!" Somebody had scrawled swastikas on the Lubyanka. Although the building was dark, the curtains inside were seen to twitch: Armed guards were in place to resist any effort to storm the place. Several men scaled Iron Felix and draped wire ropes around his neck and arms. Others applied a blow-torch to the brass rods securing him to the monument's base. The idea was to attach the ropes to a truck and pull down Iron Felix in a resounding crash. But Moscow city officials, who had rushed to the square on getting word of the gathering, begged the crowd to resist. The officials understood the popular desire to "shatter totalitarianism," as one later put it, but they were worried that a toppled Iron Felix could rip a gaping hole in the square and possibly harm the demonstrators as well. They bargained with the crowd, promising to send for a crane to take Iron Felix away safely.

After several hours, two cranes arrived. As legend has it, one of them came from a construction site at the U.S. embassy, a few miles away on the Garden Ring road. According to one version of the tale, American officials at the embassy happily offered use of the crane for such an agreeable purpose as getting rid of Iron Felix. According to a second version, it was actually the leaders of the Lubyanka Ploshad crowd who somehow managed on their own to snatch the crane from the embassy site. None of these stories was true: A Moscow city official at the scene borrowed both cranes from an Austrian businessman using them for a hotel construction project. The legend, though, was understandable, because the American superpower was widely believed to have a hand in everything happening to bring an end to the Soviet regime. President George H. W. Bush had strongly associated America with the street hero of the moment, Boris Yeltsin, who three days earlier had stood on a tank outside the Russian parliament building to denounce the coup plotters. Appreciative Muscovites had filed past the American embassy chanting, "Bush! Bush! Yeltsin! Bush!"

Again a cable was draped around the neck of Iron Felix, and now one of the cranes lifted the giant statue off the pedestal. For several minutes Iron Felix dangled, suspended in the air as if by a hangman's noose. His shadow appeared on the Lubyanka, the apparition cast by the bright lights of the television crews at the scene. As the crowd burst into applause, fireworks exploded in the Moscow skies. "I am a World War Two veteran. I lived through lies all my life, but I am glad I lived long enough to see this," a spectator, Alexander Lipich, told an American journalist. A British foreign correspondent later wrote that "to be part of such a crowd was to be given the nearest thing to grace in a world from which God had long since departed." Iron Felix was spat on and kicked and then carted away, facedown, on a flatbed truck. In the light of the morning after, young fellows chipped away at the granite base. They were looking for souvenirs—and maybe something more valuable: Rumor had it that the Communist Party's gold was buried under Iron Felix.

Two years earlier, young people a thousand miles to the west had chipped away at the fallen remains of the Berlin Wall. Iron Felix's demise was Moscow's "Berlin Wall" moment, and for amazed Americans watching the pictures on CNN, this was another reason, even a bigger one, to exult. After all, this was not a distant frontier of the Soviet empire—this was ground zero. There was relief and satisfaction all over the country. "The Trail of Freedom Reaches Tyranny's Epicenter," the *New York Times* declared in a headline. The new head of the KGB was "a democrat whose passions include Elvis Presley," the *Atlanta Journal-Constitution* reported. Two months earlier, on his maiden trip to the United States, Yeltsin himself had extolled America as the model for a democratic revolution in Russia. "We're only toddlers compared to you; we have a lot to learn," Yeltsin said to applause from his audience at the National Press Club in Washington.

Polls showed that three-quarters of Russians had a favorable view of America. The year had already witnessed America's quick and decisive victory against Saddam Hussein's forces in Desert Storm, the first Gulf War. With the Soviet Union headed toward the ash heap, it was hard to think of any reason why

America's global influence should not rise still higher. "Should the United States want it to, the moon could become the fifty-first state," Aftab Iqbal, a writer from Pakistan, declared in his 1990 book, *Seatbelt*, based on a visit to America. It turned out not to be so. Iron Felix was lifted from his pedestal of stone on Thursday, August 22, 1991, at 11:28 p.m. Moscow time, 4:28 p.m. in Washington, D.C. This was the high-water mark of the American Century.

Introduction

Early in 1941, Henry Robinson Luce, the founder of *Life* magazine and a man who commanded a large audience in America among both elites and ordinary folks, spoke in Tulsa, Oklahoma, at a dinner hosted by an association of oilmen. His subject, as ever, was America, and more particularly the prospects facing the country with Europe plunged into the war started by Adolf Hitler. Pearl Harbor was still nearly a year away. Luce, though, had a vision of America's global destiny in a world that seemed bent on destruction. "Ours is the power, ours is the opportunity—and ours will be the responsibility whether we like it or not," he declared. In February, these remarks became the basis of "The American Century," a still-famous five-page editorial in the pages of *Life*, in which Luce, as one biographer noted, "equated a happy future with American hegemony." In his exhortation, which began on a page opposite an advertisement for Texaco's Havoline Motor Oil ("distilled and insulated...against heat...against cold"), Luce expanded on America's unique role as a cultural and economic lodestar for a planet that had become hooked on American jazz and Hollywood films and was no less awed by the affluence of America's middle classes. Luce called America "the powerhouse from which the ideals spread throughout the world." America would reign supreme in the world—and America, and the world, would be blessed for it.

Henry Luce was right to predict the coming of the American Century— America had already achieved an economic and cultural global preeminence, and after World War II the country attained a military one as well. But he was clearly wrong to see it as a culmination of history. Luce was driven by missionary impulses, and his view of America as the child of providence ignored the fundamental fact that the rise and fall of civilizations is an organic matter, not one based on destiny or providence. As a great civilization, America is not immune from the life cycles that all civilizations undergo. Their health depends on their internal vigor but also on changes, over which they have limited control, in the external environment. America is a civilization that, like all others before it, cannot operate outside of these principles; America, in short, cannot exist outside of history.

This is not, it seems, an easy lesson to absorb. In an essay published in the summer of 1989, shortly before the fall of the Berlin Wall, Francis Fukuyama, a U.S. State Department policy analyst with a taste for the philosophy of Hegel, echoed Henry Luce in declaring an "end of history." Fukuyama's vision was of the arrival of an American-dominated liberal world order, with no ideological rival in sight. Americans, in their triumphal moments, seem prone to history-ending visions.

Reality has intruded. America is now having its rendezvous with history: American civilization has reached the end of its long ascendancy in the world. The breakdown of American dominance can be seen across the military, political, economic, and cultural dimensions of influence. In the case of the military component, America's ebbing clout is illustrated by its inability to achieve decisive victories in Iraq and the tribal borderlands of Pakistan and Afghanistan. In the meantime, America is finding itself less able politically to bend outcomes to its interest, as seen in its difficulties in persuading powers like China and Russia to take collective action to keep Iran from developing nuclear weapons. In the summer of 2008, Washington watched helplessly as Vladimir Putin's Russian military effectively dismembered Georgia, the small former Soviet republic that provoked Russia's ire by seeking a military, political, and economic alliance with America. In surveys, peoples around the world, including in traditionally America-friendly places like South Korea and Poland, reject "the idea that the United States should continue to be the world's preeminent leader." In these circumstances, American jurisprudence is losing its prestige: Decisions of the U.S. Supreme Court are less frequently cited as guidance in rulings of judges in countries like Canada and Australia, while the work of other legal bodies, like the European Court of Human Rights, is attracting growing global attention. A chief justice of the Supreme Court of Israel has said that the U.S. Supreme Court "is losing the central role it had once had among courts in modern democracies."

America's reduced political leverage is a function in part of its mounting economic liabilities. Foreigners, including the Chinese government, hold more than 50 percent of total U.S. Treasury debt, thus making U.S. foreign policy potentially hostage to the willingness of geopolitical rivals to finance America's borrowings. The dollar is losing its longtime status as the leading currency for global transactions, while a rising share of global output is claimed by the burgeoning economies of Asia, like India's and China's. Institutions established by Washington at the end of the Second World War to manage the global economy, like the International Monetary Fund, are becoming irrelevant. By early 2009, no less an American business icon than General Motors had become a ward of the federal government, while the Obama administration, projecting a $1.75 trillion annual budget deficit, had effectively nationalized Citigroup, the floundering banking giant. The U.S. economic model of deregulated capitalism—the model offered to the world as superior to all others as a way to raise living standards—seems discredited. And on the dimension of cultural influence, the collapse of American hegemony can be seen in the "lost pillar" of Hollywood. What was once perhaps the preeminent means by which American-style values were communicated beyond America's shores has now become, in response to commercial imperatives, a global creator of multicultural product for a culturally diverse marketplace.

A fluid world is entering an interregnum—a period between acts. What comes next—what will be the contours of an "After America" world, of the world in which America is no longer the dominant influence? And how can Americans adjust to a world in which their civilization is no longer dominant? These two questions are at the heart of this book.

My starting premise—that American civilization, broadly considered, has come to the end of its long climb to global preeminence—is a staple in corners of the global intellectual and political elite that *hope* this will prove the case. This is not a surprise: There have always been people who are resentful or envious of America's rise in the world. But there is also a growing consensus behind this premise among those who wish America well—among those who believe that the time of American dominance has been very good not only for America but also for the planet. America has few better overseas friends than the likes of Michael Stürmer of Germany, a historian who in the 1980s was a close advisor on foreign policy to Chancellor Helmut Kohl of the Christian Democratic Party. Stürmer knows everyone in the Washington foreign policy establishment; his name was suggested to me by Richard Burt, a former U.S. ambassador to Germany, for a balanced foreign perspective on America. We met for drinks and dinner on a warm evening in May of 2007 in the executive dining room of the Berlin corporate headquarters of the Axel Springer media conglomerate. Stürmer writes a weekly column for one of Springer's papers. He is a courtly man with a mop of white hair, a taste for fine wines, and a decidedly conservative take on global politics and culture. From our perch on the nineteenth floor, we sipped a glass of Riesling or two and ate poached salmon and asparagus while watching a pale orange sun set over the dome of the Reichstag.

"America's cultural supremacy has been lost," Stürmer told me, describing the widespread hostility to the cowboylike style of George W. Bush as "a thin veneer of something deeper" in the global psyche. As for America's ability to keep world order through its massive military presence, Stürmer again shook his head. "Iraq will be the nemesis of American hubris." He pointed to a building in our line of sight: the new U.S. embassy, then under construction, just across from the Brandenburg Gate. The building is a massive, ugly fortress, withdrawn from the street—and hated by the architects who have added dozens of jewels to Berlin in the rebuilding spree after Germany's reunification in the late 1980s. "That's the end of the Pax Americana—the embassy embodies it," Stürmer said. "It goes away from the people—it is built not with the representation of America in mind but for security, for defensive purposes. It is a kind of Maginot."

In political circles in America, it is not uncommon to hear liberals make the case that America's global influence has peaked. But that perspective is shared as well by cold warriors like James Schlesinger, a steward of the American Century. Schlesinger, who was born in New York City in 1929, served as director of the CIA under Richard Nixon, as secretary of defense under Nixon and then under Gerald Ford, and as secretary of energy, the first to hold that job, under Jimmy Carter. He has a reputation for being acerbic, but even his detractors concede his brilliance. We got together at his offices at the Northern Virginia campus of the MITRE Corp., a nonprofit contractor for the Pentagon and other agencies in Washington. From the window could be seen the next-door building of Northrup Grumman, the defense giant. I replayed for Schlesinger my talk with Michael Stürmer, and he nodded his head. "After World War Two, we were the fairy godmother" for a world on its knees, Schlesinger said. But this could never be a permanent situation, because the rest of the world, contrary to what many Americans think, does not want to be "like us"; in fact, "they never particularly wanted to be like us," and now "the world is going to quite ostensibly pay less attention to what America thinks." Schlesinger's concern is that Americans will have trouble recognizing how things have changed from the past—even now, he said, America is living "an illusion" with a mind-set that is "a kind of mental illness." He asked me if I had read *Buddenbrooks*, the 1901 novel by Thomas Mann. In Mann's tale, the fortunes of the once-grand Buddenbrooks, a mercantile family in the North German port of Lübeck, erode over the course of four generations. By the story's end, one member of the family, Christian, has become "more and more subject to uncanny delusions and morbid hallucinations," while in the case of Frau Permaneder, "the more depressing the present appeared, the more she strove to depict the elegance of the life that went on in the houses of her parents and grandparents." The Buddenbrooks are hopelessly mired in a life of make-believe; the world around them has changed and, as Schlesinger noted, "They don't know it. They don't acknowledge that the prestige and the power of the family has declined." And that, he said, is going to be a problem for Americans, who must make cognitive adjustments to adapt to new realities beyond their capacity to alter.

While all this may sound terribly gloomy and painful, the After America world does not have to be a disaster for America and for Americans. In fact, it could even be a liberating moment; it is not hard to see circumstances in which the country and the people could thrive in an After America era. But now I am getting ahead of my story. First it is necessary to put in perspective how America came to be the world's dominant civilization: how America acquired its founding myth of American Exceptionalism, its sense of being unique and apart from all that had come before; how America rose to be the world's dominant economic and cultural power; and how America came to possess an Accidental Empire. This is the subject of part 1 of the book. Part 2 explores how America came to its present straits: how America, which has always prided itself on being a land of tomorrow, has become a middling in various modern respects, including the uses of everyday technology; how the American Goliath has overstretched its imperial frontiers in places like the Middle East; how countries once thought hospitable to the American model, like Russia, are instead rediscovering their own cultural and political roots.

Part 3 casts the question of what comes next, After America, into the future. The short answer is, we don't know, but it is possible to build some plausible narratives. Indeed, the second major premise of this book, following on the first premise that the American influence has peaked, is that After America narratives are *already* being constructed, all over the planet. The world is pregnant, not with one possibility for what might come next, but with multiple possibilities. These embryos exist in parallel with one another—although at some point a "victor" will presumably emerge, we are still probably a long way from reaching that point. My approach to part 3 is to take each of these plausible possibilities and suggest how they might emerge in a fuller-fledged form.

The scariest narrative is a dark chaos, a new Dark Ages, as large parts of the world experienced after the collapse of the Roman Empire. This is the sort of prospect that worries the Michael Stürmers of the world, knowing that there is no ready replacement for America as a global policeman. Parts of the Middle East—a supposed American patrol zone—are already in a semi-anarchic condition, and it is conceivable that instability could spread through Turkey and into Europe itself. But there is another way to look at chaos. I also will consider the possibility of a happy chaos, in which the world, without *any* Big Daddy, takes advantage of new technologies of personal empowerment that allow individuals to make their own connections in an After America setting.

Another possibility, the scenario that many geopolitical analysts consider most likely for a post-American world, is a multipolar order of nation-states in which America would assume a scaled-down position as one great power among others. A twenty-first-century multipolar order would be a first for the world—unlike the Eurocentric balance of power of the nineteenth century, this arrangement would bring into play a mix of the world's great civilizations, including China and India. I explore a rising India, with its ambition of developing a blue-water navy to police the far reaches of the Indian Ocean, as a test case for the proposition of a new kind of multipolar order. A stronger India, with interests broadly aligned with America's, might help America by lightening its load of global-policeman responsibilities. But a multipolar world is by no means assured, because the foundation on which it would rest—the modern system of nation-states—is battered and besieged by those who would seek to subvert or bypass it, from the "nonstate" terrorist group to the multinational corporation and supranational tribunes of human rights. The state must reestablish its primary role in global life for a new multipolar order to take root.

Nor is it assured that a multipolar order would be stable. It may be that the world, as politically incorrect as this sounds, needs a hegemon, a recognized alpha dog to keep order in the pack. China is the most obvious candidate to replace America in that role. After all, if there was a somewhat accidental character to the arrival of the American Century, then the trajectory for a Chinese Century could follow a similar line. In its planetwide search for raw materials, China may already be sowing the seeds of an imperium that extends to America's own backyard of Latin America. I explore Chile, whose treasure trove of copper deposits is the basis for an intensifying political, economic, and cultural engagement with China, as a case in point of China's expanding global reach. Although the Chinese foray in places like Latin America may sound threatening to Washington, the Chinese, unlike the Americans, are not known around the world for trying to impose their values on distant civilizations. A capitalism-friendly, trading-oriented Chinese Century would not necessarily put in jeopardy America and the American way of life.

Perhaps the time is past for the age of empires as well as for the age of the nation-state. This scenario considers the possibility of a new age of global city-states. History suggests a precedent: After the collapse of the Roman Empire, and once the Dark Ages had run their course, it was the city-states of Europe, not the nation-state (that invention came later), that became the bulwark against the chaos of the medieval countryside. The most successful of them, in Italy, gave birth to the Renaissance. In the twenty-first century, the global city, in our age of economic globalization, is already a powerful force—think New York, London, and Hong Kong, and toss in an invented city like Dubai and a rising ancient one like Bangalore—and the global city could become the defining feature of an After America era. In that kind of era, America, which has already given the world such distinctive urban landscapes as Los Angeles and Las Vegas, both with global orientations, would stand to be a prime participant, so long as twenty-first-century America does not allow itself to be subsumed by its fear of the immigrant. The one key to the success of the great city, through the millennia, is its openness to the outsider, the newcomer, as a source of creative energy and an antidote to provincialism.

And finally, there is a path that leads first to a universal civilization of "global people" and ultimately to global government. Such people already exist in growing numbers, operating in globally oriented business and finance, in global regulatory institutions, in "transnational" human rights and environmental groups, in the arts, academia, and the media. They constitute a cosmopolitan elite, stronger than anything that has existed in any past chapter of history. Even though official Washington tends to be opposed to global institutions that threaten the system of state sovereignty, or at least America's sovereignty, many prominent Americans, like Al Gore on the issue of climate change, already function as global people, as post-Americans in an After America world. And a rising generation of young people is being taught to think globally by prestigious universities like Harvard, which has migrated from a national to a global identity. For subscribers to the vision of Henry Luce, who died in 1967, there can be no more painful irony than the fact that the After America world is a project that Americans and American institutions are helping to build.

The bottom line is that America needs to reflect on and mentally prepare for a world in which it is no longer preeminent. The concluding section of the book, part 4, returns the story to my conversation with James Schlesinger. The transition to an After America world entails a monumental paradigm shift. For segments of the political class based in Washington, in particular, the end of the American ascendancy augurs nothing short of a crisis of identity. It is possible that America, following the example of the waning British Empire, will experience a Suez-like disaster from a failed attempt to flex its muscles. An After America nation could drip nostalgia into the stream of politics like a poison. But there are also much brighter possibilities. California, America's most plastic, most future-oriented, and most successful place, is *already* starting to exit the American Century and remake itself as a global actor in a world that does not revolve around the American sun. The relatively cosmopolitan, Euro-friendly Democratic Party is showing signs of a more graceful adaptation to the After America world than is the relatively provincial Republican Party, with its attachment to the notion that it is always morning in America. And there are steps that individual Americans can take, practically speaking, to prepare for the After America world.

This, then, is the arc of the book: the rise of America as the world's preeminent civilization; the passing of the American Century, evident in the here and now; and, at the heart of the exploration, the question of what life will be like for the planet and for Americans as their dominance continues to ebb. The first part of the book is a narrative drawn from history; the rest of the tale is shaped by the materials I gathered and impressions I formed in my travels around various reaches of the world, from the Pacific shores of California and Chile to the Arabian seacoast of India, with stops in between in places like Moscow and Dubai and the Anatolian plain of Turkey.

The book is informed by what I am fond of calling an organic interpretation of how change happens. By organic, I mean from the ground up, from the soil of global political, cultural, and economic life. Americans in particular, but not only Americans, like to read their history as a tale of great men and great deeds. The "larger than life" personality can make for an easy or at least an enticing way of spinning a narrative. Hence the bookstores of America are piled with bestselling biographies of Thomas Jefferson and John Adams, Abraham Lincoln and Theodore and Franklin D. Roosevelt, Harry Truman and Ronald Reagan. Much as I enjoy such books myself, my own sense of how history works, as bottom-up and contingent, comes more from the likes of Fernand Braudel and Leo Tolstoy. Braudel, born in Lorraine and educated in 1920s Paris, was a historian of civilizations whose main focus was on the evolution of the modern world from "the enormous mass of history barely conscious of itself." Tolstoy, a classic autodidact, outlined his conception of history in the philosophy-oriented epilogue of *War and Peace*. He described history as an "ocean" in which grand personages, like Napoleon and Tsar Alexander, may appear to be masters of the currents but in truth are mastered by them. We often see modern renditions of this dynamic. It was Tolstoy's masses that flooded Lubyanka Ploshad in August 1991 and gave the Moscow city government essentially no choice but to haul down Iron Felix, thus drawing the curtain on the Soviet era in history.

I don't mean to say that leadership or vision has no role in determining what comes after the American ascendancy—even Tolstoy had an idea of the heroic, in the anti-Napoleon figure of General Kutuzov, the unglamorous Russian commander who sometimes fell asleep at briefings by his aides and was fond of sayings like "When in doubt, my dear fellow, do nothing." The closest American parallel to Kutuzov is the stolid but unyielding General Ulysses S. Grant, whose portrait, by the Civil War photographer Alexander Gardner, hangs on my office wall. My point is to suggest a corrective to the conventional view of events that assigns too large a role to big-idea leaders and central governments.

Americans both individually and collectively will shape their After America futures—but within certain boundaries. Or to put it another way, just as scientists are now discovering with respect to their exploration of the human brain, "free will" may be as much an illusion for a nation and for a civilization as it appears to be for an individual person. Maybe the best answer to why Americans act as they do is because it is in their character to do so. And it would be helpful for Americans to grasp that, because the illusion of free will can itself be a cause of damage: Both human beings and civilizations can be less dangerous with a sensible realization of their limits. In the affairs of humankind, there is no such thing as a pure actor as a driver of events: Even the biggest of actors is acted upon. Subject and object dissolve into an unfolding tale whose conclusion is elusive, a matter of probabilities rather than certainties.

It is impossible to approach a project like this one without some aspect of the personal creeping into the story. My perspective is as a child of the American

Century. I was born in 1957 in a hospital on a U.S. Air Force base in Bangor, Maine, used as a refueling depot for the B-52 bombers of the Strategic Air Command. My father worked as a doctor at the base, which is now a commercial airport. In the early 1980s, when I left my native New England to attend graduate school in London, I felt that I had a passport to see the world and would be welcome nearly everywhere. And so I was, sleeping undisturbed on a blanket next to a bedouin camp on the shores of the Red Sea on the Sinai Peninsula. As a journalist, I have spent much of my career in Washington, D.C., writing about managers of American might from Ronald Reagan to Barack Obama. I have also lived and worked on the margins of America's influence, in the lands of the post-Soviet Russian empire. In 2007, nine years after I married my wife in her native Tashkent, I watched her raise her right hand and take an oath to become an American citizen. She was joined by fifty other new citizens in a ceremony at a government office building not far from our home in Northern Virginia. The After America world will be mine, hers, and most of all, our two young children's.

PART ONE

The Ascendancy

L ike the story of any civilization, the tale of America's can be told as a series of what-ifs. A primal reality of life in the New World was the lethal contact between the settlers from Europe and the Native American population. The greatest threat came not from the settlers' muskets, although they were a threat, but from their germs, like the smallpox, influenza, and measles that the colonists carried to seventeenth-century Virginia, to which the Indians had no immunity. American civilization would have acquired a different character had the Indians, quite literally, proved more resistant to the arriving Europeans. And it would have been different if Jesuit missionaries from France, rather than Puritans from the British Isles, had established a foothold in the land that became known as New England. While the British monarchs had an interest in exporting "unruly members of Protestant sects" across "the herring pond," the French authorities, as a French historian noted, mistakenly "feared that France might be depopulated" and so had no interest in "peopling" North America.

Then, too, the American colonists might not have succeeded in their rebellion against King George III without the forceful intervention of France, Britain's great imperial rival of the eighteenth century. And what if, nearly a century later, the South had achieved its bid for independence in the Civil War? It is only the distance of time, and the illusion that distance affords, that makes the South's defeat look inevitable. The conventional wisdom at the outset of the conflict ran quite in the other direction. "Just as England during the revolution had to give up conquering the colonies, so the North will have to give up conquering the South," the military analyst for the *Times* of London wrote in mid-1862.

And consider one last what-if. What if Hitler had not invaded Stalin's Soviet Union in 1941, a fateful error that led to the smashing of the German war machine? The Second World War probably still would have been won by America and its Western allies, but at a considerably greater cost in blood, resulting in a very different geopolitical environment at war's end.

With the what-ifs all breaking in favor of America, with the misfortune of others sometimes amounting to the good fortune of the new civilization, the arc of America's rise to global preeminence from the early seventeenth century to the mid-twentieth is an almost unbroken one. There are no defeats of great consequence, no hard lessons that America had to learn from a crushing failure. Part 1 of the book charts the American ascendancy. Chapter 1 delineates the essential character traits of American civilization—a mix of qualities, both borrowed from the Old World and more or less invented by the new society, crowned by the founding myth of American Exceptionalism, the notion that America was a unique creation in world history. Chapter 2 traces the circumstances that led to America's economic and cultural preeminence, capped by Henry Luce's call for an American Century. And chapter 3 shows how the new superpower operated as an Accidental Empire, a role for which it had no preparation and only one approximate role model, the British. The empire gained, the American ascendancy attained its peak with the collapse of the Soviet Union in the cold war. From Captain John Smith's arrival in Jamestown in May of 1607 to the hauling down of Iron Felix on Lubyanka Ploshad in Moscow in August of 1991, nearly four centuries—three hundred and eighty-four years, to be precise—had passed.

Chapter One

"Never Imitate": A Civilization Is Born

And why need we copy the Doric or the Gothic model? Beauty, convenience, grandeur of thought, and quaint expression are as near to us as to any, and if the American artist will study with hope and love the precise thing to be done by him, considering the climate, the soil, the length of the day, the wants of the people, the habit and form of the government, he will create a house in which all these will find themselves fitted, and taste and sentiment will be satisfied also.

—Ralph Waldo Emerson, "Self-Reliance," 1841

Times were hard in the southeastern counties of early-seventeenth-century England; hard enough, one inhabitant reported, that "there are many thousands in these parts who have sold all they have even to their bed straw, and can not get work to earn any money. Dog's flesh is a dainty dish." The jails were filled with petty thieves, the almshouses were overcrowded with beggars, and even those in the upper classes were feeling the pain brought on by European wars that drove down the value of money and took from England her cloth markets. "This England grows weary of her inhabitants, so as Man is here of less price amongst us than a horse or a sheep," complained John Winthrop, a country squire of Suffolk, who tended a small estate. Like so many others, Winthrop thought of emigration: "I wish oft God would open a way to settle me in Ireland, if it might be for his glory."

It was not nearby Ireland that was to receive John Winthrop, but the remote shores of the "New World," where he was to become the first governor of the

Massachusetts Bay Colony and its dominant presence for nearly two decades. John Winthrop is best known in American history for the sermon he delivered to his fellow émigrés in Southampton in March of 1630, shortly before the departure of their ship, the *Arbella*, on its transatlantic passage. He reminded them of their covenant with God and their vows to one another, and beyond that, of their example for posterity, "for we must consider that we shall be as a City upon a Hill. The eyes of all people are upon us." His sermon conforms to a strict biblical interpretation of the planned colony as a New Jerusalem, an understanding to which some Christians in America subscribe to this day. Winthrop's words also have been handed down as a secular creed describing America's earthly purpose, often invoked by its leaders to remind their fellow Americans of their "great responsibilities" to act wisely with the understanding that "at some future date the high court of history sits in judgment on each one of us," as president-elect John F. Kennedy said in a speech at the Massachusetts statehouse in January 1961. Or as President Ronald Reagan said in his farewell address to the nation from the Oval Office in January 1989, Americans must keep the portals of their "city" "open to anyone with the will and the heart to get here." Winthrop's words resonate as one of the earliest briefs on behalf of a missionary purpose, religious or secular or both, for the settlers of America.

It is on these terms that America is often apprehended—as a mission, as the template for an idea, as an experiment for working out certain convictions about what the world on earth is or can or should be. America was a mission. But it was not only a mission. And to see America only from the standpoint of a mission—of an "errand into the wilderness," in the phrase of the historian Perry Miller—is to miss quite a bit. And a lot is missed, too, when America is viewed, as it often is, simply as a nation-state. The schoolchild who pledges allegiance to the flag "and to the Republic for which it stands, one nation . . ." is of course not wrong to see America in these terms. But the broader framework of a civilization is more useful because it offers the widest possible perspective on the American experience. A civilization is an intricate, complicated, multifaceted thing—a messier construct than an experiment in ideas, embodied by a republic, which suggests a neat elegance. A civilization typically has both lofty and earthly dimensions; it tends to be guided by mythic quests but also by the pursuits of wealth and power. A civilization is powerfully shaped by its natural environment, settlement patterns, and frontiers. A civilization in certain respects is akin to a living thing, say an animal, which can prosper through guile but also through the misfortune of others. Accident can shape a civilization as much as genius or vision. A civilization develops habits and reflexes of which it is sometimes only dimly aware, like the man who forgets his tendency to pull on his earlobe when he's nervous. Buried traditions, likewise, can shape a civilization long after their origins are forgotten. A civilization tends to have a prevailing mind-set—not a single way of thinking, but a set of mental attributes toward which it is disposed. Civilizations become distinctive according to how they differ from others based on this package of qualities. Great civilizations tend to acquire empires, which become the political and military expressions of their personalities.

The study of civilizations acquired a bad name from the likes of Oswald Spengler and Arnold Toynbee. Writing in the early twentieth century, at a time when European civilization seemed to be collapsing, they developed sweeping, highly schematized theories of development that attempted to make civilizations conform to certain basic laws and propositions. It was Toynbee who famously wrote, in typically dramatic fashion, "Civilizations die from suicide, not by murder." This effort to make the rhythms of civilizations conform to a general theory proved a sterile exercise. But in the hands of a historian like Fernand Braudel, who made no claims to being a scientist and did not try to fit his facts into any particular ideological cubbyhole, the framework of a civilization is useful and indeed invaluable.

Braudel likened civilizations to organic "cultural zones" with permeable borders: "Every civilization imports and exports aspects of its culture." He was not especially given to metaphor, which can distance a thing from its real properties and yield the generalizations he tended to dislike, but he did once say that "at first sight, indeed, every civilization looks rather like a railway goods yard, constantly receiving and dispatching miscellaneous deliveries." In this conception, the signature mark of a civilization lies in what it has rejected or refused from others. For Braudel, America was a distinct civilization, and that is itself an important notion. Spengler and Toynbee, and decades after them, Samuel P. Huntington, the author of the famous 1996 treatise *The Clash of Civilizations*, all viewed "the West"—a rather grandiose term in itself—as a single civilization of which America was but a part. With more attention to everyday habits, beliefs, and styles of living, Braudel more sensibly, if less poetically, divided what he called "European civilizations" into the "American civilization" of the United States and the civilizations of Latin America, Russia, and Europe itself. He did not believe that American civilization was unique—he did not believe that of any civilization—but he did acknowledge that "as a civilization, it was for a long time a traveler without baggage, convinced that the future would forever grow brighter and that seizing it was simply a matter of willpower."

In the beginning, in the day of John Winthrop and the Puritans, America was not yet a distinct civilization in Braudel's terms, but the properties of the civilization it was to become could already be seen. Indeed, nearly all of these properties could be discerned in the life and person of John Winthrop. He might have gone to Ireland but, to the good fortune of the New World, which needed men of his caliber, he did not. He was a man of God but also a man of ordinary needs and desires. It was not only his thirst for a more authentic and less constrained spiritual life that led him to Massachusetts but also the severity of his financial circumstances: "My means here are so shortened (now my three eldest sons are come to age) as I shall not be able to continue in this place and employment," he informed his friends. The Massachusetts Bay Colony over which he presided was not only a religious proposition but also a business one, with origins in a small group of investors from Dorchester whose interest was in financial profit. The wind in the sails of the *Arbella* and her many sister ships of this era was the wind of modern global capitalism, which grew out of the Protestant Reformation in sixteenth-century northern Europe and came into its own in seventeenth-century England with a proliferation of joint stock companies of small investors pooling their stakes. The glory of such enterprises was not only to God but also to the British Crown, which typically granted the joint stock companies the right to a monopoly over certain regions or commodities.

This is not really a contradictory picture. There is a single thread that connects the motives of John Winthrop as he made way for America—the thread of optimism. Whether the spur was mostly spiritual or mostly practical, he believed he was leaving England for a better destination. Optimism stands out as a signature trait of the American mind-set. American optimism can be seen as a temperament disposed toward buoyancy, or alternatively as the absence of a tragic sense of life. The European temperament was notably a tragic one and understandably so. The Puritans left behind an England on the brink of civil wars engulfing the religious communities of the Stuart kingdom, a set of conflicts that were part of a broader bloody struggle involving dynasties, Protestants, and Catholics on the European continent. German agriculture and industry were devastated; in the recovery after these wars, starting in the 1680s, large numbers of Germans began migrating to America, at first to New York and Pennsylvania. As for the shiploads of Scots-Irish that entered the ports of Boston and Philadelphia early in the eighteenth century, these migrants were removing themselves from oppressive rents, lengthy droughts, and laws banning the export of their wool and cloth products. In the face of these known miseries, optimism about an unknown America made sense.

Optimism also made sense as the arrivals to the New World gazed westward at the marvelous expanse of land available for settlement. The frontier, and its potential for development, also separated America from Europe; only Russia, which in the early seventeenth century was still not much more than a collection of city-states west of the Urals, faced a similar stretch of undeveloped land. As historian Frederick Jackson Turner observed, the frontier became central to the American mind-set. It gratified the restless pioneer possessed of a "love of adventure" and offered a sweet economic reward: "Year by year the farmers who lived on soil whose returns were diminished by unrotated crops were offered the virgin soil of the frontier at nominal prices." In political terms, the frontier was an incubator of a libertarian spirit—it offered an opportunity to escape governmental controls. Like the Russian pioneers who made their way eastward across Siberia in the seventeenth century, some at the tsar's command but many others on their own initiative, the settlers of America were determined to move westward across the North American continent with or without the sponsorship of their leaders.

A third quality setting apart life in the New World from life in Old Europe was the emergence of what became known as the melting pot. This was the rising civilization's most significant *conscious* rejection of European traditions.

Early on, before America separated itself from Britain and became a republic, American society sought to distinguish itself from Europe with an emphasis on the melting away of ethnic identities as a mark of a new American identity. This concept was new; America can fairly be said to be the inventor of the melting pot, perhaps its greatest invention ever. It was J. Hector St. John de Crèvecoeur, an immigrant from France to the American colonies in the 1750s, who eyed his fellow settlers, a mix of English, Dutch, Swedes, Germans, and others, and noted, "Here individuals of all nations are melted into a new race of men." Crèvecoeur, a farmer in Orange County, New York, was not talking about "multiculturalism," a looser mix of ethnic and national groups within a society. He was talking quite specifically about Americans as a "promiscuous breed" dedicated to or unable to resist a mixing of blood. One of his models was a family with an English grandfather who took a Dutch bride and had a son who married a French-woman. The melting pot philosophy embraced gross hypocrisies—American Indians were excluded, and so were plantation slaves from Africa, although their blood mixed with the rest of America's as a result of the rape of female slaves by their white owners. And yet the ethos, as time went on, strengthened itself and surmounted whatever legal barriers and rank prejudices stood in its path.

Other distinguishing features of American civilization are better thought of as modifications of the spiritual or mental baggage—the imports—brought to the new land by the settlers. This is a lengthy list of attributes—some positive, some not—which collectively cast the new America as a place with more of a foot in the Old World than is generally conceded by interpreters of American history, with their emphasis on the novel aspects. In particular, America's founding religious tradition was just that, an ingrained set of customs and beliefs imbibed directly from Protestant dissenting communities scattered throughout Europe. America proved fertile ground for such communities—without doubt more fertile than Europe, with its cruel monarchs bent on enforcing orthodox practices. But the religious beliefs and customs themselves, the faith in Jesus Christ the Lord and sectarian practices of groups like the Calvinists, were products of a long-standing period of European incubation. Quite different spiritual beliefs, of a pagan sort, were practiced by the Native Americans, the "heathen" Indian tribes, but these beliefs had very little impact on the spiritual psyche of the settlers. The periodic Great Awakenings, the first of which swept the American colonies in the 1730s with sermons by John Edwards on topics like "Sinners in the Hands of an Angry God," were revivalist events firmly grounded in the European Christian tradition. The new American evangelicals, who spread their mission to the frontier of Appalachia and the lands stretching toward Mississippi, were latter-day proselytizers in the tradition of Paul bringing his gospel to his native Anatolia in what is now Turkey. This was the old world encroaching itself on the new, and it was precisely because the settlers had brought their religion with them, from "over there," that the religious domain proved the ripest point of cultural conflict in the Huntington-like "clash of civilizations" that played out between the settlers and the Indians over several hundred years, until Indian civilization was at last vanquished.

Likewise, the European settlers—some of them, anyway—brought slavery to the American colonies. As Condoleezza Rice has said, "Africans and Europeans came here and founded this country together—Europeans by choice and Africans in chains." But America's "birth defect," as Rice called slavery, was not a specifically American invention—the slave system was borrowed in its entirety from standard European imperial and commercial methods, with only practical adjustments made for the particular features of American land and climate. The early Southern plantation owners were comically imitative creatures—as W. J. Cash noted in *The Mind of the South*, they were desperately eager to fashion themselves as European-style country gentlemen in the cavalier tradition of the novels of Sir Walter Scott. And just as the slave system's cultural overlay was of a borrowed sort, so was the economic engine at the core of American slavery. Slavery came to America not because European settlers were especially racist and cruel beings, compared to others in Europe, but because the slave trade was embraced by its practitioners as a "modern and economically successful system," as the historian David Brion Davis has noted. Although Africans were doled out the cruelest treatment, the capitalist barons who exported slavery to America cast their eyes to the European labor pool as well. For the Virginia Company, determined to wring profits from its investment in Jamestown, a form of indentured servitude, snaring English boys typically as young as fourteen, was an element of the business plan.

Likewise, the settlers brought with them war-making skills and technology.

The musket was as familiar to the Puritan as his Bible; John Winthrop was a commander of a militia regiment of the Massachusetts Bay Colony. The colony engaged veterans of European wars to wage attacks on Pequot Indian tribes in response to killings of English colonists; Indian lands were laid waste— wigwams burnt, canoes destroyed, cornfields razed—in tactics reminiscent of England's wars in Ireland. In one engagement, as many as seven hundred Pequot were killed, including women, children, and the elderly. A historian of the colony likened the savagery of such events to the Peasants' War of the German states in the sixteenth century. These first wars anticipated the later series of "French and Indian" wars, targeting despised French Catholics and Native American tribes. To keep their guard, the colonists formed the likes of "Rogers' Rangers," a counterinsurgency unit in New Hampshire under the leadership of Captain Robert Rogers. The Rangers "equaled the Indians in stealth, skill with canoe and bateau, scouting, taking prisoners, and killing sentries—and Rogers was not above a little scalping, too," a sympathetic chronicler later wrote. American civilization's capacity for war was considerably strengthened with the arrivals in large numbers of the Scots-Irish, who had a fierce war-making tradition of their own, a clannish, backwoods style, honed over the centuries in their native land. That tradition had an important influence on the U.S. Marines. But the Scots-Irish American who was "born fighting," as James Webb, the Scots-Irish senator-soldier, has described him in his book of that title, was a European inheritance only modified by American terrain.

If this seems like an unsavory list of America's borrowings, consider the most ennobling and important borrowing of all, the Enlightenment tradition. The Enlightenment was a movement hatched in the seventeenth century on the British Isles and the European continent. The giants were men like Sir Isaac Newton, for whom the scientific quest was part of a liberal and quite radical intellectual creed intended as a deliberate break with superstition and unexamined religious faith. "He saw, and made people see; but he didn't put his fancies in place of truth," Voltaire said of Newton, whose funeral he attended in 1727. Newton's example was a thrilling one for the great pioneers of American science, like the kite-flying Benjamin Franklin, with his pathbreaking experiments on the properties of electricity. Franklin was enormously proud to be honored for his discoveries by the Royal Society of London for Improving Natural Knowledge, founded in 1660. The European model in education was likewise a source of American imitation: The first great universities, such as Harvard, founded in 1636 by a vote of John Winthrop's Massachusetts Bay Colony, were based on the English university types of Oxford and Cambridge, both of which had been created hundreds of years earlier. Perhaps no one among the Founding Fathers was a fuller-fledged subscriber to the Enlightenment tradition than Thomas Jefferson, an unabashed Francophile with more than a streak of Voltaire in his makeup. Asked by a young man why science should be studied, Thomas Jefferson briskly replied in a letter in 1799 that "the idea that the human mind is incapable of further advances" is "cowardly," for "it is impossible for a man who takes a survey of what is already known, not to see what an immensity in every branch of science yet remains to be discovered." Jefferson pronounced himself confident, though, that America would avoid the "cowardly" path: "Thank heaven the American mind is already too much opened, to listen to these impostures."

The Enlightenment advanced not just modern science and education but also that project known as modern "Western" democracy. Is the American democratic tradition, in this sense, a borrowed one? Yes and no—American democracy is a mixed bag of the borrowed and the invented, with the accent, as time has passed, on the invented. Well before the "American democratic idea" received its muscular expressions in the colonists' rebellion against King George, the virtues of democracy were among the philosophical speculations of Enlightenment thinkers like John Locke in England and Montesquieu in France. (The former died in 1704, the latter in 1755.) Jefferson in particular was intimately acquainted with such thinking. His radical ideas about liberty, set forth in his first draft of the Declaration of Independence in June of 1776—the notion that "all men are created equal" and thereby "derive rights inherent & inalienable"— started to become common currency in the streets of France in the summer of 1773. (The French phrase was *droits de l'homme*, or rights of man.) That said, with the break from the British Crown and the intensified effort to settle the American frontier, American civilization molded the democratic idea taken from Europe into a more distinctive, populist form. The decisive break with European-style politics came not in the age of the founders, when the likes of Jefferson and John Adams were at the helm, but in the age that followed them, the age of Andrew Jackson.

Andrew Jackson was a frontiersman from the Carolinas who fought the Indians and fought the British, and when he entered the White House as president, in 1829, he let the people, clad in their muddy boots, have the run of the joint. Eastern establishment sorts despised his type and his example: His predecessor, John Quincy Adams, the son of John Adams, called him "a barbarian who could not write a sentence of grammar." Anger and resentment from this quarter was understandable, because the Founding Fathers and their brood had imagined and hoped for a national leadership class closer to their own Old Worldish, aristocratic ways. But with American civilization developing as it was, into a raucous frontier society, the ascension of a figure like Andrew Jackson was ordained. "Old Hickory," as he was known, was indeed a crude specimen of American democracy, but he also was an authentic one, an early representative of the future direction of things.

These, then, were the signature traits of American civilization, and they had all come together by the age of Jackson. As in all civilizations, there were seeming contradictions, in this instance between the religious disposition, especially in its evangelical form, and the secular-oriented Enlightenment disposition. True Voltaireans scorned religion. But for European travelers to Jacksonian America, the combined package invariably struck them as something quite novel. One particular visitor, Alexis de Tocqueville, a young French aristocrat who arrived in America in 1831 in order to make a survey of the country's prisons, immortalized the new civilization as a sharp departure from Old Europe. On a journey lasting nine months, Tocqueville wound his way from New York City to Buffalo by way of Albany, saw something of "lower Canada," and managed to get in parts of New England as well as Philadelphia and Baltimore, Cincinnati and New Orleans. In volumes that he later published, known as *Democracy in America* (part 1 came out in 1835 and part 2 in 1840), he latched onto features of American society that seemed to define America as so very different from his own land. The most important such trait, in his mind, was set forth in the very first sentence of the first volume: "Among the novel objects that attracted my attention during my stay in the United States, nothing struck me more forcibly than the general equality of condition among the people."

Tocqueville overdid it. Not even Jacksonian America, more different from Old Europe than the young America had ever been, was a total break. "Equality of condition," as painstaking research of tax records and other archives by modern historians of Jacksonian America has demonstrated, was not a universal characteristic of this society. In fact, as one such historian, Edward Pessen, has authoritatively presented the findings, there was a somewhat Old World, European-style pattern to the distribution of wealth in Jacksonian America—and what is more, this distribution became even more unequal as the era progressed. "In the great cities of the northeast, the top 1 percent of wealthholders owned about one-fourth of the wealth in the mid-1820s and about half the property by midcentury," Pessen found, and for the smaller cities and rural parts of Jacksonian America, "the proportions were not very much different." These facts do not reveal any bad faith on Tocqueville's part; they simply underscore, as Pessen concluded, that "his interest was not in facts but in their meaning. America was to him a kind of generalized case study of *démocratie*, the civilization of the future." America, as has been its lot, was again being interpreted as the platform for an idea.

Ideas, of course, can have great consequence, especially when they are interwoven with emotion to form the fabric of a myth. And Jacksonian America proved to be the creator—or at least the completer—of America's most cherished myth, the myth of American Exceptionalism. This myth almost had to be born, because the sad fact—sad, that is, to influential members of America's nascent intellectual class—was that American society was *not* as different from the Old World as they wished it to be. This was a great point of anxiety to a new class of thinkers and writers in America who were determined to wrench the civilization from its European roots. Among them was Ralph Waldo Emerson, a graduate of the Harvard Divinity School and a former minister of the Second Church of Boston, who was establishing himself as an original poet-essayist on the American proposition. In "Self-Reliance," which he published in 1841, at the age of thirty-eight, Emerson produced a biblical-style lamentation on America's woes, which he attributed, in a tone of disgust, to a shallow propensity for imitation. "Our houses are built with foreign taste; our shelves are garnished with foreign ornaments; our opinions, our tastes, our whole minds, lean, and follow the Past and the Distant, as the eyes of a maid follow her mistress," Emerson wrote. "As our Religion, our Education, our Art look abroad, so does our spirit of society. All men plume themselves on the improvement of society, and no man improves," he continued. How best to combat such vanity, such foolishness? "Insist on yourself; never imitate," Emerson advised.

Emerson's dictum can be read as an imperative to the individual—any individual—to cultivate "that which each can do best," a command that came from his faith that "every great man is a unique," as he put it. ("Where is the master who could have instructed Franklin, or Washington, or Bacon, or Newton?" he asked rhetorically.) It can also be read as an imperative to a collective "we"—a message to all Americans to be participants in the creation of something unique. He made a special appeal, in this vein, to the American artist, whom he asked to create a new kind of house, not yet another copy "of the Doric or Gothic model." He was asking, in effect, for all aspects of American society, from its arts to its form of government, to fit a test of uniqueness. The great task of American civilization was not necessarily to be the best or the biggest but to strive to be original. The point was for America not to out-Europe Europe but to create a standard of its own.

"Self-Reliance" was a powerful and inspiring appeal, and Emerson was just getting started. Three years later, in the essay "The Poet," he complained of searching "in vain" for the bard who could do justice to America as "a poem" whose "ample geography dazzles the imagination." He finally found his man in Walt Whitman. In 1855, Whitman sent Emerson a copy of a first collection of poems, *Leaves of Grass*. It was undoubtedly enough for Emerson to read the long first poem, which came to be known as "Song of Myself," to see the fulfillment of his plea for an original American composition. About a third of the way into the poem, Whitman warbled:

> *Of every hue and caste am I, of every rank and religion,*
> *A farmer, mechanic, artist, gentleman, sailor, quaker,*
> *Prisoner, fancy-man, rowdy, lawyer, physician, priest.*
>
> *I resist any thing better than my own diversity,*
> *Breathe the air but leave plenty after me,*
> *And am not stuck up, and am in my place.*

At the heart of the American Exceptionalism myth was Emerson's notion of leaving behind "the Past and the Distant." This was a vision that an earlier generation of like-minded Americans had similarly extolled: "We have it in our power to begin the world over again," the pamphleteer Thomas Paine had proclaimed in 1776, adding that "the birth day of a new world is at hand." But the Jacksonian period gave much fuller amplification to these ideas—as noted earlier, Founding Fathers like Jefferson and Franklin were happily Europhilic in many of their attitudes and ideas and were eager to see European transplants set root in America. Now the Paine-Emerson-Whitman leitmotif seeped into the mainstream of a postaristocratic, populist democratic culture. And the myth was hitched to some of the great political causes of the day—namely, the annexation of Mexico as part of the "Manifest Destiny" of the United States to unfurl its settlements all the way to the Pacific Ocean. The coiner of the Manifest Destiny phrase, John O'Sullivan, a founder of *United States Magazine and Democratic Review*, took his cue almost word for word from Paine in his editorial refrains. Of America, O'Sullivan wrote, "We have, in reality, but little connection with the past history of any [nation] and still less with all antiquity, its glories or its crimes. On the contrary, our national birth was the beginning of a new history." As a result, "we may confidently assume that our country is destined to be *the great nation* of futurity."

This was history as therapy—aimed at uplifting and empowering American spirits. O'Sullivan was going well beyond Emerson, who sometimes wrote for the *Democratic Review*. Emerson had not said, as O'Sullivan asserted, that America had *already* accomplished this magnificent feat of cognitive separateness from Europe—it was indeed Emerson's great worry that an intellectually lazy and slavishly imitative civilization had failed to do so. But as the myth of American Exceptionalism evolved, as it perhaps had to evolve, there was an insistence on a virgin-birth conception of America as an infant dropped from heaven. Part of the appeal of the myth was that, like John Winthrop's vision of "a City upon a Hill," it could be subscribed to in literal religious terms—America as the creation of providence—or in strictly secular ones—America as a blank canvas in a new era of Enlightenment. This notion of America as a blank slate was a classically utopian idea—it is the essence of utopian thinking to see the entire universe as a blank slate. Founding Fathers like the worldly Alexander

Hamilton, who prided himself on his realist thinking, on his appreciation of the inherent wickedness of mankind, had no such reading on the new America as a departure from the laws of human nature.

But there was no stopping the idea of an immaculate birth, which found its most resonant expression not in lyrical poetry or beseeching prose but in the pleasing pictorial images of a new type of allegorical landscape painting, typified by Thomas Cole, a founder of the Hudson River school of artists. The Cole movement cropped up at the start of the Jacksonian era and came to dominate American art. In Cole's *Sunrise in the Catskills* (1826), "Hudson River school artists invested the land with a sense of national identity, the promise of prosperity, and the presence of God," as an art historian later noted. A later example, John Gast's famous *American Progress* painting of 1872, is even more mythically explicit. An allegorical young maiden, in long blond hair, pale skin, and wispy white robe, a book and a string of telegraph wire in hand, is shown floating high over a landscape of pioneers, covered wagons, and a railroad train, all pushing westward.

The American Exceptionalism myth was a supple one, accommodating itself to nationalistic and somewhat jingoistic sentiments as it became evident that, contrary to John O'Sullivan's initial hopes, tasks like the annexation of Mexico were unlikely to be accomplished without military action. The spilling of blood, when it came, was interpreted in some quarters not as a notice that God was out of sorts with the American project but as a sign that the project must go on, without fail. "God has predestinated, mankind expects, great things from our race; and great things we feel in our souls. The rest of the nations must soon be in our rear," Herman Melville proclaimed in his novel *White-Jacket*, published in 1849, three years after the outbreak of the Mexican-American War. (Emerson, along with his New England writing mate, Henry David Thoreau, opposed the war out of concerns that newly acquired territories would come into the union as slave states.) America of course won the Mexican-American War and annexed the territories of Texas and California; both of these successes could indeed be seen as confirmation, providential or otherwise, of the exceptional qualities of America. In such winning circumstances, doubters were paid little heed.

As in all effective myths, there was plenty of truth in this one. American

Exceptionalism, in its varieties, covered the bases in its homage to the new civilization—its democratic spirit, its sense of a religious quest, its economic and ethnic diversity, its unspoiled frontier wilderness, its optimistic outlook. And yet, these attributes did not add up to the audacious proposition that America was a gift from God or an experiment liberated from history. No matter. Myths are deliberately selective, and their whole point is to inculcate belief. This one did, with the aid of confirming events. A civilization had been born, and so had its presiding myth.

Chapter Two

America Preeminent

Chicago, when it finally dawned on him, came with a rush on the second morning. . . . This raw, dirty town seemed naturally to compose itself into stirring artistic pictures. Why, it fairly sang! The world was young here. Life was doing something new.

Theodore Dreiser, The Titan, 1914

America believed itself to be exceptional, but the greatest power of the nineteenth century, the British Empire, felt the same way about its character and role in the world. And France subscribed to a similar myth of Exceptionalism, a mind-set that managed to survive the country's crushing defeat in the Napoleonic Wars. "French civilization is so above and apart from that of all other peoples," Victor Hugo said, "that my countrymen need not shrink from encouraging people like those of the United States in their ambition to imitate the glories of France." As the nineteenth century took its course, there was no great danger of Americans chasing the French model; while France was declining as a great power, America was mounting a challenge to Britain's global preeminence. The America of this age gained in confidence, even acquiring a bit of swagger, not because American Exceptionalism was such a brilliantly woven myth, but because America's awesome economic performance in the nineteenth century, its leaps-and-bounds improvements in material living standards, powerfully validated the myth. No society could rival America as a fountain of optimism because the ordinary American understood that his children stood to live far better than he did. It was from this material base that America launched its cultural and political onslaught on the world. Long before American culture became a global force, long before America's voice counted for much on the globe's diplomatic stage, and very long before America became the world's dominant military force, America became economically preeminent.

It happened, by the standard of such things, quite rapidly. In 1840, the U.S. economy was but half the size of the United Kingdom's, the world's largest, as measured by gross domestic product. In 1872, only seven years after the conclusion of the Civil War, the total output of America's economy surpassed that of the UK's. By 1880, the UK's economy was only four-fifths as big as America's, and by the turn of the century, in 1900, Britain's was only three-fifths as big. America's economic spurt was in part a function of its growth in population, from 24 million in 1850 to 76 million in 1900. Over this period, the UK's population grew more modestly, from 27 million to 41 million. But the American economy's growth well outpaced the increase in population, and by 1905 the world's biggest economy also was the richest one, eclipsing the UK in "per capita GDP," the standard measurement of national wealth. That trophy won, America was poised to become universally dominant in global affairs, to commence what Henry Luce was to proclaim as the American Century.

The tale of America's global economic ascension is not, as might be imagined, a story about how Americans overtook their Anglo cousins across the Atlantic through a superior application of timeless rules of economic behavior that any nation can follow to prosperity. This is not a story about the magic of the free market; it is, rather, a story that has a great resemblance to the chronicles of roughhouse economic life that nowadays come from the rising lands of China and India. Granted, the American colonies took from their British masters a tradition of contract law and property rights; and America, once a sovereign republic in her own right, made this tradition a principle of her own economic and legal affairs. And yet the hallowed principle of rule of law, enforced by impartial courts and regulatory bodies, though always an accepted ideal, was widely flouted, and nowhere more so than in America's great economic expansion during the nineteenth century. The prevailing practice in the most dynamic industries of the era was not the rule of law but the rule of cliques of "robber barons," along with smaller-time shady operators who manipulated the law to their own selfish ends with impunity. This was particularly the case in the defining achievement of the age: the establishment of a nationwide railroad system, which knitted together not only the economy but also a society previously divided into separate provincial pieces. The transcontinental railroad was a stupendous accomplishment, "perhaps more responsible than any other development for the emergence of modern America."

American railroad financing and construction, which greatly accelerated in the 1850s, was to its core afflicted with dirty dealing that government was either powerless or not disposed to stop. The railroad promoters raised enormous sums of capital from American and European investors, often bilked "through watered stock, security speculation, dummy construction companies, padded costs, and a host of other questionable devices." The 1860s and 1870s are usually thought to be the peak of railway corruption, but even in the latter part of the 1880s the *Economist* of London was warning British investors to stay clear of American railways securities given the "malpractices" that "have been carried on for a series of years."

To advance what was basically a system of oligarchic capitalism, an unregulated Wall Street emerged as a global powerhouse of finance. And this happened, paradoxically enough, during America's greatest upheaval, the Civil War. The war took the lives of 620,000 soldiers, devastated large parts of the South, and destroyed permanently the Southern way of life built around the slave plantation. But the main battles took place no farther north than Gettysburg, in southern Pennsylvania, leaving untouched the North's great centers of population, finance, and industry. In fact, the war as a whole was an economic boon for the Union, as the federal government poured massive amounts of borrowed money, obtained from bonds sold to the public, into the private sector—into not only railroads but also shipyards, iron and textile mills, shoemakers, and many other enterprises. The production of iron railroad rails, a standard measure of industrial strength of the time, climbed from 205,000 tons in 1860 to 356,000 tons in 1865. Wall Street grew to become second only to London in the volume of its securities markets. With brokers reaping up to ten thousand dollars a day in commissions, a writer of that period noted, "New York never exhibited such wide-spread evidences of prosperity. Broadway was lined with carriages. The fashionable milliners, dress makers and jewellers reaped golden harvests. . . . Never were such dinners, such receptions, such balls." And with the business of national government also booming, the Civil War "transformed Washington from a sprawling town into a swarming city," its population growing by 74 percent in the 1860s.

Not only the railways but virtually all important projects of industry and finance were part of this American phase of crude capitalism. Consider the amazing rise of Chicago in the second half of the nineteenth century as a magnet for job seekers from all over America as well as from Europe. Like Shanghai of the late twentieth century, mid-nineteenth-century Chicago was among the world's great construction projects, built by ruthless financiers who got their way with municipal officials through threats and inducements ranging from cash bribes to prostitutes. The architects were brilliant rogues like Charles T. Yerkes, the son of Philadelphia Quakers, who built the famous Chicago "Loop" transit system and whose life is immortalized in a vivid trilogy of finely detailed realist novels by Theodore Dreiser. As a boy growing up in Philadelphia, the Yerkes character, Frank Cowperwood, is fascinated by a fish-tank exhibit in which a lobster, in successive bites over a matter of days, devours a squid. "The incident made a great impression on him. It answered in a rough way that riddle which had been annoying him so much in the past: 'How is life organized?' Things lived on each other—that was it." And yet Dreiser's Cowperwood is not a repellent character; he has a Rhett Butler–like magnetism irresistible to women, and the vision of success he has for himself becomes part of a larger vision of success for his adopted city of Chicago, to which he moves after being convicted of embezzlement in Philadelphia. His fellow schemers are no better or no worse—what they are is *vital*. At a meeting in a private dining room in Chicago, Cowperwood takes his place among men "with eyes and jaws which varied from those of the tiger, lynx, and bear to those of the fox, the tolerant mastiff, and the surly bulldog. There were no weaklings in this selected company."

Cowperwood's relentless energy and determination, his steady nerves in the face of failure, his disinclination to look back, even his division of the universe into the strong and the weak, shorthand for the capable and the incapable, was a practical American formula for prosperity. "To a man with great social and financial imagination," Dreiser wrote, the continental spread of America "gave him a sense of the boundless commercial possibilities which existed potentially in so vast a realm." As for the real-life Yerkes, even his fiercest critic, Chicago mayor Carter Harrison, Jr., had to concede, "He was the stuff great war heroes are made of." Toward the end of his life, Yerkes, like many of the robber barons, came to philanthropy; in his case, his grand present was a magnificent observatory in Lake Geneva, Wisconsin, given to the University of Chicago.

In this fashion, nineteenth-century America, taking its own society as the arena of competition, reflected a Darwinian survivalist ethos. But the America of this age did not adopt this attitude toward the outside world. Although Wall Street sucked in foreign funds for investment in the railways and other capital-intensive projects, America was not of a mind to make a level playing field as regards, say, its manufacturers and those in Germany. In fact, America was determined to stack the deck in its favor and did just that. There was little appetite for the British-style laissez-faire philosophy of minimal government interference in the economy, as championed by the likes of David Ricardo, the classical British economist whose theories predicted that a system of free trade was best for all nations. In 1846, mighty Britain repealed its infamous "Corn Laws," which set high import tariffs against foreign grain to protect British corn growers. "We seriously believe that *free* trade, free intercourse, will do more than any other visible agent to extend civilisation and morality throughout the world," the founders of the *Economist* declared in their support for repealing those laws. But across the Atlantic, America's political class advised against the British example as unsuitable for America's vulnerable economy, at that time smaller not only than Britain's but also than France's and Germany's. "Abandonment of the protective policy by the American Government, must result in the increase of both useless labour, and idleness; and so, in proportion, must produce want and ruin among our people," Abraham Lincoln of Springfield, Illinois, a freshman member of the House of Representatives, declared in 1847.

Lincoln's mind-set represented a standard worldview of the time that can be called economic nationalism. Economic nationalism was in the first instance a set of public policies, including high import tariffs and direct government subsidies to crucial industrial sectors like the railroad builders. Economic nationalism also was a set of chauvinistic political attitudes that appealed not only to the manufacturing magnates but to their workers as well. Recognizing the appeal of this plank, Lincoln's new Republican Party, established in the 1850s, made economic nationalism a core element of its identity.

This protectionist mind-set endured for as long as it had to—until America was the greatest industrial economy on earth. Economic nationalism prevailed from the passage of the high-tariff Morrill Act in 1861, after Lincoln's election as president, to the reversal of this policy in 1913 under the leadership of Woodrow Wilson, a Democrat. Until Wilson's triumph, Republicans had won eleven of thirteen presidential elections going back to Lincoln's victory in 1860. Grover Cleveland, the Democrat who broke a string of six consecutive Republican presidential victories with his win in 1884, lost his reelection bid in 1888; Republican cartoons, playing on his support for free trade, portrayed him as "England's Candidate for the American Presidency." Fatuous rhetoric on the tariff issue was commonplace. Nevertheless, the protectionist United States of 1870–1913 had an economic rate of growth roughly double that of Britain. From 1870 to 1880, America enjoyed an average annual growth rate of 4.8 percent, compared to 1.9 percent for Britain; from 1900 to 1913, the difference was 3.9 percent versus 1.9 percent.

As legend has it, America's robber barons finally met their match in Theodore Roosevelt, who knocked them down a few pegs and smoothed the sharp-toothed edges of American capitalism. Few figures in American history are more invested with romantic sentiment, with a larger-than-life character, than is Teddy Roosevelt. Overcoming a sickly boyhood through sheer will and rigorous physical exertion, he became famous for stalking big game in the wilds of Africa. He is one of those figures said to mold an entire age of history. But it was the times themselves that created a vital figure like Roosevelt—just as the times created the great barons of capitalism. He shared many of their character traits in the intensity of his aggression, in the wide scope of his imagination, and in his embrace of a survival-of-the-fittest ethos. "One of the prime dangers of civilization," he explained to the Germans, who perhaps did not need the reminder, was "the loss of the virile fighting virtues, of the fighting edge." TR was an embodiment of Muscular Christianity—the Victorian-era movement, crossing over from England into America, that sought to harmonize traditional masculine strivings, in rugged sports and other fields, with Christian ideals. The

YMCA—the Young Men's Christian Association, founded in 1840s London—is an example. While Roosevelt enacted the reform agenda of the Progressive movement, a movement that arose in reaction to the manipulative excesses of the robber barons, his role was more that of a consolidator of the system that drove America's economic rise in the nineteenth century. Under his rule, America obtained a regime of nationally regulated railroads—long after the transcontinental connections had been established. And economic nationalism was his creed as well. "Thank God I am not a free-trader," he wrote a friend in 1895. "In this country pernicious indulgence in the doctrine of free trade seems inevitably to produce fatty degeneration of the moral fiber."

Roosevelt had a big heart; he did not like to see the weak stomped on. This separated him from the most venal and cynical of the robber barons. But after becoming president in 1901, he looked back at the spectacular economic run America had enjoyed since the time of the Civil War and evinced satisfaction. "These forty-odd years have been the most prosperous years this Nation has ever seen; more prosperous years than any other nation has ever seen," he declared.

Even as America's economy grew at a breakneck pace, even as America became a preeminent magnet for Old World migrants looking for a new start in life, cultured Europeans had spent the better part of the nineteenth century looking down on their cousins across the Atlantic as uncouth and immature. Typical in this regard were Frances Trollope and her novelist son, Anthony, who on their visits to Britain's former colony took issue with virtually every aspect of the American "persona," including the demand of the "adult infant" for "fresh ice in his water." This rote brand of snobbery, spiked with envy and resentment, never fully abated, but as the century drew to its close, a tipping point was reached, as it finally dawned on the European intelligentsia that American civilization was not only about muscle and material pleasures but also about the finer parts of life. The soul of the country was finding expression in cultural marvels distinctly different from anything produced by Europe. It was a fulfillment, conscious or unconscious, of Emerson's dictum that America must stop copying and insist on itself.

In Braudel's terms for how civilizations mix, America was becoming a cultural exporter, while Europe was increasing its imports. Thus, American ragtime, a precursor to jazz, became a sensation in Europe. The French composer Claude Debussy turned to ragtime in "The Golliwog's Cakewalk," composed in 1906, and ragtime sheet music sold well in the shops of Paris and London. The real cultural breakthrough came, fittingly enough, in an aesthetic symbol of America's industrial might: the skyscraper. The world's first skyscrapers, built in 1880s Chicago, were made possible by improvements in the safety of elevators (courtesy of the American inventor Elisha Graves Otis) and the availability of cheaply produced steel. The more notable of these edifices, like New York's Woolworth Building, completed in 1913, made America a symbol not only of economic strength but also, as Europeans were to acknowledge, of modernity itself. A European historian called the Woolworth Building "the most ambitious edifice, perhaps, since the Pyramid of Cheops."

Even American-style philosophy was in fashionable demand in the land that had long looked to thinkers like Plato and Aristotle, Descartes and Locke, for wisdom in this quarter. In 1907, William James published *Pragmatism*, his bible of commonsense thinking drawn from his lectures at Boston's Lowell Institute and Columbia University. The book sold a remarkable sixty thousand copies in Europe. Unlike his younger brother Henry James, who resided in London and wrote elaborate novels of manners distinctively in the European style, William James lived in America and embraced in his philosophy a brisk, businesslike style of thinking. He was a graduate of the Harvard Medical School, with a deep interest in human physiology and psychology, and his emphasis was on concrete experience, not on airy metaphysical ideas. And while European philosophers often used their writings and lectures to showcase their erudition, James adopted a style that was straightforward and easy to digest. Philosophy, he said, is "not a technical matter; it is our more or less dumb sense of what life honestly and deeply means. It is only partly got from books; it is our individual way of just seeing and feeling the total push and pressure of the cosmos." His unadorned way of conveying his meaning anticipated the widespread admiration in Europe for the stories of Ernest Hemingway in the 1920s. The French philosopher Henri-Louis Bergson called *Pragmatism* "the philosophy of the future."

Europe was turning to America because America was fresh and original but also because Europe was becoming conscious of its own exhaustion. The age of Europe as the center of the modern world was coming to a close. Early in the twentieth century, Europe plunged into the conflict generally known as the First World War but which in hindsight is better seen as a type of civil war, engaging societies closely linked by cultural traditions and ties of blood. America had no role in provoking the war "over there," which was even more senseless than most wars are, and probably would not have taken part if the Germans, bent on breaking a British blockade, had not torpedoed American merchant vessels more than two and a half years after the conflict started. America was not a large actor in the global imperial games that obsessed the Europeans in the nineteenth and early twentieth centuries. The Spanish-American War, fought with a frail European power without the will to hold on to its Caribbean possession of Cuba, was a sideshow incited by the jingoistic lords of the yellow press, led by William Randolph Hearst.

The First World War cost Europe the deaths of 8.5 million soldiers and 5 million civilians. The elite of European society—including half of the men in France between the ages of twenty and thirty-two—went to their graves. In geopolitical terms, the only "winner" to emerge from this bloodbath was the United States, which suffered some 115,000 military deaths, about a fifth of the toll claimed by the Civil War. In the killing fields of the Marne was lost whatever sense of inferiority Americans might have felt to the supposedly more sophisticated and polished European way of life. At least America's Civil War served the moral purpose of bringing an end to slavery—and the practical purpose of saving the American Union. After the First World War, it was plain, notwithstanding Oswald Spengler's portentous musings about "the decline of the West," that the European and American story lines had parted.

Among those in Europe who grasped how thoroughly America had evolved away from its bosom in the Old World was D. H. Lawrence. His novels, with their lush descriptions of human beings captive to nature and their animal, sensuous selves, evoked what he liked to call "the spirit of place." In *Studies in Classic American Literature*, a slim volume published in 1923, Lawrence paid homage to artists like Whitman and Melville as prophets whose work emerged from the soil of American experience and foreshadowed an American-defined epoch in world history. And now, he said, that moment had arrived. With "Europe destroyed," he wrote, "America will begin."

D. H. Lawrence was a romantic, and the idea of the American Century, even though it was rooted in the solid reality of America's astonishing climb in the world, was a quintessentially romantic one. It was not an especially original notion: What rising civilization does not imagine itself as one day astride the world? Otto von Bismarck's unification of Germany in the second half of the nineteenth century spurred fantasies of a coming German Century. Japan's humiliation of tsarist Russia in the war of 1904–5 nourished an imperial dream of dominance in Asia—and beyond. Henry Robinson Luce did not have a copyright on the idea of an American Century, even though he became its single greatest proselytizer. Still, in his life and times can be seen the elements that made the call for an American Century such a persuasive one. And while he may come across as an eccentric figure, the timing of his message was magnificent, pitched to a weary world eager to hear that America had arrived to play a central role on the global stage.

Harry Luce, as he preferred to be called, was born on April 3, 1898, in Tengchow, a port city in northern China. His parents had arrived there a half year earlier to pursue Christian missionary work. Luce's father, the Rev. Henry Winters Luce, descended from a settler from Britain who had arrived in the British colony of Massachusetts in the mid-seventeenth century. His father took up the study of law at Yale College in preparation for a career in commerce, but in 1892, shortly before he was due to graduate, he had an epiphany "that inspired him to seek the Kingdom of God." He devoted himself to studies at a seminary and applied for overseas service to the Board of Foreign Missions of the Presbyterian Church, in Princeton, New Jersey. American Protestants of the Reverend Luce's stamp saw missionary work as "more than a religion; it was a summons to social activism." Late-nineteenth-century China, dominated by European and Asian imperialists, was seen by American missionaries as in need of America's inspiration, optimism, and energy to defeat superstition and disease, to "help ease China's passage into the modern world." As a Luce biographer, Robert E. Herzstein, noted, there was even a phrase in the reverend's family for this "can-do" American cocktail, called "native Lucepower."

The reverend's firstborn, Henry Robinson (three children were to follow), was a natural believer in Lucepower. A devout Presbyterian who as a child imagined himself as a Christian soldier in the games he played in his family's walled compound, he did not on maturity enter a seminary as his father had but always considered himself a kind of amateur theologian. He drew his faith in America's global potential from both religious and secular quarters in roughly equal measure. As a boy, repelled by the sight of Chinese workers abused by their British overseers, he boasted that Americans were different because they "overpaid their coolies." Perhaps so, but as is often the case for the children of expatriate families, he seemed to gain, as a result of his experience in this foreign land, an overdeveloped or exaggerated sense of American identity, of the qualities that supposedly made the American so fundamentally different from the member of any other society. He was like a lot of Americans in his sense of national distinctiveness, only more so.

Luce's parents enrolled him at the British China Inland Mission School in the city of Chefoo. At this "smelly old prison," as Luce called it in a letter to his parents, the Brits ruled and there was an active, bullying contempt for Americans and American customs; on Sundays, all children, including the Yankees, "dressed in imperial white pith helmets and white suits with knee-length pants and marched to Church of England services." In 1913, at the age of fifteen, Luce came to America for the completion of his precollege studies at the Hotchkiss School, a Connecticut boarding school founded in 1891 and in Luce's day attended mostly by the boys of wealthy, Presbyterian, Republican-leaning families. He excelled at Hotchkiss, becoming captain of the debating team and challenging himself to master a tendency to stammer.

Luce was precocious, coming into possession of his lifelong political views at an age when most boys have other things on their mind. At the age of sixteen, with the First World War barely under way, he was predicting "America's leadership of the world at the close of the European war." At twenty, while attending Yale University like his father before him, he celebrated American patriotism in a prizewinning essay calling for "American business ideals" to be "recognized wherever the trader goes" and for America to help "the lame, the halt and the blind among nations." He was an ardent Republican but scolded classmates for identifying with the party out of narrow reasons of economic class. And he backed American intervention in "every international difficulty." The cynicism and sense of aimlessness that afflicted so many members of his generation after the carnage of the First World War was entirely foreign to his nature. Some became fellow travelers, sympathetic to the Russian Revolution and its utopian aims, but Luce was viscerally revolted by atheistic Bolshevism.

While Luce was having trouble making a sale to his own countrymen, the view he held on America's global abilities found receptive ground overseas. A harbinger that the American Century brand would travel well came in post-Ottoman Turkey. The First World War had destroyed the Ottoman Empire and the decayed institution of the Moslem sultanate, based in Istanbul. An ascendant band of Turkish nationalist reformers were in desperate search of a formula to modernize their society. France was one place to look, but America was another. One of the reformers, Riza Nur, had in mind an American rescue mission. His dream was for America to assume a League of Nations mandate for Turkey, in effect to administer Turkey until a new Turkish republic, based on democratic, secular values, could stand on its own feet. "If America were to accept the mandate and behave in a just and honest manner, it could within twenty years bring us to a degree of development which Turks, left to themselves, would not be able to achieve in a century. It would make Turkey prosperous, rich and happy and turn Turks into a strong and civilized nation," Nur believed.

The U.S. Senate declined to ratify America's membership in the League of Nations; there would be no U.S. mandate in Turkey. But Nur's plea underscored that Luce was right to sense that the world, at least some parts of it, not only felt inspired by the American model but also desired a hands-on American involvement. Luce was a peddler of America to the outside world, but much of his business was walking through the door. He became a media mogul, a natural ambition for someone of his particular ambitions. With his creation of *Time* and *Fortune* in the 1920s and *Life* in the 1930s, he had mass-market outlets for amplifying a matured version of the same basic perspective he had held since his teenage days. He was, of course, deeply opposed to the isolationist movement, which could claim a majority in Congress and was determined to forgo any

American involvement in a European conflict threatened by Hitler's rise to power. Under his direction, Time Inc. made a movie, *The Ramparts We Watch*, that played up German crimes in the First World War and concluded with an image of Plymouth Rock, a rendition of "The Star-Spangled Banner" supplying the sound. In 1940, he helped sell President Franklin Delano Roosevelt on a proposal by which the United States would give naval destroyers to Great Britain in return for bases held by the British Empire in the Western Hemisphere, in America's backyard. Roosevelt bought the politically controversial idea, which came with the pledge that Luce's magazines would promote the plan. *Time*'s several million readers were treated to a four-page essay, maps included, making the case for the bases as essential to America's national interests.

"The American Century" editorial in the February 17, 1941, pages of *Life* became instantly famous, not because the message was novel but because so many Americans were prepared to heed it, as they had not been in the 1920s and 1930s. Luce scolded his countrymen for an inexcusable failure of vision and offered a remedy:

> Whereas their nation became in the 20th Century the most powerful and the most vital nation in the world, nevertheless Americans were unable to accommodate themselves spiritually and practically to that fact. Hence they have failed to play their part as a world power—a failure which has had disastrous consequences for themselves and for all mankind. And the cure is this: to accept wholeheartedly our duty and our opportunity as the most powerful and vital nation in the world and in consequence to exert upon the world the full impact of our influence, for such purposes as we see fit and by such means as we see fit.

To buttress his point, and perhaps to shame his fellow Americans, Luce noted that across the seas, in beleaguered Britain, there was an understanding that America's time had come, and no question of America, in any wartime alliance with Britain, being anything other than the top dog. He cited a comment from the London *Economist*, that respected voice of the British political and financial establishment: "If any permanent closer association of Britain and the United States is achieved, an island people of less than 50 million cannot expect to be the senior partner. . . . The center of gravity and the ultimate decision must increasingly lie in America. We cannot resent this historical development. We may rather feel proud that the cycle of dependence, enmity and independence is coming full circle into a new interdependence."

A half century later, the Washington-centered group of policy activists, pundits, and intellectuals known as neoconservatives were to offer a robust post–cold war vision of American global dominance, of American ideals married to American power, along the lines of the unapologetic Luce formula of exerting influence around the world "for such purposes as we see fit and by such means as we see fit." The neocons were champions of the U.S. invasion of Iraq in 2003 as a way to bring American-style democracy to the Middle East. Henry Luce, in retrospect, might be called the first neocon—there was certainly no one who came after him who had a more ambitious idea of America's purpose. This was old-fashioned American Exceptionalism, of the Manifest Destiny variety developed by the publicists of the Jacksonian era. Against the age-old wisdom that power corrupts, no matter who is wielding it, was his faith that America was different—different not only from the empires of the Ottoman Turks and the Chinese emperors, he said, but also from the empires of Rome and the British. "We need most of all to seek and to bring forth a vision of America as a world power which is authentically America," he wrote in the *Life* editorial. And that meant not only a vision of military triumph, starting with entry into the war and the defeat of Hitler, but also a vision of the American business and cultural model creating, just as it had for Americans, a world of economic abundance. America must send to the world, as part of this global Americanizing mission, its "engineers, scientists, doctors, movie men, makers of entertainment, developers of airlines, builders of roads, teachers."

There was praise for the editorial not only from East Coast political and business leaders but also from the Hollywood baron Samuel Goldwyn, who said Luce had hit "the nail on the head." Many ordinary Americans were also smitten with the piece, as *Life* was pleased to show in a string of Letters to the Editor. "Your article is magnificent. It is historic. Best of all is your use of the word 'powerhouse' as opposed to 'sanctuary' for the ideals of civilization," wrote Robert E. Sherwood of Sasabe, Arizona. "While other men idly finger lumps of lava, Mr. Luce uncaps the volcano," wrote Bob Wronker of Tuckahoe, New York.

Henry Luce–like thinking even seeped into the pages of *Partisan Review*, the cherished highbrow publication of New York City's left-oriented intellectuals. The prose was packaged into a different form—*Life* was a strictly bourgeois product, in *Partisan Review* terms—but the message was the same. The deliverer of the gospel was the influential art critic Clement Greenberg. Greenberg was a tireless champion of a style of "drip" painting, Abstract Expressionism, pioneered by Jackson Pollock, as *the* new wave in modern art, and a distinctively American one. For the first four decades of the twentieth century, abstract painting had been dominated by Europeans like Picasso and Miró. That era was over, Greenberg announced in the pages of *Partisan Review* in March 1948. With the ascendancy of the Pollock group, he wrote, "the main premises of Western Art have at last migrated to the United States, along with the center of gravity of industrial production and political power."

Clement Greenberg was a proselytizer, just as Harry Luce was. Both had become caught up in an intoxicating moment, the American moment, and it was not hard to see why. Across the Atlantic, from European intellectuals, came even headier toasts to the American possibility. "America is one of those places in the world where, despite everything, humanity's *potential* continues to flourish," the French writer Claude Roy wrote in his 1949 treatise, *Clefs pour l'Amérique* ("Keys to America"). "Coming back from the United States, one is completely confident that a new kind of people can be born, more certain of their ability, more imbued with wise, down-to-earth, practical contentment. We may make fun of the refrigerators and vitamins, the accumulation of gadgets. . . . But I do not believe that we have the right to make fun of a certain type of American who has already mastered the art of living and asserted the power of humanity over what once seemed ineluctable fate."

Was there no one willing to rain on this parade—to suggest, in a thoughtful way, that perhaps America had not mastered "what once seemed ineluctable fate"? Walter Lippmann, who had the credentials for the job, gave it a good try. Lippmann was a Wise Man of the East Coast foreign policy establishment. Born in New York City in 1889, nine years before Luce, he was equally precocious, becoming an informal foreign policy advisor to President Woodrow Wilson seven years after graduating from Harvard. Lippmann, too, was drawn to journalism and the penning of treatises, and he admired some of Luce's writings; like Luce, he believed America was headed for global political preeminence after the Second World War. But Lippmann had a profoundly different sensibility, especially in his view of history. Lippmann saw America's ascension as a function of, yes, certain auspicious American qualities, but even more so of the particular circumstances of the time. Lippmann was a reflective person, a public intellectual, with a subtle cast of mind, and he did not believe, as did Luce, that God or fate had dealt America a for-all-time winning hand. Unlike Luce, Lippmann was not a religious man, and he did not possess a missionary temperament: Although his family belonged to upper-crust German-Jewish society in New York, Lippmann chose to ignore his Jewish identity. He prided himself on being a cosmopolitan, equally at home in the salons of Europe and in Washington and New York.

Lippmann had no particular political ideology; as an analyst he operated in the tradition of the "realist" style of thinking, a legacy of Europe's going as far back as the sixteenth-century philosophy of Machiavelli and tending to view humankind through a tragic lens. Lippmann recognized that Luce's vision of America as the all-powerful champion of an American Century lacked grounding in the way that history tended to work. "Great as it is, American power is limited," Lippmann wrote in 1945, shortly after America obtained the nuclear bomb—four years before Stalin's Soviet Union broke the U.S. atomic monopoly with a successful test of a bomb in Soviet Kazakhstan. He worried that America, with "our moral and political immaturity," failed to see that its immense power still rested on contingent circumstances in the world and could be dissipated if unwisely directed.

Lippmann's commonsense skepticism was shared by other Americans. Luce's own publication, *Life*, printed a small note of dissent from "The American Century" editorial, a letter from Carl Adams of Shrewsbury, Massachusetts. "We must clarify our position before we team up with anyone to save the rest of the world," Adams wrote. "We must first convince our own people of the right direction before we can become an effective force in any direction. When we have clothed, fed, and washed the face of that unfortunate 'one-third' of our people"—the portion of Americans acknowledged by Luce not to be living in material comfort—"and have brought faith in Democracy back to them, we shall begin to show a semblance of unity and incidentally have something desirable to show the rest of the world." (In a response to Adams, *Life* said that "as American social reform becomes more and more effective, America would seem to have ever more to offer the world.")

But however many people might have agreed with Walter Lippmann and the Carl Adamses of the *Life*-reading public, the energy and the enthusiasm were clearly on the side of Luce. America on the whole, and admirers abroad, preferred to believe in an illusion—in the fantasy that history had been obliterated. That moment did not last forever: As the years of the American Century rolled on, revisionist appraisals of America's climb to these global heights became common currency, not least within America itself. An oral history of reminiscences of America's "good war," assembled by Studs Terkel in the mid-1980s, made for, at times, painful reading. "You must realize we were not a worldly people," said the wife of an engineer who worked on the Manhattan Project. "We didn't know much about the Japanese and Japanese culture. They were yellow, they had squinty eyes, and they all looked evil. They were always evil in the movies, characters slinking around knifing people. You began to think of them not as human beings but as little yellow things to be eradicated." Against the popular mythology that Americans had saved their European brethren, single-handedly, from the triumph of the Nazis, military historians pointed out that the fight against Hitler's armies took its decisive turn not on the beaches of Normandy in June 1944 but in the frozen warrens of Stalingrad in 1942–43. It was there that Hitler's war machine was met head-on, and repelled, by the Red Army.

The Allied wartime leaders all knew the realities of these events. Winston Churchill himself said, in 1944, that Stalin's troops "tore the guts out of the German army." But the regard of the postwar world, understandably enough, was less for a brutal communist dictatorship than for the planet's most vibrant democracy and greatest industrial power. And as a practical matter, the non-communist world urgently needed America to fill a geopolitical vacuum. With Europe in ruins, with Stalin menacing the borderlands of an expanded Soviet Union, America got drawn into a much wider set of global responsibilities. However America had arrived at this point in its history, it was becoming obligated to keep order in a large chunk of the world beyond its shores. At hand was the pressing business of running a new global empire.

Chapter Three

Accidental Empire

The principal imperialism the American exercises is the imperialism of attraction.

Max Lerner, *America as a Civilization*, 1957

Postwar America was an unrivaled global superpower, the only power of the moment with nuclear weapons—but it was not a global empire of the classical variety. After all, America lacked a formal system of colonies—in fact, its sole colony, the Philippines, acquired in the Spanish-American War, was granted independence by Washington in 1946. In a conversation at Argentia Bay, off Newfoundland, four months before Pearl Harbor, Franklin D. Roosevelt angered Winston Churchill by blaming the colonial practices of the British Empire, particularly the onerous economic policies, for the peoples of the Indian subcontinent and Africa being "still as backward as they are." As Churchill started to object, Roosevelt interjected, "I can't believe that we can fight a war against fascist slavery, and at the same time not work to free people all over the world from a backward colonial policy." A truculent Churchill said there could be "no tampering with the Empire's economic agreements" with its colonies, since those agreements are "the foundation of our greatness." The dispute embodied a tension between the political cultures of the two countries, which were in sympathy on so much else. Imperial Britain had a popular consciousness of empire, with its poets and pageants proudly attesting to the splendor and grandeur of the imperial life. The Colonial Office in Whitehall featured a façade with representative human and animal figures from the five continents of empire. In 1865, at a comparable moment of

British global preeminence, the British economist W. Stanley Jevons could not conceal his excitement as he wrote, "The plains of North America and Russia are our corn-fields; Chicago and Odessa our granaries; . . . Peru sends her silver, and the gold of South Africa and Australia flows to London; the Hindus and the Chinese grow tea for us." These were not the notes struck by the Washington political elite or the American people at the start of the postwar world, when America might have felt entitled to a bit of imperial crowing. Americans collectively tended to see themselves, because of the origins of their republic in an underdog rebellion against a British king, as an anti-imperial type of people.

Nevertheless, "empire" is a useful and even necessary way to think about the transformation of America from a rising nation-state to a globally dominant power with imperial-like interests needing protection. John Lewis Gaddis, the dean of cold war historians, and certainly not to be confused with left-wing critics of America who use "empire" as a label of opprobrium, has helpfully written that, after World War II, "the Americans constructed a new kind of empire—a democratic empire," in the sense that the system, like federated America itself, accommodated a fair degree of autonomy in the provinces. This was empire with a light touch, by historical standards—the American empire was a creation that many *wanted* to join, unlike the Soviet version of the time. America maintained the empire through a traditional system of overseas military bases, a global blue-water navy, and an army capable of rapid planetwide deployment. America was the leader of the permanent NATO alliance of European states and had protectorates, formally designated or not, like Israel, Japan, Taiwan, and South Korea. On the financial side, the "almighty dollar" established itself as *the* reserve currency for the world economy, as good as the gold to which it could be converted at a fixed price. America was the guarantor of liberal postwar order, propped up by new multilateral institutions like the International Monetary Fund, based in Washington. In keeping with the "democratic" aspect of the empire, America brought in the Europeans as major stakeholders.

As these examples suggest, America had no choice but to improvise as it cobbled together its Accidental Empire—the global empire that it never sought, as a conscious matter, to possess. Some practices were imported from the British—the nascent American intelligence services, in particular, were stocked with Anglophiles who learned a great deal from their more experienced counterparts in London. But this edifice was fundamentally an American one, reflecting American values and interests. As time went on, as Washington's imperial managers got more accustomed to the work, the character of the empire became less a matter of improvisation and more a matter of rote planning and routine. The imperial class, a bipartisan one, took great pride in their accomplishments, even if the term "empire" remained mostly verboten. And however different in character the American empire was from its predecessors at the dawn of the American Century, the gap began to close. Great power, it might be said, tends to make its practitioners more or less the same.

It may seem like a stretch to present America's postwar global empire as the result of an accident rather than as the calculated product of lust and yearning, in the traditional manner of empire formation. And yet the history on this point, now more than six decades old, continues to hold up. The postwar empire evolved out of a series of defining moments—opportunities, not necessarily asked for, when Washington had to decide, sometimes in a matter of days or even a day, what to do about some matter. These moments kept occurring, in the first instance, simply because the British Empire, however much it may have still wanted to be an empire, was exhausted and bankrupt and could no longer play that role in the world. And there was nowhere the Brits could turn except to their Anglo cousins in America, in whom they invested their fondest hopes. "Only the English-speaking peoples counted," Churchill, ever the unapologetic imperialist, told an American statesman in the 1950s. "Together they could rule the world." A first urgent attempt at a handoff came with respect to Greece and Turkey, British allies in danger of being drawn into the widening communist orbit of Stalin's Soviet Union. Early in 1947, the U.S. State Department received from "His Majesty's Government" two messages that were fairly called by Dean Acheson, a senior American diplomat, "shockers": notices that British aid to Greece and Turkey would cease within six weeks. Might not rich America, the British asked, assume the burden? The answer, Washington quickly decided, could only be yes. "We and we alone were in a position to break up the play" of Stalin, Acheson later wrote in his memoirs, and surely, as the matter looked from Washington's vantage point, he was right.

Whatever London might have hoped for, Washington did not simply carry on in the way that the British might have, had they continued to rule. The American empire would be stamped with the personality of America. One of the misconceptions about empires is that they are interested in little more than the amassing of power and wealth. But there is a third traditional imperial pursuit—present in some empires more than in others—which is the projection of values and culture. An early decision that defined the character of America's global empire was in this values tradition: the recognition of the new Jewish state of Israel. It was another of those long-simmering issues that suddenly became a crisis. The British had a mandate, dating from World War I, to run Palestine, but they abandoned it (in part due to pressure from Jewish insurgents), thus leaving another patch of the planet in Washington's hands. President Harry Truman's national security advisors were on the side of *not* recognizing Israel, and they grounded their argument in conventional realpolitik terms, such as the nineteenth-century European great powers habitually employed. "There are four hundred thousand Jews and forty million Arabs" in the Middle East, the secretary of defense, James Forrestal, argued. "Forty million Arabs are going to push four hundred thousand Jews into the sea. And that's all there is to it. Oil—that is the side we ought to be on," Forrestal said.

Truman got the point, but was mindful of other issues, including the need to lock down the Jewish-American vote in the presidential election that fall, and also his own personal legacy. One of his oldest and closest friends was a Jewish American, Eddie Jacobson. The pair had been business partners and served together in the First World War. Jacobson assiduously lobbied the president on the need for a Jewish homeland for survivors of the Nazi Holocaust. At one point Jacobson walked into the White House, without an appointment, to get Truman to agree to meet with Chaim Weizmann, the president of the World Zionist Organization. "You win, you baldheaded son-of-a-bitch. I will see him," Truman told his buddy. When the crucial moment came, in May of 1948, he sided for recognition, and however close the call might have been, he did not regret it. Later introduced to an American-Jewish delegation as the man who "helped create" Israel, Truman took umbrage and shot back, "What do you mean 'helped create'? I am Cyrus, I am Cyrus!" A Baptist like Truman knew his Bible—knew that Cyrus the Great was a ruler of the Persian Empire of antiquity who won honor among the Jews, and biblical acclaim, for his decree in 538 BC permitting Jewish exiles in Babylonia to return to their homeland in Israel.

Harry Truman was the American Century's first imperial president, the first in a long line to come. He may not have seemed right for the part. He had been the operator of a failed men's clothing store in Kansas City who got his start in politics as a tool of a local political machine. He became president when FDR died in office, in the spring of 1945, of a cerebral hemorrhage. Nevertheless, Truman's presidency laid the foundation for the Imperial Presidency, which deserves its capital letters because it became a keystone institution of the Accidental Empire. The essential feature of the structure was the concentration within the office of the president of an enormous discretionary power in the domain of national security. In this scheme, Congress, notwithstanding its Article One constitutional power to declare war, was a bit player. And that was the most remarkable thing about the Imperial Presidency—not the grasp of the executive for kinglike powers, but the utter submission of Congress. Branches of government don't normally yield their prerogatives without a fight, but in this case that is exactly what happened. The defining precedent was the crisis over Korea. On June 25, 1950, the armies of North Korea's communist regime invaded the Republic of South Korea. North Korea's regime had the backing of Stalin in Moscow. As a review of declassified records showed, years later, Truman's first response was to go to Congress: "He personally consulted repeatedly with the joint leadership of Congress, asked repeatedly to address a joint session of Congress on the crisis, and even provided a draft resolution of approval for Congress to consider." The leaders told him to put the resolution in his desk. "If a burglar breaks into your house," Texas's Tom Connally, the chairman of the Senate Foreign Relations Committee, told the president, "you can shoot at him without going down to the police station and getting permission." It proved a lasting image—the U.S. president as global sheriff.

Congress accepted a diminished war-powers role in part because of the exigencies of the moment but also because of an institutional self-abasement that was not unearned. In the 1930s, Congress was the seat of an isolationist policy that sought to keep America out of World War II. The isolationists were blind to the vulnerability of America to foreign attack—they truly believed, as one of their publicists, Phillips Bradley, wrote in 1937, that "we are insulated by water against effective attack." The surprise Japanese attack on Pearl Harbor destroyed isolationism as a credible national security strategy. Doubts about the wisdom of Congress in foreign affairs now infected the institution itself: Senate Majority Leader Scott Lucas was among those who opposed calling back Congress from a recess to debate a response to North Korea's invasion of the south.

While FDR was certainly capable of acting imperiously, even deviously, America entered World War II on the strength of Congress's constitutional power to declare war. There would be no such formal declaration in the case of Korea or in succeeding conflicts entered into by the imperial presidents of the American Century. It is tempting to view the Imperial Presidency as a personality-shaped institution. The archetype, in this way of thinking, is the ultra-devious and secretive Richard Nixon, whose actions led to the 1973 book by the liberal historian Arthur M. Schlesinger, Jr., *The Imperial Presidency*, that made the term a staple of the political lexicon. But as Schlesinger himself wrote, Nixon's presidency was "not an aberration but a culmination" of institutional trends favoring greater executive power going back to the Truman presidency. Both the Democratic and the Republican party contributed to the gallery of imperial presidents. Even when a president entered office with a deliberate anti-imperial style, as in the case of Jimmy Carter, elected in 1976, he exited as an upholder of the imperial tradition. Carter, in the wake of the Nixon Watergate scandals, made a point of carrying his own luggage and preached loudly on behalf of U.S. support of global human rights. But when the Soviet Union invaded Afghanistan in late 1979, toward the end of his presidency, he put on a global sheriff badge. "Any attempt by an outside force to gain control of the Persian Gulf region will be regarded as an assault on the vital interests of the United States of America, and such an assault will be repelled by any means necessary, including military force," he told a joint session of Congress in his fourth and final State of the Union Address. The so-called Carter Doctrine is one of the great exhibits of the Imperial Presidency. As the *Washington Post* editorial page noted with regret, Congress had played no role in the formulation of a "historic and structural" enlargement of the security commitments of the United States. No matter. The Imperial Presidency overrode the usual checks and balances of the American system of government. Carter's audience greeted his line-in-the-sand pronouncement with bipartisan applause.

The imperial president needed imperial stewards. Every empire requires managers of its far-flung operations who collect and safeguard its secrets and do all else that is needed to keep chaos at bay and the enemy off balance—all that is required to maintain an order friendly to the empire's interests and, if possible, faithful to its ideals. Lacking the formal institutions of empire, Washington in effect sourced the job to an informal clique of action-intellectual types, largely drawn from an East Coast Anglo-Saxon Protestant elite. From wartime service, many already had close ties to British intelligence and related services.

The group included largely forgotten names like Richard Bissell, Frank Wisner, Tracy Barnes, and Desmond Fitzgerald—together constituting an "invisible government" for a new national security state. If Henry Luce supplied the ideological foundation for the American Century, these folks got their hands dirty installing the wiring, maintaining the plumbing, and knocking down the occasional wall. They were based in Washington, helping to transform that city into a global center for political intrigue, just as New York had already become a preeminent center of finance and Los Angeles of popular culture. They filled the upper management ranks of newly created agencies like the Central Intelligence Agency, the successor to the wartime Office of Strategic Services. "We didn't talk like it, but we felt like we were at the center of the world," Susan Mary Alsop, a prominent Washington hostess (and descendant of the Jays, one of America's oldest families), later told the Washington author Evan Thomas, who chronicled the first generation of CIA men in his 1995 book, *The Very Best Men*. "The feeling then was, it's our responsibility," Alsop said. "What should we do about the Italian elections?"

As often happens in the court of a king, the advisors to the imperial president tended to think more imperiously than the man on the throne himself. While Truman, during the Korean crisis, was willing to go to Congress for a resolution, his secretary of state, Dean Acheson, barely hid his disdain for the legislative branch and its prerogatives. "We are in a position in the world today," Acheson said at the time, "where the argument as to who has the power to do this, that, or the other thing is not exactly what is called for from America in this very critical hour." In diminishing Congress, in building up the powers of his boss, Acheson was shoring up his own clout. His disdain was quite keenly felt and indeed was a staple of his identity. It was the disdain of the cosmopolitan man, who thinks in global terms, for the man of the provinces, who cannot help but think in terms of local horizons. Congress was dominated by provincials, especially the "people's body"—the House of Representatives, whose members typically devoted the balance of their energies to projects like getting a new road or government office building for their district. One of the sad consequences of the birth of the Accidental Empire was that this enduring divide in American life, between cosmopolitans and provincials, was accentuated, as America became responsible for parts of the world that a great many ordinary citizens, apart from soldiers who had served overseas, would have trouble locating on a map. Dean Acheson was a snob who felt wholly justified in his snobbery.

America has always had its cosmopolitans—the Founding Fathers, with their European affinities, were charter members of that club. The clan that rose to prominence after World War II had its own distinct pedigree in American history. Besides Acheson, the group comprised lesser-known figures like Richard Bissell, a top figure at the CIA. Bissell and his mates have made for easy fodder, even ridicule, for revisionist critics, but his example is worth considering for an appreciation of the situational difficulties, including the moral hazards, faced by the new men of empire. Bissell wrote a memoir, *Reflections of a Cold Warrior*, published in the mid-1990s after his death, which is unapologetic and yet also regardful of the dilemmas he confronted.

Richard Bissell was descended on his father's side from a line of Bissells who came over from England to Windsor, Connecticut, in 1636. The Bissell family was a prominent one in the affairs of the colony, helping to establish churches and fight the Indians. One ancestor was a spy for George Washington in the American Revolutionary War. Richard Bissell's father and grandfather made money and attained social prominence as executives in the insurance business. Born in Hartford in 1909 (in the Mark Twain house on Farmington Avenue), Bissell was afflicted with "severely crossed eyes," as he recalled in his memoirs, which required him to wear glasses from the age of six months. Summers were spent in Maine, where he gained his lifelong passion for sailing. There were frequent trips to Europe—typically to Venice and Paris and once, in about 1919, to the First World War battlefields of northern France. That trip made a strong impression on the boy. "The July heat was intense, and the scene was dreary . . . there were very few trees," he later recalled—"all had been destroyed by the war. I formed the impression of World War I as a cataclysm. The sights surely spurred my interest in history; they may also have contributed to my becoming increasingly isolationist in the 1930s, when I was horrified at the idea of America's being involved in a war like that again."

Bissell attended boarding school at Groton in northern Massachusetts. An Episcopal academy for boys founded in 1884 by Endicott Peabody, a clergyman from a famous old-line Massachusetts family, Groton became a hatchery for prominent empire managers-to-be, including Dean Acheson, Paul Nitze, and Averell Harriman. The school's Latin motto, adopted from the Anglican Book of Common Prayer, was *Cui servire est regnere*, which translates as "whose service is perfect freedom." For Bissell's generation, the dominant figure was the Reverend Peabody, who served as rector for a half century. Peabody created a Spartan environment at Groton, reminiscent of English boarding schools with its cold showers, austere dormitory cubicles, and emphasis on athletics and other tenets of Muscular Christianity. Bissell suffered from homesickness and got on poorly with his classmates: "I was shy, I wasn't a good athlete, and I was scared of them." In time he made friends, and even though Bissell found Peabody to be something of a bully, the rector succeeded in producing in him, as in so many others, an aspiration toward public service.

Bissell studied history as a Yale undergraduate and stayed in New Haven to earn a Ph.D. in economics and then to teach at the university. During the Second World War, he worked at the War Shipping Administration, helping to arrange for the efficient allocation of vessels for civilian and military use. He planned to go back to teaching after the war but instead was virtually conscripted to join in the administration of the massive Marshall Plan of economic recovery aid to Europe. Through school ties and other personal contacts, he knew many of the senior people involved in the early operations of the CIA, which had been created after the war, and he started to become immersed in intelligence work as well.

At first, Bissell worked as a consultant for the CIA, helping out as a "troubleshooter" for the agency's covert campaign to overthrow the regime of President Jacobo Arbenz Guzmán in Guatemala. Arbenz was suspected by Washington of having communist sympathies, and his toppling, in 1954, along with the successful CIA-sponsored coup against Iran's Mohammad Mossadegh the year before, produced a feeling of invulnerability among the spymaster crowd. At the White House, the thinking was that covert operations were a low-cost, low-maintenance way to accomplish America's foreign policy aims. Known for his calm under pressure and his skill at bureaucratic politics, Bissell rose to become the head of the CIA's covert-plans department. He authorized a plan to use the American Mafia to assassinate Fidel Castro. The Mafia seemed a "reasonable partner" to him because it had once controlled gambling casinos in Cuba and wanted to get them back and presumably had the contacts for carrying out the job. Although Bissell had no desire to be personally involved, "mainly because I was not competent to handle relations with the Mafia," his secretary fielded calls from the likes of the mobster Joseph "Joe Bananas" Bonanno.

Bissell was an architect of the anti-Castro Bay of Pigs invasion of Cuba in 1961—a spectacular failure that cost him his job. He accepted that he had made mistakes but believed the operation might have succeeded had President John F. Kennedy authorized a bolder military plan. Ironically, he had rooted for Kennedy's election in the fall of 1960 because, as he told a friend, "I think Kennedy is surrounded by a group of men with a much livelier awareness than the Republicans of the extreme crisis that we are living in. . . . What I really mean is that I believe the Democrats will be far less inhibited in trying to do something about it." He was inspired by Kennedy's "hard-line" inaugural speech, although mindful that, with the stakes so high, "any prospect of presidential vacillation in the face of Communist expansionism risked a loss of confidence in America's leadership of the West."

Bissell grasped the moral road he was traveling. "My philosophy during my last two or three years in the agency was very definitely that the end justified the means, and I was not going to be held back," he acknowledged in his memoirs. Such sentiments were common among the Groton crowd; Paul Nitze once said that as the Greeks regarded the Persians, he regarded the communists, as "barbarians" against whom everything is permitted. There was a religious inflection to this sentiment: "In history, every religion has greatly honored those members who destroyed the enemy," Nitze observed, and "Groton boys were taught that." And communism, after all, was an aggressively atheistic movement, finding its greatest expression in civilizations, in Russia and China, that Americans generally regarded as alien.

Over the course of his life, Bissell had gone from being a committed isolationist, a supporter of Charles Lindbergh's prewar America First Committee, to a subscriber to the "overwhelmingly obvious" proposition that "we are deeply concerned with the internal affairs of other nations and that, insofar as we make any effort to encourage the evolution of the world community in accord with our values, we will be endeavoring purposefully to influence these affairs." He had come to view the United States as the world's natural upholder of an "international order" to "preserve democracy and protect human rights." He acknowledged the tension between a culture of democracy and a culture of secrecy but still came down on the side that "publicity is the enemy of intellectual honesty, objectivity and decisiveness." He was, to the last, a man of empire.

Richard Bissell and the Groton fraternity represented the first generation of imperial stewards. They cast the mold for the job—which remained intact even as, over the course of the American Century, the clout of the Anglican elite declined in the East Coast foreign policy establishment. At its senior management echelons, the Accidental Empire drew sustenance from that greatest of all American social institutions, the melting pot. The crossover figure was Henry Kissinger. Dean Gooderham Acheson was the Connecticut-reared son of an English-born Church of England priest. Henry Kissinger was a German-Jewish refugee from Nazi Germany who attended high school in Manhattan's Washington Heights at night while working in a shaving-brush factory for eleven dollars a week during the day. Only in America. A summa cum laude graduate of Harvard, Kissinger scaled the ladder of the national security establishment with the help of his brains and a remarkable talent for cultivating powerful patrons, starting with New York's Nelson Rockefeller, the rich grandson of the American oil baron John D. Rockefeller, Sr. Among the members of Richard

Nixon's inner circle, no one was better than Kissinger at managing the boss's insecurities. Kissinger was without any doubt a cosmopolitan, and he was followed by another cerebral and worldly first-generation immigrant, Zbigniew Brzezinski, the international relations academic who served as Jimmy Carter's national security advisor. Brzezinski was born in 1920s Warsaw, where he was raised in a strict Catholic household, and educated in North America, at McGill University in Montreal and then Harvard. His father was a Polish diplomat. He taught international politics at Columbia in New York and was a cofounder with David Rockefeller, a brother of Nelson, of the Trilateral Commission, a private group of financial and intellectual types from North America, Europe, and Japan that sparked oddball anxieties, expressed by provincial sorts in America, of a global elite's conspiracy to manage the world.

Kissinger and Brzezinski, both of whom spoke English with what a native midwestern American would notice as a foreign accent, may have struck many Americans as exotic figures. Nevertheless, they fit comfortably into the imperial role as it had been shaped by their Anglican elite predecessors—and indeed, with their sense of history, both as academics and as men who had grown up in a turbulent Europe, they proved to be cunning imperial gamesmen. Brzezinski had a visceral antipathy—the equal of anything felt by a Groton man—of the Kremlin's godless empire, which was extended to his native Poland after World War II. He was an architect of the Carter Doctrine and devised the plan of covert military aid to the anti-Soviet Afghan mujahideen.

Even as the cast of imperial presidents and functionaries changed over the years, the basic mind-set of the American empire displayed certain constants, familiar in varying degrees to empires in all times. With the premium put on secrecy, the Accidental Empire was a fairly regular liar to the American people—and to the world outside America—about its actions. Lying is endemic to politics and especially to imperial politics. As Richard Bissell found, when the stakes are so high and the moments of crisis never seem to stop, it becomes easier to believe that the ends justify the means. Notwithstanding America's democratic foundation, resting on the "consent of the governed," as Jefferson put it, the imperial class felt an entitlement to lie in America's own best interests. America's journalists often understood that they were being lied to—a seminal analysis of the new regime of imperial lying came in the 1964 book *The*

Invisible Government, by David Wise, the Washington bureau chief of the *New York Herald Tribune*, and Thomas B. Ross, a Washington correspondent of the *Chicago Sun-Times*. (The CIA, David Wise later said, considered buying up the entire print run from the publisher, Random House, to keep the book from getting out.) But the exposure of a lie generally came when things no longer mattered to the government. Lying was a bipartisan practice of the imperial class, and the lies were big ones, bona fide whoppers. On the matter of the Washington-directed coup in Guatemala, which ousted the democratically elected leader Arbenz, Dwight D. Eisenhower's Republican secretary of state, John Foster Dulles, told the public: "The situation is being cured by the Guatemalans themselves." On the matter of the plot to overthrow Fidel Castro, John F. Kennedy's Democratic secretary of state, Dean Rusk, declared: "The American people are entitled to know whether we are intervening in Cuba or intend to do so in the future. The answer to that question is no." The disposition to lie degraded America's democratic government during the American Century, contributing to a climate of public cynicism toward Washington that in varying degrees has prevailed ever since.

A less obvious but no less harmful feature of the Accidental Empire was its cultural blind spot. Dean Acheson and Richard Bissell, Henry Kissinger and Zbigniew Brzezinski, were cosmopolitans, but it is hard even for worldly and brilliant men to know everything worth knowing about the world, to see everything worth seeing. Their intimate acquaintance was with Europe, where the Groton men had spent their summers and where Kissinger and Brzezinski had been born. They understood Europe not as an abstraction but as a kaleidoscope of cultures with distinct histories. They had faith in Europe's core values, as the values that had helped give birth to America. The Marshall Plan was a product of their faith and their acuity of vision. Recipients of U.S. economic aid had considerable discretion in their use of the money: The plan was not a one-size-fits-all blueprint but an accommodation to widely divergent political and economic conditions in countries ranging from Britain to Italy. It was a spectacular success—the gold standard of postwar aid programs.

The blind spot applied to the world outside Europe—and especially the world that lay beyond predominantly Christian societies. The problem was in part a racial one—a tendency to see "the natives," wherever they happened to live, as an undifferentiated mass of non-European poor people, the "underprivi-leged." The leaders of the Accidental Empire were raised to help the less fortu-nate, and they did not lack compassion—the United States was a principal force in the establishment of the World Bank, which had its headquarters in Wash-ington. But like the British Empire, which took up "the white man's burden," the American empire failed to appreciate that good intentions did not tend to di-minish the sensitivity of the locals to the intrusive presence of the "foreigner." Whereas America liked to see itself as a spreader of hope in the "third world," itself a patronizing term, others were apt to see the spear of a conspiracy.

Early on, it was evident that the blind spot that would most harm Washing-ton was in the Islamic Middle East. The American Century's imperial presi-dents and managers included Baptists and Episcopalians, a Catholic and a Jew, but not a Muslim among them. That was a pity, because a Muslim, steeped in either Arab or Persian culture, surely could have provided a map of the cultural minefields confronting America in the Middle East. The British Empire had sparked great resentments from Arabs and Persians, who sensibly enough viewed the British as an obstacle to their economic and political aspirations of self-determination. America, as Britain's close wartime ally, and as an "Anglo" civi-lization founded by Christian white people, naturally was viewed with wariness as it took over for the British in the Middle East. Nevertheless, Truman's suc-cessor, Dwight D. Eisenhower, the army general who had plotted the Allies' D-day invasion of Europe, found himself at a loss to understand such senti-ments. Soon after taking office in January of 1953, Ike was informed by advisors that the Iranians might choose to align themselves with the Soviet bloc rather than the American one. Eisenhower asked why it was not possible "to get some of the people in these down-trodden countries to like us instead of hating us." Eisenhower authorized the CIA coup that toppled Mohammad Mossadegh, the Iranian leader who had outraged the British by nationalizing their Anglo-Iranian Oil Company (the precursor of British Petroleum). The British, who were in on the initial planning, were delighted by the coup—their belief, in keeping with their imperial-commercial tradition, was that Mossadegh had taken one of their assets without fair compensation and deserved what he got. It was the Americans who looked naïve—for believing in a communist Iranian threat that in hindsight looks exaggerated. The legacy was a lasting Iranian bitterness toward the United States that helped form Iran's anti-American Islamic revolution in the 1970s.

A streak of mendacity plus the affliction of a blind spot does not make for a particularly attractive picture of the Accidental Empire. It might seem puzzling that the empire proved as globally successful as it did. And yet America's "democratic empire" was less oppressive than the British global empire, with its system of colonies, and by many orders of magnitude less cruel than earlier empires that had stomped through ancient battlegrounds like the Middle East. Imperial Americans of the mid-twentieth century did not take slaves back to the metropole to cook meals and wash clothes, as the ancient Romans did, and they did not raise a military corps of Janissaries by stealing away young boys from home, as the Ottomans did. And against the example of the American empire of the mid-twentieth century was the counterexample of the Soviet empire. That was the plausible alternative of the time, not some imaginary ideal empire—and it is hard to imagine a better foil for the American empire in terms of highlighting the attractive qualities of American civilization.

The convention among international relations analysts is to describe the period between the Soviet nuclear bomb test in August of 1949 and the expiration of the Soviet Union in December of 1991—that forty-two-year stretch of geopolitical time—as a bipolar world. As a portrayal of the military balance between the United States and the Soviet Union during this period, that description is a roughly accurate one. The two great powers had the capacity to destroy each other with their atomic weapons, and that military fact was a central element in the recurrent political crises of the era, notably the Cuban Missile Crisis in the fall of 1962. Lesser powers for the most part had little choice but to align themselves with one or the other superpower.

But from a broader perspective, that of the prism of civilizations, the bipolar portrait is not an adequate one. Even as they remained "tied" with the Soviets in ICBM counts, and even though the cream of Soviet defense science was able to get a satellite, Sputnik, into orbit before the elite of American military science made that happen, the Americans dominated in most other categories that mattered to ordinary people around the planet as they apprehended how life was lived in the United States and how life was lived, as best as could be known, in the USSR. From 1950 to 1960, the output of Japan's economy more than doubled while the economies of Soviet-dominated Poland and Hungary each grew by just under 60 percent. In 1960, a rebuilt Western Europe, the preserve of NATO, had a per capita GDP two and a half times that of communist Eastern Europe's.

And if American-style consumer capitalism was not to everyone's taste, including that of some Western Europeans, what could the Kremlin's leaders put up against it? The boasts of Nikita Khrushchev—"our color televisions are better"—were transparently preposterous. The Soviet Union had starved millions of its citizens in the famine in Ukraine in the 1930s and imprisoned millions of others in its vast gulags. By contrast, the ugliest features of America's society—like the slums of its great cities—were open to foreign inspection. Indeed, the foreign expert, in a tradition going back to Tocqueville's visit to 1830s Jacksonian America, was invited to visit and judge: The Carnegie Foundation recruited and funded the Swedish political economist Gunnar Myrdal to assemble his devastating study of race relations, *An American Dilemma: The Negro Problem and Modern Democracy*, published in 1944.

"Throughout the world there is a fear of the current American stress on arms and money. Yet it remains true that the principal imperialism the American exercises is the imperialism of attraction," Max Lerner, a journalist and professor of American civilization at Brandeis, wrote in his 1957 book, *America as a Civilization*. "If he is not admired he is envied; and even his enemies and rivals pay him the homage of imitation. People throughout the world turn almost as by a tropism to the American image," Lerner marveled. Even a French critic of the American imperium, the writer Emmanuel Todd, later conceded that "most of the world consented to the rise of American hegemony, despite the patches of sympathy for communism among peasants, the working class, and many individuals."

As for the American people, their attitude toward the Accidental Empire was ambivalent. Many were upset about the lies that were told about events like the

Bay of Pigs. And yet the American public, like its representatives in Congress, generally submitted to the rise of an Imperial Presidency. Truman's decision to go to war in Korea without even a debate in Congress did not spark a popular rebellion. (Truman's popularity plunged later in his presidency, when the war bogged down.) Probably the main reason that Americans submitted to what might seem like an un-American system of government was fear—the cold war was a genuinely scary time, with Americans taking quite seriously the possibility of a nuclear rain. But there was also an element of seduction. The powerful president, with his finger on the nuclear button, became a figure of mystique. The media's obsession, and the obsession of the politically minded intellectual elite, was with the awesome responsibilities of the man in the Oval Office. He was "the leader of the free world," in a cosmic narrative pitting good against evil. On his good judgment rested "our" lives. Nothing like that could be said of any other person in American life.

The Accidental Empire, in all the years between the end of the Second World War and the collapse of the Soviet Union, faced only one serious crisis of identity. That was over Vietnam. Vietnam was not an outlier in the American Century—it was not a rogue operation out of character for the Accidental Empire, as might be thought, but an apt illustration of the empire's main personality traits. There was, to start with, an improvised quality to the initial phase of the venture, which began in the 1950s as a stopgap, to fill a geopolitical vacuum left by the withdrawal of the French, the longtime colonial rulers of Vietnam. There was the blind spot: Washington never developed a good purchase on Vietnamese society—it never, in particular, was able to separate the communist strands of the Vietnamese rebellion from the anti-imperial, nationalist strands, and it failed to appreciate how much popular resentment of the U.S. role in Vietnam was based on perceptions that America, far from being an agent of freedom in a cold war theater, was simply another foreign intruder. America's leaders were at times painfully aware of the limitations of their vision, but the problem had no ready solution. In 1965, as he pondered the merits of a pause in the bombing of North Vietnam, President Lyndon Baines Johnson, a native of the Texas Hill Country, confessed to an aide that he was finding it just about impossible to put himself into the shoes of his counterpart, Ho Chi Minh, to gauge how the North Vietnamese might respond to such a step. "I don't know him," LBJ told the aide. "I don't know his ancestry or his customs or his beliefs. It is tough, very tough."

And there were the lies, told by one imperial president after another, LBJ included. His administration resorted to deceit to prod Congress to authorize an expansion of the war—a blank check, in effect—after an attack on a U.S. destroyer in the Gulf of Tonkin in 1964. Contrary to Defense Secretary Robert McNamara's claim that the destroyer, the *Maddox*, had been "carrying out a routine mission of the type we carry out all over the world at all times," the vessel in fact had been on an intelligence-collection mission, within North Vietnamese waters, at a time when U.S.-trained South Vietnamese commandos were assaulting communist North Vietnamese facilities.

Still, for all that, Vietnam would not have precipitated an imperial identity crisis had Johnson's war not bogged down, with a rapid increase in the deaths of American soldiers, at a time when the United States still used the draft to raise its armies. By the late 1960s, America, with Vietnam as the bloody case in point, finally engaged in a full-blown public debate on the implications of the global security role the country had assumed after World War II. An aging Walter Lippmann now found a wider audience for his critique, sharper than it had ever been, of the Henry Luce vision of an America that would intervene virtually anywhere and everywhere freedom was under attack in the world. In 1967, Lippmann addressed his colleagues in the press at a dinner in Washington to mark the end of his career as a columnist. The crucial question for Americans, he told the group, was "how wisely, how gracefully, how skillfully and how constructively they would adjust themselves to the reality of power and to being first among equals; to living with the fact that while we might still be the strongest power, we could not and should not wish to be omniscient, omnicompetent, omnipotent; that we were not the leader of mankind and not the policeman of the world." Lippmann, who had spent a lifetime at court as an informal foreign policy advisor to presidents, had by then broken with the Johnson White House over the war. "Put not your trust in princes," he ruefully told his fellow journalists.

That message got through to the people and to their representatives in Congress. Legislators, after more blood was spilled, finally voted to cut off funds for the Vietnam War. And they approved a War Powers Resolution requiring Congress's express approval to keep troops in combat. But as it turned out, this was the high-water mark of the challenge to the Accidental Empire, and it was not a lethal one. The winding down of the Vietnam War and the shift in the 1970s from a draft to an all-volunteer force for the military sharply curtailed public criticism of America's continuing global-policeman role. The War Powers Resolution came to be seen in Washington, even on Capitol Hill, as a dead letter. With the cold war grinding on, from Jimmy Carter's covert program to arm the Afghan mujahideen to Ronald Reagan's secret scheme to sell weapons to Iran and use the money to fund the anti-communist Nicaraguan Contras, Congress did not have the political stomach or the political inclination to end the Imperial Presidency. "Frankly, if I were president, I would thumb my nose at the legislation," the majority leader of the Senate said of the War Powers Resolution in 1988, at the end of the Reagan presidency. The speaker was a veteran Democrat, Robert Byrd of West Virginia, usually known for his defense of legislative prerogatives.

A visitor to Washington in 1990, at the cresting of the American Century, would have been hard put to identify the face of empire. The U.S. State Department was in a nondescript building in a neighborhood, known as Foggy Bottom, that featured a charming sculpture of Albert Einstein. On the Washington Mall was a Vietnam memorial, but its main feature, a conjunction of two polished black granite walls on which were inscribed the names of the dead or missing, was somber and austere. (Not until 1995, forty-two years after the fighting had stopped, did Washington dedicate a separate memorial to the veterans of the Korean War, known as America's "forgotten war.") And yet this picture was misleading. By this time, forty-nine years after Roosevelt had lectured Churchill on the evils of imperialism at Argentia Bay, an imperial consciousness was as deeply etched into the mind-set of Washington as it was into the London of the British Empire. America's global empire, for the governing class, was much like what the British Empire had been for the British governing class, an "elaborate abstraction of ideas, loyalties, fancies, bluffs [and] aspirations."

On these terms, Francis Fukuyama's famous essay on the "end of history," published in mid-1989, stands out as a quintessential imperial document—and a rather smug one at that. Fukuyama, the son of Japanese immigrants, was born in Chicago in 1952. He wrote his Harvard doctoral dissertation on Soviet foreign policy and was serving on the State Department's policy planning staff, as deputy director for European political-military affairs, when he made his pronouncement. The end of history boiled down to the continuation of the American imperium—a liberal American-ruled order, with no apparent rival as the Soviet Union faded from the picture. China? "Chinese competitiveness and expansionism on the world scene have virtually disappeared," Fukuyama wrote, in one soon-to-be-disproved observation. He believed there was no limit to America's reach, to its "imperialism of attraction," in Max Lerner's phrase, and so did many of his peers in the Washington imperial class. "One of these days, the American people are going to awaken to the fact that we have become an imperial nation," Irving Kristol, known as the godfather of neoconservativism, wrote in the 1990s. Awake or not, the public was largely along for the ride—which in the post–cold war "unipolar" world would prove an unexpectedly bumpy one.

PART TWO

End of the Ascendancy

T here is usually no easy way to tell when a civilization has reached a peak of influence. If the peak is followed by a steep decline, that is one thing, but the path typically leads not to a cliff but to a plateau or a slope of gradual decline. Russian civilization spread its influence first through the "white" empire of the tsars and then through the "red" empire of the Soviet leaders. The empire imploded in the 1980s, with defeat in a war in Afghanistan and anti-Russian nationalistic rebellions along the periphery. But its global prestige, along with the prestige of Moscow and of Russian civilization generally, had been waning for decades amid a serious case of economic, political, and cultural sclerosis. The high point, in retrospect, may have been the launch of the Sputnik satellite in 1957, a feat that surpassed anything that America or anyone else at that time had accomplished in outer space. The British Empire—the global expression of the British way of life, and a singularly proud achievement of the British people—dissolved after the Second World War, when London begged Washington to take over its global responsibilities. But its twilight probably began in the Edwardian period, before the cataclysm of the First World War and that war's devastating toll on the British economy and on Britain's confidence as the world's greatest power. Islamic civilization flowered between the eighth and twelfth centuries. It lost its position of global leadership in the thirteenth century, as Christian Europe began to regain control of the Mediterranean and the Mongols invaded from Asia. As for Roman civilization, historians are still debating when it reached its apogee; by some accounts, the decline, drawn out over centuries, lasted longer than the rise.

"Declinism" can be a lazy habit of thought, more a mood than an actual system of analysis, but there is laziness and a lack of rigor on the other side of the intellectual coin as well. Those who hold to the belief that what goes down must come up, that the pendulum swinging in one direction must of necessity start to swing in the other, are not good students of history, which is not a physical science. Great civilizations have their ebbs and flows, their cyclical rhythms, but at some point the peak is reached. As the nineteenth century gave way to the twentieth, a British journalist posed the question, "Will the Empire which is celebrating one centenary of Trafalgar survive for the next?" The answer turned out to be a resounding no. The "declinists" were right.

Part 2 of this book focuses on the strong signs of a passing for the American Century—for that crowning moment of an ascendancy that goes all the way back to the British settlement of the New World. Just as America's rise showcased the strengths of American civilization, the end of this centuries-long incline is an illustration of the weaknesses and the limitations of the civilization. But this "end" is also about how others have come up in the world. Chapter 4 shows that America in important respects is no longer preeminent in ways that it aspires to be and thus has a diminished claim to being the face of tomorrow. Chapter 5 focuses on a paradox of power: America retains the world's preeminent military arsenal but has overextended the frontiers of its Accidental Empire and is mired in a bog of its own making. Chapter 6 illustrates a case in point—post-Soviet Russia—of how Henry Luce's American Century lost its magnetic appeal. Russia and other societies have begun gravitating away from the American sun and evolving according to their own patterns.

Chapter Four

Middling America

"It isn't supreme—that's what's the matter with it, and I hate anything middling," said Pandora Day.

Henry James, *Pandora*, 1884

Fernand Braudel did not share the prejudices that so many intellectuals of his generation in France felt toward America. Perhaps this was because Braudel had an especially wide frame of reference gained from his study of diverse civilizations, as well as practical knowledge of the world gained from his varied travels and experiences, among them being held as a prisoner of war by Nazi Germany. He might have stayed comfortably put in Paris after taking his degree in history from the Sorbonne in the 1920s, but instead, in the 1930s, he moved to Brazil to help start a university in São Paulo. "I met black people in an atmosphere that reminded me of *Gone With the Wind*," he later wrote. In the early 1960s, he published one of his more topical books, later translated into English as *A History of Civilizations*, which sketched comparisons between the world's great civilizations, with an assessment of their contemporary strengths and weaknesses. "America, still so young, has grown a little older," he wrote. "The Vietnam War has aged it still more. It has become conscious of its history. . . . Certainly, the past is beginning to weigh on its shoulders." And yet Braudel remained, on balance, bullish on American civilization, seeing nothing that came close to surpassing it: "But let us not forget that America lives in advance of modernity. It is still the country of the future—and that, at least, is a sign of hope and a proof of vitality."

Braudel died in France in 1985. His proposition from the 1960s—"America lives in advance of modernity"—no longer holds up. America's traditional claim to being exceptional on these terms, as better than others in terms of "progress" and "the good life," as America herself measures these signposts of modernity, is foundering. America can no longer claim to be the dominant pacesetter civilization—the standard setter of the benchmarks of excellence. It is by no means universally second best—its military is still the global benchmark—but part of what it meant to be "the powerhouse from which the ideals spread throughout the world," as Henry Luce called the America of the 1940s, was supremacy across a broad spectrum. No other civilization has replaced America in this role, at least not yet; instead the benchmarks are scattering around the world. It is possible, given the nature of globalization, in which ideas and talents move so quickly, that there will never again be a single benchmark civilization, like America of the twentieth century, Great Britain of the nineteenth, and Rome long ago. In the meantime, the world is looking increasingly to a range of different models in its search for the best, with America but one among many others in this exploration. And this undermines, fatally, the American Century's conception of American civilization as *the* standard for tomorrow.

One reason the benchmarks are scattering is that there was always something rather artificial about the dominance that America came to possess at the end of the Second World War, when so much of the planet was either in ruins or still shackled by colonial rule. That situation simply could not last. Consider the trajectory of modern research science. There was a time when a rising young scientist in America would feel an absolute obligation to put in a few years at a preeminent laboratory in Europe, as did the physicist Robert Oppenheimer, the father of America's atomic bomb, who did postgraduate work in the 1920s at a leading center for theoretical physics in the medieval German town of Göttingen. In the decades following the Second World War, European scientists felt a similar need to burnish their careers and broaden their minds with a stint at a place in the United States like Harvard or Berkeley. Those times have passed. These days, America is no longer "the center" of the scientific world, noted the geneticist Gerry Rubin, a Boston native who is the founding director of Janelia Farm, a biomedical research facility in Northern Virginia funded by the Howard Hughes Medical Institute. There is no longer, Rubin told me in an interview, *any* center; there are nodes of excellence scattered in cities and regions all over the world, including new entrants like Singapore, which is spending a lot of money to attract world-class biomedical researchers in an audacious bid to achieve global preeminence in a matter of years. America still has more nodes of scientific excellence than anyone else, but the gap is closing.

If the story of middling America is told this way, as a matter of the natural rise of the rest of the world, it may not sound all that troubling. But while this is one dimension of the tale, it is not the only one. Middling America is also a matter of deficiencies in the American model. Most glaring are the chronic ailments in the realm of the economy. The first three-quarters of the twentieth century showcased the United States as not only the world's most affluent society but no less remarkably also a society in which the gap between rich and poor steadily narrowed. As a result, America was able to avoid, for the most part, the severe class divisions that wrecked prospects for social and economic progress in so much of Latin America and parts of Europe and the Middle East. But America's pacesetting role as an egalitarian society began to come to an end in the mid-1970s. Since that time, income inequality has been widening for a number of reasons, not least the failure of America to supply all its citizens with a first-class education, starting in primary school. A study published by the Federal Reserve Bank of Boston in 2002 found that since the 1970s U.S. families have been significantly less likely to move up the income ladder, prompting questions that "go to the heart of our identity as a nation." A 2007 study by the Pew Charitable Trusts found that economic mobility was actually higher in Denmark, Canada, and Finland than in America, and by some measurements, mobility is also higher in the United Kingdom and perhaps even in Germany, despite its reputation as a sluggish society. Should these trends continue, "Old America" could supplant "Old Europe" as a breeder of the envies and resentments that inevitably are nourished by growing income inequality.

The widening income gap suggests a broader failure of the laissez-faire approach to capitalism that has been a distinctive feature of U.S. economic policy, especially over the last thirty years. During that time, America has offered a model of deregulation as a solution for the problems of more state-controlled economies. But what lessons are there for the world to draw? The spectacular meltdown of America's financial markets in 2008—forcing the government bailout of humbled Wall Street firms—was caused in part by weakly regulated lenders who underwrote risky products poorly understood by consumers. By March 2009, federal guarantees and other government aid to rescue banks and other financial institutions exceeded $1 trillion. The crisis followed others in which weak or nonexistent government regulation was evident, as in the meltdown of the energy conglomerate Enron in a deregulated electricity marketplace. America's financial markets long have been hobbled by a patchwork system of federal and state regulation dating back to the 1930s. The state-of-the-art regulator is generally conceded to be the Financial Services Authority in London, a "unified" regulator in charge of oversight across the spectrum of financial industries.

Nor does the U.S. model of corporate management stand as the twenty-first-century benchmark for the world. The American business manager once was thought to be without peer in his ability to harvest profits from the global marketplace. Not just the Soviet Union but Europe and nearly everywhere else seemed to stand for mediocrity compared to the American example—and it was the American business organization that stood for the virtues of teamwork, planning, and efficiency. In Billy Wilder's 1961 movie, *One, Two, Three*, Jimmy Cagney, playing the role of C. R. MacNamara, Coca-Cola's top man in Germany, offered a comic portrayal of that sort of "all for the team" executive. The role worked because the image was based in reality. America's fall from this perch is most painfully evident in the sad saga of Detroit. The once-preeminent U.S. auto industry has been in decline for at least thirty years. It is a story of a failure of vision, of bureaucratic stagnation, and of an erosion of a commitment to quality, which was all laid out by the renegade GM executive John DeLorean in his 1979 indictment *On a Clear Day You Can See General Motors*. In July of 2008, GM had a stock-market capitalization of $6 billion—compared to $163 billion for Toyota.

A final testament to America's fall from the economic heights is the decline in status of the U.S. dollar. As a global currency of first choice for the world's traders, the dollar has had an amazingly long run, dating from its triumph over the British pound in the first half of the twentieth century. But that run now appears to be over. It is surely only a matter of time before the oil kingdoms of the Middle East shift from their long-standing practice of denominating the price of oil in dollars to a new system in which the price is pegged to a basket of currencies, including the Euro. No currency has displaced the dollar as the unit of global choice—not yet, anyway. But the once hegemonic status of the dollar is yielding to a more multipolar financial arrangement in which a variety of currencies have credible standing in global markets. For the global investor, the world is no longer a U.S.-centric one.

While these economic barometers stand out as unmistakable signs of a loss in America's role as a benchmark society, there are less obvious but no less real examples in the domain of culture. I got an inkling of America's readjusted place in the cultural cosmos on a 2007 visit to Berlin. Weimar Berlin of the 1920s, famous for its outward, experimental disposition, was a frank admirer of the American example. The Germans were no slouches when it came to scientific and technological inventiveness, and yet one of Berlin's inhabitants, returning to the city after a five-year absence, eyed its new motorways and airport hangars and called Berlin "an apostle of Americanism." No longer. I spent the better part of a day with a prominent young architect, Gesine Weinmiller, a native of Bavaria who had studied in Munich and opened an office in Berlin in 1992. At that time, three years after the fall of the Berlin Wall and with the city no longer divided, Berlin was developing into a vast construction project for the latest and most vital in architecture. Architects from all over the world were invited to submit designs for the most interesting projects. I was curious to see what touches of the "new Berlin" had an American reference point, and the answer was, almost none. Weinmiller took me on a long driving tour of the city; we looked at newly constructed foreign embassies, office buildings, apartment houses, and monuments. Only once, at the sight of the DaimlerChrysler skyscraper at Potsdamer Platz, did she point her finger at an unmistakably American reference—an example of the Chicago style of the late nineteenth century, which a European historian once called "a conspicuously distinctive American gift to the world."

Open and friendly, Weinmiller was dressed casually in khakis, her blond hair pulled back behind a beret. As a practicing Lutheran, her dream was to design a church, she told me. (She was a finalist in the competition to build the

Holocaust memorial in Berlin.) In 2000, she spent two months in America on an Eisenhower fellowship, the prestigious award given by a foundation in Philadelphia, since 1954, to "emerging leaders from around the world." She visited Los Angeles, Chicago, New York, Phoenix, and El Paso, among other spots. The idea of the fellowship was to give something of America for recipients to take back to their home countries, but in the case of Weinmiller, the program did not quite work according to plan. "I saw less good architecture in two months than I see in two days here," she told me, making clear that she was referring not to the marvels of American architecture of a century or so ago but to structures built by her contemporaries.

America's present-day architectural middlingness is most evident in its public works—in the structures necessary to everyday life and commerce that also show a face to the world. In the industrial age, the supreme statement of this type was made by the railway station, and America contributed gems like New York's Grand Central Terminal—the Beaux Arts design of the Minnesota firm of Reed & Stern, which opened in 1913. Nowadays, the international airport is looked to for the same kind of message. America's veteran architecture critic, Paul Goldberger, has asked the question, "Can anyone design a nice airport?" His answer is yes—but not, it seems, in the United States, where "the last thing that cash-starved airlines and airport authorities want to think about is aesthetic appeal." Airports built in the last generation, in line with the Denver and Atlanta models, "enhance the sense that the whole thing is less a piece of architecture than one big machine." But the situation is different, he noted, in Europe and Asia. "The best new airports in the world," he said, are in Beijing, where the British architect Norman Foster has designed an enormous $3.65 billion terminal, and on the outskirts of Madrid, where the British Richard Rodgers Partnership has contributed a new terminal. In the Beijing airport, with its "sensuous curves," Foster has delivered "an aesthetically exhilarating place," Goldberger said—he has "done for airports what the architects Reed & Stern did for train stations with their design for Grand Central."

One of the more exasperating proofs of the waning of America as a benchmark civilization comes to the mind of the American expatriate who plugs into the

Internet or places a cell-phone call in countries like Japan, South Korea, Finland, or Norway. Things there work *faster* than they do in America, and this is, historically speaking, a rather shocking thing. Americans have long prided themselves on being a speed society. America did not invent the automobile, but Detroit and Madison Avenue, with help from the American road-building industry, turned early-twentieth-century America into the world's preeminent example of a motorways civilization. And this was essential to America's image as a society that did things at a lickety-split pace. America, likewise, was a pioneer in jet transport and landline telephone connections. In January 1878, New Haven, Connecticut, beat London by twenty months in the race to be the first city in the world to open an exchange for the new landline telephone. The English critic G. K. Chesterton, musing about a trip to New York City, attributed the American ability to be "efficient" in "the fashionable thing" to an attribute of youth: "We can imagine a very young person forgetting the old toy in the excitement of a new one."

For the likes of Mark Twain, a journey to late-nineteenth-century Europe was a chance to make sport of a society that, compared to America, lived in slow motion. "In all these years, the American fountain pen has hardly got a start in Europe," Twain wrote in the early 1890s, a few years before he turned sixty. "There is no market for it. It is too handy, too inspiring, too capable, too much of a time saver," he said. "Then there is the elevator, lift, *ascenseur*. America has had the benefit of this invaluable contrivance for a generation and a half, and it is now used in all our cities and villages, in all hotels, in all lofty business buildings and factories, and in many private dwellings. But we can't spread it, we can't beguile Europe with it. In Europe, an elevator is even to this day a rarity and a curiosity. Especially a curiosity." He concluded with barbs aimed at the European railway and postal services.

Considering the age he lived in, Twain probably would have found it inconceivable that the day would come when the Americans—"always alive, alert, up early in the morning"—would be slower than the Europeans, as well as other peoples, to take advantage of the "invaluable contrivances" of the modern world. These days, speed has to do with the pace and quality of digital connections, and America is very far behind the pack. Consider one standard measurement of digital speed: the time it takes to download data from the Internet to a personal computer device. Japan leads the world with a "median download speed" of 64 megabits per second (mbps), and the ranks go down from South Korea at 50 mbps to Finland at 22, Sweden at 17, the Netherlands at 9, and Portugal at 8. America is the world's fifteenth fastest country, at 5 mbps. Thus, the average user in Japan can download an iTunes movie in about two minutes; for the American user, nearly half an hour is needed. What's more, access to broadband networks is about four times cheaper in Japan than in America. And this is not just a matter of consumer convenience: Digital speed is a basic ingredient for product innovation. Whenever such surveys are published, critics often point out that America is so much bigger than the places against which it is compared. And yet no American state, no region within any state, not even any city, is as digitally well equipped as the Baltic nation of Estonia—eStonia to its admirers around the world. Those admirers include *Wired*, the San Francisco–based magazine that specializes in mapping the terrain of California's Silicon Valley but seems to have found heaven elsewhere. Noting Estonia's virtues as a place in which almost all bank transactions are done over the Internet, where the government has adopted online voting, and "cell phones can be used to pay for parking or lunch," *Wired* was forced to conclude: "Someday, the rest of the world will be as wired as this tiny Baltic nation." Is Arizona, say, a more formidable technological-infrastructure challenge than Norway? A cellular phone signal is available virtually everywhere in Norway, even with its long coastline of mountains and fjords. That's not the case in flatter Arizona, which has a similar population density.

Speed, of course, is not everything, but how about health? America has "the world's best medical care," John McCain said as he wrapped up the Republican presidential nomination in March of 2008. So America's politicians often say—McCain's promise was to protect America's health-care system from liberal efforts to destroy it—but America of the twenty-first century has neither the world's best medical care nor, by any stretch, the world's healthiest people. "Happily for Western Europe, its peoples today enjoy a literally vital demographic edge in health and mortality over almost all the rest of the world.... On a country-by-country basis, U.S. life expectancy at birth is not utterly below the levels seen today in Western Europe, but it is near the bottom, with only Portuguese men and Danish women reporting shorter lives." These withering lines come not from the Michael Moore documentary *Sicko*, his broadside attack on the U.S. health-care system, but from a 2007 publication of the American Enterprise Institute (AEI), the Washington think tank known as the home of America's neoconservative movement. The authors, Nicholas Eberstadt, a past member of the Board of Scientific Counselors for the U.S. National Center for Health Statistics, and Hans Groth, a Swiss physician on the board of Pfizer, have impeccable professional credentials.

Sometimes America's unimpressive statistical portrait is attributed to the wide disparities in its melting pot society. But this argument doesn't wash, either. "America is a famously multiethnic society," the AEI authors noted, "marked by equally famous ethnic disparities in health—yet even life expectancy for so-called 'white' Americans does not rate particularly well in European comparisons. Of Western Europe's eighteen countries, fourteen national populations report higher male life expectancy and all eighteen report higher female life expectancy than are reported for contemporary American 'whites.'"

The state-of-the-art health-care system is generally conceded to be France. France spends 11 percent of its gross domestic product on health care, compared to 15 percent for America, and yet life expectancy both at birth and at age sixty-five is higher in France than in America. France's strength, and America's weakness, is in primary care—the basic package of health care that patients get as part of their regular checkups, before they develop a serious (and often preventable) disease that requires hospitalization or other costly treatment. In one study, Victor Rodwin, a professor of health policy at New York University, contrasted Paris to Manhattan, a "like to like" comparison between two big urban areas, each with some of the most prestigious hospitals and medical specialists in the world, with both extremely rich people and extremely poor people, and with large numbers of foreign-born. Focusing on primary-care standards, he examined conditions for which hospitalization is avoidable, like diabetes, pneumonia, and asthma. His finding: In Manhattan, there were two and a half times as many hospital admissions for avoidable hospital conditions, which suggested that Manhattan was suffering from a relatively poor regime of primary care.

America is often considered to have a demographic advantage over Europe because of America's higher birth rate. But in coming decades America could suffer economically relative to Europe if it turns out that healthier Europeans, men and women in their fifties, sixties, and even seventies, are able to work more productively than Americans of the same ages. In both societies, with work becoming less physically arduous, the race is apt to be won by the most mentally alert, not the most muscular. "Although it is now commonplace to bemoan Europe's demographic handicaps," the authors of the AEI report observed, "the fact of the matter is that the European health and mortality profile is a tremendous blessing—and a potentially powerful economic springboard."

America's failure to keep pace on modern benchmarks like speed and health is indicative of a deeper failure in what might be called applied social imagination. It is difficult to account for this, as America retains preeminent universities and Americans are certainly not without creative ideas. The key, perhaps, is the "applied" part of this equation—the follow-through on the idea all the way to its execution.

One possible explanation is the shortcomings of American democracy. There are many good ideas about how to improve the health-care system; the problem is that the political system, like a faulty transmission belt, seems incapable of putting them into practice. Americans justly celebrate their society as the inventor of mass, popular democracy, but their democratic experience in recent decades has come to compare unfavorably with the rest of the pack. The 2000 Bush versus Gore presidential election, decided on partisan lines by the U.S. Supreme Court with the vote count in murky Florida up for grabs, was a global embarrassment—produced by the same country that sends trainers all around the world to advise on the building blocks of democracy. For the half century following the Second World War, just about every so-called first-world or modern, democratic country averaged a higher turnout of voting-age population in its national elections than America. Australia was at 84 percent, Germany at 80 percent, Spain at 76 percent, and the United Kingdom at 74 percent. The United States averaged a 48 percent turnout—a poor performance by its own historical yardstick: In the latter part of the nineteenth century, turnout in American presidential elections averaged nearly 80 percent. High turnout in an election is not a guarantee that desirable change will follow, but it was in the time of high turnout, in the Progressive Era of the late nineteenth and early twentieth century, that Washington made the kinds of comprehensive reforms in industry, bureaucracy, and social welfare that it has proved unable to make in the latter part of the twentieth and early part of the twenty-first century. In the 2008 elections, for all the excitement over the candidacy of Barack Obama, turnout, at 61.6 percent, only slightly exceeded the share in 2004.

Obama's election was a historic one, breaking a color barrier that for more than two centuries had kept the American presidency for white people only. There was widespread applause from foreign audiences, who took hope from America's demonstration of democratic opportunity. Still, America remains a laggard on another measure of political inclusiveness—the election of women to office. Since 1964, women have represented a majority of the American electorate, and yet in the U.S. House of Representatives in 2008, only 74 of 435, or 17 percent, of members were women, compared to 45 percent in the Swedish parliament and 38 percent in Norway's. In her nearly successful bid for the Democratic presidential nomination in 2008, Hillary Clinton came closer than a woman ever had before to becoming America's head of state—a goal that women have already achieved in other democratic countries, including the United Kingdom, Germany, Israel, Chile, and Liberia. It is worth recalling that "second wave" feminism in the twentieth century began with the French writer Simone de Beauvoir, who published *The Second Sex* in 1949, fourteen years before Betty Friedan, a suburban housewife in Rockland County, New York, published *The Feminine Mystique*. In her first chapter, "The Problem That Has No Name," Friedan pays tribute to de Beauvoir's early insistence on addressing questions of female emancipation that, Friedan noted, had been widely ignored in postwar America.

A second, not incompatible, explanation for America's failure to keep pace with other societies on standard benchmarks of modernity is that America has become transfixed by power. A paradox of American civilization is that as it became more powerful, as its brute strength became a defining characteristic, it became less impressive in other capacities. Perhaps the lesson is that a civilization may seek to be either powerful or original, but it is difficult to be both. The cold war hid the fact that America, even though superior to the Soviet Union, was becoming something less than the beacon of modernism that it clearly was at the start of the twentieth century. Even one of America's most impressive "speed" projects of the era, the construction of the Interstate Highway System, was launched in the 1950s on grounds of national security, to enable America's tanks to trundle from coast to coast. In the thaw that followed the end of the cold war, in the melting of the ice, America was exposed not as a universal ideal—a clearly superior way of organizing political, economic, and cultural life—but as a laggard.

Consider another postindustrial category in which America might seem to be a natural standard setter: robotics. America, as a self-styled futuristic society, has a rich literature of science fiction, and its technological potential is second to none. Everyone understands that the robot is going to occupy a prominent spot in the world of tomorrow—the robot will be as central to digital life, Bill Gates has said, as the personal computer has been. America, as might be expected, is the world's leader in military applications of robotics. But outside that sphere, in the domain of everyday life, the Japanese are the world's leaders. This is not simply because the Tokyo political-business elite, "Japan Inc.," has made a strategic decision to install a robot in everyone's home. The interesting thing is that the Japanese are having a cultural love affair with the robot. Whereas the American mind has fastened on the robot as a military tool, the Japanese mind is more apt to see the robot as a creature of fun.

This is how pacesetter civilizations are formed—not at the top but from the organic depths of a society. You cannot tell people what to love or what to latch on to as cool; there is, by definition, no such thing as a bottled formula for producing cool. The flowering of American jazz in the early twentieth century was not a government-funded program launched by a Washington group focused on making America a cultural superpower; it emerged from the quarters of New Orleans and the smoky clubs of Chicago and New York. Sometimes a civilization is simply more in sync with the modern—with the cutting edge—than at other times. America's religious evangelical streak was a powerful spur to the abolitionist movement of the early nineteenth century—the movement, often strident in tone, that forced reluctant politicians to confront the society's original sin of slavery. In the twenty-first century, the frontier of the modern civil rights movement has shifted to another controversial domain—the question of whether same-sex couples should be permitted to marry. And on this frontier, America is a middling, with opposition to gay marriage led by cultural conservatives who claim that the Bible is on their side. The pacesetter on gay marriage is the world's most secularized patch of ground, in the northern reaches of Western Europe. In 2001, the Netherlands became the first country on the planet to legalize same-sex marriage. That was two years before the Massachusetts Supreme Judicial Court, and seven years before the California Supreme Court, struck down bans on gay marriage. And by May of 2008, when New York's governor, David Paterson, directed state agencies to start recognizing same-sex marriages performed in other jurisdictions, gay marriage was already legal not only in the Netherlands but also in Belgium, Spain, Canada, and South Africa. Public-opinion surveys suggest that time is on the side of gay marriage in America. Among Americans aged eighteen to twenty-nine, about half are in favor of laws allowing gays to marry, compared with paltry support among those sixty-five and older. But at this rate, it may take America another decade to reach the point pacesetters have already attained.

The same can be said on another twenty-first-century marker of modernity—progress toward a green society. Green is the new cool, which suggests a fashion, but this is a case of a fashion being aligned with an imperative. No project of the contemporary world is more profound than the creation of an ecologically friendlier way of life. Technologically inventive America might have been expected to set the benchmark. After all, if it could set the global standard for the mass-produced motor society, why not for the mass-produced green society? America was blessed with brilliant visionaries who apprehended the perils of the hydrocarbon age. Decades before the OPEC oil shocks of the 1970s, and long before Al Gore had declared that Earth was "in the balance," the designer and inventor R. Buckminster Fuller was captivated by the possibilities of energy-efficient cars and houses. Fuller was a distinctive American character—born in Milton, Massachusetts, in 1895, with relations going back to Margaret Fuller, the American transcendentalist, feminist, and friend of Ralph Waldo Emerson. Expelled from Harvard for "irresponsibility," he went on to claim twenty-eight U.S. patents for his original designs, and he was a source of inspiration to a new generation of ecologically minded Americans like Stewart Brand, the Stanford-educated biologist who founded the *Whole Earth Catalog* in the late 1960s. In their tribute to Fuller in the pages of the catalog, the editors wrote that "with . . . empirical curiosity, and New England perseverance Fuller has forged one of the most original personalities and functional intellects of the age."

Fuller died in 1983, leaving behind a vision of a green society that lay largely unfulfilled, notwithstanding the growing clout of the American environmental movement, with its roots in 1960s liberal activism and exposés like Rachel Carson's groundbreaking report, published in 1962 in *Silent Spring*, on the ecological damage, especially to birds, wrought by the indiscriminate use of industrial pesticides. Powerful as this movement was, it faced determined opposition from large corporations, like agribusinesses and oil companies, rooted in the hydrocarbon economy; and many American citizens seemed to buy the line that environmentalism was some kind of left-wing creed that would do terrible damage to the American capitalist economy. The benchmark for energy conservation became Denmark. Over a thirty-year period, Denmark managed to double the size of its economy without increasing its consumption of energy. The average Dane was 80 percent as wealthy as the average American but used, in a year, less than half the electricity. The benchmark for wind power was set in Spain: In 2007, wind supplied more than 9 percent of Spain's electricity needs but only about 1 percent of America's. The benchmark for the use of ethanol as a source of biofuel in automobiles was set in Brazil, despite America's enormous potential for ethanol production. In 2007, American automobiles actually traveled on fewer miles per gallon than they did twenty years before. The burgeoning "sustainable tourism" movement, which embraced global standards for best environmental practices by hotels and others in the tourism industry, was pioneered by the United Kingdom in the 1990s. It was the UK model to which tourism planners for the state of Hawaii turned in 2005 as they began to develop a framework for a sustainable tourist "system" for their islands. Meanwhile, one of the world's most intriguing green initiatives is happening in, of all places, the Persian Gulf city-state of Abu Dhabi, in the land of the oil well. There, Norman Foster has been given a commission to build Masdar City, a 2.3-square-mile car-free, zero-carbon "sustainable development" being billed as the world's first green city. It may be only a demonstration project—but it has become a worldwide conversation piece already.

Western Europe is ahead of America in green initiatives in part because the Europeans are more accepting of a role for long-range government planning than Americans are. The usual pattern of American history is for bursts of government-spurred reforms to alternate with periods of stasis or reaction during which the reforms are consolidated. But as noted earlier, this cycle seems to have broken down as part of the seizing up of the gears of popular democracy. The last period of major progressive reforms was the 1960s. Since then, the country has experienced waves of antigovernment sentiment—as in the conservative Reagan era of the 1980s—but no new popular consensus on how government, outside the crown-jewel national-defense sector and state-of-the-art medical research, should reassert itself in society in a positive, helpful way. American innovation thus resides chiefly in the hands of the market, which generally has done a good job in creating wealth for the people but is not producing a dominant set of world-class firsts. It was the economic crisis greeting the Obama administration that created an opportunity for Washington to assert a role as an innovator in depressed sectors like automaking.

Pacesetter civilizations generally show a unity of purpose and a restless nature that demands concrete achievements. For a very long time, settlement of the frontier supplied the role of a consensus mission in American life. At the Chicago World's Fair of 1893, when Frederick Jackson Turner declared that "the frontier has gone," by which he quite literally meant "the existence of an area of free land" for settlement, he also prophesied that the pioneer impulse would remain a defining mark of America's character. "The American energy will continually demand a wider field for its exercise," Turner said. But in the twenty-first century, there is, in fact, no obvious and certainly no agreed-upon frontier for America. The space program has lost cachet; in fact, the United States has lost the commanding lead it once held over all others in space-related domains as China, Russia, Europe, India, and others invest heavily in fields like satellite launching. This loss, painful as it may be to NASA and others in the U.S. space sector, is not the cause of any great national consternation. The frontierlike idea, championed by neoconservatives, of spreading liberty to the world at the point of a gun, if necessary, is a divisive one; ideas like ending poverty at home win applause but do not have any programmatic substance behind them. Cyberspace is an exciting and evolving frontier, but a dispersed global one, not an American possession. In the meantime, massive energies are consumed trying to protect existing national frontiers from the encroachment of illegal immigrants. The completion of a high-tech fence on the southwestern border would be a kind of benchmark, but surely not the sort that Turner had in mind. It may be that America, as a function of its age, success, or sheer size, is moving into a postfrontier stage of its development. To the extent that frontiers are explored, they may be largely personal ones as self-empowered individuals haul metaphorical Conestogas to their own personal vistas.

The absence of a muscular frontier project suggests a more subjective barometer of America's middling status. Let's call this the risk-tolerance quotient. I don't have in mind a tolerance for financial risk—America remains, as it has been from the very beginning, an entrepreneurial civilization in which great numbers of talented people are willing to risk losing their shirts in pursuit of a business proposition that could yield a pot of gold. I am thinking specifically of risk to life and limb. An acceptance of that kind of risk was an essential ingredient of the pioneer spirit—had that acceptance been lacking, few might have left the relative comforts of the Atlantic seaboard settlements for destinations west, toward Appalachia and beyond. America of the twenty-first century has migrated away from this kind of risk tolerance. The society, especially at the elite level, has become a cosseted Nanny State. No household device is considered free of the need for a warning sticker; no suburban child is ever to be let outdoors on a bicycle, even a three-wheeled one, without protective headgear. As a parent of young children, I observe such practices myself; they are a part of neighborhood life, even if I managed to survive my own early childhood years, in the 1960s, without the bike helmet. Perhaps the explanation for this state of affairs is simply modern America's penchant for tort lawsuits; perhaps it has more to do with a condition of affluence and the development of a postindustrial society that has atrophied America's blue-collar working class. An elementary school in an upper-middle-class area of Northern Virginia, not far from my home, banned the playground recess-time game of tag, enjoyed by boys and girls alike, as too aggressive. I am confident that I am not the only parent who believes the school is being overly protective, and yet this coddling approach has the support of a professional class of education experts whose findings often seem to trump parental sentiments. "Tag may look OK socially, but it can be a double standard because kids can use it to bully a certain student," and there is "potential for *some* victimization," a psychologist with the National Association of School Psychologists has said. Dodgeball is under similar suspicion—banned by schools around the country and debated in the *Journal of Physical Education*, which posed the question, for an academic symposium: "Is There a Place for Dodgeball in Physical Education?"

The ready counterargument to the proposition that America shirks risk is the modern U.S. military—made up of brave young men and women, every one of them volunteers, willing to risk life in battle all over the world. But the all-voluntary military confirms the point that America, on the whole, has shifted away from a tolerance for bodily risk. This military has become a distinct sub-culture of American life. All Americans "support the troops," but relatively few citizens have any contact with them. Young people grow up secure in the knowledge that they are not going to be forced to walk point on a battle line, that someone else will be recruited to ensure their safety. That someone else is not necessarily a person with the same choices in life. As the wars in Iraq and Afghanistan ground on, desperate Pentagon recruiters were forced to meet their quotas by signing up a growing number of high school dropouts and con-victed felons. In America's Civil War, 68 percent of the Harvard Class of 1861 served in the Union military. Harvard's Memorial Hall was built to commemo-rate the university's war dead. In today's times, as noted by Richard Miller, the author of a history of a Union regiment dominated by officers hailing from Har-vard, "even if the university wanted to honor recent graduate-veterans, it would have relatively few to name. And what is true of Harvard is equally true for a cultural elite of which Harvard University is emblematic."

The pioneer society, and the America of the robber barons, as held up to the mirror by Theodore Dreiser in his Frank Cowperwood series of novels, was a coarser society in which social Darwinism, the ethos of survival of the fittest, prevailed as a mind-set. That society is forever gone—and good riddance, it is easy enough to say. But a civilization that invests too much in risk avoidance can expect to be challenged by scrappier ones. These days, the setting for

Dreiser-type stories of hard strivers has moved to sharper-elbowed lands like India. The stories are being told by the likes of Rohinton Mistry, a Mumbai-born writer who immigrated to Canada in the mid-1970s. In novels like *A Fine Balance*, Mistry supplies a gallery of beggars, con artists, and rogues with a heart. His India is often cruel and pitiless, but it is immensely vital.

Perhaps the most poignant benchmark loss that America is suffering is the loss of its place as the standard setter on the dimension of optimism. From the beginning, optimism has been America's signature characteristic as a society. No people on the face of the earth were said to be more optimistic than Americans. That trait has certainly not disappeared, but optimistic sentiments about the future are now less widely held by Americans. One traditional measure of optimism is whether people envision better long-term prospects for their children. In a 2007 survey of forty-seven nations by the Pew Research Center, in Washington, D.C., only 31 percent of Americans said that they believed their children's lives will be better, down from 41 percent in 2002. It is possible, to take the most pessimistic case, that these numbers reflect long-standing trends that will be difficult to reverse, like the steady decline in economic mobility for U.S. families over the last three decades. But perhaps the numbers in that survey reflected no more than a temporary unhappiness with issues like the war in Iraq; let's stipulate that once America gets past things like the downturn in the housing market, the numbers will rebound to over 50 percent, maybe even to 60 percent. That would certainly be a recovery of optimism and a demonstration, once again, of American resilience. But it would not be enough to restore America as the world's optimism leader, because in other parts of the world optimism is even higher than that. China is in the throes of an optimism boom: The Pew survey found that 86 percent of Chinese said that their children's lives will be better than theirs. In Bangladesh the figure was 84 percent, in Morocco 67 percent, in Slovakia 68 percent, in India 64 percent, in Chile 62 percent. Only the Palestinians, certain West Europeans (especially the Italians, French, and Germans), and the Japanese are significantly less optimistic than Americans are about the future of their children.

This reversal of optimism roles is surely *not* a temporary phenomenon. The rest of the world was so down for so long, while Europe, America, and Japan prospered, that almost any forward progress is fair cause for optimism. There is a rational basis for the relatively greater optimism of the Indians and the Chinese compared to the Americans or, say, the Germans: From 2003 to 2007, per capita income increased by 10.2 percent in China and 6.8 percent in India, against 1.9 percent in America and 1.4 percent in Germany. If only because of the good things happening in the societies for so long "to the rear" of the United States, America may be doomed to remain an optimism middling for the remainder of the twenty-first century and beyond. However well America does, some other society will undoubtedly be viewed as more dynamic, as feeling sprightlier, with more of a bounce in its step. This is part of what it means not to be young anymore. But surely the loss of the optimism benchmark is no cause for sustained commiseration in America. America never wanted to be number one while everyone else felt miserable, did it? And more than that, it can be said that America—through its own example, as the world's most successful society ever—helped to spur the rest of the planet to try to improve itself.

A civilization that is not the world's foremost producer of benchmarks of excellence is not necessarily a failed civilization. Australia and Canada have spent virtually all their lives as second or below second in the benchmark departments—never once enjoying the preeminent moments of their European ancestors—and yet they are both highly successful societies. Peoples from Asia, the Middle East, and even parts of Europe pine to move to either country; in some barometers of social well-being, like the level of crime, both societies are better off than America is. It is tempting to think that America, stripped of its role as the preeminent benchmarks producer, could settle into the happy existence of a Canada or Australia. But it won't be that easy. The problem, as I explore in parts 3 and 4, is psychological. The idea that "the past is beginning to weigh on its shoulders," as Braudel delicately put it in the 1960s, is not one that Americans like to contemplate.

Chapter Five

Goliath Bound

One takes what one can get, up to the limit of one's strength.

F. Scott Fitzgerald, "The Bridal Party," 1930

Paul Kennedy was born in 1945 in the northeast of England in the shipbuilding town of Wallsend. This was ground that could remind one of the impermanence of empire: The Romans built a fort in Wallsend to protect the eastern end of Hadrian's Wall. Kennedy went to grammar school in Newcastle and attended the University of Newcastle before studying for a doctorate in history at Oxford. He was teaching at the University of East Anglia when, in the mid-1970s, he came out with his book *The Rise and Fall of British Naval Mastery*. By 1987, when he published *The Rise and Fall of the Great Powers*, the tome that made him famous (or notorious, depending on one's perspective), he was a full professor of history at Yale. He began with the rise of the Western world, shifted to the Habsburg bid for mastery, and did not even get around to the sensitive matter at hand, "The United States: The Problem of Number One in Relative Decline," until past the five hundredth page, just before the epilogue. Kennedy wrote that "decision-makers in Washington must face the awkward and enduring fact that the sum total of the United States' global interests and obligations is nowadays far larger than the country's power to defend them all simultaneously."

The American foreign policy establishment was in no mood for this message. Victory in the cold war was at hand, and Kennedy was dismissed as a gloomy and heretical declinist, as if he had somehow failed a test of bullishness on behalf of America, his adopted country. Not the least of his sins was his un-Exceptional treatment of America as a classic "Great Power," subject to the same laws of history, "the age-old dilemmas of rise and fall," that govern all such powers. Moreover, Kennedy also had the impertinence to inform Washington's imperial class, which tends to see the world as a ball at its fingertips, that there was only limited scope for maneuver: "These are not developments which can be controlled by any one state, or individual." He was offering, in the tradition of Braudel and Tolstoy, an organic, bottom-up perspective on global change, and he wound up his book to this effect with a paraphrase from Bismarck: The Great Powers travel "on the stream of Time," which they can "neither create nor direct," but upon which they can "steer with more or less skill and experience." A more un-American summation is hard to imagine.

These days, the "relative decline" view is a staple of Washington establishment thinking among career professionals in the foreign policy, national security, and intelligence communities. In the 2004 report *Mapping the Global Future*, published by the National Intelligence Council and drawing on the advice of analysts at the CIA and elsewhere, the authors concluded that the United States, out to 2020, "will see its relative power position eroded." The supporting analysis read like an update of Kennedy's discussion of the rise of new powers like China. "The likely emergence of China and India, as well as others, as new major global players—similar to the advent of a united Germany in the 19th century and a powerful United States in the 20th century—will transform the geopolitical landscape, with impacts potentially as dramatic as those in the previous two centuries," the authors wrote. "In the same way that commentators refer to the 1900s as the 'American Century,' the 21st century may be seen as the time when Asia, led by China and India, comes into its own." The assessment was put together by Robert Hutchings, a veteran U.S. diplomat, who has moved on to teaching history at Princeton. We got together for lunch at the Princeton faculty club. The son of a U.S. naval officer, Hutchings was born in 1946 in central Florida, and in various positions he served the George H. W. Bush, Bill Clinton, and George W. Bush administrations. "I don't think of myself as a declinist," he told me, "but the salience of the alliance we are leading is fading fast." It had occurred to him that he might get fired from the National Intelligence Council for forecasting a deterioration of America's global position, but what happened instead was that his bosses in the George W. Bush White House simply chose to ignore the assessment.

The conclusions of the Hutchings-led team were validated four years later by a new crew of U.S. intelligence analysts, tasked with examining future trends to the year 2025, who concluded that the ebbing of U.S. dominance was proceeding "at an accelerating pace." There are two main features to the predicament of "relative decline." One of the features—the economic and military rise of new powers like China—is a function of the broad sweep of history and in no way reflects a failure or shortcoming of America. China was bound to recover at some point; America was never destined to maintain a 40 percent share of global GDP, as the United States had in 1945. The other feature, though, reflects a particular problem of U.S. empire—of empire generally—and demands close scrutiny.

Paul Kennedy cast this predicament in terms of the classic malady of "imperial overstretch," also suffered by Spain, France, and Great Britain in earlier times. Kennedy focused on a mismatch of economic means and imperial aspirations. On the surface, his assessment may look misplaced. As big as America's defense budget is, at more than $700 billion annually, the budget is only 4 percent of the nation's gross domestic product, compared to just below 6 percent in the late 1980s and nearly 10 percent at the peak of the Vietnam War in the late 1960s. Still, America's current financial position in fact is a serious impingement on its ability to carry out, unhindered by other powers, a big-stick foreign policy. The problem is one of debt. In June 2008, the United States achieved a dubious milestone. For the first time ever, foreign ownership of U.S. Treasury securities surpassed domestic ownership: foreigners held $2.71 trillion of total Treasury liabilities of $5.27 trillion, according to U.S. Federal Reserve statistics. Back in the 1970s, the foreign share of Treasury debt was below 20 percent. Much of the debt is held by the central banks of rising powers like China, and it is likely that the foreign share will continue to increase in the years ahead, as Washington depends on the Chinas of the world to buy the bonds that fund the rescue of the U.S. financial system. This is a matter of leverage, of the upper hand that a lender has on a borrower, applied to the fluid arena of geopolitics. For example, Washington may want Beijing to stop its bullying ways in resource-rich African countries like Sudan, but just how far can Washington push, knowing that Beijing has the option of shifting its huge pool of financial reserves to markets in Europe and elsewhere? Likewise, how much pressure can a debt-burdened Washington exert to get China to support sanctions on Iran to keep the mullahs from gaining a nuclear bomb? "The linkage can be subtle—it is not absolute," but America's growing indebtedness to foreigners is rapidly emerging as "an important constraint" on U.S. foreign policy in the twenty-first century, the economist Roger Kubarych, a former head of international research at the New York Federal Reserve Bank, told me.

In the case of the indebted British Empire in the mid-twentieth century, there was no subtlety at all. Brad Setser, a former U.S. Treasury official, began a 2008 analysis of "sovereign wealth and sovereign power" with a discussion of how America, as a creditor nation to the UK, gave British prime minister Anthony Eden no practical choice but to meet U.S. demands and withdraw British forces from the Suez Canal Zone in the 1950s. "The lesson of Suez for the United States today is clear: political might is often linked to financial might, and a debtor's capacity to project military power hinges on the support of its creditors," Setser wrote in a paper published by the U.S. Council on Foreign Relations.

Beyond the impediment of overstretched finances is the problem, at least as serious, of overstretched frontiers. Imperial America's cultural blind spot, so evident in the twentieth century in places like Vietnam, remains. In fact, the empire's current entanglements are even more vexing than the bind of Vietnam. The Islamic Middle East is an obvious example; a less obvious one is the former Soviet South Caucasus. After the 9/11 attacks, Washington embraced the ex-Soviet republic of Georgia as a new ally in the "war against terrorism." At a Georgian military base littered by abandoned Soviet tanks, I watched raw Georgian recruits being drilled by U.S. Green Beret trainers. "We're going to raise their potential exponentially," a Green Beret major told me. Nearly six years later, invading Russians cut Georgia's troops to pieces—as Washington watched helplessly. "Where are our friends?" a retreating Georgian soldier asked a U.S. journalist. America had built up and encouraged an ally that the United States was in no position to help in crunch time.

Whether this state of affairs is a result of historical fate or of errors and miscalculations is hard to say. Probably the answer is that the fate could not have been avoided but was hastened by bad decisions, like the decision to invade a country, Iraq, which had not attacked America. Looming largest, though, is the destiny part of the equation. Once America made the leap, however inadvertent, from continental to global empire, it was inevitable that cultural frictions would begin to strike sparks. The frontiers were bound to become, as they are now, "frontiers of insecurity," in the apt phrase of Christopher Layne, a professor at the Bush School of Government and Public Service at Texas A&M University. Or as a U.S. naval officer put it to me on the sidelines of a conference in New Delhi, "the white man thing"—the association of the United States, fairly or unfairly, with the tradition of European imperialism—is a very difficult barrier to overcome. Even when right is on the side of U.S. might—as in Afghanistan, which served as a base for the 9/11 plotters—Americans are widely seen as interlopers. America is confined by cultural perceptions that took centuries to form and are unlikely to change anytime soon. The American imperial soldier occupies much the same position as the imperial policeman George Orwell found himself in decades ago in India—at the mercy of natives who demand that he shoot the elephant. In the twenty-first century, the American empire, viewed by some in Washington as a spur for the liberation of the oppressed peoples of the world, is a global prison from which there is no easy exit.

Not everyone, of course, accepts these practical limitations on American power. There are two schools of thought on how America can stay very far ahead of everyone else through the leveraging of its military preeminence. It is worthwhile to sift through the arguments, because they actually serve to flesh out the point that America is facing an unsolvable cultural-frontiers problem.

First is the argument for America as the global policeman. This is the soft version of the case for America's military supremacy, and in U.S. foreign policy circles it tends to come from Democrats, like Vice President Joseph Biden or former UN Ambassador Richard Holbrooke, who might be called liberal war hawks or liberal imperialists. In his 2005 book *The Case for Goliath*, the Washington analyst Michael Mandelbaum likened America to a world government for the society of nations, providing necessary "public goods." The most important such good is global security—which America is in a position to supply, he notes, with some seven hundred military bases in foreign countries around the world and military forces operating in about 150 of the world's 193 countries. Mandelbaum is not arguing that America is motivated by altruism—he is saying that America, in following its own global interests, is benefiting everyone. He offers this analogy:

"The owner of a large, expensive, lavishly-furnished mansion surrounded by more modest homes may pay to have security guards patrolling his street, and their presence will serve to protect the neighboring houses as well, even though their owners contribute nothing to the cost of the guards. This is what the United States does in the world of the twenty-first century."

It is a clever analogy, but it breaks down. A security guard, or policeman, needs to be well armed, or at least to have access to superior force in the case of trouble, and America certainly has that part of the job down. But for a policeman truly to do his job, he needs not only firepower but a public recognition and acceptance of his role as an enforcer of order. When this recognition is lacking—whether in certain bad neighborhoods of Los Angeles or in the bad neighborhoods of the Middle East—"crime" flourishes. It may have been the case in the cold war that a large portion of humankind was accepting of a police role for America, as the "leader of the free world"; that level of acceptance is now lacking.

For one thing, even if Washington views the battle against an Islamic style of totalitarianism as a reason for a continuation of the American police role, others do not. The "free world" is generally not buying the idea that Islamic fascism represents a threat on the order of Stalin's Soviet Union. In a poll published in the spring of 2007 by the Chicago Council on Global Affairs, publics in eight foreign countries were asked the question "Do you think the United States has the responsibility to play the role of 'world policeman,' that is, to fight violations of international law and aggression wherever they occur?" The answer, in seven of the eight countries, was a resounding no, with that response supplied by 79 percent of Australians, 70 percent of Armenians, 69 percent of Ukrainians and Indonesians, and 60 percent of South Koreans.

The survey was taken in the midst of the U.S. war in Iraq and no doubt was partly a reflection of that war's global unpopularity and also the unpopularity of the Bush administration in so many foreign countries. But these attitudes are unlikely to dissipate in a post-Iraq, post-Bush era. Christoph Bertram, a former head of both the International Institute for Strategic Studies in London and the German Institute for International and Security Affairs in Berlin, can be considered a card-carrying member of the "transatlantic" national security establishment. For more than two decades, Bertram has been a participant in the security debates involving Washington and European capitals, and in those debates he has been a consistent advocate for the position, resisted by some in Europe, by which Europe and America, as part of the same "West," must try very hard to stick together in their approach to global issues. These days, he is still committed to his idea of European-American unity but doubtful of its prospects. "Americans do not realize the extent to which their international position has been weakened," he told me. "They still think that with a new person in the White House their role and the respect they used to enjoy will return as if nothing has happened. I think they are wrong in this belief/hope. Something more than just the reputation of one administration has been shattered. It is the image of an America which is good for the world." As Barack Obama prepared to take office in January 2009, the outgoing Bush White House prepared for him "more than a dozen contingency plans" for an international crisis in his first few days on the job, *The New York Times* reported, including possibilities like "a North Korean nuclear explosion, a cyberattack on American computer systems, a terrorist strike on United States facilities overseas or a fresh outbreak of instability in the Middle East."

In part, the Accidental Empire is paying the price for its preferences. Harry Truman and his advisors well understood that a decision to recognize a Jewish state of Israel could harm perceptions of America in Islamic lands. So it has. It is understood everywhere in the Middle East, and beyond, that the Jewish state has the status of being an informal protectorate of America. The great majority of Americans, by all the measures, endorse this preference—this is not an instance of the imperial class imposing its own values on U.S. national security policy against the will of the people. It is generally considered good politics for a presidential candidate to play up U.S. support for Israel—Hillary Clinton, in the 2008 presidential campaign, offered an especially vigorous illustration of this principle in her stated threat to "obliterate" Iran if the mullahs attacked Israel with nuclear weapons. But America's preference for Israel tends to be seen in the tribal Middle East as a premium on Jewish blood over the blood of all others. The preference rankles and always will. In explaining how America is no longer able to be a global peacemaker, Ahmet Hasyuncu, a Turkish textile magnate with whom I spoke in his hometown of Kayseri, in central Anatolia, invoked the analogy of a referee at a soccer match. "If the referee is fair," he said, "the spectators are not provoked. The referee of the world is not a fair referee. It says 'offside' when there is no offside. A penalty when there is no penalty. For how long can the spectators bear this?" He cited an old Turkish saying, *Zulum ilea bad olan berbat olur.* That translates as "The one who persecutes will disappear."

Global opinion, it might be argued, is ephemeral stuff. But consider this: If America is truly the world's policeman, providing "public goods" from which everyone benefits, as "the case for Goliath" goes, then why are rising powers like India and China investing so heavily in their own navies in order to develop, as they see it, the means to protect the vital lines of sea commerce on their own? In part 3 of the book, I will examine the Indian and Chinese examples in detail. The point I would like to make here is this: Even in a country like India, in which public opinion tends to register a fairly favorable view of the United States, there is a major push for a blue-water Indian navy to project power from the choke point of the Strait of Malacca on India's east to the Persian Gulf on the nation's west. It would be naïve for Washington to see this effort as some kind of security subcontracting scheme in which the Indians play the hired hand of America as the general contractor. The Indians, with centuries of hard colonial experience behind them, mainly at the hand of the British, are beyond that subservient role in the world. They have decided that it is not prudent to count on the good intentions of the American policeman. They'd sooner trust their security to themselves.

There is a final problem with the model of the global policeman, which has to do not with the demand for his services but with his willingness to supply them. The model suggests that the cop, at least when asked, is willing to perform his job. A policeman, after all, is of little worth if he is prepared to chase down criminals in one neighborhood but not in others. But even at the height of its "unipolar moment," in the first years after its cold war triumph, America suffered qualms. If ever there was a time for the global-cop doctrine of the liberal war hawks to be asserted, it was in Rwanda in 1994. In one hundred days of slaughter—a genocide—an estimated 800,000 Rwandans were killed. Bill Clinton's White House closely monitored the situation but, to its enduring sorrow, never intervened. The failure to do so, Clinton later wrote, was his greatest regret as president. There were of course logistical obstacles to any rescue attempt by U.S. forces, but at the heart of the failure to intervene was the absence of a conviction that the Rwanda crisis, however bloody, posed a direct threat to the security of America. The universalist rhetoric of the global-policeman idea did not match the reality: For "the indispensable power," as Madeleine Albright, a secretary of state under Clinton, once called America, certain parts of the planet remained off-limits.

The second, quite different, argument on behalf of the staying power of the Accidental Empire is what might be called the "America as Rome" brief. A prominent exponent of this point of view, which tends to find favor among big-stick Republican conservative types, is Victor Davis Hanson, a historian of ancient Rome and Greece with a specialty in military affairs, and a man to whom the George W. Bush administration, and in particular Dick Cheney, was known to listen. After the September 11, 2001, attacks on America, Hanson wrote that "moderation in war is imbecility" and that victory for Americans, in the coming wars in the lands of Islam, would be nothing less than "the absolute annihilation of their adversaries."

About four years after the start of the Iraq war, I attended a luncheon for Washington journalists, sponsored by Stanford's Hoover Institution, at which Hanson was the guest speaker. We gathered in the oak-paneled Franklin Pierce Room of the Willard Hotel, two blocks from the White House. In person, Hanson came across not as fierce and grave—not as the modern-day Spartan evoked by his prose—but as mild and rumpled, like most academics. Still, his criticism of President Bush's war policy in Iraq was withering. The president, after raising expectations with tough rhetoric—"smoke them out, dead or alive"—had fought the war with "half measures" that amounted to "braggadocio with a little stick." In war, Hanson explained, as to a classroom of students, "you defeat, you humiliate the enemy," and then and only then do you "become magnanimous."

And America has this capability: "This is the most powerful country in the history of civilization," Hanson reminded; the only limits on what we can do are "psychological."

Months earlier at a forum in Washington I had heard much the same from Princeton's Bernard Lewis, a historian of the Islamic world and another academic with close ties to the Bush-Cheney White House. In a venomous essay in the *Wall Street Journal*, Lewis contrasted America's history of weakness in the Middle East to the strength displayed by the Soviet Union in that region during the cold war. "If you did anything to annoy the Russians, punishment would be swift and dire," Lewis wrote. "If you said or did anything against the Americans, not only would there be no punishment; there might even be some possibility of reward, as the usual anxious procession of diplomats and politicians, journalists and scholars and miscellaneous others came with their usual pleading inquiries: 'What have we done to offend you? What can we do to put it right?'"

The "America as Rome" brief echoed in some military quarters. "Thus I have had many 'Defense World' conversations," one veteran Washington military analyst has noted, "that have ended with: 'the time may come when we will have to kill millions of Muslims,' or 'history shows that to win over a people you have to kill at least 10 percent of them, like the Romans.'" Similar sentiments were expressed in military quarters during the Vietnam conflict. Air force general Curtis LeMay was of the opinion that the North Vietnamese could be defeated by being blasted "back to the Stone Age." Still, this mind-set—that America is a more or less traditional imperial power and needs to act like one—was largely foreign to the Accidental Empire as it took shape after World War II. In his "American Century" editorial, Henry Luce, perhaps mindful of how he had been bullied by his British schoolmates in China, insisted that America would be different from the dominant world powers of the past because, "unlike the prestige of Rome or Genghis Khan or 19th century England," America's prestige throughout the world was derived from "faith in the good intentions" of the American people. It was the 9/11 attacks on the American homeland, not the Pearl Harbor attacks of sixty years earlier, that crystallized a classically imperial way of thinking about the hazardous security environment beyond America's shores. After the attacks, Juan Alsace, a career U.S. Foreign Service officer who had served in such stations as Karachi and Istanbul, wrote an essay for a journal of the U.S. Army War College titled "In Search of Monsters to Destroy: American Empire in the New Millennium." The title was a twist, and a rather sharp one, of the admonition of John Quincy Adams, back in 1821, when he was secretary of state. America's "glory" was "not dominion, but liberty," Adams said in a speech to the U.S. House of Representatives. Therefore, America "goes not abroad, in search of monsters to destroy." Alsace recast the admonition as an imperative: "Those who argue the United States has no empire to uphold whistle past the graveyard, ignoring the historically unparalleled confluence of political, economic, military and information power that have come together in the American imperial construct.... Only the United States has the capability to restore order, imposing its will when and where necessary. This imperial path holds danger and difficulty, but it is a choice the nation must embrace, even if reluctantly and at certain cost."

Post-9/11, sympathetic images of American empire also seeped more widely into the mainstream media. Unlike the British, America had never developed a popular literature of empire. Indeed, American writers had often mocked the imperial pretension as ill suited for the casually democratic American sensibility. But in his 2005 book, *Imperial Grunts*, the reporter Robert Kaplan departed from this tradition with a romantic, stylized portrait of the American imperial soldier. Using as a model a marine officer bound for duty in the Persian Gulf, he described this soldier as a superior version of the Roman soldier of old: "His skin was the color of clay under his high-and-tight crew cut, with taut cheeks and a get-it-done expression: an ancient sculpture in digital camouflage, except for the point of light in his eyes. The Romans, by their rites of purification, accepted and justified the world as it is, with all its cruelty. The Americans, heir to the Christian tradition, seek what is not yet manifest: the higher ideal. Thus, he was without cynicism." And so was Kaplan's soldier sanctified and sent out to the world to do his duty, with others to follow, who knows where, for "by the turn of the twenty-first century the United States military had already appropriated the entire earth, and was ready to flood the most obscure areas of it with troops at a moment's notice."

But for all of America's might, there is no reason to think that Goliath can win its battles by acting like Rome. The Romans held their empire, in part, through terror—wiping out towns that refused to surrender to a siege, selling captured soldiers into slavery. America began its 2003 invasion of Iraq with a "shock and awe" campaign of bombing that led to the toppling of the Saddam Hussein regime but failed to pacify the country. Instead, a vicious anti-American insurgency cropped up. The insurgency was tamped down, in 2007 and 2008, not by Rome-like tactics to out-terrorize the terrorists but by efforts to create security partners among the local Iraqi populations. There would be no American conquest of Iraq, no regionwide object lesson in humiliation. The best the United States could hope for, as it contemplated a drawdown of its forces, was a fragile peace that kept Iraq from becoming an anarchic breeding ground for anti-American Islamic terrorists. "This is a good-bye kiss from the Iraqi people, dog," an Iraqi journalist shouted before throwing his shoes at Bush during a news conference in Baghdad in December 2008. The gesture of contempt made him an instant folk hero in the Arab world.

Nor is there reason to think that the act-like-Rome formula can pay dividends in other hot spots. Afghanistan? The relentless Taliban, seven years after being toppled from power by the U.S.-led coalition in 2001, mounted a comeback. Errant U.S. military strikes that killed Afghan villagers threatened to turn the civilian population in the rural areas against America. Like the British troops in the nineteenth century, American forces in the twenty-first had no easy solution to the advantages that Afghanistan's mountainous terrain conferred on guerrillas who knew the land so well. As in Iraq, it seemed unlikely that U.S. forces would be defeated on the battlefield—but equally unlikely that they would succeed in delivering a crushing blow to the enemy. Nuclear-armed Pakistan? It is no secret that the Taliban, al-Qaeda, and various other anti-American bands have taken refuge in the lawless tribal lands bordering Afghanistan. Pakistan's army has shied away from engaging these groups. America, with its tens of thousands of troops in Afghanistan, has the military capability to launch an across-the-border invasion, but not even hard-line Washington neoconservatives are recommending that step. They recognize the risk that an inflamed Pakistan, already suspicious of America's intentions in the region, could end up in the hands of Islamic radicals. Iran? To keep the mullahs from gaining nuclear weapons, America could go ahead and "bomb bomb bomb, bomb bomb Iran," as John McCain half-humorously suggested in a ditty he sang to the tune of the Beach Boys song "Barbara Ann." A bombing strike, perhaps, could set back Iran's nuclear ambitions. But surely it would mobilize tens of millions of prideful Iranians against America. What then?

Any modern adaptation of the humiliation principle in the end rubs up against what may be the most vexing problem of all. The anti-American terrorists of the twenty-first century, unlike the barbarians who aimed to bring down Rome, are able to create globally dispersed networks by virtue of the Internet and cell phones and the ease of jet travel. They have no need to mass along the borders of the hated American homeland in preparation for invasion, because their goals would be served by the detonation of massively destructive weapons—biological, chemical, even nuclear—that had no parallel in ancient times. While it is true that even the twenty-first-century terrorist must find some safe place to live and work, that place may be no more than a fringe neighborhood in some poorly policed section of a city in Europe. In this type of mobile, "asymmetric" warfare, the object of humiliation tends to be a fleeting one. Act-like-Rome U.S. imperialists tend to disparage the conception of the war on terror as a multilateral law-enforcement job involving American gumshoes working closely in concert with peers all around the world. This is indeed a prosaic, small-stick approach to the task, not the dramatic, big-club approach favored by these imperialists. And it makes American security dependent, in part, on the police work of foreigners. Modern conditions, though, suggest no better alternative. The Rome formula is fantasy.

Great militaries have always inspired mythmaking lore, from Sparta's and Rome's armies to the British Royal Navy. For superpower America in the digital age, the totem of supremacy is a technological marvel like the F-22 Raptor, touted by the U.S. Air Force for "its combination of stealth, supercruise, maneuverability, and integrated avionics," all making for "an exponential leap in warfighting capabilities." The "primary function" of the craft is "air dominance," the air force says in its picture-studded "fact sheet," the military-industrial complex's equivalent of the glossy buy-this-home brochures churned out by real estate agencies. But why does military supremacy, all through the ages, tend to be fleeting? Why can't it last longer? One answer is that military greatness calls too much unfriendly attention to itself, unlike mediocrity, which is unthreatening. In Joseph Heller's *Catch-22*, set on an American-occupied island in the Italian Mediterranean in the Second World War, the young Lieutenant Nately visits a local brothel and is baited by an old man who says, "Yes, I am quite certain that Italy will survive this war and still be in existence long after your own country has been destroyed." Shocked to hear such "blasphemies," Nately shouted, "America is not going to be destroyed!" The old man replied, "Rome was destroyed, Greece was destroyed, Persia was destroyed, Spain was destroyed. All great countries are destroyed. Why not yours? How much longer do you really think your own country will last? Forever?" Nately "squirmed uncomfortably" as "the jeering old man with keen, sadistic zest" drove his point home: "The frog is almost five hundred million years old. Could you really say with much certainty that America, with all its strength and prosperity, with its fighting man that is second to none, and with its standard of living that is the highest in the world, will last as long as . . . the frog?"

Joseph Heller began writing *Catch-22* in 1953 as a sideline from his day job creating copy for a small New York advertising agency. That was a time when ordinary Americans were just getting used to the idea of their country as the most powerful military force the world had ever seen. The book, which finally came out in 1961, was prophecy dressed up in a cloak of humor—all drawn from an insight, a serious one, that the new American empire was not all sunshine but cast its own large shadow on the global landscape. (Heller was eight years ahead of Kurt Vonnegut, who highlighted a similar theme in his 1969 novel *Slaughterhouse-Five*.) *Catch-22* was a way of saying that the myth of an America liberated from history stood to be punctured; it was also a way of saying that the belief of Americans in their own innocence was a trap. Although Heller's story was rooted in America's greatest ever military success, World War II, his tale anticipated misadventures like Vietnam and Iraq—in the sense that he grasped an essential disconnect, like a missing gear, between means and ends, between the possession of supreme power and the ability to direct that power toward desired purposes. Vietnam suggested a possible end to the American global military ascendancy, and Iraq and Afghanistan have confirmed that the end of the ascendancy has indeed been reached. Further along, in part 3, I will explore the implications of this "end"—which range from the possibility that the world, as supporters of American empire believe, will get a lot messier without a dominant America to maintain security, to the alternative possibility that various new ways of keeping order can be found. Heller's vision, not really of the actual destruction of America but of the eclipse of a certain idea of America, as a hegemonic force in the world, had a firm grounding in the history of all empires, but did not tell what might come next.

Chapter Six

The Return of Russia

The Russians have a disturbing effect on the peoples of the West.

Russian philosopher Nicolas Berdyaev, *The Russian Idea*, 1946

It is "last bell" day—graduation time—for the young cadets of the Aksaisky Military School, a boarding school operated by the legendary Don Cossacks of southwestern Russia's Don River basin. Outside, on a sun-baked field bordered by poplars, the one hundred pupils, outfitted in their wide-brimmed caps (some too large for their small heads) and formal regimental uniforms (navy blue for most of them, cream with red piping for the drummers), sweat through a procession of speeches. They are plainly suffering but, then, a good Cossack is taught to endure suffering. Their Orthodox chaplain, Father Michael, an unsmiling fellow in an ankle-length black frock, calls on them "to be devoted believers." All stand for a recorded rendition of the Russian national anthem; the roll of graduates is called; and then begins the entertainment portion of the program, which starts with choir singing of patriotic songs and is followed by Cossack-style dancing. One young man squats close to the ground and, hands on hips, juts his legs to the fast-paced rhythms of the folk music. The festivities end with a concert of drums, guitars, and an electric organ. As an honored guest, I am presented with a large bouquet of yellow roses.

The Cossacks are a kind of martial brotherhood, sharing a heritage and certain ideals and customs. They were repressed early on in the Soviet period but began to regroup as soon as the Soviet Union collapsed. The Aksaisky school, about twenty miles from the provincial capital of Rostov-on-Don, illustrates what Cossacks are about. In the lobby is inscribed the Cossacks' motto: "Surrender life to motherland, soul to God, and honor to nobody!" Education in the Russian Orthodox faith—the only accepted religious belief for Cossacks—is a core part of the curriculum; there are icons in many rooms, and prayers are said before meals. The cadets, who are exclusively male, partake of ballroom dancing (with girls from an outside local school), training in the martial arts, and target practice at shooting ranges. They are taught the history of the Cossacks; they also learn how to use computers. The academy is popular—with only one slot for every twenty applicants. About three-quarters of the pupils come from orphanages or other vulnerable circumstances, and pay no money. The provincial government helps fund the school.

"I am proud of my children—this is the future of Russia," the school's director, Vasily Dontsov, a retired Russian army colonel and paratrooper, told me as we chatted in his office before the ceremonies began. Many of the graduates will enlist in the military, but that is not mandatory—they can also become tax or customs inspectors or pursue careers outside the state. Some may join the local police patrols guarding this part of Russia from Chechen terrorism and other threats. "I want to become a good protector of the motherland—I want to pursue a military career and, yes, I am ready to do it with guns," Sergei Kisselov, fifteen, who comes from a long line of Cossacks on his father's side, explained to me. He had blond, Viking-like features, unlike the black-haired, dark-eyed Alexander Shevchenko, fourteen, who is also of Cossack descent and who asserted, "a Cossack means a free man and also a very well brought-up one." It might be that Schevchenko has Turkish blood—Cossacks of olden days sometimes stole away Turkish women as war prizes.

After the ceremonies, I drove back to Rostov-on-Don for a meeting, in the city's main cathedral, with Father Vadim, responsible for the church's dealings with Cossacks in the region. A large man with a kindly face, he greeted me with a kiss on the cheek and got one from me in return. We chatted, standing up, just inside the main entrance to the cathedral, which was packed with afternoon worshippers. Midway through our talk, Russia's most famous ballerina, the golden-haired Anastasia Volochkova, her red face peeping out of a white shawl, stooped to kiss Father Vadim's hand. She was performing in the city that evening. "Our Cossack movement is flourishing because the local authorities support us," Father Vadim told me. "We must not only revive traditions but have someone to pass them on to." I tried to draw him out on the special role that the Orthodox church plays in Cossack life. "We want decisions to be taken jointly by Cossack and church leaders," he began. He then offered a "poetic image"—a river, a town on the river, and the threat of a flood. "The idea is to keep the river in its channel," Father Vadim said, with the job of the church to provide a "frame" to keep the river from overflowing its banks—to keep Cossacks' democracy, a good thing, from becoming anarchy. "If there is no frame, there is anarchy," Father Vadim pronounced.

The new Russia, it turns out, looks a lot like the old Russia. It is a society's willful return to old architectural patterns, in shades largely of White. Traditions like political authoritarianism, a suspicion of foreigners, and a rather chauvinistic nationalism are returning to the fore, and this is not something for which Russians feel they need to apologize. "It's a revival of Russian identity," an official in Vladimir Putin's Kremlin once explained to me. Americans may feel committed to an ethos of the novel, of an idea of their country as a constant work in progress, but Russians tend not to feel that way. "This is not something new," the official said of the features of today's Russia, because the country's citizens "carry the genes of our whole Russian history."

In the American mind, this was not the turn Russia was supposed to take after the Soviet collapse. Amid the demise of communism as a global ideology, Soviet satellites like Poland and Hungary eagerly sought to replicate the American model of popular democracy and freewheeling capitalism. Post-Soviet Russia, led by Boris Yeltsin, the country's America-friendly president and the man who had stared down an attempted KGB-led coup to preserve the USSR, also was receptive to the U.S. example. As Russia began to drift away from that example, some in Washington started to ask: Who lost Russia? It's the wrong question, because Russia was really never America's to lose.

The Arab fighter against the U.S. military occupier in the Middle East, the Islamic holy warrior in Pakistan who burns with a hatred for America—they represent the most obvious challenge to the American global ascendancy.

The Russian challenge is of a different character. Russians are departing from the American model not out of some great antipathy toward America but out of a natural liking for their own ways of organizing their politics and their culture. They are not so much confronting the model as bypassing it, and their ability to do so is a marker of the diminishing power of the American tropism. The Russians are not alone; America's "imperialism of attraction," as Max Lerner called it in the 1950s, is of declining intensity in many parts of former Soviet Central Asia and, closer to home, in Latin America. This movement away from the American example may prove more consequential to the passing of the American Century than the revolt of the men with guns and the suicide bomber. An analogy from the area of technology is illustrative. The once-hegemonic powers of Microsoft did not erode because some rival took direct aim at Microsoft and dealt a crippling blow (although many tried). The Microsoft-makes-the-rules universe began crumbling when the Googles and Yahoo!s of the world entered the picture and began creating popular alternatives to Microsoft products. The Microsoft model is being not so much defeated as supplanted, and the same thing is happening to the American model in the world of global politics.

While Americans may find this tale of Russian rejection disheartening—a vote against the American model—they at least ought to appreciate a central irony: It is a vote. Societies like Russia are exercising a popular preference, the kind of choice that is at the core of the American democratic faith. Americans may not like this choice—there is plenty not to like. But they are fooling themselves if they imagine that resistance to the American way of doing things is lodged in the recalcitrant leadership of these societies and not in the people themselves.

In the fall of 1982, the body of Leonid Brezhnev was laid to rest on a hallowed spot of Soviet ground: in front of the Kremlin wall on Red Square and directly behind the Lenin mausoleum. Nearby were the remains of Stalin himself. Vice President George H. W. Bush, representing the United States at the funeral ceremonies, kept his eye on Brezhnev's seventy-four-year-old widow, Viktoriya. Before the lid on her husband's coffin was closed, she leaned forward and made the sign of the cross over his body. "I was stunned," Bush later wrote, because "it was visible proof that despite official policy and dogma for over six decades, God was still very much alive in the Soviet Union." Bush was right: One of the immediate consequences of the downfall of the Soviet Union nine years later, by which time he was president, was the formal restoration of religion's traditional place in society.

From the beginning, from the earliest signs of the weakening of Soviet rule, not one narrative but two competing ones were playing out in Russia. The familiar narrative, at least to the American ear, of a "new" Russia poised for integration into a U.S.-led international order built on democracy, human rights, and free markets was a real one. Behind Yeltsin was a group of intellectuals and political advisors, many from St. Petersburg, Russia's most outward-looking city, who grasped the Soviet collapse as a historic opportunity to launch Russia into the orbit of Western society. These individuals believed that a reforming tsarist Russia, before the tragedy of the Bolshevik coup in 1917, had been on such a trajectory; and now it could be resumed. Yeltsin himself was a mercurial figure of complicated and somewhat contradictory parts, but one of those parts was of the same fiber as the liberal radicals, as they were known. His Kremlin, of the early 1990s, was solicitous of American economic advisors, including the Harvard economist Jeffrey Sachs and senior policymakers at the U.S. Treasury in Washington, who encouraged the radicals not to waver in their determination to bring a "big bang" of reforms to Russia. Yeltsin sacrificed some of his political popularity by agreeing to let prices for consumer staples like bread float up to their market levels. All this was revolutionary for Russia and in the spirit of an American-style formula to create a dynamic private economy separate from the heavy hand of the state.

For some of Russia's new rags-to-riches businessmen—the oligarchs, as they were called—there also was an open admiration of America. When I lived in Moscow as a foreign correspondent, from 1999 to 2003, I used to talk about this with the oil baron Mikhail Khodorkovsky. He liked to say that the future for Russian business was to look at how America did things—the European route, of state planning and heavy regulation, was a barren path. Although he didn't quite put it this way, I think he saw himself in the tradition of the American robber-baron magnates of the nineteenth century. I know he believed, as did the liberal radicals, that all too many Russian traditions were debilitating ones—

products of a superstitious, peasant-dominated culture distrustful of modern ways. The American formula represented Russia's chance for a great leap forward. Khodorkovsky sounded weary when talking about how things worked in sluggish Russia; both for practical business reasons and also, I came to think, because of a genuine regard for America, he cultivated contacts in places like Washington and Houston and made frequent trips to the States.

But Khodorkovsky and the liberal radicals were not broadly representative of the Russian people. There was, in the early 1990s, an initial attraction to America propelled by widespread disgust with the geriatric condition of the Soviet Union in its final stages. But this attraction did not prove sustainable. The State Department's own polling of Russian public opinion showed a steady decline in approval of the United States—from about 75 percent in 1993 down to 54 percent in 1999 and further down to 48 percent in 2000. An American diplomat who worked in the political arm of the U.S. embassy in Moscow during this period attributed this backlash to a feeling on the part of ordinary Russians that they were "being treated like laboratory rats" and that "many of the scientists conducting the experiments were not even Russians, but were people sitting in offices in Washington, in the U.S. Treasury and the IMF."

Khodorkovsky's fall from grace was a revealing measure of the public mood. After Boris Yeltsin, at the end of 1999, left the Kremlin in the hands of the group led by Vladimir Putin, Khodorkovsky bridled at a new set of Kremlin rules designed to keep oligarchs like him from interfering in political matters. Intemperately, he suggested there was corruption in Putin's Kremlin, and he also began to consider selling his oil assets to a multinational like ExxonMobil. Lest other magnates get the same idea, the Kremlin made an example of Khodorkovsky. With great fanfare, he was arrested and convicted on charges of fraud and tax evasion and carted off to a jail in Eastern Siberia, where his face was slashed by an inmate. Tax authorities seized his choicest oil holding and handed it over to a Kremlin-controlled company chaired by a Putin aide. The spectacle was savored by the Russian people. This was the game played according to traditional Russian rules, in which money and power are joined and the loser, to make sure he does not make a comeback, is spat on and humiliated, on occasion jailed, sometimes shot. And Khodorkovsky was an outsider: a clever guy, whose father was Jewish, who had figured out how to make money from the crack-up of the Soviet Union. In his comeuppance, the Russian people saw not a gross injustice, not the abandonment of the cherished Western notion of the rule of law, but an overdue restoration of a familiar order.

This second narrative of post-Soviet Russia was becoming ascendant. The disintegration of Soviet society was an opportunity for the revival not only of the long-thwarted dreams of the liberal radicals but also of the visions of the Old Russia traditionalists, who looked to pre-Soviet Russia as the basis for the post-Soviet one. While Bill Clinton's team in Washington was throwing in its lot with Yeltsin—to the point that U.S. political consultants friendly to Clinton worked urgently on behalf of Yeltsin's reelection as president in 1996—Russia was restoring tsarist-era imperial symbols like the double-headed eagle, reconstructing buildings in a neo-Byzantine style, and restoring street names from pre-Soviet times. The new rich flocked to places like Tsarskaya Okhota (Tsar's Hunt), a restaurant on the outskirts of Moscow. Yeltsin himself was increasingly acting in a tsarlike way, preferring to rule by decree rather than submit to a "reactionary" parliament opposed to his reforms. At the same time, nationalistic sentiments became a more resonant current in Russian politics—reflecting the mood of a hurt, humiliated people who saw themselves as the butt of jokes in the affluent and triumphant West, such as when the popular U.S. late-night television host Jay Leno used his opening monologue to make comic light of the new Russia's depleted store shelves. Few Americans actually bore any deep ill will toward Russia or its people; in fact, few Americans thought about Russia at all. This was simply the age-old if rather cruel way in which a gloating winner tends to mock a battered loser. But at a time in Russia when many people were forced to grow their own food to survive, the barbs hit a nerve and contributed to an anti-Western mind-set. Especially among the Moscow political elite, a tightly knit group, the idea took root that America preferred to keep Russia weak and would, as in the cold war, regard a resurgent Russia as a threat.

As Russians recovered their pride, they became even more determined to return to the past—their past—in the search for solutions to their predicament. One Russian writer complained in the mid-1990s that "we are restoring the pillars" of prerevolutionary life—"the nobility, the Cossacks, Orthodoxy, Autocracy." "We are infected with nostalgia," he said, "idealizing 'the Russia we lost'" and "failing to see that we have lost it forever." But the renewed attention to the past could also be seen as the search for an anchor. Russia has a complex set of inheritances, the most important one of which is not from the European West but from the Byzantine East. The crucial event in Russian history took place in the tenth century, when the tsar, followed by his people, converted to Orthodox Christianity—the religion of the Eastern branch of the Roman Empire, based in Constantinople. After the Ottomans overran Byzantium in the fifteenth century, renaming Constantinople Istanbul, Moscow saw itself as the Third (and last) Rome, the guardian of Orthodoxy. Even as the level of religious feeling at times abated, Russia never lost a sense of itself as culturally separate from the Europe that had evolved from the first Rome. The Renaissance, the Protestant Reformation, the Enlightenment—these defining events for Europe met with ambivalence in Russia or, as in the case of the Reformation, with an enduring hostility.

In rejecting its Red heritage, or at least aspects of that heritage, post-Soviet Russia had a natural interest in revisiting the basis of the White critique of Soviet ideology—and it did so with renewed attention to prerevolutionary philosophers like Ivan Ilyin, who was imprisoned by the Bolsheviks for his anti-communist activities, sentenced to death, and later expelled along with other prominent White intellectuals. Ilyin believed Europe was rotting with the anti-Christian, secular creeds of Friedrich Nietzsche and Karl Marx. He saw Orthodox Russia as a gift to the world for overcoming this disease. Russian history, in his view, was the story of "morality triumphing over difficulties, temptation, danger and enemies." He embraced the traditional idea of Russian separateness and tended to see the West as conspiratorially aligned against Russia. And he believed that the Russian character was in need of a strong, guiding paternal hand: "Not having a mature, strong-willed nature himself, the Russian demands that his ruler have a will," Ilyin wrote.

The post-Soviet revival of Ilyin began in the early 1990s with strident nationalist politicians like Alexander Rutskoi and Vladimir Zhirinovsky extolling his sayings. His promoters also included the Russian actor and filmmaker Nikita Mikhalkov, whose anti-Stalin film, *Burnt by the Sun*, won the Oscar in 1994 for the best foreign-language film. Mikhalkov propagated Ilyin's writings and successfully campaigned for the reburial of his remains at the Donskoy Monastery in Moscow in a ceremony attended by such luminaries as Patriarch Alexy II, the head of the Russian Orthodox church, and Yuri Luzhkov, the mayor of Moscow.

During the cold war, Americans embraced the anti-Soviet dissident movement, partly because it was an acute point of vulnerability for the Kremlin but most of all because the movement appeared to spring from the values of freedom and human rights so dear to the American heart. The dissident movement, though, had different factions, and in Russia some of them were not particularly approving of the United States or of American values. Among the most powerful opponents of the Soviet regime was Alexander Solzhenitsyn, the winner of the Nobel Prize in literature in 1970 "for the ethical force with which he pursued the indispensable traditions of Russian literature," as the Nobel Academy said. Sent to the gulag for making critical remarks about Stalin in a letter to a friend, Solzhenitsyn wrote about the moral crimes and inanities of the Soviet Union in books like *One Day in the Life of Ivan Denisovich*, which were banned in his homeland but won a wide following in America and elsewhere. Exiled in the mid-1970s, he retreated to rural Vermont, whose climate and forests resembled Russia's. He lived there for eighteen years as a recluse. Solzhenitsyn detested America's consumer-oriented society, and he was not an admirer of American-style democracy, either. He hated the Soviet regime because it was godless. He hoped to see the Soviet Union replaced by a traditional Orthodox Russia, led by a benevolent tsarist-type leader. He returned to Russia in 1994 to "be of at least some small help to my tortured nation," as he explained at a rare appearance at a Vermont town-hall meeting, at which he thanked his neighbors for forgiving "my unusual way of life." In time he joined his voice to the chorus of conservative nationalists as they became increasingly critical of America. NATO, Solzhenitsyn said, had "preparations for the complete encirclement of Russia." He praised the foreign policy of Vladimir Putin, who likened America to a "wolf," as "forward looking." Solzhenitsyn came from a family of Cossack intellectuals in the Rostov-on-Don region; the young cadets of the Aksaisky Military School of the Don Cossacks, with their old-fashioned honor code and homage to God and the motherland, were in a sense his children.

Boris Yeltsin's embrace of the American formula for Russia became a source of his unpopularity with the Russian public. His successor, Vladimir Putin, did not make that mistake. Rather, Putin accumulated popularity by appropriating the public's chauvinistic sentiments and making them a mark of his rule. He proudly proclaimed that Russia was not going to become a second edition of Great Britain or America. I once had the chance to talk with Putin's confessor, Father Tikhon, who was in charge of an Orthodox monastery in central Moscow. He railed against Yeltsin as a drunken atheist and praised Putin as a sober, hardworking leader. In America and Europe, I told Father Tikhon, Putin was coming to be seen as a betrayer of the cause of democracy in Russia. I cited Putin's termination of the system of popular election of the governors of Russia's provinces, instead making the governors subject to the Kremlin's appointment. "It is a step forward, it is progress," Father Tikhon responded with vehemence. Many of the governors were corrupt and were acting "like tsars," he said. In Russia, there can be only one tsar.

Putin's Russia was embracing what might be called Patriotic Orthodoxy. The flavor came across in a visit I once paid to the Moscow headquarters of a youth group, Moving Together, organized by the Kremlin. The group presented itself as against abortion (Russia has one of the highest rates in the world) and took care to inform recruits of the Orthodox tradition of having large families. Members helped out at orphanages and handed out small crosses on street corners. The group's recommended-reading list steered clear of edgy post-Soviet writers and instead featured reliable old masters, such as Pasternak and Chekhov. "The Russian national idea is Orthodox, and it is very beautiful," Moving Together's chief librarian, twenty-year-old Irina Shevalkina, told me.

The recovery of Russian identity extended to the contemporary arts as well. I received an enthusiastic e-mail on this theme from a friend in Moscow. Andrey Isserov is a young history professor at Moscow State, Russia's most prestigious university. His specialty is America of the early nineteenth century; he is fluent in English and has lived and traveled widely in the United States. These are the credentials of a typical member of the liberal Russian intelligentsia—but unlike so many of these types, Isserov is not captivated by the idea of Russia importing its ideals and culture from the West. "Among the most spectacular recent developments are the renaissance of Russian prose and poetry," he told me, "and the renaissance of cinema." He cited film directors like Alexander

Sokurov, whose credits include *Alexandra*; Andrey Zvyagintsev, *The Banishment*; and Pavel Lungin, whose 2006 film, *The Island*, was praised by the Russian Orthodox church. *The Island* is set in mid-1970s Soviet Russia at a remote settlement of monks in the icy White Sea. The hero is a distinctive Russian type, a "holy fool" (the *yurodivy*), who years earlier attempted to murder a man to save himself and now is a blunt foreteller of the future to his fellow monks and others who, aware of his reputation, make the trek to his door for advice. He scares a young Russian woman away from an abortion, telling her that she will never marry, with or without the child she is carrying, so must keep her "golden boy," as God commands. Movies like *The Island* suggest a shift away from the moral and social anarchy that seemed to engulf Russia in the wake of the unexpected Soviet collapse. "I hope one day we will have powerful and unforgettable artistic images that will interpret perestroika and 1990s reforms," Andrey told me.

On a visit to Moscow in 2006, I looked up Yegor Gaidar, a champion of free-market reforms who served as an acting prime minister in the early 1990s until a beleaguered Yeltsin fired him. Gaidar was ill used and had cause to be bitter, but I found him less caustic about Russia's development than were most observers in America. He cheerfully told me that Russia's "liberal moment," following the Soviet collapse, the moment when Russia was ripest to penetration by American ideas, "was a historical accident." How so? "The liberals would never have been in power except for the collapse of the Soviet Union," Gaidar explained, and the Soviet Union wouldn't have collapsed but for gross mismanagement by its economic planners. Russia, after a good deal of disorientation, had found a balance likely to last for a generation. And the balance, despite what was being said in America and Europe, did not represent a return to Soviet ways. "It's not Soviet at all," Gaidar told me. "It's Russian."

The essential Russianness of the Putin era could be seen in his Kremlin. He worked out of a corner office in the Old Senate, a mustard-colored neoclassical building commissioned by Catherine the Great in the 1770s. Down the corridor, in a remodeled set of rooms that once contained Stalin's living quarters, was a small, candlelit Orthodox chapel with icon paintings on the walls. In the long, narrow hallways of the section of the building in which Putin and his top aides worked, the ambiance was distinctly Old Russian. On one wall were portraits of Nicholas II, Russia's "last tsar"; General Mikhail Skobelev, a nineteenth-century conqueror of Central Asia for the Russian empire; Catherine the Great; and Catherine's devoted lover and aide, Grigori Potemkin.

On a visit to Moscow in 2007, I met one-on-one for nearly an hour with Putin's first deputy prime minister, Dmitri Medvedev, who, on the strength of Putin's personal recommendation and the political muscle of the Kremlin, would be elected president in March of 2008. Someone who had worked with him referred to him as "the kid," and it was easy to see why. He stood five feet five inches tall, looked like he could not weigh more than 150 pounds, and had a clean-shaven face that appeared younger than its forty-one years. My first impression was of a miniature—a figure that could be pulled out of a *matrioshka*, a Russian nesting doll. The doll-like effect was magnified by his large eyes, a bit too big for his small, oval face. Born in St. Petersburg (Leningrad) in 1965, Medvedev had studied and taught law there. His father was a scientist, his mother a teacher—he was a product of the educated classes, not the working classes that spawned so many Soviet leaders, including Stalin and Khrushchev. I suggested that, like some others of his generation in St. Petersburg, Russia's most European city, he might have become part of the intelligentsia and pushed for radical changes in the Soviet Union. No, he answered. He referred me to a distinction made by Alexander Solzhenitsyn between an intelligentsia—a special Russian institution that has tended to pit itself against Russia's political establishment and traditional Russian values—and the "well-educated people" of the establishment elite. He identified himself with the latter.

The Western European and U.S. press made hopeful note of Medvedev's reputation as an "economic liberal" and the fact that, unlike Putin and many in the Putin crowd, Medvedev had not been an officer in the security services. He was even a fan of the English hard-rock band Deep Purple. But my main impression was that he shared the control-oriented thinking of a typical Russian leader. We talked at length about what Medvedev called "a special problem in Russia"—the potential, realized a number of times in the country's history, for its elites to fracture and plunge the society into chaos. "Whole empires were wiped off the face of the earth when their elites lost a unifying idea and engaged in deadly battles," he had told a Russian magazine back in 2005. On a piece of paper he drew for me a diagram—an equilateral triangle with the government elite at one corner, the business elite at the second, and the "humanitarian intelligentsia" at the third. These three elites must have harmony for Russia to be stable, he told me.

I cannot imagine a senior government official in Washington, D.C., or one in London, for that matter, drawing this sort of diagram. At the core of the Anglo-American ideal of checks and balances is the idea that competition in society and especially within the political sphere is a healthy and indeed necessary condition for preventing a worrisome concentration of power. Medvedev, though, was entirely in earnest. History has conditioned Russia's rulers to worry that a system of checks and balances is an invitation to a destructive and probably violent struggle for power and wealth. The notion of "consolidation" is not a Putin-era idea but one deeply rooted in the Russian experience. As a decision maker, Medvedev is loaded, consciously or not, with cultural DNA, and that matters a lot more than an affinity for Deep Purple.

Russian tanks rolled into the former Soviet republic of Georgia in the summer of 2008, a few months after Medvedev was inaugurated as president. In a matter of days, Russia's armies forced Georgia's U.S.-trained and -equipped troops out of the Russian protectorate of South Ossetia—and then the Russians moved into Georgia proper and dismantled Georgia's military infrastructure. The world saw images of a swaggering Russian army, half joking about the prospect of making a move on the Georgian capital of Tbilisi. This was not the same Russian army I had observed six years earlier on edgy patrol in the Russian breakaway province of Chechnya. At that time, I wrote about baby-faced Russian conscripts in the burnt-out capital of Grozny who lived in terror of a nighttime that belonged to the rebel forces. But Moscow, employing brutal methods, eventually squashed the Chechen rebellion—and the morale of the army was restored. Russia was back as a military power.

As U.S. and European criticism rained down on the team of Medvedev and Putin (at this time operating as prime minister), there was no doubt that the hearts of the Russian people were with their leaders and their soldiers. Georgia was a restorative not just for the army but for the nation. "I hope that now the West learns a lesson," one Russian woman in Moscow said. "Now we will be more respected," another woman, a doctor, commented. Like so many times before in its history, Russia had found communal pride in strength—in this case, in a display of might calculated to humiliate not only a small neighbor but also that neighbor's muscle-bound patron in Washington.

The lesson of post-Soviet Russia is the same lesson that Henry Luce might have learned, but failed to, about pre–Communist China of the early twentieth century. Societies are not plastic to the American touch, or to anyone's touch. Americans like to think about history as a straight line, with an upward trajectory, but history in a place like Russia looks more like a circle, a continuous tacking back to origins. Or, to put it another way, Russia tends over time to recapitulate itself, creating, as time moves on, not exact copies of earlier ages but recognizable likenesses. Thus, while elites in Western Europe, parts of Asia, Canada, and even America are moving toward a postnational universal civilization, a trend I explore in part 3 of this book, Russia remains more rooted in historical patterns.

In America, Russia's return to type is now widely acknowledged, and it is generally decried as a retreat from freedom. While there is a basis for this criticism, Americans might profit by asking *why* it is so difficult for societies like Russia to be free, in the Anglo-American tradition. The problem is not simply that Russia has had wicked rulers, fond of tyranny, but that the Russian people, broadly speaking, have a complicated relationship with the Jeffersonian ideal of freedom, defined as individual liberty, the freedom to pursue one's own happiness, so long as no one is harmed.

It is not that Russians are uninterested in the pursuit of happiness—it is just that they tend to have a collective concern about where this road can lead. In the nineteenth century, as Enlightenment notions of freedom coursed through Western Europe, "the Russian feeling for "freedom" was connected with anarchism rather than with the strict principle of liberalism," as the Russian philosopher Nicolas Berdyaev noted in his book *The Russian Idea*. *Svoboda*, a Russian word for "freedom" popularized in American and European media coverage of the collapse of the Soviet Union, comes closest to capturing what the Enlightenment philosophers meant by individual liberty. But even that word is problematic—in medieval times, *svoboda* had a communal connotation, having more to do with the freedom of a settlement rather than with the freedom of the individual. Moreover, there is another word in Russian that relates to freedom, *volya*, and it has an edgier connotation. *Volya* suggests uninhibited behavior—it is more about the engagement of the senses than of the mind. For example, for the prisoners of the gulag, *volya* represented the "fulfillment of desires that you yearn for when in a situation of nonfreedom."

In these terms, a "free Russia," were it ever to arrive in full measure, might be something of a revelation for Americans who can imagine nothing but good coming from their most cherished ideal. As the Cossacks, with their wild ways, also remind us, the free man may not be the "enlightened" one. And yet the Cossacks enjoy recurring seasons of celebration in the Russian mind because they embody a certain definition of what it means to be free. In Tolstoy's laudatory novella, *The Cossacks*, a young Russian army officer, weary of artificial Moscow life, is stationed in a Don Cossacks village. The officer says, admiringly, "The people live as nature lives: they die, are born, unite, and more are born— they fight, eat and drink, rejoice and die, without any restrictions but those that nature imposes on sun and grass, on animal and tree . . . these people [are] beautiful, strong and free."

PART THREE

After America Worlds

T he end of the American ascendancy is giving rise to a planetwide obsession with "what's next." Depending on one's perspective, the prospects are
frightening—or exhilarating. The future is China—or India. The future is Dubai.
The future is the global citizen. The future is global "flashmobs" of roving
criminal or terrorist gangs. (This last possibility is a vision of the Development, Concepts and Doctrine Centre of the British Ministry of Defence.) The
anything-is-possible giddiness of today's times recalls the "futurist" movement
in Europe of one hundred years ago. In 1909, Filippo Tommaso Emilio Marinetti, the Italian poet, novelist, and polemicist better known as F. T. Marinetti,
published his "Futurist Manifesto" in the Parisian daily *Le Figaro*. Marinetti
proclaimed: "We are on the extreme promontory of the centuries! What is the
use of looking behind at the moment when we must open the mysterious shut-
ters of the impossible? Time and Space died yesterday." He outdid any American of his time in hailing the world-altering possibilities of the motor vehicle,
much as today's technophiles hail the promise of cybertools. While Marinetti
may have had an irrational exuberance about the future, he was not wrong in
sensing a hinge point of history. A global order long dominated by European
monarchies and aristocracies and their imperial rivalries was nearing a spectacularly bloody end.

The "what's next" question, though, is a tricky one. There were "After Britain" possibilities for the planet other than an American Century. In 1909, from
the vantage point of a Marinetti, a fair bet could have been laid on the emerging
juggernaut of Germany, which Bismarck had unified several decades earlier.

While American-style popular democracy bid for the support of the common man, so did Karl Marx's communism. The Bolshevik Revolution was only eight years away. Fascism—the odious philosophy that Marinetti also came to support, in the Italian form—was another competitor for the allegiance of the masses in an age of brute industrialism. History teaches, if it teaches anything, that there is no "doctrine of inevitability," the historian Henry Steele Commager observed.

It likewise pays now to consider a range of "what's next" possibilities—if only because of the certainty that "accidents" will play an important role in determining which path, of the number of plausible ones, the After America planet will take. In hindsight, it looks like the X factor of the first half of the twentieth century was how the working classes would respond to unregulated capitalism. America itself could have taken a socialist detour during the Great Depression had FDR not saved capitalism from its more savage features. As for the first half of the twenty-first century, surely one large X factor is the nexus of issues associated with climate change and the availability of resources from basic foods to hydrocarbons. The question may be whether calamities like mass famine and the flooding of coastal population centers as the polar ice caps melt engender bloody anarchy or global cooperation. But if I had to bet, an even more important unknown may turn out to be how core questions of group identity are resolved. Am I first and foremost a member of a nation, a city or region, a tribe or religious group, or the global community? That existential question is in flux as perhaps never before—and how people answer it will have a profound impact on the character of the After America era.

Chapter 7 considers the possibility that the current chaos in the global system will spread and become a defining trait of an After America world. The world might then pine for the days of the Pax Americana—unless it turns out, as is also possible, that the chaos of global life without a hegemon, any hegemon, turns out to be a happy one. Chapter 8 looks at the ways in which a multipolar order might emerge, focusing on a rising India as an example of a player in such a system. Chapter 9 examines how a Chinese Century might evolve out of the inroads that the Chinese have already made in the world, including in America's backyard of Latin America. Chapter 10 looks at the emerging global city-state, including invented cityscapes like Dubai, as the most important feature of life after the American Century. And Chapter 11 looks at how a world government could emerge from the seeds of Dante's hoped-for universal civilization, now sprouting in such fertile patches of the planet as the environs of Harvard University in and around Cambridge, Massachusetts.

Chapter Seven

Chaos

The only thing standing between order and chaos is us.
Team America: World Police, the 2004 movie by the creators of *South Park*

The Cosmos Club of Washington, D.C., has the sedate ambiance and quaint customs of a bygone, pre-air-conditioned, age. One of the rules is that "gentlemen" must at all times wear jacket and tie, except in the summer, when the tie can be shed. Its home since 1952 has been an ornate French Renaissance building, set amid wisteria and magnolia trees, on a boulevard, Massachusetts Avenue, known for its foreign embassies. The walls of a hallway outside the main dining room are lined with framed portraits of Washington luminaries, including many of the iconic figures in the making of the American Century. Paul Nitze, Robert McNamara, and Henry Kissinger are represented, and this photographic gallery includes the most thoughtful and prescient critic of Henry Luce's idea of a globally omnipotent and omnipresent America—Walter Lippmann.

This felt like a good setting in which to discuss the potential of the American Century to unravel into some form of chaos. On the afternoon I dined there, the front-page, upper-right-corner headline of the *Washington Post* laid out for members on a table in the lobby was "As British Leave, Basra Deteriorates." It sounded like something out of 1920s Iraq. My host was Michael Vlahos, a historian and strategic studies specialist and a member of the National Security Analysis Department at the Johns Hopkins University Applied Physics Laboratory in Laurel, Maryland. The lab was one of countless appendages of Washington's national security establishment. Vlahos, whom I had met back in the 1990s when he was an informal advisor to the Republican politician Newt Gingrich, was a participant in a government working group set up to contemplate the future of "asymmetric warfare"—that is, violent conflicts pitting America against various types of stateless groups, from religiously motivated terrorists to heavily armed criminal gangs. "I think the universalist phase of the American mission is over," he told me as we scanned the menu.

So what's next? Vlahos shrugged. He'd been doing a lot of reading on "transitional" periods in history like the fifth to seventh centuries AD, when the western part of the Roman Empire disintegrated. That was certainly a time of chaos, as it often is when empires start to crumble. That was true of the British Empire in the mid-twentieth century, especially in the Indian subcontinent and in Palestine. It was also true of the Soviet empire in the 1990s, when civil wars broke out in the former republics of Tajikistan and Georgia, Chechen rebels mounted a violent insurgency to win independence from Moscow, and Armenians and Azeris fought over the disputed territory of Nagorno-Karabakh in the South Caucasus. A generalized economic collapse in post-Soviet Russia, with the disorder extended even to the streets of Moscow, bred gangster groups, forced many citizens to survive on homegrown vegetables and barter trade, and came close to returning the communists to power.

A dark chaos could accompany the passing of the American empire as well. The Pax Americana was always a fragile proposition and never a universally achieved one; even at the height of the American Century, some patches of the planet, like West Africa, never quite emerged from a miserable postcolonial chaos. The possibility of an After America chaos is a wider vacuum in which no one is able to step forward to take the role that America has played in keeping at least a modicum of order in places like the Middle East. There could emerge new zones of chaos as an isolated America is forced to retreat from military bases it has occupied as an imperial power for decades. If badly managed, the withdrawal from Iraq, pledged by Barack Obama, could reignite a civil war between sectarian factions.

In the era of the suitcase bomb, the envelope filled with anthrax, and other modern artifacts of "weapons of mass destruction" (WMD), America itself could become a zone of chaos. Experts on nuclear proliferation assess the chances that terrorists will succeed in detonating a nuclear device in some American city within the next ten years to be as high as 50 percent. The likeliest targets are New York City and Washington, D.C. According to one such scenario, a crude, Hiroshima-type atomic bomb, "small enough to fit into a medium-size truck" and detonated in America's capital city, at a stop halfway between the White House and the U.S. Capitol, could be expected to kill fifteen thousand in the first few minutes alone, with the blast immediately flattening the Justice Department and the National Gallery of Art. Some two hundred thousand people could be exposed to lethal radiation doses over the first twenty-four hours, and "with perfectly average weather—a big assumption, the fallout spreads to the east and north along a path 200 miles long and 25 miles wide, drifting out to sea north of Atlantic City." Electric fuses blow: "Well into West Virginia, Pennsylvania, Delaware, and New Jersey, all the lights go out." What then? There would surely be pandemonium, and if the shock were great enough, a temporary state of chaos could become a prolonged one—even "a permanent climate of fear in the West" and "the reversal of globalization," one writer has suggested.

The WMD that could plunge America into chaos also might come in the form of one of those esoteric financial products—like the so-called CDS, credit default swaps, derivatives—about whose destructive capacities the legendary investor Warren Buffet has long warned. (In the case of the CDS, traders bet enormous sums on contracts that promised to insure against various forms of credit default, but it turned out that the insurers lacked the funds to deliver on the promise.) In the fall of 2008, an economic collapse was avoided as the federal government stepped in to rescue an overleveraged Wall Street, but this was a stopgap measure. The era of panics may be only just beginning—especially because America's indebtedness has left it so vulnerable to borrowers, like China, who may not wish the United States well. The analogue to the breakdown of America's global military empire is the breakdown of the U.S.-managed post–World War II economic order. That order no longer exists—today's financial universe is akin to an unpoliced global jungle. It is possible, as I show in the following chapters, to glimpse the forms of alternative orders, but so far, no alternative has firmly established itself. Wall Street's Barton Biggs, the former chief global strategist at Morgan Stanley and a longtime market bear, has written that investors should adopt a new ethos of survivalism: "You should assume the possibility of a breakdown of the civilized infrastructure. Your safe haven must be self-sufficient and capable of growing some kind of food. It should be well-stocked with seed, fertilizer, canned food, wine, medicine, clothes, etc. Think Swiss Family Robinson."

It is tempting to argue that an After America chaos pump has been primed by one particular regime in Washington—by the George W. Bush regime, which destabilized the Middle East with its invasion of Iraq in 2003 and seemed to be blind to the hazards of a laissez-faire approach to economic regulation. But this is too narrow a view of things. The wellspring of an After America chaos, in both its economic and its geopolitical possibilities, is systemic. Economic deregulation was embraced by the Republican Reagan administration in the 1980s and the Democratic Carter administration in the 1970s—and its merits have long been preached to the world, in the formula known as the "Washington consensus," by mainstream American economists. With its emphasis on risk taking, this model always offered the possibility of rapid gains, but also, by definition, the possibility of severe losses. And the model contained a strain of the antigovernment philosophy that has long been an element—often a beneficial one—of American civilization. If the American Century was a global advertisement for the strengths of this model, an After America time of economic chaos might represent an illustration of its inherent weaknesses.

As for the Iraq war, it does not stand out as a radical departure from the established traditions of the Accidental Empire. While the venture was championed by the Republican-affiliated camp of the neoconservatives, support for the war cut across the political establishment, including liberal interventionists, the so-called liberal war hawks, of the Democratic Party. And the neocons are properly understood as heirs to an interventionist tradition of which Henry Luce, also a Republican, was himself a part. Some leading neocons, like William Kristol, were part of a Washington-based group calling itself the Project for the New American Century.

In any case, the chaos pump, even before the Iraq venture, was not lacking for supplies. All empires, even relatively benign ones like America's, engender resentments. As I can attest from my own global travels, it is common to hear a complaint against America's role in the world that starts with the invasion of

Iraq and treatment of the Palestinians but then segues into a litany that includes Vietnam and Yanqui imperialism in Latin America. The anti-imperial narrative—the counternarrative to the story of America's purpose as told by Henry Luce and his followers—has deep roots in the global soil. It turns out that not even a "democratic empire" can escape eternal imperial dichotomies like boss/bossed and ruler/ruled.

And there is an irrational element to the anarchic energies that have accumulated against America over the decades. America has stirred pathological hatreds and envies simply by being her modern, wealthy, successful self. The philosophical father of the 9/11 bombers was the Egyptian educator Sayyid Qutb, who spent one year, in 1949, traveling "in this large workshop called the New World," as he later wrote in a book, *The America I Have Seen.* Like so many foreign visitors, he was dazzled by America's accomplishments in science, technology, and industry and by the material abundance, "like dreams of the promised paradise," on display practically everywhere he set foot. But he was viscerally revolted by America's popular culture and its pastimes and everyday rituals of behavior—as seen in sports and other entertainment and especially in the conduct of the sexes: "In everything that requires brains and brawn the American genius is foremost. As for what requires soul and feelings, America is primitivism personified." Qutb became a martyred hero of the Muslim Brotherhood, and his litany of American culture's supposed diseases is the rote fare of al-Qaeda's anti-American taunts these days.

While some form of After America chaos is a plausible possibility for the American homeland, the likeliest chaos prospects lie elsewhere, on the margins of the empire. America's imperial frontier largely coincides with what could be called an arc of chaos—a vast swatch of territory stretching for more than two thousand miles across the Eurasian heartland, from Central Asia to Eastern Europe, with the Middle East in between. The region suffers from tribalism, sectarianism, religious fanaticism, tyranny, political corruption, poverty, and a plague of gangsters peddling narcotics and weapons. The American imperium is by no means the only enemy of the assorted criminals, terrorists, and rogue regimes that populate the area—but it is a huge and vulnerable target. With the possible exception of stretches of Africa, there is no more fertile ground for an After America chaos—a chaos that surely would not be contained in this region alone.

In the east, the arc begins in the remote Chinese region once known as Chinese Turkestan. This is the home of the Uyghurs, a Turkic-speaking Muslim people whose feelings of oppression at the hands of the majority Han Chinese have at times exploded into violent rebellion. Moving westward, the arc swings into the Fergana Valley, a lush agricultural region, also a breeding ground for Islamic militants, shared by the former Soviet republics of Uzbekistan, Kyrgyzstan, and Tajikistan. Uzbekistan and Tajikistan share a border with turbulent, opium-rich Afghanistan, which in turn backs into the lawless tribal lands of Pakistan, in which Taliban and al-Qaeda fighters have taken refuge. Western Afghanistan borders on Iran and the former Soviet republic of Turkmenistan— the latter a black hole that rivals Stalin's Soviet Union in its secrecy and xenophobia. Iran gives way to Iraq, whose western region extending on into Turkey is the home of a guerrilla band of Kurdish separatists, the PKK, in thrall to secular Maoist-tinged ideology. Across the Caspian Sea from Turkmenistan lies the Caucasus mountain region, a tinderbox of ethnic and tribal rivalries, involving in various theaters Georgians, Azeris, Armenians, Chechens, Abkhazians, Ossetians, and Russians. The Caucasus slopes down to the Black Sea and to Ukraine, which remains, as ever, a land divided between its European-leaning and Russian-leaning populations.

Over the centuries, great empires, including the Russian, the British, the Chinese, and the Persian, have attempted to control large chunks of this region to their strategic advantage. In the twenty-first century, America is the single most powerful actor, with a string of military bases extending from Kyrgyzstan on China's border all the way west to Turkey. From the perspective of Washington's imperial class, there are vital interests to protect—not only the security of fledgling democracies like Iraq and Afghanistan but also access to the region's vast reserves of hydrocarbons in Iraq and also Kazakhstan, Azerbaijan, and Turkmenistan. In the 1990s, over the objections of a weakened Russia, Washington persuaded Azerbaijan, Georgia, and Turkey to agree to a new pipeline, to be operated by British Petroleum, which would ship oil out of the landlocked

Caspian along an east-to-west route, drawn to skirt Russian soil, terminating in the Turkish Mediterranean port of Ceyhan.

But Washington's grip on this region is becoming more tenuous, as seen in Russia's dismemberment of Georgia, the resurgence of Iran, the rekindling of the Taliban movement in Afghanistan, and the fall of Pervez Musharraf, the autocrat on whom America bet so much in nuclear-armed Pakistan. In Uzbekistan, the local dictator, Islam Karimov, evicted U.S. troops from a military base in 2005 after Washington criticized his violent crackdown on political and religious dissidents. While Russia boasts of reestablishing a traditional "sphere of influence" along its southern underbelly, China quietly is amassing influence in energy-rich states, including Kazakhstan. The U.S. imperial project in Eurasia is in danger of wholesale collapse, possibly leaving this region a total mess.

How might chaos spread? My interest in the *potential* for greater chaos in an emerging After America world took me to one such plausible candidate: Turkey, and in particular, the Anatolian plain, for millennia a bridge between East and West and, as such, one of the most contested grounds on the planet. For better than half a century, Anatolia has served as a key listening post and staging ground for America's global kingdom. But as I learned on my visit, this is exactly the kind of place in which a seemingly entrenched American presence rests on the shakiest political and cultural ground.

The American military arrived in Anatolia in 1951, settling down in Adana, a town less than an hour's drive north of the beaches of the Mediterranean and about six hours' drive east to the Habur gate at the border with northern Iraq. The Roman emperor Hadrian built a sixteen-arch white stone bridge, still in use today in Adana, to span the shallow green waters of the Seyhan River. The Americans built a nine-hole golf course on the outskirts of town. Golf is not a big sport in Turkey; at the time, it was the only course in the country. A short distance from the course, the land, containing fig orchards, was bulldozed to make room for an airstrip. So began the construction of Incirlik Air Base, a joint project of the Turks and the Americans. (Incirlik, with the "c" pronounced as a "j" in the Turkish language, refers to "the place of the fig.") Anti-communist Turkey, which was already fighting, with the Americans, against the Stalin-backed communist forces on the Korean peninsula, joined NATO, becoming the southeastern flank of the alliance.

With its proximity to the Soviet Union and the cold war sparring grounds of the Arab and Persian Middle East, Incirlik was a precious asset for America. The base served as the main stationing ground for the CIA's U-2 spy plane program, the brainchild of Richard Bissell. (The flights over the USSR came to an abrupt halt when the U.S. pilot Gary Powers was shot down by the Soviets in 1960, while flying over the Ural Mountains in Soviet airspace.) On the Turkish side, a generation of officers received training in America, many learning to speak English. And the Turks received plentiful supplies of American arms and military equipment. There was a reservoir of goodwill between the two sides generated by their shared fight in Korea, where Turkish soldiers fought in hand-to-hand combat against the Chinese, the Turkish sidearm sword, or "long knife," pitted against the Chinese bayonet.

Incirlik is a Turkish-run base of which the Americans are tenants. The Americans sometimes chafed under the Turkish military's petty bureaucratic ways but lived there happily enough by turning their portion of the grounds into a suburban miniature of what might be found in their country. When I visited Incirlik on a warm October day, I found, in addition to the golf course and a driving range, a bowling alley, softball fields, charcoal grills under gazebos, and suburban-style detached houses with carports, where the U.S. top military brass lived. A portable basketball hoop had been set up on a cul-de-sac. Sprinkler systems watered the manicured green lawns and the rosebush hedges. On the Pentagon's global American Forces Network, the American community could watch NFL football games along with *Wheel of Fortune* and *Hardball with Chris Matthews*.

For an American soldier stationed overseas, Incirlik is considered good duty. Couples can live with their children on the base, and the children, from pre-K on up through high school, study in air-conditioned schools run by U.S.-accredited teachers. I found the children excited about the approach of Halloween; pumpkin cookies were being baked in one of the classrooms. Turkish nannies and gardeners are cheaply available. For vacationers, Paris, Rome, and London are just a few hours away by plane, and the base chapel offers trips to religiously important spots in Anatolia, like the well at which Paul of Tarsus (born Saul) was said to have preached the Christian gospel. "Turkey is such a biblical place," Sgt. Susan Edmonds told me. She dipped a finger underneath her T-shirt and showed me the crucifix dangling from the gold chain around her neck.

The United States keeps tactical nuclear weapons at Incirlik—possibly several dozen B-61 gravity bombs, each as much as ten times more powerful than the Hiroshima bomb. Incirlik is also a sanctuary from attack. The grounds include a hospital with an underground bomb shelter, set below ten feet of concrete and equipped with filters to protect against fallout from the use of nuclear, biological, or chemical weapons. The shelter contains a seven-day supply of food, water, and electricity, and sewage storage tanks made to hold out for a week. The facility, planned in the 1980s during the cold war, when the Soviets were believed to present a threat of germ warfare, began operating in the 1990s. Even though the Soviet threat no longer exists, unconventional methods of attack, like germ warfare, are high on the list of hazards presented by the likes of al-Qaeda. The American troops at Incirlik run a drill in which they don their hazard-protection suits and masks, which must be within easy reach at all times, and repair to the shelter—the "best decontamination facility in the world," an Incirlik hospital administrator boasted.

For how long, I asked an American diplomat, will Incirlik be needed as a base for U.S. troops and military operations? "For as long as the Middle East is unstable," the diplomat replied. In the skies over Incirlik I saw a jumbo C-17 cargo plane coming in for a landing. Incirlik was the principal cargo hub (since 2005) for resupplying U.S. forces in Iraq and Afghanistan. I asked a classroom of second- and third-graders why U.S. soldiers, their parents, needed to be here. Quinlin, a girl in the second grade, raised her hand. "They protect America so that the people who want to destroy America won't get in," she answered.

"Location, location, location" is why Incirlik remains important to America's strategic interests, Col. Kenneth Stefanek, vice commander of the U.S. forces on the base, told me during a talk in his office. A banner from Notre Dame, his alma mater, was tacked to the wall behind us. Stefanek has a feel for the Middle East; he attended an elementary school in prerevolutionary Iran, where his father worked for B.F. Goodrich. Iranian kids in his Tehran neighborhood, who didn't like the American habit of keeping dogs as house pets, sometimes threw rocks at him. "You can't beat having an air base" so close to places like Iraq and Lebanon, he told me.

When I turned our conversation to wider currents in Turkish society, Stefanek acknowledged that the Americans at Incirlik are "isolated a little bit" from those currents. That is an understatement—and it underscores a painful irony for the American tenants. When the Americans arrived in Adana in the 1950s, Turkey was still a country run in the secular-autocratic image of Atatürk, the French-admiring founder of the modern Turkish republic after the First World War. The Turkish military was the chief guardian of that republic, which had abolished the Islamic caliphate and sultanate and insisted on European styles of attire. Responding to popular protests in Anatolia against his ban on the wearing of the Muslim fez as headgear, Atatürk declared, as if by decree, "We will become civilized." But as post–cold war Turkey has become more democratic, more in tune with popular sensibilities and less beholden to the generals and the judges of the Atatürk mind-set, the American presence at Incirlik has become more controversial; many Turkish citizens would just as soon not have any American soldiers stationed in their country. The time may be approaching when the leaseholders at Incirlik ask their American guests to pick up their belongings and leave. "We've had to think about that," Stefanek acknowledged.

Muslim Turkey and Judeo-Christian America have always been an awkward fit, notwithstanding the cold war alliance that held the two together. Had Atatürk's vision of a secular Turkey anchored in the West succeeded, the relationship might have worked out smoothly enough. But Turkey is drifting away from that vision, as was evident in my travels around Anatolia. In the city of Kahramanmaraş, a two-hour drive northeast of Adana across the pine-covered Taurus Mountains, I spent an evening talking to two young women who covered their heads with scarves in the traditional Islamic fashion. The head scarf has become an enormously contentious issue in Turkish politics and society—secularists in Istanbul and elsewhere have struggled to keep in place a ban against a woman's wearing the scarf in public buildings, like a government office or a public university, as an essential pillar of the Turkish republic. The two women, both of whom were teachers, were joined by their husbands. We met at one of the couples' homes in a suburban apartment house whose walls were adorned with framed Koranic verses in Arabic. Eylem Akgun, twenty-eight years old, worked at a privately operated school for mentally retarded children. She refused to work at a publicly run school, she said, because she would be required to remove her head scarf. Eylem was wearing a cream-colored scarf, a maroon blazer, and a blue cotton skirt that flowed down to her shoes. Only her face and her hands were uncovered. Why, I asked, was wearing the head scarf so important to her? Her dark eyes met my gaze. "First, it's an order from Allah, and I don't question an order from Allah, I just do it," she said. I asked her if Turkey would be stronger and healthier, as a society, if it showed more Islamic faith. Yes, she replied, "Iran is an example of this," and that country, ruled by Islamic clerics, was a good model for Turkey. Which came first for her, her identity as a Muslim or her identity as a Turkish national citizen? Her Muslim identity, she replied, as her husband, also a teacher, added his agreement.

Suppose, I continued, she could choose for a neighbor in her apartment block a German, an American, an Iranian, or an Israeli. What would be her order of preference? First the Iranian, she said, followed by the German, and then the American, and last the Israeli, with whom she could "never" be a neighbor, because the Israelis are even worse than the American "imperialists." They act in a manner that is barbaric, "not human," she said. There was general agreement in the room with her negative view of the Israelis, which seemed also to incorporate a pernicious view of the character of Jews: The husband of the other woman in the room chimed in, "Jews believe others must serve them." He said this in a matter-of-fact way, not as a point of debate but as a declaration of the obvious. When his twelve-year-old daughter, practicing her English, asked me what nationality I was, it occurred to me to say Jewish American, but I decided to leave things at "American."

It was just one evening of conversation, but typical of the direction in Turkish society. Public opinion surveys indicate that a sense of religious identification is increasing, with just over half of all Turks viewing themselves as Muslims first and Turks second, a finding that would have particularly appalled Atatürk. The surveys also suggest that hostility toward Christians and especially toward

Jews is mounting, with Jews viewed favorably by only 15 percent of the people. Attitudes not only toward America but toward the West generally are increasingly negative, with Westerners being associated with traits like "greedy," "selfish," and "violent." In this atmosphere, Turkey also is becoming more vulnerable to radical Islam—to organizing both by groups linked to Iran and by al-Qaeda. Turkish-based al-Qaeda cells were responsible for suicide attacks launched in Istanbul in 2003 against a pair of synagogues, the British consulate, and the HSBC bank headquarters.

Nor is the Turkish military, the supposed secular bastion of the republic, immune from the shift toward a greater religiosity in everyday society. At Incirlik, American commanders grapple with issues like whether it is acceptable to continue to serve alcohol at receptions with Turkish officers at the base. In the past, this was not a debatable matter—Atatürk was a proud, even boastful, drinker of raki, the traditional anise-flavored liquor, and many a Turkish general followed his example. Colonel Stefanek told me that religious issues have become the "third rail" in Turkey—too sensitive for him to bring up in conversation with his opposite number at the base.

I could see why. The religious-political sensibility is fusing spiritual beliefs with aggressive, warlike ones—directed at all those deemed "other." America is inevitably part of this mix. It is blamed, for one thing, for stoking the flames of Kurdish nationalism. There are about 14 million Kurds in Turkey, mostly in southeast Anatolia, out of a total population of 72 million; and 5 million more Kurds live across the border in northern Iraq. Even though the Kurds are Muslims, they speak a language related to Persian and are seen by many Turks as outsiders. Kurds in Turkey and elsewhere generally welcomed the U.S. invasion of Iraq: Saddam Hussein had brutally suppressed their aspiration to run their own affairs in northern Iraq. But ethnic Turks, who overwhelmingly opposed the U.S. plan to attack Iraq, worry that the Kurds, as part of their aspirations for a separate state, plan to take a territorial bite out of Anatolia. Those anxieties are nourished by borderland attacks on Turkish soldiers by the PKK, the separatist Kurdish rebels, who operate from bases in the mountains of northern Iraq.

During my visit, a spontaneous wave of rallies urging the government toward war was sweeping Anatolia in response to the killings of Turkish soldiers by the PKK—on the day before my arrival in the country, there had been an especially nasty ambush, killing at least seventeen Turks. A Western diplomat who had witnessed one of these rallies told me they seemed like something out of 1914 Europe, when publics fervently demonstrated all over the continent in support of war. I could see what he meant, but I was struck more by the religious element of the war fever. Turkish soldiers were being asked by their people to be prepared to perish in battle against the PKK not only for their country but also for Allah. A common slogan at the rallies was "Martyrs don't die"—which I saw on the headband of a young girl preparing to march in Kayseri. Seeking to pump up demonstrators, organizers of the rally were playing Ottoman martial music through loudspeakers, simulating the bands that marched in front of the *gazi* jihad warriors in the days of empire. The refrain went: *Ileri, ileri, hep ileri.* "March on, march on, always further."

At a rally in the nearby town of Niğde, the public square, marked by a statue of Atatürk mounted on his horse, felt more like a makeshift mosque. About a thousand people, running the gamut from elderly pensioners to small children accompanied by their mothers and fathers, spilled out from the square. A little boy next to me waved the red Turkish flag as the speaker at the podium, shouting into a microphone, called for "revenge" against the PKK and for Allah's damnation of the *kafir*, the Arabic term for the infidel. With their palms turned out, as in prayer, the crowd responded with a chorus of amens. The speaker, who was probably part of the Grey Wolves, a notorious group with fascist views, launched into an ugly anti-Western tirade, declaring that the West had feasted on "the rubbish" left behind by the Ottomans.

One demonstrator carried a sign reading PKK, USA & EUROPEAN UNION: YOU ARE NOT POWERFUL ENOUGH TO DIVIDE US. The speaker asked for punishment of "the traitors inside our country" and finished by asking Allah to "accept our prayers like those offered in Mecca." Anxious for my safety, and perhaps his own, my translator, an Istanbul resident raised in Anatolia, asked me to take off my sunglasses—he said I looked like a CIA agent.

In this noxious atmosphere, just about the only group in Turkey *not* taking an anti-American line is the Kurds, who view the American presence as the one thing standing between them and Turks intent on taking revenge for the PKK killings. "For us, first is Allah, second is America," Abdullah Cece, a Kurdish

field-worker, told me at a teahouse in the back streets of Adana. At a second teahouse, I asked Suleyman Gergin, also a Kurd, whether chaos would ensue if
America were to withdraw from Turkey and Iraq. "Yes, yes, yes, yes," he said, his
rapid hand movements matching the urgent pace of his words.

I don't mean to suggest that a chaotic bloodletting is a certain or even a
probable future for Turkey. But it is a plausible one, the way things are going—
and it is an organic possibility that America is more or less helpless to thwart.
How bad could it get in Turkey? The darkest turn that political conversation
takes is toward the theme of civil war. This discussion is not as neat as "Western" (secular) Istanbul versus "Eastern" (Islamic) Anatolia—Anatolia itself is
divided between towns like Kayseri, known for the Islamic orientation of their
business and political elite, and others, like Mersin, known for a more secular,
liberal disposition. If the military is still thought to be largely secular, the local
police forces in Anatolia are thought to have sympathy with the religious side.
And since Turkey, like America, is a gun culture, with many folks apt to keep a
weapon at home, civilian-based paramilitary forces are another likely factor in
any breakdown of civil order.

Civil strife would likely shut down the U.S.-backed Caspian-oil pipeline that
terminates in Anatolia—now pumping about 1 million barrels of oil per day into
global markets—and inevitably would spill over to Europe as well. Germany
alone is home to some 2 million people from Turkey, including half a million
Kurds. And perhaps most disastrously of all, a meltdown in Turkey would be a
significant accomplishment—a triumph—for the forces of radical Islam. With
the collapse of order in Turkey, Islamic militants in the border states of Iran,
Iraq, and Syria, as well as in Turkey itself, would have an easier time exporting
their ideology and weapons into the Balkans. Depending on the outcome of a
civil war, Istanbul could once again serve as a launching pad for jihad into Europe, as it did six centuries ago with the capture of Constantinople by the Ottomans. That is how bad things might get.

The possibility of a black chaos tends to be taken most seriously by those who
have experienced the worst that history can offer. That's why the Jews and the
Kurds take chaos so seriously, as do, for that matter, the Palestinians, driven

from their ancestral homes when Israel was established in 1948. Notwithstanding the creation of Israel as a sanctuary, Jews in Israel and elsewhere still take very seriously the possibility of chaos, as indeed they should with American power on the wane. Theodor Herzl, the modern philosopher and founder of the Zionist movement, sincerely believed that the establishment of a Jewish homeland in the Holy Land would solve the age-old problem of anti-Semitism by providing Jews with a route out of the cauldron of Christian Europe. "The Jews, once settled in their own State, would probably have no more enemies," he wrote in his 1896 manifesto *Der Judenstaat*. The cruel truth has turned out to be quite the reverse: Israel's Jews, the target of anti-Semitic ravings from WMD-aspiring Islamic terrorist groups as well as Mahmoud Ahmadinejad, the president of Iran, are at greater risk than Diaspora Jews in countries like America, Canada, Great Britain, and Australia. In the After America world, with the ebbing clout of Israel's longtime protector in the Middle East, Israel's sense of embattlement stands to intensify. While Israel possesses a nuclear arsenal, that arsenal has failed to deter sworn enemies like Hamas, whose weapon of choice is the rocket and the suicide bomber. "This place could turn into a massive killing ground," Benny Morris, a prominent historian of Zionism who lives in Jerusalem, told me on a trip to Israel in 2004.

It is also in the disposition of Europeans, with their ingrained appreciation of the tragic, to take chaos seriously. The historian Jacques Barzun, who spent his childhood in his native France of the First World War and came to the United States in 1919, at the age of twelve, was a connoisseur of disorder, of which there are about as many varieties as of vintage champagne. In an essay written in the late 1980s, "Towards the Twenty-First Century," he observed that "history shows both big and little decadences," a word that means "falling off." Sometimes it is possible for a civilization to experience one of these small decadences "without wrecking the entire fabric," as in the transition from the High Middle Ages to the Renaissance. "But it can also happen," he noted, "that not enough new ideas, no vitalizing hopes, emerge, and civilization falls apart in growing disorder, mounting frustration, and brainless destruction." As he observed, "The tremendous endings of Greece and Rome are not a myth."

For those Americans who have known little of life outside America, a scary, free-fall chaos is generally not part of the world they have inhabited. Americans tend to think, as they generally have been taught, that history is all about progress. The Great Depression that followed the stock market crash of October 1929 caused great hardship but was surmounted—it was not, as was feared at the time, the start of a long slope of decline, or the spark for a crisis in capitalism that could make America turn to European-style socialism. In the pantheon of American leaders, Abraham Lincoln, who was prone to bouts of depression and evinced a European-like sense of the tragic in his most profound speeches, stands out for taking chaos seriously. Given the Civil War, and the real possibility that the Union side could lose, Lincoln perhaps had no choice but to peer over the edge of the precipice and try to imagine what a "falling off" might look like. It was when things looked darkest for the Union, in December of 1862, that Lincoln, in an address to Congress, called America "the last best hope of earth." Those words spoke to his abiding belief in America's greatness but also conveyed his sense of the world's predicament as fragile and precarious, as if the planet were a ticking time bomb that only America could defuse.

Although generally foreign to the American experience, brooding about the prospect of chaos is now becoming a fashion. At a concert at Carnegie Hall in 2006, Randy Newman sang:

> *The end of an empire is messy at best*
> *And this empire is ending*
> *Like all the rest. . . .*

I suspect that this will be a permanent and unavoidable psychological consequence of the transition of America from the American Century to the After America world—even if chaos does not, in fact, become the main feature of that world. The basic reason is anxiety, and especially, though not only, the anxiety aroused by the 9/11 attacks on the homeland. "When we go under, Western civilization goes under," Colorado congressman Tom Tancredo pronounced in a televised debate among Republican presidential candidates in the spring of 2007. Whatever one makes of that prediction, the anxiety is not without a rational base—in the sense that, in the emerging After America world, America *by definition* will be in less control of its destiny.

American-generated chaos scenarios invariably have helplessness, a sense of powerlessness, at their root. One wellspring for such scenarios stems from Christian millenarians. In the best-selling Left Behind series of novels, the Antichrist is represented by a new head of the United Nations who gathers all of the world's nuclear weapons in his hands and lays waste to Washington, D.C. In *Jerusalem Countdown*, a book by John Hagee, the controversial Christian Zionist pastor who endorsed John McCain for the presidency in 2008, the Antichrist is head of the European Union. A less obvious source of chaos scenarios is the voice not on the margins of the establishment but deep within it. Listen to the Lincoln-like bass note sounded by the liberal imperialists, intellectuals, and others who argue that the American empire, for all its faults, is in fact all that prevents a global-systems breakdown that could swamp America itself. One bearer of this point of view is Niall Ferguson, the Glasgow-born, Oxford-educated historian who teaches at Harvard and is a senior fellow at Stanford University's Hoover Institution. His July/August 2004 cover story for *Foreign Policy*, a magazine published by the Carnegie Endowment for International Peace, a prestigious Washington, D.C., think tank, was a litany of horrors of the sort that comes in less polished form from the religious apocalyptic. "Critics of U.S. global dominance should pause and consider the alternative," Ferguson began. "If the United States retreats from its hegemonic role, who would supplant it? Not Europe, not China, not the Muslim world—and certainly not the United Nations. Unfortunately, the alternative to a single superpower is not a multilateral utopia, but the anarchic nightmare of a new Dark Age." This time of "apolarity," Ferguson ventured, could turn out to mean "an era of waning empires and religious fanaticism; of endemic plunder and pillage in the world's forgotten regions; of economic stagnation and civilization's retreat into a few fortified enclaves."

Talk of a twenty-first-century version of a Dark Ages cannot be dismissed—there really was, after all, a medieval Dark Ages, at least in Europe, and it was every bit as horrible as it sounds—with French peasants reduced to eating grass. If the twenty-first century turns out to be only one-quarter as bad as "the calamitous 14th century," as the historian Barbara Tuchman called this "violent, tormented, bewildered, suffering and disintegrating age, a time, as many thought, of Satan triumphant," then it will be a very bad time indeed. A modern example of how quickly things can unravel is the hyperinflation of Weimer Germany in 1923. The American writer Pearl Buck witnessed the events:

"They had lost their fortunes, their savings; they were dazed and inflation-shocked and did not understand how it had happened to them and who the foe was who had defeated them," she said of the German people. "Yet they had lost their self-assurance, their feeling that they themselves could be the masters of their own lives if only they worked hard enough; and lost, too, were the old values of morals, of ethics, of decency."

As stark as these examples from history are, the more alarmist warnings of today's chaos purveyors need to be kept in perspective. These warnings, in particular those emanating from the political and financial elites, contain an echo. The stewards of the British Empire also sincerely believed that large tracts of the world could not manage without them. If the British left India, Winston Churchill warned in the early 1930s, India would "fall back quite rapidly through the centuries into the barbarism and privations of the Middle Ages." As it turned out, India's turbulence in the wake of the British departure proved temporary—and the transition to India's independence surely would have been less bloody had the British done a better job of managing their exit. The British belief was a self-serving one, born of a false sense of racial and religious superiority. Empires tend to manufacture myths of indispensability.

Is chaos always so terrible? Strictly speaking, chaos is a state of nature with an inherent randomness or unpredictability, which is not the same as instability. A chaotic system is therefore not necessarily an imbalanced one, much less a horrible void. So let's consider this: The end of the American-enforced global order might generate chaos, but this chaos would not necessarily be of an awful kind. The After America world would be one in which there is no Big Daddy—no omnipotent force, no "God" to enforce order and set standards and rules of conduct. And yet this world, for all its potential to go awry, actually turns out to function like a system of more or less happy chaos. Yes, happy chaos.

A happy chaos scenario might take its cue not from gloomy mythic poets like T. S. Eliot, or from the Bible, which depicts chaos as a rebellious beast, but from modern science. The chaos of science is value-neutral and altogether unromantic. Chaos theorists look for clues about its qualities by studying flows and processes of everything from weather and highway traffic patterns to the evanescent dissipation of a swirl of cigarette smoke. A system of chaos is all about sequences and chain reactions. The outcome of such sequences can be unpleasant, as in the famous Butterfly Effect, coined by the zoologist Konrad Lorenz, in which the beating of a butterfly's wings in Brazil is said to set off a tornado in Texas. But the same logic suggests that chain reactions can lead to positive results.

For those who scoff at the prospect of a happy chaos, who believe that all disorder is basically bad, think about an example that is close to the American bone: migration. The greatest settlement in American history, the settlement of the frontier West, was a profile in chaos, not the master plan of a grand visionary. The settlers were at the mercy of climate and unfamiliar landscape and often ended up in a place different from the one for which they started out. And the spurs to settlement had a haphazard quality. Who could have predicted the fallout from the discovery of gold in 1840s California? It was as if a global pistol had been fired; the migrants raced in from everywhere, pans in hand, and they brought with them a swarm of tricksters and charlatans, as well as legitimate entrepreneurs, who hoped to profit from the boom. "Gold fever" was a social and economic revolution that transformed San Francisco from a runt village into one of America's most dynamic cities and ports. California, which was admitted to the American union as a full-fledged state in 1850, was born in a whirlwind.

Nor is chaos absent from the homeland of twenty-first-century America. America is still the world's preeminent power, but for the last quarter century it has not been in control of its southwestern borders. Millions of immigrants have entered the country without legal permission—they can be thought of as the starter agents of a chaotic sequence of unpredictable events still playing itself out but that may end, if it ever does end, happily. The Latino immigration narrative at first was about the Hispanic resettlement of borderland areas like California, Texas, and New Mexico—to critics, it looked like an effort to retake lands seized by the United States in the nineteenth century. But the immigration story has turned out not to fit such a neat historical pattern as Latinos settle in places like Iowa and Georgia and go from being seasonal migrants to a

permanent presence in the Rocky Mountain West. Among the "corrido" ballads, set to the rhythms of a snare drum, in the onion fields of Idaho, one goes:

> *Now they are putting up barriers in front of us so we don't return*
> *But that is not going to block us from crossing into the United States*
> *We leap them like deer, we go under them like moles*

The long chain of Latino migration is transforming the Rocky Mountain West
unpredictably—just as that region, once the province of Native American tribes,
was forever changed by European settlers. It is an irreducibly chaotic event.

Saskia Sassen, a sociologist who taught at the University of Chicago and the
London School of Economics before moving to Columbia University, is best
known for her work on the global city. But Sassen's true subject, as she explained in a conversation at the Waldorf-Astoria in Manhattan in 2007, is how
things break down—what she likes to call "the disassembly of territorial
framings." She pointed to the emerging "economic-cultural region" encompassing parts of Mexico and America as an example. "A lot of what we are trying to
understand as an integrated system is closer to what chaos theory would predict," she said. "What we are seeing," she told me, are the "reassemblies of bits
and pieces that were part of the nation-state."

Sassen was born in the Netherlands in 1949, lived for a time in Rome, and
came to America in the late 1960s at the age of nineteen. The "golden moment"
for America was the growth of its vast middle class in the decades after World
War II, she said. But now she views America as "an agent" in the global breakdown of the nation-state. Seated across from me in the lobby of the Waldorf,
with her white hair and purple shawl and penchant for bracing pronounce-
ments, she slid easily enough into the timeless archetype of a prophet. But she is
no Jeremiah. Sassen views chaos not as a cataclysm but as "the worming of
norms." Should we be afraid of where this all leads? "I am an adventurer. I think
this is very interesting," she said.

In the first half of the twentieth century, the economic philosopher Joseph
Schumpeter thought along similar lines. Chaos was an integral part of the formula of "creative destruction" that he identified as the key to capitalist progress,
and America was his favorite exhibit. Americans were as willing as any people

to endure the chaos of moving from the horse-and-buggy age to the times of the railroad and the motorcar, and of shifting from the age of steel to the age of the transistor. Detroit and Pittsburgh withered while Silicon Valley cropped up on the redwood forest coast of California. Chaos was a bittersweet process of misery for some and opportunity for others.

Happy chaos is the sort of notion that the managers of a nation-state, any nation-state, find unorthodox and distasteful, not to mention oxymoronic. History, it has to be admitted, is generally on their side. It is indeed hard to think of any time when the absence of political control, the absence of government as a restrainer of the worst tendencies of humankind, has created a positive sequence of events. Typically what happens is that periods of chaos, even those that may on balance be happy ones, like the settlement of California, tend to invite central controls.

The main reason to consider that the future could be different is technology—which Schumpeter regarded, above all, as the catalyst of creative destruction. The argument is this: The new technologies of personal empowerment can subvert centuries of political tradition. Happy chaos has a possibility in the emerging postindustrial world that did not exist in the receding, top-down industrial one. The arc will be from unipolarity to infinite or near-infinite polarity, from a dominant point of power to billions of such points. This sort of happy chaos would not be a world of total randomness—just as the weather, for all its unpredictability, is not a totally random system, either. Rather, the distinguishing feature would be the ability of technology-equipped individuals to form their own connections, their own social patterns, absent controlling influences.

A happy chaos of the twenty-first century would be proof of the idea that small is beautiful, that diversity and dispersion is a good thing, and that it is the control freaks of the world, whether in the form of an autocratic parent or a hegemonic global power, that account for the greatest miseries on earth. For believers in the American Goliath, that sounds like a heretical notion, but it was embraced, late in life, by one of the architects of the American Century, the diplomat George Kennan. In the late 1940s, Kennan helped map the political strategy for containing Soviet expansion. But in the early 1990s, with the cold war won and the Soviet no more, he startled readers with a book, *Around the Cragged Hill: A Personal and Political Philosophy*, embracing the notion that

America had become "a monster country," like China and India. And "there is a real question as to whether 'bigness' in a body politic is not an evil in itself, quite aside from the policies pursued in its name," Kennan wrote. In the venerable American tradition of eighteenth-century anti-federalists like Patrick Henry, who opposed the creation of a powerful national government as a threat to personal liberty and a recipe for empire, Kennan suggested breaking up America into a dozen constituent republics, and "to these entities I would accord a larger part of the present federal powers than one might suspect—large enough, in fact, to make most people gasp. . . . There would be much room for local innovation and for departure from older national norms." This train of thought was not a passing fancy for Kennan. In 2001, on the eve of his ninety-seventh birthday, he wrote a letter of encouragement to the leader of the Vermont independence movement. "There can be no doubt of the closeness of many of our views. But we are, I fear, a lonely band," Kennan noted. He died four years later, at the age of 101.

The modern prophet for this outlook is Leopold Kohr, the Austrian philosopher, born in 1909, who believed, as he wrote in his 1957 treatise, *The Breakdown of Nations*, that "wherever something is wrong, something is too big." He took the contrarian view that the Soviet Union, because of its enormous size, was inherently fragile at a time when America's leading "Sovietologists" felt confident that the USSR was a stable entity that would long endure. This kind of thinking—likewise dear to the hippies of 1960s San Francisco and the Dada crowd of Weimar Berlin, as well as to anarchists like Mikhail Bakunin of the nineteenth century and Noam Chomsky of the twenty-first—now has some actual technological muscle wrapped around its spine. "Who needs Goliath?"—"Who needs *any* Goliath?"—is the question for which happy chaos demands an answer.

Against the neocon view of war as a policy tool of desirable change, the mind-set of happy chaos suggests the personal computer. At a Washington, D.C., cocktail party, I once heard a senior federal judge (a Democratic appointee) say the Islamic world might start to find a way out of its troubles if every woman had a PC—so she could escape the boundaries of whatever failed state she was living in and become conscious of herself as a member of a modern, global society of unlimited horizons. Chaotic systems are about far-flung interconnections—which is precisely what the Internet and Internet-based search tools like Google are all about. These technologies of linkage, also including YouTube and MySpace, are in their infancy. We don't know what the everyday digital tools of five or ten years from now will be, but it is an easy prediction that they will increase, probably dramatically, our possibilities for leading more mobile and interconnected lives. For the European futurist Marcel Bullinga, "a Dutch net pioneer," as he calls himself, the year "2020 is filled with nomadic people in a constant flow of short and semi-permanent stays all over the world, creating a constant brain and workplace circulation."

A twenty-first-century nomadic life could be enabled by new energy technologies that, in freeing the planet of dependence on fossil fuels, also liberate the "end user" from the electric grids controlled by megacorporations. Breakthroughs in photovoltaic research, for example, could quite literally empower individuals to move about the earth with their own private energy source. "In a solar future, your mode of transportation—and even the clothes you wear—could produce clean, safe electric power," according to no less an authority than the U.S. Department of Energy. For those who preferred to live in a permanent dwelling, buildings, too, could produce their own energy.

In a post-hydrocarbon age, with the ultimate imperial commodity, oil, no longer a reason for nations to go to war, the Persian Gulf would become geopolitically marginal. Conventional geopolitics, a nineteenth-century construction nourished by the age of oil, might itself become irrelevant. Even as things are now, the idea that the oil lanes need to be guarded by a state or group of states is dismissed by some libertarian thinkers as an anachronistic fixation of the control-freak crowd. Oil shipments do not need protection of military power any more than trade in computer parts does, Ivan Eland, a senior fellow at the Independent Institute, a libertarian-oriented think tank, likes to argue.

Unlike orthodox anarchists, market-oriented libertarians believe that in a happy chaos, private property rights would remain. The main thing, both agree, is that the state would recede as no longer necessary. John Bolton, who served as George W. Bush's ambassador to the United Nations, has a reputation for being a hard-power guy, willing to use military force to take out bad guys, but he also has a pronounced libertarian streak. "The logical conclusion of free trade is no government. That would be fine with me," he told me.

I am a skeptic about the prospect of a happy chaos, but I have explored its possibilities in part because the discussion is a necessary antidote to the faith-based and ahistorical conviction of the believers in American empire that a dark chaos, and only a dark chaos, is the alternative to America as the global policeman. Surely the world has a higher chaos tolerance than the control freaks think it does. As for my skepticism, it is grounded in doubts about the ability of technology to alter the basic human equation in a radical way. The big question about happy chaos is whether human beings would be equipped to make it endure, to make it last beyond a passing moment. It is precisely the question posed by Immanuel Kant, who lived in pre–computer chip Enlightenment Europe. Kant spent all his days on the shores of the Baltic Sea in Königsberg, where he was born in 1724 and died in 1804. He was not an anarchist; in fact, he was on the whole an admirer of his king, the Prussian ruler Frederick II ("Frederick the Great"), a brilliant conqueror but also an ardent reformer who abolished torture and corporeal punishment and met the philosopher's standard of being a ruler "who is himself enlightened and has no dread of shadows." And yet in Kant's philosophy lies the only possibility for believing that an After America chaos would not go badly awry.

In the fall of 1784, five months after attaining the age of sixty, Kant wrote a short essay, "An Answer to the Question: What Is Enlightenment?" The answer came in the first sentence: "Enlightenment is man's emergence from his self-imposed immaturity," he wrote. "Immaturity is the inability to use one's understanding without guidance from another," Kant explained, and "laziness and cowardice are the reasons why so great a proportion of men, long after nature has released them from alien guidance . . . nonetheless gladly remain in lifelong immaturity, and why it is so easy for others to establish themselves as their guardians. It is so easy to be immature. If I have a book to serve as my understanding, a pastor to serve as my conscience, a physician to determine my diet for me, and so on, I need not exert myself at all." And yet Kant was at heart an optimist who believed that the "essential destiny" of "human nature" lay in "progress" that man could achieve by releasing himself from his harness. "If only they refrain from inventing artifices to keep themselves in it, men will gradually raise themselves from barbarism," he concluded in his essay.

Some of what Kant hoped for came to pass. Over the centuries, the cathedrals of his native northern Europe changed from man-made repositories of spiritual direction to, for many, little more than interesting specimens of an earlier age of architecture. But industrialization, which was starting to gather force in Europe in the last years of Kant's life, created the factory town and many other systems of paternal control that for ordinary people were very hard to resist. What he meant by enlightenment remained largely in abeyance.

What, though, if the problem with humankind is not "immaturity" but something ineradicable—a seed of evil (in theological terms) or a drive for power (in secular terms)? The tragic perspective on human affairs has as much standing as the optimistic one, and this perspective suggests that digital technology may not be enough. Still, the fact that something like happy chaos can even be part of the discussion of an After America world is in itself a remarkable thing. It is now possible, for the first time in the modern era, to consider the prospects of a stateless, empireless planet. First implodes the Soviet Union and next the American Goliath? If a world of happy chaos manages to endure, America will come to be seen as the last of its type, a dinosaur representation of an age that no longer has a reason for being.

Chapter Eight

Multipolar World

The world must be multipolar; domination is unacceptable.

Russian president Dmitri Medvedev, August 2008

If the General Assembly of the United Nations were asked to vote on their preference for a plausible alternative to an American-dominated world, then the choice of a multipolar order—in which power was dispersed and balanced among nation-states, rather than concentrated in America or any one other state—surely would snare the most votes, even on a secret ballot. The idea is appealing, not only to the Russias of the planet, with their longing for a time when they mattered more, but even to many of America's best friends. "A multipolar system will benefit the world," Afghanistan's ambassador to the United States, Said T. Jawad, told me. We were chatting in his office at the Afghan embassy in a mansion in the leafy, upscale Kalorama neighborhood of Washington. Soon after we had settled into red leather chairs, a white-jacketed aide arrived with a pot of green tea and a bowl of pistachio nuts. The ambassador was dressed in Western business style, in a finely tailored dark suit and a red silk tie, and he spoke impeccable English. A native of Kandahar, he moved in the 1980s to the San Francisco area, where he worked as a lawyer. His country owed everything to America for the toppling of the Taliban, he acknowledged, but America was shouldering too much of the world's security burden. The Europeans, the Japanese, the South Koreans—all were taking advantage of the U.S. security umbrella when they could be doing more on their own. The Europeans, he added, acted as if the global war on terrorism was a U.S. war, rather than a challenge they needed to confront directly with their own lives on the line. And it would be a good idea, he continued, for America to remove its troops from the South Korean side of the Korean peninsula, because then South Korea, an affluent nation of 50 million, more than twice the population of impoverished North Korea, would be forced to provide for its own defense. He did not foresee the chaos that the Washington political and military establishment envisioned in a U.S. exit from that region.

The prospect of a multipolar world is a monumental one—nothing even remotely like it has ever existed. The closest analogue, the nineteenth-century "balance of power" among the great nation-states of that time, was a reflection of a profoundly Eurocentric order. A new multipolar arrangement would be truly global in sweep, engaging America and Russia and also the rising powers of the East. Not only India and China but also Iran—possibly a nuclear-armed Iran—could emerge as anchors. Brazil could be a weighty player. A twenty-first-century multipolar world could make for an empowerment of large patches of the planet that for centuries have been regarded by the West as barely capable of organizing themselves.

It is easy enough to play with this conception, as in the board game Risk. No doubt new and improbable-sounding alliances would form, as they did in the nineteenth century, when Queen Victoria's Great Britain and Ottoman Turkey paired up to thwart Russian expansionism toward the warm waters of the Black Sea and the Mediterranean. Perhaps in a twenty-first-century "balance of power," a post-Ottoman Turkey and a post-tsarist, post-Soviet Russia would team up to press their interests in regions like the Middle East. In this kind of fluid geopolitical environment, categories like "North and South" and "East and West" might become less meaningful. This could be a new age of realism, and possibly of regional hegemonies, in which the nation-state, cold of heart, would have no permanent friends but, rather, a shifting cast of allies and rivals. Then again, perhaps like-minded states, let's say the democracies of America and India, would team up to counterbalance the nondemocratic states, like China. That prospect would warm the hearts of many a Pentagon planner, worried about the overstretching of the American military.

But let's not get carried away. There is nothing that organically ordains a multipolar world. If a multipolar world was such an obvious and appealing way to order the planet, then how to explain the rise, acceptable to a large chunk of the world, of a unipolar empire like America's? For there to be a multipolar world in the twenty-first century, the modern nation-state, a battered and aging creature owing its birth to the Peace of Westphalia in mid-seventeenth-century Europe, must reassert itself as the essential actor in global politics. It must become *the* barrier to a dark, After America chaos. It must have octane—a national spirit—to power its gears. It must have efficient machinery—such as modern surveillance techniques—to keep WMD out of the hands of nonstate terrorist groups and to keep anarchic cyberwarriors from fouling up vital national security and financial communications networks. It must have effective navies to combat pirates on the high seas.

And the nation-state will have to rise outside of the land of its origins, Europe, in places like India that are coming on line in the twenty-first century. India, with its rapidly growing economy, a relatively youthful population of 1.2 billion, and ambition to project itself onto the global stage in a large way more than a half century after winning independence from imperial Britain, is an excellent test for the future prospects of a multipolar world. That world cannot exist unless a prominent state like India has a major place in it. But can India fulfill that expectation? Given the country's immense poverty, much of the analysis of that question is understandably devoted to India's long-term economic prospects. Considerable analysis, too, is dedicated to India's ability to achieve a harmony of purpose in a multicultural, multilingual society messily divided into numerous subnationalities. (V. S. Naipaul titled a 1990 book *India: A Million Mutinies Now.*) In the pages that follow, I start with an exploration of a matter that gets less scrutiny: India's ability to assert itself as a "hard power," the term that geopolitical strategists use to rate a nation-state's military prowess. For all that is written about China's ambitions to amass hard power, India also aims to be one of the great military powers of the twenty-first century. But that goal is fraught with difficulties and far from being realized.

Martin Luther King, Jr., visited India for a month in 1959 and wrote and spoke rapturously about the moral fiber of the civilization that had given birth to his slain hero, Mahatma Gandhi, whose philosophy of passive resistance had won

India's freedom from imperial Britain—and would win genuine civil rights, King hoped, for America's black community. On departing India, King suggested the country could help teach both America and the Soviet Union about how to get along in the atomic age. "I wish to make a plea to the people and government of India," he said. "It may be that just as India had to take the lead and show the world that national independence could be achieved nonviolently, so India may have to take the lead and call for universal disarmament, and if no other nation will join her immediately, India should declare itself for disarmament unilaterally. Such an act of courage would be a great demonstration of the spirit of the Mahatma and would be the greatest stimulus to the rest of the world to do likewise."

Reverend King was giving voice to a standing American image of India as a symbol of spiritual high-mindedness in a land of unfathomable suffering and want. India, it was said, had demonstrated the power of argument—if only the rest of the world could live by that precept as well. India itself has encouraged this perspective. It was India's first prime minister after independence, Jawaharlal Nehru, a Mahatma Gandhi protégé, who offered an idealistic vision of "peaceful coexistence" to a skeptical world. Nevertheless, today's generation of Indians is tired of this stress on India's supposedly unique qualities; the national conversation is very much a post-Gandhian one. An American who broaches the idea that India can be different—"better"—than the rising powers of the past is apt to have his knuckles rapped. The idea "that India must be pure and be a moral beacon" is "contemptible" coming from a place like America, which has shown no hesitancy to use the gun to advance its realpolitik interests, the Indian historian Ramachandra Guha, the author of *India After Gandhi*, lectured me. India lives in a world of hostile nation-states and must have the "hard power" it takes to survive and make a mark in this world, Guha said. India, he was telling me, just wants to be normal.

I might have been spared the lecture, for I agreed with him. Notions of Indian Exceptionalism are undoubtedly as off base as notions of American Exceptionalism. It's not fair to hold India to a higher standard than other societies—and it is not at all surprising to see a change in Indian attitudes toward military power. Consider the evolution of American thinking about hard power from the idealistic days of the early nineteenth century, when Jefferson, six years into his presidency, said that "the spirit of this country is totally adverse to a large military force." There is no more intimate association in history than the bond between the nation-state and military power. The state is not expected to produce great culture, and almost never does, but it is expected to produce a capable force of arms. Indeed, the history of the modern state and the history of modern armaments go hand in hand: The most awesome state creations, for better or worse, have tended to come in the field of weaponry.

And India has already learned, to her pain, that a position of moral superiority does not count for much in the trenches. It was embarrassed by China in a small border war, in the Himalayas, in the early 1960s—a defeat that engendered popular scorn of Nehru's dream of "Asian brotherhood." In *Such a Long Journey*, Rohinton Mistry's novel of the India that followed those times, the narrator bemoans "such a humiliating defeat, everywhere people talking of nothing but the way China had advanced, as though the Indian army consisted of tin soldiers."

India, of course, already possesses nuclear weapons; it conducted its first nuclear test, Smiling Buddha, in 1974, amid conflict with Pakistan and censure by the United States, which tilted toward the side of Pakistan. But while a nuclear arsenal may be a necessary condition for a nation-state to become a serious power in the world, it is not a sufficient condition, as perpetually troubled Pakistan, which also obtained the bomb, illustrates. Hard power is about having a wide range of credible military options—not only last-resort ones. It is about having a tool of coercive diplomacy in the hope no shot will ever be fired. And for India, with a 4,350-mile coastline fronting some of the world's most politically turbulent waters, hard power is about having a first-rate blue-water navy.

It was with this goal in mind that India's admirals, in the mid-1980s, conceived Project Seabird, a plan to build the largest naval base on the planet east of Suez on a plot of real estate stretching for sixteen miles along the Arabian seacoast of southwestern India. The northernmost point, the town of Karwar, lies some 550 miles south of Mumbai. The INS Kadamba, as the base is known for a local tree that blossoms in the monsoon season into apricot-colored spiny balls (and also for an ancient ruling dynasty that took its name from the tree), is a natural fortress. The approach from the water is protected by a string of small islands, which also afford relief from the lashes of the monsoon, which starts in June and lasts for four months. The waters, unusually for the western coastal area, are quite deep, and at the rear, the base backs into the Western Ghat mountains, which abound with monkeys and may contain a tiger or two. Submarines can be concealed by enclosures cut into mountain-face rock. At the time of my visit to the area, a cloudless day in February of 2008, a gentle breeze blew in from the west and a destroyer lay in dock. Eagles and falcons circled the skies above emerald green rice paddies. On a beach to the north of the base, past groves of mango, coconut, and cashew trees, Indian boys stripped to their shorts played cricket with wickets planted in the soft white sand, the outfielders standing ankle deep in the warm foam of the waves.

This is the Indian navy's first-ever base devoted exclusively to military purposes. All others, like the one up in Mumbai, are shared with commercial users. Unlike the Mumbai base, the INS Kadamba is large enough to accommodate an aircraft carrier, which can be dry-docked for repairs. A hydraulic lifting station, built by Rolls-Royce, is capable of handling a ten-thousand-ton vessel. The docks are constructed to receive as many as three dozen warships at a time, and might in the future play host to a fleet of nuclear-powered subs. India, in the past, has had to lease such vessels from Russia, but the navy aims to make them on their own. There are also plans to build a naval airstrip.

The Karwar site was selected by an Indian vice admiral, K. K. Nayyar, who is now retired from the navy but is still a prominent voice in maritime policy. "The insufficiency of India's seapower changed the history of the world," he told me, by allowing the European powers to colonize India and then the rest of Asia. Every Indian schoolchild knows the story. Until the twelfth century, India was a maritime power. Its ability to protect its shores began to erode with the advances of the Arabs in seafaring prowess—and then was shattered by the Europeans. On May 28, 1498, the Portuguese explorer Vasco da Gama made landfall in Calicut, to the south of Karwar. The Portuguese ships were the first men-of-war with mounted cannon to enter India's seas. Indian seamen resisted the thrust, but they were overmatched. In the early sixteenth century, control over India's shores passed from the Portuguese to the Dutch, for a brief interlude, until finally residing in the hands of the British. The Royal Navy's supremacy, sealed in the mid-eighteenth century, was to last for nearly two hundred years, until India gained its independence from Britain in 1947.

Imperial Britain made good use of Indian shipbuilding skills and timber. Malabar teak was superior to British oak and elm; the docks of Bombay turned out some of the finest vessels of the Royal Navy and the East India Company. But the British had no interest in turning out Indian naval commanders, who London well understood could be a threat to Britain's naval hegemony. "By all means, let us have Indian admirals, but not too many of them, please," Churchill is reported to have said during the Second World War. After independence, India's martial energies went into building up its armies to counter the threat presented by Pakistan, to the north. It was not until 1956 that the Indian navy gained an admiral.

In the twenty-first century, this time of privation is over. In 1950, the navy's share of India's defense budget was a mere 4 percent, and from the 1950s through the 1980s the navy procured a 12 percent share. But in 2004, spending on the navy constituted 18 percent of the defense budget, which currently totals $27 billion, eleventh highest in the world. New Delhi's greater attention to naval priorities reflects not only a bid to recover lost maritime pride but also a cold assessment of the security picture. The vast majority of India's economic trade is seaborne—more than 90 percent by volume. The Indian economy depends on tankers shipping oil through the Strait of Hormuz and on cargoes moving through the Indian Ocean's other prominent choke point, the Malacca Strait, bordered by Singapore and Malaysia. India imports 70 percent of its oil; its share is expected to surpass 90 percent by 2020. One growing problem is piracy—tankers sometimes disappear from the Malacca Strait without a trace. "We are a big country. We cannot act small," retired vice admiral Madanjit Singh told me in a meeting in New Delhi. He presided over the navy's western command, including the Karwar base, from 2003 to 2006.

The Indian Ocean has been an American lake ever since the U.S. Navy took over for the British Royal Navy in the region after the Second World War. America's navy continues to be the leaseholder of the British-owned island base of Diego

Garcia, and the U.S. Fifth Fleet is based at the former British protectorate of Bahrain in the Persian Gulf. And yet, far from being alarmed about India's ambitious plans for a blue-water navy, Washington's defense planners and State Department foreign policy strategists sense an opportunity. Their hope is that the Indian navy can lend a helping hand, as a kind of junior partner, in the increasingly burdensome task of maintaining security in the Indian Ocean region.

These hopes are understandable. Consider how the IO theater, as it is known, looks from the vantage point of the global security planners in Washington. They regard these waters, first of all, as a central zone in the Long War—their term for the struggle between Islamic holy warriors on the one hand and America and all other democracies on the other. Almost every one of the key countries in which there is an effort by the jihadists to subvert the ruling regime—Saudi Arabia, Iraq, Pakistan, Indonesia—has a coastline on or leading directly into the Indian Ocean. This makes the IO a prime route for smugglers' ships loaded with weapons sought by the militants. Theocratic Iran, too, is an Indian Ocean power—and its small navy is a growing source of harassment to U.S. ships patrolling the Strait of Hormuz. And finally, U.S. defense planners have a wary eye cast on China. The Chinese also are dependent, like India and America, on oil supplies from Persian Gulf countries, and they have their own ambitious blue-water navy program with a reach extending from the Pacific to the Indian Ocean. In what the Pentagon calls the "string of pearls" strategy, the Chinese are building seaports in Sri Lanka, Bangladesh, and Myanmar, extending westward in an arc, going around India all the way to the Chinese-built naval base of Gwadhar on Pakistan's Arabian seacoast, across from the Strait of Hormuz.

In this picture of things, India is indeed the obvious candidate to link up with America. China feels threatening to America's national security managers in a way that India does not. This is partly because India is a democracy, while China remains under authoritarian rule, but also because the British imperial legacy has given India "Anglo" political institutions that are familiar to the Washington political class. A senior defense official with experience in George W. Bush's Pentagon told me that, just as London was able to hand responsibilities off to Washington at the end of the Second World War, America could attempt a similar strategy, on a smaller scale, with respect to the IO region and India. Also behind this thinking is Washington's conviction that New Delhi, as a geopolitical matter, ought to share Washington's concern about problems like Islamic terrorism, Iran's bid for nuclear weapons, and China's "string of pearls" naval buildup.

Washington's hopes of establishing a strategic partnership with New Delhi were boosted by the approval of the U.S.-India nuclear deal in the fall of 2008. Under this pact, reached after several years of hard negotiations, Washington reversed its long-standing policy against cooperation with India in the nuclear field because of India's (continuing) refusal to sign the 1968 Nuclear Non-Proliferation Treaty. Now the United States, along with other outside powers, stands to become a supplier of nuclear fuel to India. Still, Washington's vision of an enduring American-Indian concert seems likely to fall short. To start with, this vision suffers from the cultural myopia that warped Washington's view of the Arab and Persian Middle East in the early years of the American Century. Although practically minded Indians, including navel officers, are eager to learn techniques from U.S. military forces, the Indians, like the Iranians, have not let go of the idea that the Americans are the successors to the British imperialists. Among the older generation of Indian navy officers, in particular, there is skepticism that America can tolerate a meaningful security role for the Indian navy, no matter what pleasing words Washington may shower on India. "I have a theory that the Anglo-Saxon people will never tolerate competition at sea," the retired vice admiral M. P. Awati wrote in an essay in 2005. In the British-American mind, he continued, "the sea is an Anglo-Saxon preserve. They must remain supreme on that medium because they honestly believe that the future of their materialist, free enterprise, market-based civilization depends on supremacy at sea, their supremacy. Mahan is alive and well. Any attempt by India to regain her maritime primacy in the North Indian Ocean is unlikely to be tolerated by the New World Order unless we endorse its agenda."

This may sound like paranoia, but try putting yourself in the position of an Indian reading, say, *God and Gold: Britain, America and the Making of the Modern World*, a 2007 book by the U.S. geopolitical analyst Walter Russell Mead, which credits much of the planet's progress over the last four hundred years to the globalization of Anglo-Saxon ideas and culture. While Washington has never ruled India, as London once did, Washington is capable of expressing an equal measure of disdain and heartlessness. In 2005, the U.S. National Security Archive released a trove of documents relating to the White House's tilt toward Pakistan in the India-Pakistan conflict of the early 1970s. In private conversation, America's president, Richard Nixon, called the Indians "a treacherous and slippery people" and sarcastically suggested that India could benefit from "a mass famine."

In any event, Washington and New Delhi differ in important respects in their assessment of the security threats in the Indian Ocean region. On China, while Washington's sentiments lean toward hawkish and suspicious, New Delhi's are mixed. India has its China hawks but also its China doves. Some Indian strategists fear that China is pursuing a strategy of global hegemony that includes the naval encirclement of India in the IO region as part of the competition between the two countries for scarce natural resources. Other strategists say that Sino-Indian conflict is a thing of the past and that, with the rise in fortunes of both economies, the conditions are better than ever for a healthy, cooperative relationship. China has already replaced America as India's top trading partner. Tarun Khanna, an Indian-born Harvard Business School professor who specializes in the Asian economies, believes that India and China are shaping up to be economic and cultural collaborators and notes an easing of distrust on the security front, with the reopening in 2006 of a Himalayan mountain pass closed since the war in the early 1960s. While Khanna's may be an overly optimistic view of the relationship, Washington might take note that Indians are not necessarily betting on the odds of America's remaining the global hegemon. Citing America's economic ailments, an official in New Delhi suggested to me that "the U.S. could become a client state of China in fifty years—why not?"

It is on the ripe question of Iran that the American and Indian mind-sets are furthest apart. Washington is united in seeing Iran, under the rule of the mullahs, as one of the great security perils of our time. But New Delhi, notwithstanding its distaste for theocratic government, does not share Washington's anxieties about the mullahs. "Iran is not a threat," retired army lieutenant general H. Lai told me bluntly as we chatted over lunch in a New Delhi hotel. Others in the Indian elite assured me that it will probably take many years for Iran to obtain nuclear weapons, and even if it does, India will survive, just as it has in a neighborhood that already includes a nuclear Pakistan, a nuclear China, and a nuclear Israel. New Delhi hopes to strike deals with Tehran to ship Iran's natural gas supplies to India's energy-thirsty market. The Indians have conducted exercises together with the Iranian navy, just as they have with the U.S. Navy, and India is helping Iran to upgrade the Iranian naval port of Chabahar, on the Gulf of Oman, which is Iran's best point of entry to the Indian Ocean.

The strongest ties between India and Iran are those of culture. The Persian and Indian civilizations have been mixing for many centuries, to the point that separation is simply not possible. A small example is India's assimilated Parsi community—of Persian descent and with a traditional belief in the ancient religion of Zoroastrianism—which has played an important role in India's business, science, and arts. A large example is music. "Indian music is inconceivable without Persian music—we feel it in our bones," an Indian intellectual told me. The sitar and the sarod, the stringed instruments so prominent in Indian music, are of Persian origin, and the Urdu language, a staple in Indian music and poetry, has Persian roots. India's cultural affinity with Iran seldom comes up in conversations in Washington about the role that India might play in a twenty-first-century multipolar world. Culture is generally assumed to matter less than security or economic considerations in relations between nation-states. But just as cultural mistrust—a sense of the American as an Anglo imperial intruder—may keep India apart from Washington, cultural fraternity may keep India close to Iran.

If an American-Indian concert is an illusion, what then is the Indian vision of its role in a multipolar world? The Eurocentric multipolar world of the nineteenth century was a world of shifting alliances. The Indians, though, say they want none of that. "We are not going to be in alliance with anyone—not with the Russians, not with the Americans, not with the Chinese," retired vice admiral Singh told me. The nonalignment posture has its roots in the cold war, with New Delhi's determination to stand apart from the power-politics games of the Washington- and Moscow-led blocs. The continuing influence of this mind-set can be seen in the vision that India has of its blue-water navy. There are actually two visions: a soft one, emphasizing cooperation and collective security, and a harder-edged one, envisioning India as more of a regional alpha dog. Elements of both visions were evident at a forum of naval chiefs of staff from around the region, organized by the Indian navy and convened in New

Delhi in early 2008. Naval brass attended from littoral countries including South Africa, Oman, Indonesia, and Australia. Representatives from the United States and several European countries came as observers. Iran was invited but chose not to attend, while China was not invited. The Indians permitted me to attend as a guest delegate from the U.S. media.

This was the first gathering of the Indian Ocean Naval Symposium, which the Indians aim to turn into an annual event. In a speech to the group, retired Indian admiral Arun Prakash recounted the history of Western colonial exploitation of the Indian Ocean region and said it was time for the region's countries to take the matter of security into their own hands. He likened the symposium to a *panchayat*, the local council for governance in an Indian village, the "basic building block of democracy in India." India's aims, he said, were to help capture pirates and render humanitarian aid, as India did after the tsunami that devastated Indonesia in 2004, when India's ships arrived on the scene, as its naval officers note with pride, three days before the U.S. Navy. As for those who might worry that India aimed to dominate the Indian Ocean region, the admiral declared, "I would suggest that hegemony in the context of a developing nation like India is an oxymoron, and we need to beware of mischief makers who spread such canards."

Much of this, of course, was rhetoric, and on the sidelines of the conference, there was talk that India, in fact, does aspire to be the master of the seas. Don't believe the *panchayat* line, an Australian naval officer advised me as we sipped tea. The Indians, he said, "want to be known as the most dominant power in the Indian Ocean region." An Indian naval officer, a Sikh, echoed what I had been told by the Australian. It will take time—perhaps fifteen years—but India eventually will be number one in the Indian Ocean, more powerful than all others, outside powers like America and China included, he said. "India is rising." That sounded boastful, but a U.S. naval officer, a "fly on the wall" at the symposium, told me that India, with its stress on nonthreatening tasks like mounting humanitarian missions in the Indian Ocean, was going about its strategy of becoming regionally preeminent in a very smart way. He was skeptical, though, about India's insistence on avoiding alliances—in practical terms, he said, India will discover that it cannot be everyone's friend.

Which vision of Indian naval power is likely to triumph—the soft or the hard one? The answer depends in part on the trajectory that Indian nationalism takes. Indians are starting to take national pride in their navy. On the eve of the symposium, NDTV, a leading Indian television channel, teased the event with screen crawlers like "Indian Navy Takes Charge" and "Is India Stretching Its Legs in an Effort to Isolate China?" No other country has an ocean named after it, Indians are apt to note. At the same time, Indian nationalism has not taken a particularly pugnacious form. Right-wing Hindu nationalists, with their hatred of Gandhi's nonviolent philosophy and their determination to rewrite Indian school textbooks to suit their mythic narrative of Indian history, have at times provoked riots against Muslim communities; however, they have failed, at least so far, to capture the imagination and sympathies of the broader public. The single noteworthy episode of seafaring imperialism in India's history—when Hindi navies, in the seventh and eighth centuries, helped colonize Sumatra, Java, and the Malay Peninsula—is more than a thousand years old. The most resonant aspects of Indian nationalism are lodged outside the military sphere. These have to do with a recovery of Indianness, of a distinct Indian identity, outside the West. In the 1980s and 1990s, there was an infatuation, particularly among Indian men, with British and American styles of dress. Now Indian men are apt to come to weddings in places like Mumbai and New Delhi dressed not in a suit and tie but in *churidar* and *kurta*. It used to be that Indians would boast of obtaining a British or an American passport; now it is asked, "What is wrong with an Indian one?"

I asked the deputy chief of mission at the Indian embassy in Washington, Raminder Singh Jassal, a Sikh who had served in the Ministry of Defense, whether the revival of Indian nationalism was a temporary fashion or something likely to endure. "Yes, it's a real thing," he answered. One source, he explained, was "a better sense of self-esteem among Indians." In the chaotic years after independence, India watched how rapidly Japan, Korea, and Singapore grew their economies, while its own seemed moribund. In their schools, Indians neglected study of their native languages, instead focusing only on English. But now, he said, while India's youth still is learning English, there is a greater interest in speaking a second native tongue as well—and this points to a restored pride in things Indian. (More than thirty languages and some six hundred dialects are spoken in India.) A second source of nationalism, Jassal continued, was the "better living conditions" in India. As bad off as many Indians still are—some 300 million are illiterate, he noted—everyone agrees that the overall trend lines are improving. And a third source of nationalism, he said with a smile, is India's "greater ease and comfort" on the world stage in dealings with the planet's greatest powers.

While India's rulers aspire to possess the "hard power" attributes of a great power, the execution of that plan is another matter entirely. Project Seabird illustrates the gap between reach and grasp. Back in the mid-1980s, when the project was conceived, villagers were informed that the government would soon be acquiring land, but this effort languished amid other priorities, and the process of getting people off their land to make way for construction did not get rolling for another decade. By that point, a number of the villagers, led by a group of fishermen, launched a campaign of resistance, including hunger strikes. Landholders complained that the state was not giving them enough money for their plots, and the fishermen said they were losing their prime fishing ground to the navy, which would no longer allow them in the waters, teeming with kingfish and prawn, extending out from the base. Eventually everyone was moved, but several thousand of them banded together to file lawsuits, under India's national Land Acquisition Act, to force the state to increase the level of compensation. The fishermen got the government to build them a small new harbor, outside the base, along with a facility on land for ship repairs. It took until 2005 to complete Phase One of the project, while the rest, including the naval airfield, might not get finished until 2020.

After chatting with some of the fishermen, I made an appointment to visit with a local lawyer, R. V. Bhat, whose family had lost land to the base and who was representing a number of the complainants in the lawsuits. I drove down from the north, but what I expected to be a ninety-minute journey turned into nearly five hours. The highway was blocked, with burning logs and tires, by protestors demanding that the state make promised road improvements. On my arrival in Karwar, Bhat showed me the tiny courtroom, framed with a portrait of Gandhi, in which the train of lawsuits got started. Over hot *chai* in his office, just up from a vacant lot strewn with garbage, he gave me, from the litigants' perspective, the good news and the bad news. The good news was that successive courts had ruled in favor of his clients, so the monetary awards would indeed be greater than the government's initial offer. The bad news was that most of the claims, nearly fifteen years after they had been filed, had still not been resolved: They were pending before the Indian Supreme Court in New Delhi. So how many people, I asked, have hard currency in their pockets in compensation for the land taken from them? Only four or five extended families have actually received money, the lawyer told me with a shrug.

Project Seabird attests not only to the Indian state's sloth but also to its inability to ride roughshod over the people. "The Chinese would just shoot down the people who objected" to this kind of project, retired vice admiral Nayyar, the architect of the Karwar installation, told me. "We must have the goodwill of the people around the base." He added: "The difference between China and India is enormous—this is a country with very vigorous human rights organizations. There is rule of law."

His point is well taken, but it is India's merchant ships that are forced to go to Chinese yards for repairs for lack of capacity in India's antiquated facilities. Even though the Indian navy has been warning for years of the need to modernize and expand the country's shipyards, they remain in bad shape. "Our choice of materials is poor, reliability of indigenous machinery is low and internal management shoddy. Our shipyards are over-manned [and] have low productivity," one admiral has publicly complained. Japan's shipyards are ten times more efficient, labor-wise.

India's democracy tends to subvert grand visions, Ramachandra Guha, the historian, told me. The system of multiple parties and the absence of a tradition of bipartisanship in foreign policy make it tough to get big things done. In India, "you cannot have a vision for twenty years, like the Chinese have," Guha said. "There will always be someone undermining it." The Indian writer Arun Shourie, who has also served in government in New Delhi, has likened the Indian state to "a tree hollowed by termites." India was a "soft state," he told me when we met at his home on the outskirts of New Delhi. As if on cue, the front pages of the newspapers, on the day after we talked, featured headlines about a daring raid by heavily armed Maoist rebels on police armories in the impoverished eastern province of Orissa. The surprised cops were outnumbered; and while some offered resistance, others fled their positions, permitting the guerrillas to make off with more than a thousand weapons, including pistols, AK-47s, and other rifles. After the attack, some of the rebels lingered to take a meal in a restaurant and pack food for their colleagues; they reportedly took care to settle the bill before leaving town. Eight months after my visit to India, a band of terrorists with links to Pakistan mounted a spectacular assault on luxury hotels and other sites in Mumbai. The terrorists arrived by sea, in a powerful demonstration of the inadequacies of India's naval defenses.

Outside the labyrinth of the Indian state is another India—a vibrant and creative India. This is the India whose software engineers, filmmakers, bankers, lawyers, and surgeons are tying cities like Mumbai and Bangalore into the global economy while making India a research-and-development magnet for multinationals like Microsoft, General Electric, and SAP. The Indian state benefits, of course, from all this economic activity, but the story here—the organic story—is not really the rise of the Indian nation-state so much as the ability of certain talented Indians, and certain regions of the country, to make their own imaginative and profitable connections to the outside world. This dynamic is creating within India a new class of cosmopolitans who feel much less rooted in a particular regional or ethnic identity than do most Indians. In the long run, this class, with its planetary outlook, may make its greatest contribution not to the Indian state but to the development of global institutions and standards in fields like finance and software. This India may contribute a Bangalore to an emerging world of global city-states or perhaps a treasury minister or even a president to a future world government. It is already contributing multinational corporations, like the Bombay-based Tata Group, to a league that has been dominated for many decades by American- and European-based players. Tata, with holdings like America's Eight O'Clock Coffee Co. and the UK's Tetley Tea (as well as Jaguar and Land Rover), is on a path to becoming no more of an "Indian" company than Coca-Cola or Halliburton is an "American" one. The founder of the Tata dynasty, Jamsetji Tata, is from a Parsi family, with ancestral roots in Persia. Because India is such a multicultural civilization, it may prove better at hatching true multinational companies than Japan, Korea, or even China.

Typecast Western images of Indians as captive to a passive Buddhist ethic, in which the life of spiritual contemplation is elevated above the sweaty pursuit of material gain, obscure the complex reality: Indians have their own style of pluralism, messily interweaving the religious, cultural, and commercial strands of their traditions. The Indian brand of pluralism is more chaotic than American-style pluralism—India sometimes has the feel of an experiment in barely controlled chaos. But this, too, is a milieu that can hatch entrepreneurs. While Indians sometimes deride their entrepreneurial classes for thinking too small, like shopkeepers, the opportunity Indians now have to prove themselves on a global playing field seems to be a stimulus to large ambition. A new generation of entrepreneurs is emerging, determined to shatter traditions. The Indian millionaire Alok Kejriwal escaped from "the shackles," as he has put it, of his family's unionized sock-making business and, with money borrowed from his grandparents, founded C2W.com, an innovative marketer of global consumer brands. His cheeky marketing strategies—the subject of a Stanford University business study—tend to be mocking of the ascetic India embodied by "marble" figures like Gandhi. "I don't really care about Gandhi—Gandhi is retrograde," he has said.

As the basis of the global economy continues to shift from making physical products like steel to the fashioning of what Alan Greenspan has called "conceptual products"—the valuable new ideas, in fields like technology, the media, and finance, that gain the status of intellectual property—the Indians may truly excel. The English philosopher Francis Bacon of the late sixteenth and early seventeenth centuries is generally credited with coining the aphorism "Knowledge is power"—that staple of postindustrial thinking. Indian culture, though, has operated on this principle for millennia. As noted in a 2006 report by an analyst for SAIC, the U.S. contractor that often does work for the Pentagon and the CIA, the premium that Indians have traditionally placed on "deep thought," in particular, is of enormous value in an economic environment in which entrepreneurial success increasingly depends on intellectual innovation. The contemplative strain of Indian culture—however much it goes against the grain of Ben Franklin's "Time is money" axiom—may prove a competitive advantage in the twenty-first-century globalized economy. After years of limiting their investments in India to older, more established firms, the world's venture capitalists are starting to make bets on unproven start-up companies offering little more than a promising idea. In September 2008, Sequoia Capital, a prominent venture-capital firm based in California's Silicon Valley, announced the establishment of a $725 million fund for investment in start-ups in India.

While the global economic downturn is expected to result in a contraction in the American and European economies in 2009, the Indian economy, after average annual growth of 9 percent in recent years, is still expected to grow at a rate exceeding 5 percent. Like China, India is able to draw on an enormous pool of domestic savings available for investment. In 2007, the personal savings rate in India averaged 28 percent of post-tax, disposable income, compared to 24 percent in China, 11 percent in Germany, 3 percent in the United Kingdom—and 0.4 percent in the United States.

India has the potential to tell the world a story about itself that is even better, or at least more compelling, than the story of the rise of America. After all, the colonists of the American New World, from the Pilgrims and the settlers of Jamestown onward, faced a much less formidable set of hurdles than India did after, say, its independence. Once resistance from the Native American tribes was overcome (and disease, remember, was the number-one killer of the tribes), the settlers had a sparsely populated continent, rich in natural resources, to exploit. India had no such good fortune. It had suffered the wrenching experience of partition and already had far too many mouths to feed. For a time after independence from colonial rule, the heavy hand of the state, under the influence of soft-socialist, Fabian-style ideology, trapped the economy in anemic rates of growth. For this India to surpass Japan, say, in economic output, as some economists predict could happen within a quarter century, would be an amazing achievement, all things considered—and a powerful example to poor societies in Africa and elsewhere. "India is a microcosm—the problems it needs to solve are the world's," an Indian-American management consultant told me.

Still, something more will be needed for a rising India to become one of the principal power brokers in a multipolar world. Unless the usual rules of statecraft are suspended, India will need to show a cunning and a willingness to play the game—the cynical game—of great-power politics. So far, it seems reluctant to do so. Its insistence on not forging permanent alliances of interest is not how these games are generally won. The American example is instructive. Notwithstanding its own professed disdain for European-style geopolitical maneuvering and a penchant for instructing the world on the blessings of freedom, America learned to play a good hand of realism. No one played the game with more relish and skill than Franklin Roosevelt, who during World War II courted "My Dear Mr. Stalin," as America's president addressed notes to the dictator, and pushed the Washington bureaucracy to ship massive quantities of military aid to the Soviet Union to help the Red Army defeat the Nazis. India has produced its Mahatma but not yet its FDR.

If India stands as an example of the state "flesh" being weak, even though the nationalist spirit may be willing, how does the rest of the world stand, in these terms? Europe suggests an opposite example. In northern Europe, in particular, lie the world's most efficient and well-organized states, adept at things like collecting taxes and building high-speed rail systems. The European Union, as a project in state-building, now with a central bank and the Euro as a common currency for most members, is already much further along than many people thought it would get. But there is little in the way of vitality when it comes to the exercise of power. Americans may be casualty-conscious these days, but nowhere near as much as the postnational Germans are when it comes to deaths in a far-off place like Afghanistan. European statesmen are painfully aware of the predicament. In an anguished talk at the Brookings Institution in Washington, Hubert Védrine, a former French foreign minister, said Europe risked looking like "the global village idiot" for its apparent willingness to tolerate the disrespect of others:

> The French are enamored with the notion of Europe as a power, "l'Europe-puissance," but they are pretty much the only ones. Generally speaking, public opinion in Europe is uncomfortable with this notion of power. A majority of Europeans want to be like a giant Switzerland, that is a place where you are safe, free, incredibly prosperous, where you have plenty of rights, very few duties and obligations and where you hope that

things will stay that way despite what is going on elsewhere. This can only work if the world is made up of Western Europeans. Of course, this is not the case: History continues, and so does its cruelty, and we have ahead of us demographic, geopolitical, energy, and environmental crises so this will obviously be quite difficult.

Védrine went on to say that it is possible that the world's lack of respect "and the painful emergence of a multi-polar world will awaken the Europeans.... This might awaken a spirit of power." Perhaps. A Europe vulnerable to shame may yet prove a contributor to a multipolar world. Or perhaps Europe simply needs to feel more vulnerable—it conceivably could be awoken by a Russian imperial revanchism, a plunge back to the Balkan wars of the 1990s, a sustained wave of Islamic terrorist attacks on the European homeland, a breakdown in civil order in Turkey. Europe's oldest prejudice is that chaos comes from the East, from those "hooded hordes swarming / Over endless plains, stumbling in cracked earth," as T. S. Eliot called them in "The Waste Land." Perhaps Europe will need to get a fresh taste of a bloody chaos before the steel returns to its spine.

For Washington, a revival of Europe's "spirit of power," applied to critical security missions like the policing of Afghanistan, would be a relief, but nobody is counting on it. At a small dinner party at a Washington restaurant, I listened to a former U.S. national security advisor bemoan how Europe remains "exhausted." There is no real prospect, he said, of Europe becoming a major player in the security architecture of places like Afghanistan. He sounded not so much angry about this as resigned. Ordinary Americans, he said, still have no real idea of how much the world wars of the first half of the twentieth century cost Europe.

The same might be said about Japan. Even with widespread popular resentment of the long-standing presence of American troops in Okinawa, Japan still prefers to outsource its security to Washington. And although the heyday of the post–World War II Japanese pacifist movement has passed, Article Nine of the postwar Japanese Constitution remains in effect: "Aspiring sincerely to an international peace based on justice and order, the Japanese people forever renounce war as a sovereign right of the nation and the threat or use of force as means of settling international disputes.... The right of belligerency of the state will not be recognized." In New Delhi, I heard the same sorts of disdainful comments made about the Japanese as I commonly hear in Washington with regard to the Europeans. The world needs to "bring Japan out of retirement" to help deal with security problems like piracy in the Malacca Strait, a former Indian government official told me. It is possible that China's continuing military buildup will spur a wary Japan to action, but Japan has been living for decades with a nuclear China and is sustaining its economic growth through exports to the growing Chinese market. It may well be that Japan will stay in retirement, security-wise, unless it gets a very large shock, on the order of the reunification of a nuclear-armed Korea. As a former imperial ruler of Korea, over four decades in the first half of the twentieth century, Japan looks with deep foreboding to the prospect of a militarily resurgent Korea. An event of that magnitude would force Tokyo to reconsider Japan's rejection of nuclear weapons and would mark the beginning of a true era of multipolar geopolitics in Asia, engaging India, China, Korea, and presumably Japan as weighty players. But Korean reunification—with or without nuclear weapons—may yet be a generation or more away.

Russia is a different case altogether from Europe or Japan. Post-Soviet Russia is salivating at the prospect of being a consequential player in a twenty-first-century multipolar world. This yearning is suffused with nostalgia. On a visit to Moscow in the spring of 2007 I had a chat with Vyacheslav Nikonov, a historian and informal advisor to the Kremlin on foreign policy. Nikonov is the grandson of Vyacheslav Molotov, who for many years was Stalin's top foreign policy hand. As we began to talk about the outlines of an After America world, Nikonov had an assistant retrieve for me an essay he wrote in 2002, before the U.S. invasion of Iraq. The title was "Back to the Concert." For all the talk about "U.S. hegemony," he wrote, "the world is moving, and will keep moving," toward a "global concert" of powers, modeled on the "rather forgotten" European Concert, "born of joint efforts of Russia and Great Britain," that "provided a century-long peace for Europe from 1815 to 1914." This is the Russian political elite's historical memory, a default setting for thinking about Russia's role in foreign affairs, and it will probably always be so.

Russia is not absent the national will to be a great power again, and it is probably not absent the strength of state, although bureaucratic corruption is a serious problem, as bad an affliction in the Putin era as it was in the time of Yeltsin. For many centuries, going well back into tsarist times, Russia has been proficient at hatching what the Russians call *gosudardsniki*—men of state. Team Putin is composed of such types, and has done the tsars of old proud in its achievement of amassing state political and economic power in Kremlin-controlled instruments like the energy giant Gazprom.

Few play the power game with as much relish as do the Russians, as was exhibited in the invasion of Georgia and the subsequent annexation of the provinces of South Ossetia and Abkhazia, regarded by not only Georgia but also the UN as sovereign Georgian territory. Probably this game will continue—in its determination to keep Ukraine from entering NATO, Moscow can be expected to take steps to destabilize the country, perhaps by agitating pro-Russian populations in Crimea on the Black Sea. Even more vulnerable to Russian influence are the remote, landlocked former Soviet republics of Central Asia, including oil-rich Kazakhstan, which has a large ethnic-Russian population in its northern region. "I don't think we"—the Americans—"have many cards to play in Central Asia," Lt. Col. Robert Hamilton, a Russian-speaking military expert on Eurasia, told me over coffee in Washington a month after Russia's rumble through Georgia. The Russians, not surprisingly, proved the first to send a bellicose message to Barack Obama. The day after the U.S. election, Kremlin ruler Medvedev pledged to station missiles in Russia's Baltic exclave of Kaliningrad to counter the planned deployment by America of an anti-missile system in Poland and the Czech Republic.

Still, there are limits to Russia's quest to become a twenty-first-century great power in a multipolar system. Outside the state-controlled energy domain, Russia's economy remains poorly developed, thus leaving the country acutely vulnerable to a drop in oil and gas prices. Russia's people are well-educated but in terrible health—the population has steadily declined since the breakup of the Soviet Union. Efforts by the Kremlin to reverse this trend by offering cash bonuses to encourage women to bear more children seem desperate. Nor is the stability of Russia's authoritarian political system assured—when the oil boom ends, as it must at some point, a drop in living standards may lead ordinary Russians to confront the Kremlin, as they have so many times in Russian history.

With the toppling of Saddam Hussein's regime in Iraq, it has become fashionable in some geopolitical quarters to focus on next-door Iran as a coming great power in the region, possibly a regional hegemon, possibly even a great power of "global ambition," as one analyst at Washington's neoconservative American Enterprise Institute think tank has argued in a policy paper. The paper referred, for example, to Iran's challenge to the Monroe Doctrine through the formation of an "anti-American axis" with Hugo Chavez's Venezuela. This case is surely overstated—a cynic might even say that today's Washington, ever in search of a dragon to slay, is inflating Iran's power just as cold war Washington did the Soviet Union's. It's true that Iran possesses some of the attributes of a rising big power. Iran is as nationally prideful as Russia is—and like Russia, it eternally chafes at being disrespected in the world. But unlike Russia, Iran has a growing population. The country almost doubled in size from 36 million at the end of the 1970s to 66 million today, and half the population is now under the age of thirty. Iran's rulers have influence in the post-Saddam, Shiite-dominated government in Baghdad and with groups like Hezbollah in Lebanon.

And Iran may, one day, possess a nuclear bomb. That quite plausible event—like the prospect of a nuclear, reunified Korea—could be one of the great geopolitical markers of the twenty-first century. It would surely help to make for a more multipolar world; it could also make the Middle East a more volatile place by spurring other regimes, like Saudi Arabia's, to develop nuclear weapons of their own. But nuclear weapons will not magically turn Iran into a great power any more than they did Pakistan. A true great power must be an economic heavyweight, and Iran is failing that test, despite being the planet's fourth largest producer of oil. It has the world's eighteenth largest economy, by GDP, with an inflation rate exceeding 20 percent and a costly patchwork of state subsidies for basic items like sugar, wheat, and cooking oil. It has not yet recovered from the brain drain of scientists, engineers, entrepreneurs, and doctors who fled the country as the ayatollahs took over in the revolution of 1979. The business class tends to be more interested in speculating in real estate than in investing in factories. A bloated state has had little success in selling off unprofitable industries to the private sector. Iran can produce tanks, but little of interest to export markets, other than oil, and foreign investors prefer the free economic zones in nearby Gulf city-states like Dubai. In none of these respects does Iran resemble a dynamic India or China—or any of the dynamic European powers of the nineteenth century.

A better case can be made for Brazil, the world's ninth largest economy and fourth biggest democracy, with a population of almost 200 million. Brazil achieved independence from Portugal early in the nineteenth century. Like modern India, it lacks an imperial tradition; nationalism there tends to come in a softer form, with pride in Brazilian culture and the easygoing Brazilian way of getting things done, without a hard edge. The professional foreign policy cadre at Brazil's Palacio do Itamaraty—its Ministry of Foreign Affairs, in Brasilia—has traditionally cultivated a policy of nonalignment. But as Brazil gathers economic might, with a rate of growth exceeding America's, a new generation of power brokers is looking for Brazil to play a more assertive global role commensurate with the country's rising importance in the world. Brazil's troops, not America's, are playing the leading role in the UN's peacekeeping mission in Haiti, and Brazil is set on acquiring a fleet of nuclear-powered submarines. Brazil's chances of becoming a regional hegemon in Latin America are limited by its attachment to the Portuguese language, when all other countries are predominantly Spanish speaking. And there is no particularly distinctive model of Brazilian success that the country can export to the rest of the world. Brazil is achieving a growth in its middle classes, at long last, through a hodgepodge of neoliberal market-oriented and leftist state-oriented economic policies. Still, Brazil, blessed with new oil discoveries, is starting to see itself not as a power of the "third world" South but as a global power in the echelon that China and India are entering.

As this tour of the globe suggests, the best prospect for the emergence of a twenty-first-century multipolar world is the revival of nationalism, which could reinvigorate the nation-state as a dynamic actor in global politics. Modern nationalism was born in nineteenth-century Germany as a counterreaction to the French Enlightenment. Faced with the prospect of having to live in a sterile age of French hegemony, the Germans rediscovered their poetic myths and traditions. Nationalism was, and remains, a romantic movement, grounded in a sense of the nation as a mystical unit into which the mere individual can dissolve. Nationalism permits a people, linked by blood, culture, and sometimes tribe, to tell a story about themselves. In nineteenth-century Europe, nationalism also flourished in the shadow of empire; the European historian Norman Davies has noted that "popular nationalism, which grew from the grass roots, was planted like so many acorns under the dynastic states and multinational empires of the era."

With nationalism proven such a destructive force in twentieth-century Europe and Japan, it was likely, some analysts believed, to recede into memory. The idea—or the hope—was that nationalism's future in the body politic was as little more than a vestigial appendix. That prognosis was clearly wrong—it suffered in part from the failure of Westerners to understand that other peoples, in places like Asia and Africa, possessed their own national myths and stories and were eager to repossess and reanimate them. (And the Left, in a tradition that ran from Marx to Lenin to postwar socialists, made the mistake of believing that class mattered more than nation.) One of the few to anticipate that nationalism would be a potent force in the postcolonial world was Isaiah Berlin. In his essay "Nationalism: Past Neglect and Present Power," published in *Partisan Review* in 1978, he wrote, "It would not, I think, be an exaggeration to say that no political movement today, at any rate outside the Western world, seems likely to succeed until it allies itself to national sentiment."

Notwithstanding the understandable anxieties that a resurgence of nationalism in the twenty-first century would undoubtedly stoke, the case can be made that the After America world could *benefit* from more nationalism. Consider the case of Lebanon. As things now stand, Lebanon is an example of chaos supplanting American dominance in the Middle East. It is the home of a state within a state, Hezbollah, the anti-American, Iranian-aligned group that, besides its own army, also has its own fiber-optics communications network and its own system of tax collection. And yet Hezbollah is not simply, as is sometimes said, an appendage of Tehran; it has the allegiance of a fair-sized chunk of the population of Lebanon, and it has a complicated web of arrangements with the other main political actors in Lebanese society. The most hopeful thing that could happen in Lebanon would be the emergence of a stronger national identity, a Lebanese patriotism, which could weave together the country's disparate religious and cultural strands. And the same might be said of Iraq,

another nation-state whose modern boundaries were drawn by European imperialists. When and if America withdraws its forces, Iraq stands to hold together
on the strength of nationalism—on the sense among ordinary Iraqis that allegiance to their nation overrides all other loyalties. This is a tall order, especially
given sentiments among Kurds favoring a more or less autonomous republic.
Nevertheless, Iraqi nationalism may be the one thing capable of transcending
the sectarian divisions that threaten to make Iraq a permanent failed state. And
a strong Iraqi nation-state, girded by a positive sense of nationalism, may be the
best hope for keeping al-Qaeda and other transnational terrorist groups from
establishing a base in Iraqi territory.

Nationalism does not have to mean bellicosity. If a twenty-first-century
multipolar world is a landscape made up of Indias and Brazils, with their relatively soft forms of nationalism, emphasizing national pride without too much
of an accent on ancient grievances, then a multipolar order might indeed be
best for the world, even for America, as Afghanistan's U.S. ambassador told me
in our talk. For the United States, a multipolar world would certainly be prefer-
able to a dark chaos and presumably a happier alternative to a Chinese Century.
There could be tangible rewards. With America able to downsize its global-
policeman role, with the prospect of hundreds of thousands of troops returning
to U.S. soil from Europe, the Middle East, and, let's also say, South Korea (which
alone hosts thirty thousand American soldiers), the "imperial-overstretch"
problem could be solved. For the U.S. taxpayer, a "Come Home, America" strategy might mean several hundred billion dollars of annual savings—at least half
of the Pentagon budget, now totaling some $700 billion, as some analysts have
suggested. And as Latin American powers like Brazil come on line, with a willingness to shoulder a greater burden of the hemisphere's security problems,
then even the level of America's regional security obligations might be scaled
back.

I spoke with James T. Hill, a retired four-star U.S. Army general, about the
greater willingness of Latin American countries to take on security duties in
the region. From 2002 to 2004, Hill was head of U.S. Southern Command,
based in Miami, with responsibility for U.S. military operations in South and
Central America and the Caribbean. "It's a good news story for us, there's no
doubt about it," Hill said of his successful effort to persuade the Chilean navy

and others to take part in joint military exercises to practice a defense of the Panama Canal against a terrorist attack. "It's not my canal," Hill bluntly reminded the Chileans, the world's fourth biggest users of the waterway. Hill acknowledges that, similar to India, a rising power like Brazil is not going to want to serve as an adjunct of the U.S. military. "Are we ever going to be hand-holding friends with Brazil? I think the answer to that is no." Still, he's not worried, because he cannot envision a scenario in which Brazil and the United States become outright enemies. As for the prospect of America losing control of Latin America as other powers, including China, become more involved in the region, "the new reality is that the United States is no longer *the* touchstone for all of Latin America," he noted.

A multipolar world also offers a potential solution to the perennially vexing problem of Israel's place in the Middle East. America has helped to prop up the Jewish state as a regional power, but despite decades of strenuous diplomatic effort, it has failed to impose peace on the area. Perhaps the local powers could do better by sorting things out on their own. One principle that might be invoked is regional deterrence—a staple of multipolar arrangements. Everyone knows that Israel is a nuclear power, so Israel might as well make this publicly known. Suppose, then, that one of Israel's regional rivals, most likely Iran, gains nuclear weapons. Far from being a catastrophe, this might actually improve security by creating a balance of power according to the cold war formula of mutually assured destruction. India and Pakistan, it might be noted, fought three major wars *before* both obtained nuclear weapons but have not fought one since. In an After America multipolar world, the Middle East's Jews, Arabs, and Persians may need to figure out their own formula for coexistence.

For America's imperial class, accustomed to the primacy of Washington's global diplomatic agenda, a multipolar world will no doubt be seen as a retreat. Local powers will become, in effect, the policemen of their own regional neighborhoods; a power less needful of Washington's help is inevitably a power less inclined to take Washington's advice. For neoconservatives in the Henry Luce tradition, this will be an especially painful adaptation, and the suffering will be felt not only by national security policy mavens at the likes of the American Enterprise Institute but also by branches of the Washington-based national media. I am thinking in particular of opinion media, like the Luce-tinged editorial page of the *Washington Post*, which has spent much of the first decade of the twenty-first century railing against the departure of countries like Russia away from the American-style democratic model. At some point the lectures will cease as the role of global pedagogue assumed by America simply loses its force. The "students," as things are going, are already leaving the classroom, just as an earlier generation of learners did in the first half of the twentieth century when the British imperial model became tarnished.

Neoconservatives are right to be concerned that a multipolar world is unlikely to take shape in the image of America's Jeffersonian ideals. China, Russia, Iran, Brazil—all come from different political and cultural traditions; and the Indian democratic model, for all it owes to the British example, is distinctively its own. And yet, an analogy from the study of economics suggests that a multipolar world might yield America some unexpected geopolitical benefits. Economic theory, confirmed by practice, teaches that monopoly is bad—not only for the marketplace but even for the monopolist. The hegemonic economic actor becomes complacent and arrogant, a deadly combination, after the great victory over competitors is won, like IBM after it achieved dominance in the field of mainframe computers. "Big Blue" stopped thinking and missed out on the minicomputer revolution. In the same vein, unipolar America, after its triumph in the cold war, became geopolitically dumber, as illustrated by its failure to appreciate the consequences of invading Iraq after the 9/11 attacks. A more competitive geopolitical world may force Washington to wise up, diplomatically speaking, and make a more rigorous accounting of costs and benefits *before* deciding to risk its precious resources, foremost among them the lives of its soldiers. As counterintuitive as this may sound, a multipolar world actually could make America a more intelligent geopolitical actor—which would of course be good not only for the world but also for America.

Nor does a multipolar world offer any obvious threat to the economic fortunes of Americans. It needs to be remembered that America is not the only actor with an interest in a global economic order based on capitalism and trade. Canada, Brazil, Western and Eastern Europe, the Middle Eastern petropowers, China, Vietnam, Japan, Australia—even tsarist-leaning Russia, with its oligarchs—have a stake in a system in which goods and services can be exchanged. That system, of course, is at times challenged by protectionist policies brandished by assorted varieties of economic nationalists. But America itself has been guilty of protectionism at times in its history and can no longer be, in any case, the sole guarantor of a liberal economic order. Assuming that the planet does not turn sharply away from market capitalism as the best way to improve living standards, America is as well positioned as any other nation to thrive in the economy of a multipolar world. After all, America is both a Pacific and an Atlantic nation, with a community of immigrants that is among the world's most diverse. The question will be how American businesses deal with the challenge—with new competition from unfamiliar players that are coming into their own. The most successful businesses of the future surely will be those who accept that the era of U.S. economic dominance is over and find the most creative solutions to operating in a world in which not one but a half dozen or possibly more "drivers" have a hand on the steering wheel. The U.S.-based businesses that prosper are likely to be those that learn to think in multipolar terms; one step, for example, might be to recast their boards of directors to reflect the rising clout of the economies of India, China, and Brazil. As is the case in all After America possibilities, the After America entrepreneur will have to improve his knowledge of geography, languages other than English, and ways of life other than the American one.

There would be no dishonor for America and its people were the world to shift from the age of U.S. dominance to a multipolar order. Indeed, a not displeasing chapter could be added to the American narrative. Future generations of American schoolchildren could read in their history books the story of how their nation rose to the occasion as Europe started to fracture, how it helped slay the beasts of fascism and communism, and finally, how the liberal order created and policed by America enabled others to prosper and thus allowed America gracefully to retire from a role, with apologies to Henry Luce, which it was never in the country's character to occupy forever. The difficulty, of course, is that it is not in America's sole power to write this new chapter of its history. There are other authors, all across the planet, with a hand in the story.

Chapter Nine

Chinese Century

The leader of the pack is the alpha, supreme boss, Top Dog. He (or she) gets the best of everything—the best food, the best place to sleep, the best toy, etc.

Dog expert Vicki Rodenberg De Gruy

Does the world need a dominant power—a leader of the pack? The idea that the planet might benefit from an alpha dog sounds politically incorrect, but it has sometimes proved the case that socially flatter arrangements, in which there is no acknowledged leader, have produced squabbling and unhappiness and, worst of all, dangerous vacuums. The time between the first and second world wars of the twentieth century was that kind of a void—and it was not filled until America emerged from its willful isolation and asserted a consummate leadership role with its economic and military might. America, remember, did not have to elbow everyone out of the way in order to gain this station: If one path to global dominance is conquest, another is the voluntary subservience of lesser powers whose overriding interest is in safety and stability.

Americans are not easily impressed by what the rest of the world has to offer. Today's Europe, in the minds of even sophisticated Americans, is typically viewed as a museum showcase for a once glorious past, not the face of tomorrow, not a serious threat to a more muscular and dynamic America. China feels different to Americans. First-time visitors to Shanghai—including seasoned world travelers, men and women in their fifties and sixties—are awed at the spectacle of what is so clearly a massive work in progress, changing almost by the hour.

American businessmen who visit cities in remote provinces are dazzled by the quality of the modern infrastructure. Not everything is agreeable to their senses, but in their reports they sound like the foreigners who visited New York and Chicago in the late nineteenth century and were stunned (and assaulted) by the energy level on the streets. And after many years of patronizing praise for China's ability to manufacture cheap knockoff goods, the outside world, in America and elsewhere, is captivated by "Art's New Superpower," as *Vanity Fair* called China in a spread on the riot of paintings, sculptures, and other works now being turned out in studios in places like Shanghai, Beijing, and Hong Kong.

The path to a Chinese Century would in all likelihood look something like the path to the American one—a zigzag ascent driven by economic imperatives and assisted by the stumbles and miscalculations of others. The beginnings of this path can already be glimpsed. Just as the world of the late nineteenth and early twentieth centuries started to reorient itself toward America, without consciously knowing that America was destined to be the dominant power, the world of the early twenty-first century is already starting to make cultural, political, and economic adjustments to China's rising star. And as the world reaches out to China, China reaches out to the world. This encounter is happening all over the globe, including in America's own backyard, in South America, a region that America has dominated for centuries and tends to take for granted.

The Chinese are engaging politically, militarily, culturally, and, most of all, economically in South America, as a part of a planetwide search for raw materials. China's thirst for oil has led to a tightening of ties with socialist Hugo Chavez's Venezuela: Beijing is investing in oil-infrastructure projects there, and the two countries are considering proposals that include reactivating a pipeline through Panama to accommodate an increase in exports to China, possibly at the expense of the American market. Meanwhile, Chavez boasts of sending satellite technicians to China to receive training in a space-based air-defense system that presumably is intended to guard against an American military threat. South of Venezuela is Brazil, a prime source of soybeans for China; south of Brazil is Argentina, a prime source of meat; and to Argentina's west is Chile, a prime source of copper. From a Chinese perspective, it would make a great deal of sense to have a network of superhighways enabling goods to be transported by truck from Brazil and Argentina to Pacific seaports in Chile. A "bi-oceanic corridor" project is on the drawing board—with China, checkbook in hand, eager to talk about financing. If the project ever gets completed, it will be another way in which the region ends up reorienting away from Washington and toward Beijing.

The Chinese penetration in South America has gone deeper than Americans generally realize. The Chinese have arrived, and their presence is shaping up as an enduring one, as I learned in a visit to Chile. Although Chile is a small country, it is being avidly courted by China and offers a case study of what China hopes to accomplish in the region and of Chinese methods for amassing influence. The Chinese are often typecast as culturally clumsy when it comes to dealing with foreign countries, but the example of Chile suggests a suppler dimension to the Chinese approach. In Chile, the Chinese sense a historic opportunity to build alliances in a society with a legacy of distrust toward America. And despite some natural suspicions, Chileans mostly are welcoming the attention.

The seaport of Valparaiso lies on the Pacific Coast in central Chile, about a fourteen-day sail north of Cabo de Hornos, as Spanish-speaking peoples call Cape Horn, on the southern tip of South America. The town takes its name from the native village in Spain of the conquistador who planted the Spanish imperial flag here in the sixteenth century. Before the completion of the Panama Canal, early in the twentieth century, Valparaiso was a customary port of call for ships that had made their passage around the treacherous cape westward from the Atlantic side. The population spilled out from the flatlands of the port and its commercial downtown area to the steep hills beyond. The people built their homes alongside the gorges and ravines of Concepción and the Cordillera hills, and it was an arduous affair simply to get to town to buy a loaf of bread. Late in the nineteenth century, imperial Britain provided the solution: an elaborate system of mechanized "elevators" allowing the townspeople to traverse the hills in tramlike cars pulled over cable tracks by pulleys. The scheme was designed by Queen Victoria's finest engineers (one of the inventors attained knighthood) and built with cast iron imported from England's leading factories. Some of the elevators were named for Manchester, the birthplace of Britain's industrial revolution.

The elevators are still working, remarkably enough, but in the twenty-first century Valparaiso sees its future tied not to Europe or even America but to the rising economies of Asia and especially China, a fast-growing source of import-export trade for the port. And as commercial links develop, they are being cemented by cultural ones. At the Instituto Comercial Francisco Araya Bennett, a vocational high school in the center of town and a few blocks from the harbor, the students are learning Mandarin Chinese courtesy of a pilot program of the Chilean Ministry of Education in Santiago and the Chinese government in Beijing. On the day I visited in September 2007, afternoon language class was about to begin in a second-floor classroom with a spectacular view of the hills. The teacher was a slight twenty-eight-year-old woman sent from the Chinese mainland, four months earlier, to inaugurate the program. She had a round face and bright, sharp eyes and cut a striking figure in a fur-trimmed black leather jacket, a red leather handbag, and calf-high tan leather boots into which her blue denim jeans were fashionably tucked. The students, ages sixteen and seventeen, both boys and girls, wore dull blue and gray uniforms. Everyone called the teacher Luna, Spanish for "moon." It was too difficult, it seemed, to pronounce either component of her actual name, Xiau Qiong, and Luna suited her because she was an incandescent, magnetic personality with a natural charisma. She exchanged kisses on the cheeks and hugs with her charges and proceeded to a lesson practicing the four basic tones of the Chinese language. This can be the most difficult thing for beginners. For my benefit the students gathered at the front of the classroom and sang a Chinese song of "sweet love" while clapping their hands to the beat. "They are lovely, they are open," Luna told me.

Most of the students were from working-class families, with parents who could not afford a private school. Nearly all had an "Indian," or "indigenous," look—broad, flat cheekbones, wiry black hair, dark eyes, and a latte skin tone. Andrés, the star pupil, was also from a family of modest means but stood out for what in Chile would be called his upper-class, Castilian looks: light greenish eyes, wavy brown hair, and fair skin. He had just won a scholarship from the Ministry of Education to study Mandarin in China for four years. For someone of his background, this was like winning the lottery—it was a sure ticket to a good job when he came back home. He already had his plan together: He would open a sporting-goods business selling merchandise imported from China. He told me that he feels Chinese is a beautiful language. His parents were ecstatic about his good fortune, even if they stood to lose him for a time.

Luna agreed to meet me for dinner in Viña del Mar, a resort town adjacent to Valparaiso. Our rendezvous point was the local casino. She would have been easy to pick out in any Chilean crowd but in this case was unmistakable, outfitted in a long, capelike, red woolen overcoat, a fluffy white scarf that looked like a string of rabbit tails, and shiny black spike-heeled boots with pointed toes. She struck a regal pose at the top of the white steps leading to the casino's entrance. In her hand was a bag holding her tango shoes—she was coming from dance class. Over sushi, I heard her story. She was raised in the Hunan province of South China, and her mother died when she was ten years old. It was a deep shock— for three years she could not release her emotions, could not even shed a tear. Her father was a military man who helped maintain airplanes for the Chinese air force, and he was, she said, "an excellent communist." Her father remarried, and the family often moved around the country. Luna studied to become a language teacher at a Beijing institute and gained a job at one of the city's most prestigious middle schools (once touted by Bill Gates as a model of the Chinese education system). Students voted her the most popular teacher at the school. She had a comfortable life but twice almost died in car accidents. "God loves me," she said of her survival. "I have an old heart," she added, noting that in China most of her friends were quite a bit older than she was, in their fifties and even sixties.

Luna grew up on American films like *Gone With the Wind* and professed admiration for Americans' strong sense of their own beliefs and values. Chileans, she suggested, worry about gaining the favor of others and gauge their opinions accordingly, but not so Americans: "You don't mind being different." That might not have sounded like an unqualified compliment, but she wasn't talking about politics, and she clearly meant it as one. Her passion was for art and culture; only when the topic of Japan came up did she express a typical Chinese indignation over Japan's refusal to take responsibility for war crimes committed on Chinese soil. She told me that she would like to do her part to dispel popular misimpressions of the Chinese. China is no longer a nation of old men in ponytails, she said with a radiant smile.

Karl Marx understood history as proceeding from the material or hard economic base, with softer matters of culture amounting to "superstructure." In these still-relevant terms, Luna can be seen as superstructure. For the Chinese, the base in Chile is copper, and it explains nearly everything about what China is doing there and why it surely is going to remain for a very long time, possibly becoming a dominating presence. The terms of this marriage of interest are quite basic: Chile is, by far, the world's largest source of a resource vital to China's ambition to become the planet's biggest economy and a global military power.

For those who think of the twenty-first-century global economy as a package of bits and bytes, copper is a reminder of just how old-age industrial things still are. It does not have the prestige stature of a precious metal, like gold, or of diamonds, but it has countless practical uses. Pure, refined copper is strong and highly conductive, stands up well to heat, and is resistant to corrosion. It is also easily recyclable. In just about every phase of the modern industrial era, copper has played a role. In the early days of the telephone, America's Ma Bell strung copper cables between telephone poles. Copper helped make possible the age of the mass-produced automobile—a typical car contains more than fifty pounds of the metal. In the computer age, copper is used in printed circuit boards and cell phones. As for the military-goods sector, copper can be used to make bullets and engine rotors, and alloys like copper-nickel have a great many marine applications. One of the most lethal weapons used against U.S. forces in Iraq was a roadside bomb that fired off semi-molten copper slugs, capable of piercing the armor on a Humvee. A copperless future, in short, does not seem to be closing in on the world. What is happening, though, is a long-term shift in the balance of copper demand from North America and Europe to Asia. Thus as Detroit matters less to automobile manufacturing than do the new centers of production in China and elsewhere in Asia, so shifts the source of demand for copper.

Nature does not dispose of its blessings equally. Chile matters more to the global copper equation than Saudi Arabia to the global oil picture. The country's copper mines account for more than one-third of global production; and its reserves, 38 percent of the world's total, are expected to last for at least another sixty years. The *cobre* belt lies in the Atacama Desert, in between the Pacific and the Andes Mountains. It is a seismically active zone in which volcanic activity long ago pushed copper ore deposits from deep within the earth up to the crust. The Atacama is one of the world's driest places. Years can pass between rainfalls. There are no snakes, hardly any insects, almost no mammal life at all except for the guanaco, a small, caramel-colored llamalike animal that feeds on a kind of bitter sagebrush. To a newcomer the desert at first can feel forbidding, but the landscape gradually becomes a companion. The sun and the rock formations create a play of light and shadows; even during the daytime the colors change by the hour, shifting between shades of brown and pink. Especially striking are the black hills of volcanic rock, in varied sizes, shapes, and textures. From a distance they suggest abstract art sculptures. Stare at them long enough and they can bring to mind images like the rippled hide of a rhinoceros or the creviced bottom of a newborn baby. At sunset these hills change complexion from a swirl of pink to a deep violet before turning back to black. At night the sky is a bowlful of stars—a nocturnal paradise that these days attracts astronomers from all over the world to record their observations.

In the Atacama, the Chinese walk in the imperial footsteps of the Americans. America once dominated the Chilean copper industry through the Butte, Montana, mining conglomerate Anaconda Copper's holding in the famed Chuquicamata mine, known as Chuqui. Acquired by Anaconda Copper in 1923, with stockholders including members of the Rockefeller family, Chuqui became the world's single largest copper mining operation. It also became one of the most resonant symbols in the Chilean—and South American—mind of "Yanqui imperialism." Anaconda Copper ran everything at the hazardous mine in a cradle-to-grave system that contained all too much of the grave. Amid calls for nationalization, a young Ernesto (not yet "Che") Guevara toured Chuqui in 1952 with his motorcycle-traveling companion, Alberto Granado. Che reserved his greatest disdain for his Chilean guide, the "faithful dog of the Yankee bosses," as he wrote in his diaries.

Discounting for the propaganda, it was still fair to call Chile an appendage of the ascending American imperium. In 1970, direct private investment of American enterprises in Chile accounted for $1.1. billion out of a total of $1.7 billion in foreign investment. American corporations controlled the production of 80 percent of Chile's copper, which that year accounted for four-fifths of Chile's foreign exchange earnings. Grievances against the U.S. domination of Chile contributed to the election in 1970 (by a plurality) of the socialist candidate Salvador Allende, who vowed to nationalize foreign-owned mines and open diplomatic relations with the People's Republic of China and Castro's Cuba. Both promises were kept. Chuqui was taken away from Anaconda Copper and became the property of the state-owned company known as Codelco.

President Richard Nixon's administration in Washington, D.C., had tried to keep Allende from getting elected and, depending on one's read of the murky evidence, may or may not have had a significant hand in his downfall three years later and his replacement in the coup that put in power the military junta headed by the Chilean army chief Augusto Pinochet. The CIA years later acknowledged having close ties with Pinochet's repressive regime, which kept power for seventeen years, until 1990. One thing Pinochet did not do, though, was reverse the nationalization of the Chuqui complex: The mine was kept in the hands of Codelco.

And now it is the *cochinos*, as the Chileans call the Chinese, who are the talk of the copper belt—indeed the talk of the copper industry everywhere. The Chinese overtook the Americans as the world's biggest consumers of copper in 2001, and insatiable Chinese demand for *tong*, as they call copper, drove a nearly fivefold appreciation in global copper prices from 75 cents per pound in 1995 to $3.35 per pound in 2007. In the Atacama, there was chatter that the Chinese already owned some small mines and were angling to grab larger ones; chatter that the Chinese were eager to bring in their own technicians and maybe even supervisors to oversee the mines; chatter that Chinese purchases already accounted for as much as 50 percent of Chile's total copper output. Much of this talk may have been exaggerated, but there was no question that the Chinese aimed to deepen their involvement by making the jump from purchasers to investors. They wanted a piece of the mines—a piece of the profits. "Their economy is so hungry," a Codelco official told me.

The Chuqui mine still works, but it is no longer the choice copper mine of the Atacama. The Chinese have their sights set on a virgin mining project called Gaby, shorthand for the official name, Gabriela Mistral, referring to the Chilean poet, a passionate supporter of grassroots Chilean democracy, who in 1945 was awarded the Nobel Prize for literature. Gaby is in the heart of Chile's great copper vein, about sixty miles south of Chuqui. The complex can be reached only by a ninety-minute drive, much of it on bumpy dirt roads, which climb to an elevation of nine thousand feet. In the distance are the snowcapped Domeyko Mountains, eighteen thousand feet high. This area is swept by winds that can approach forty miles per hour and kick up the desert "dust devils," or *paranales*, the small, tornado-like columns of sand and dust that swirl for ten seconds or so.

Gaby is projected to produce about 150,000 tons of pure copper each year for about fifteen years. I saw no sign of a Chinese presence at Gaby and was told that Minmetals, the Chinese state-owned metals giant, had no role in the construction. I later learned, though, that a Minmetals delegation had visited the site several months before my visit. A half dozen or so officials from the Chinese mainland had come for a briefing and a look around. They were dressed informally in zip-up jackets, spoke some English but not Spanish, and sometimes huddled among themselves to talk things over in Chinese. "They acted like they were the big men on campus. . . . They came in like owners, with an ownership attitude," I was told by a senior Gaby project manager, Daniel Morales Farias, a Codelco official who personally briefed the delegation on their visit to the construction site. We were talking at his office in Santiago, and Farias emphasized that he was giving me his own impressions and not speaking for Codelco. As for the question of a Chinese stake in Gaby and other Chilean mines, he told me that some Codelco executives had concerns about how China treated its people, about the working environment in China. As he noted, the Codelco board was a diverse one, including representatives of the Chilean armed forces and copper mining unions. His own perspective was that if the Chinese so badly wanted Chilean copper, "they can always buy it on the market. . . . In the future, all of us banana republics will become stronger because we have these resources. If we start selling the ownership, we will be mortgaging our future."

I wasn't surprised to hear such sentiments. Earlier, on a visit to the Chuqui complex, I had come across a banner that one of the mining unions had put across the entrance to its headquarters: "Codelco y 'Gaby'/100% Estatal," which translates as "Codelco and Gaby/100 percent state owned." The union's president, Hilario Ramirez Gonzalez, agreed to an impromptu interview. His union represented twenty-seven hundred workers and had been formed seventy years before, when Anaconda was the owner of the Chuqui mine. Gonzalez was born in 1952 in a region south of Chuquicamata. Soft-spoken, not a table pounder, he had never worked in the mining pits; he came up in the union ranks as a university-trained financial auditor and was part of a new generation of more technically oriented, well-educated union leaders. He had a mop of black hair, sad dark eyes, and thick bushy eyebrows. In our talk he took pains to say that his union's position in favor of total state ownership of Gaby stemmed from the workers' opposition to all potential foreign or private owners, and not to the Chinese Minmetals bid in particular. Foreign ownership, he said, means the repatriation of profits outside Chile; the profits from the extraction of the nation's copper treasure should accrue to the nation's people. He expected Gaby to be a "cash cow" for Codelco, and so this project was a natural one on which the union would take a stand. He hoped to persuade Chile's socialist president, Michelle Bachelet, to keep Gaby in state hands, and failing that—Bachelet has a reputation for being indecisive—he would consider options including a media blitz on a union-owned radio station broadcasting to the mining region. There is a history of strikes and occasional violence in Chile's mining industry; Gonzalez assured me there would be "no violence" on the Gaby matter.

Although Gonzalez was seeking to occupy the high ground of political and economic fairness on the foreign-investment question, it was easy enough to see how something like the Gaby dispute could sink into the bog of populist nationalism. Chileans have a strong sense of national identity, exhibiting a boisterous patriotism that at times can turn into a strong aversion to "the foreigner." My own soundings, though, did not suggest that workers in the mining industry would, in fact, all be united behind a campaign to keep the country's copper bounty out of the hands of the Chinese. The region's big mining town is Calama, a short drive from the Chuquicamata complex. As copper prices have boomed over the past decades, so has Calama. The town is where the workers go to carouse during their periods of rest from the mines. Late on a Friday evening I stopped in at Caruso, one of a dozen or so bars scattered around Calama's main plaza. It was coming on Chile's day of national independence, always a time of prolonged festivities in the country, and a large Chilean flag, surrounded by balloons and patriotic bunting, hung from the rafters. A flat-panel video screen, barely visible through the blue-gray haze of cigarette smoke, displayed half-dressed young women tugging at each other's panties. The rhythms of Queen's "We Are the Champions" thumped from the loudspeakers.

Roberto, a master welder enjoying time off from his work at the Gaby construction site, was happy to share his thoughts. He was a swarthy fellow of thirty-two years with a few days' growth of dark stubble. A Viceroy dangled from his lips, and he was fairly well into his *piscolas*—a variation of a national drink, combining Coca-Cola with *pisco*, a strong brandy made from grapes grown in northern Chile. His drinking companion, the less talkative Daniel, was also working at the Gaby site. Roberto was a native of Concepción, a city south of Santiago, and since the age of eighteen had worked welding jobs in Chile, Peru, Argentina, and Spain. Gaby, he said, was quite good work—he was pulling in two thousand dollars a month in cash salary. He said the bosses had told the men that the first five years of Gaby production would be dedicated 100 percent to the Chinese. That was okay with him, as was Chinese ownership of a piece of the mine. The union slogan of Gaby, "100 percent state owned," was a nice "ideal," he said, but "unfortunately Chile does not have resources to develop its own endowments." Daniel assented and bemoaned Chile's lack of capacity to refine the sheets of pure copper smelted at the mines into wire products and other end uses.

The Chilean copper trail ends in the seaports in and around Antofagasta, the country's fourth largest city. In the language of an indigenous tribe that once populated the area, the city's name means "He who hides copper." Like Valparaiso to the south, this is another Chilean port with a past British imperial influence. In a downtown square lined with palms stood a scaled-down replica of London's Big Ben clock tower, presented to the city in 1910 as a gift from the British colonials living there. At the Antofagasta port, bundles of copper sheets are placed in containers that make the trip to Asia on giant vessels also holding cargoes of items like bananas. The port has been the mainstay of the copper trade for decades, but the future lies in a modern new port, about one hour's drive north, in Mejillones. At this facility, the bundles are loaded directly into the holds of ships about 250 meters in length. On a Sunday, no ships awaited loading, and the only noise was the barking of the sea lions lounging on the loading platform. Shanghai was a forty-five-day sail away.

Fidel Castro is an "hombre," a real man. So I was being told by Liu Yuqin, China's ambassador to Chile, a veteran of diplomatic postings to South America, including Cuba and Ecuador. Our conversation at the Chinese embassy in Santiago began over jasmine tea in an ornate room decorated with traditional Chinese vases and a wall-length framed calligraphy scroll of a poem composed by Mao Tse-tung. The ambassador had short-cropped hair and was fashionably attired in a maroon blazer, a green and yellow checked shirt, black slacks, and soft black leather shoes. Next-door Argentina, she confessed, was a terrific place to shop for bargain leather goods and other clothing. She had learned to speak Spanish at a Beijing foreign-language institute in the early 1970s but relied on an interpreter to converse in English.

Liu Yuqin was eager to talk about China's involvement in South America in general, and in Chile in particular. First she dispensed a short history lesson, the main point of which was that there were long-standing fraternal ties between Asians, including the Chinese, and South Americans. It might be the case, she began, that Asians and indigenous South Americans are related by blood, as scientists speculate that Asians might have crossed over to the Americas from the Bering Strait "land bridge" long ago, during a prehistoric ice age. There is a similarity in cheekbone structure, she pointed out. China's direct ties with South America, she continued, go back to the sixteenth century, when a sea route for trade in silk developed between ports in South China and Mexico by way of Manila. In the late nineteenth century, Chinese workers were among those brought in to dig the Panama Canal, a difficult project the French initiated but failed to complete, with many laborers dying of malaria and yellow fever. (The Americans took charge of the Canal Zone early in the twentieth century and finished the job under vastly improved health conditions for the workers.) After the People's Republic of China—Communist China—was established in 1949, no country south of the United States recognized the regime until Castro's Cuba did so in 1960. Recognition from Chile came in 1970, from Salvador Allende, who, Yuqin noted, had first visited China in 1954, when relations between America and "Red China" were extremely tense. Skipping ahead to the present, she said China was eager to deepen its ties with Chile, not just on the basis of copper but on cultural initiatives like Chinese-language programs.

I got straight to my point. Should Chileans be concerned about the Chinese succeeding the Spanish and the Americans as the new imperialists of South America? I was curious to see how she would counter this question. "It's not like China comes in to ransack this country of its raw materials—China pays for these raw materials," she noted evenly. When I pointed out that a union of Chilean copper workers had taken a stand against China's bid to become an owner of the Gaby mine, she said, "As in all families, brothers can have an argument." China has a policy of "noninterference" in all countries and believes in the motto "Win together." China, she insisted, is preoccupied with its own internal development: China's goal is "peaceful development, never hegemony. We don't have as much time as your country does to intervene in the affairs of others." I had asked about the sensibilities of the Chileans, but she was responding to me as an American.

And the truth, not surprisingly, is that Beijing is hopeful of extending its ties with Chile to the military domain. So far, that part of the relationship is a modest one, involving Mandarin-language training for Chilean military personnel in Santiago. The next step is a broader initiative in language and cultural training for the Chilean military, who would go to China itself for their courses. A natural step beyond that would be an officer exchange program, such as Chile and the United States had long had. Beyond that might be Chilean purchases of routine military gear, such as goggles, as well as weapons, from the Chinese. "The Chileans have told us that the Chinese are interested in a much more robust military-to-military relationship," a knowledgeable U.S. official told me. This official also said he would not be surprised to see in the long term—if not in five years, then perhaps in ten—the visitation of Chinese naval ships to ports like Valparaiso or Antofagasta. The Chinese, like the Indians, are actively expanding their blue-water navy because, as Chinese strategists say, "the oceans are our lifelines" and "if commerce were cut off, the economy would plummet." A similar logic drove the expansion of the British Royal Navy in the nineteenth century.

I asked Liu Yuqin whether China recognized the Monroe Doctrine—proclaimed by U.S. president James Monroe in 1823 to keep the Southern Hemisphere free of "essentially different" political systems, like those, at the time, of the Spanish and other European monarchies. Referencing the imperial European powers, Monroe had said that the United States "should consider any attempt on their part to extend their system to any portion of this hemisphere as dangerous to our peace and safety." It was a long time ago, but the Monroe Doctrine was one basis for the efforts of cold warriors in Washington to keep communism out of South America after the Second World War, and the doctrine remains alive for hawks in early-twenty-first-century Washington. Liu Yuqin, with a smile, first corrected me on the date of the proclamation—I had flubbed it at 1815. Then she said, "It's not a question of whether we do or do not" recognize the Monroe Doctrine, because it exists as a unilateral declaration of the United States and nothing more than that. That was something of a nonanswer answer, but she added: "The U.S. has to undergo a change of mentality, as the world has changed."

Shifting tack, she quite correctly noted that it is the Chileans who are soliciting China for an expansion of bilateral ties. This is especially true, she pointed out, in the area of language and culture. Nearly twenty of Chile's universities, including its most prestigious ones, had in recent years established Mandarin Chinese–language programs, and the country's number-one university, Universidad Católica de Chile, in Santiago, had requested the establishment of a Confucius Center for learning about Chinese culture as a joint venture with the Chinese.

We'd been talking for several hours, and it was time to move to the dining room for lunch, which turned out to be an eight-course, two-hour affair, complete with a menu printed in honor of my visit. After a clinking of glasses filled with a sorghum liquor, several notches in strength above vodka, we moved through a procession of soup, seafood, meat, chicken, and noodle dishes before concluding with preserves of the pale Asian fruit known as litchi. Our discussion turned to broader questions raised by China's encounter with South America. Is South America part of the "West" that includes European and American political and philosophical traditions? The world today is global; such classifications are not very meaningful, the ambassador said. I tried to draw her out on whether South America's Roman Catholic culture, still vibrant in countries like Chile, was in any sense a barrier for China. No, Liu Yuqin replied; even though most Chinese are atheists, they readily accept that belief may be powerful in other cultures.

And what about the vaunted difference between the Asian and Latin American work ethics? Even many Latinos, I said, tended to view their culture as a less hardworking, mañana one. (A Chilean lawyer in his sixties told me that Latin Americans had inherited from the Spanish nobility the idea that "working was for villains" and still retain "this curse of the Iberian tradition.") Liu Yuqin laughed and brought up the example of Mexicans. She said, "Mexicans like to have fun—they enjoy lots of holidays, lots of days off." They are "happy people." Our conversation was over. She signed my copy of the menu to mark the occasion, and I returned to my hotel for an afternoon nap.

The Chilean business and political elite are mostly receptive to the Chinese bid for a greater engagement with their country. There is a faction, based in the foreign ministry, who are worried the relationship might lead to an imperial domination. But most folks do not feel this way. For Chile, "the potential for opportunities in Asia is much greater than in the United States," a retired Chilean army general, Juan Emilio Cheyre, told me. As commander in chief of the Chilean army from 2002 to 2006, he issued a historic statement holding the army responsible for torture and killings under the rule of Pinochet and declaring that the military, would "never again" subvert democracy in Chile. After leaving the military, he founded a center for international relations at Universidad Católica de Chile. We met at his offices there, adjacent to a courtyard laid out in the traditional Spanish colonial style, with a fountain, a yellow-tiled floor, red rosebushes, and palms. He told me, emphatically, that he did not hold Washington responsible, as do many Chileans, for the overthrow of Allende and the takeover by the Pinochet regime. Still, "the United States has never really understood Latin America," he said. China's goal is "to penetrate the region culturally and economically," and "there is a real possibility that the U.S. can lose a lot of power." Was he worried, I asked, about how America might react to small countries like Chile shifting toward the Chinese pole? "Nobody fears the giants [of global politics] anymore. The clearest example is the twin towers," the general said.

As they try to make up their minds about the Chinese, the Chileans are drawing on impressions that are not particularly well formed, as is not surprising in a country that, with its geography of seacoast and mountains, has always had a somewhat insular mentality. On one extreme is a Chilean image of *chinos cochinos*—the "dirty Chinese," who are deemed to have an excessive appetite for garlic and a habit of spitting and burping in public. On the other extreme is the image of the Chinese as a people of Lunas—of agreeably exotic, doll-like creatures. Some Chileans use an affectionate diminutive—*chinito*, a word meaning both "little Chinese person" and "ladybug"—to describe any Asian face glimpsed on their streets. That phrase is a patronizing one; Chileans typically use Spanish diminutives in speaking to their children, maids, and pets. On balance, opinion tilts in the direction of the positive: In one survey taken in 2007 by an American polling firm, 55 percent of Chileans said China's influence was a "good thing" for their country, compared to only 28 percent who said that America's influence was a good thing.

Whether impressions of the Chinese are positive or negative, the consensus is that China is going to matter a great deal to the destiny of Chile and South America. A lawyer I met with in Santiago said of the Chinese: "They are going to be the eight-hundred-pound gorilla in this neighborhood—there is no question of that." This was not, he added, anything to feel happy about: "The Chinese are not dedicated to any proposition except China first, and China forever."

China's encounter with Chile does not answer the question of whether there will be a Chinese Century, but it offers a perspective on the obstacles the Chinese must surmount if they are to supplant America as the world's dominant power. There will not be a Chinese Century unless China manages to become the world's preeminent economic power, as America became at the end of the nineteenth century. This is a first test for the proposition of a China-dominated world and the easiest one for China to meet. Surely it has already shown the potential to be the towering economy that ends up dwarfing all others. Since 1978, China has strung together what is arguably the best thirty-year economic run that any nation, including the United States, has had, growing its economy by an annual average of nearly 10 percent. Not even the Japanese "miracle" was quite this miraculous. America, Japan, and Germany, the world's three bigger economies, as of the moment, are relative laggards: From 2000 to 2007, the American economy grew by an average of 3 percent annually, the Japanese economy by 2.2 percent, and the German economy by 2.7 percent. Even as the world's fourth largest economy, China was already, by the fall of 2007, contributing more to growth in the world's total economic output than was the United States—the same milestone that nineteenth-century America passed as it gained ground on the British economy. For the year, China accounted for a remarkable 27 percent share of the total growth in global output. The great engine of this growth is not, as is often reported in the press, exports of Chinese goods to markets in America, Europe, and elsewhere but domestic Chinese demand. Moreover, immense pools of cheap labor reserves remain in the Chinese countryside. While China may indeed be poisoning its own people with its crash program in industrialization, nineteenth-century Britain did nothing less to the children made to work in its suffocating textile mills. It would take a fairly big Chinese economic meltdown or an unexpected major surge in U.S. economic growth rates to keep the Chinese from claiming the top spot at some point.

The global financial crisis that began in the fall of 2008 undoubtedly is the most severe economic threat that China has encountered since the late 1970s—and it is a serious social and political challenge as well. As global demand for China's products fell, tens of thousands of small companies went bankrupt, and the Chinese government faced a gathering wave of labor unrest from threatened workers. With the stability of the regime itself at stake, the authorities in Beijing unveiled a massive economic stimulus plan to invest nearly $600 billion, about 16 percent of China's 2007 gross domestic product, in areas including housing, road and railway infrastructure, agriculture, and health care. While the stimulus plan underscored the seriousness of the peril to China's economic miracle, it also demonstrated the ability of Beijing to mount an aggressive and dramatic response. China's plan far exceeded America's own initial stimulus of $168 billion, about 1 percent of annual U.S. GDP, and a senior Treasury official in Washington welcomed China's plan as a "potential lift" to all countries, including America. In November 2008, the International Monetary Fund projected that China's economy would grow by 8.5 percent in 2009, compared to a contraction forecast for the U.S. economy of 0.7 percent and for Europe's economy of 0.5 percent. Global economic growth as a whole was projected at 2.2 percent. The Washington economist Albert Keidel, an expert on China's economy, calculated that China could suffer a 20 percent drop in exports in 2009 and still register growth of 9 percent. One challenge is to get China's legendary class of savers to devote a greater share of their income to spending on consumption items like television sets and restaurant meals. For all of its troubles, China remains the world's most promising engine of growth.

When might China overtake the United States as the world's top economic producer? One standard measure of economic output is called "purchasing power parity," or PPP, often used to compare standards of living between countries. The idea behind PPP is that the dollar, say, might buy only one loaf of bread in America but, converted into yuan, might buy two in China, because of bread's lower cost of production there. The same goes for the purchase of all sorts of staples in China and for locally made military goods as well. By the PPP yardstick, China could overtake America as the world's biggest economy in the 2020s. However, some economists find the PPP measurement rather dubious. So let's stick with a straightforward comparison between the size of the U.S. and Chinese economies, at regular exchange rates. Keidel told me that he expected China's economy to overtake America's in "absolute size" by 2040. That projection is based on a gradually slowing economy in China, down to 7 percent annually for the 2030s, against 3.5 percent annual growth for America's economy. By the end of the twenty-first century, a very long way off and thus much tougher to forecast with any accuracy, China's economy, according to Keidel's projections, could be twice the size of America's. And it is also conceivable, he told me, that by the turn of the twenty-second century, China could also have a per capita GDP higher than America's. China at present is vastly poorer, with a per capita GDP, in absolute terms, of $2,500, compared to $46,000 for America.

The second test for the arrival of a Chinese Century is for China to become the supreme, unrivaled power in its own backyard. Before America became a global superpower, in the twentieth century, it established itself as the regional hegemon in the Western Hemisphere. China must show that it can do the same thing, geopolitically speaking, in its own neighborhood. This test will be more difficult to meet than the test of global economic preeminence. China must deal with a wary Japan, India, and Russia, not to mention a wary America, with tens of thousands of ground troops plus the world's most formidable navy in the region. Still, China's defense capabilities are rising as it pours money into its defense budget—currently at $58 billion, behind the United States, the UK, and France. But while defense spending in Western Europe is flat, China's budget, at its current rate of growth, is projected to climb to $360 billion by 2020. Regional hegemony does not appear to be outside China's grasp. When the U.S. military offered to patrol the treacherous Malacca Strait, Singapore and Malaysia said no—because they were afraid of Beijing's reaction had they agreed, as an Australian navy officer told me. The American era of total military dominance in the region is already over; the only question is what the new order will be.

Harvey J. Feldman is one of the American foreign policy establishment's wisest China hands. A veteran of the Foreign Service, he speaks Mandarin Chinese, served in Taiwan for six years, and helped plan Richard Nixon's historic trip to mainland China in 1972. I chatted with him over lunch at a conference in Philadelphia in 2007 on the theme of "China Rising." How long would it be, I asked him, before the mainland absorbed Taiwan? He paused between bites of his salmon and replied, "It already has." Taiwan, he explained, over the years has invested $200 billion in the mainland, and the mainland is Taiwan's number-one export market. Some 1 million Taiwanese businessmen live on the mainland,

and some forty thousand Taiwanese students are studying there at any one time. If the mainland Chinese were truly good Marxists and understood that economics determines everything, Feldman continued, they would realize that Taiwan is effectively already theirs.

Geopolitical strategists take it as practically an article of faith that a rising great power must cut its teeth in a war. Imperial Japan humiliated the tsar's navy in the Russo-Japanese War of 1904–5, which heralded the ascension of Japan and the eclipse of tsarist Russia. Washington's national security planners, these days, are not unreasonably focused on the possibility of a next war, in the Pacific, involving America and China. The example of Taiwan, though, suggests that such a conflict is not ordained. For decades America's and China's hawks have circled each other on Taiwan, amid frequent predictions that a hot conflict was nearing. And yet it turns out that the mainland has swallowed Taiwan, organically speaking, without a single shot being fired. China's 1997 takeover of Hong Kong from the British was also a peaceful one.

The most difficult test of all for China is to develop a winning narrative so that a sufficient number of lesser powers all over the world will *want* to live in a world led by the Chinese. (The only alternative to a winning narrative is a global military conquest, which looks highly implausible.) The narrative part of the equation tends to be lost in all the discussion of whether China can acquire the economic or military heft to become the world's preeminent power. But as the American example suggests, this is an essential question. All aspiring Goliaths need to be able to tell a compelling story about themselves to which others can easily relate. A global giant must be more than a fist or a wallet; the giant must also be a magnet—a source of attraction and, at best, of emulation. One reason the Soviet Union never had a good chance to supplant the American hegemony was that the Russians were experienced by much of the world as a suffocating presence; they were takers, not givers.

In America and Europe, the conventional wisdom holds that the Chinese also are brute exploiters—a people absorbed by the drama of their own history, with an indifference bordering on a disdain toward the rest of the world. If this judgment is correct, then there will be no Chinese Century, just as there could not have been an American Century if Americans had been apprehended as a people with nothing useful to give the planet. The judgment, though, is premature, and it suffers from distortions. One source of distortions is the prism of race and culture. The very *idea* of a Chinese Century is worrying to some people in the West because it suggests that "yellow people" would have the whip hand over white people. In America in particular, the prospect of the "yellow peril" was an advertised fantasy of propagandists during the cold war. While attitudes toward the Chinese have improved since then, America's cultural reflex is still to regard the Chinese as an alien and worrisome presence—a source, not least, of toxic materials in imported pet food and toys. And these sentiments inform "Anglo" opinion in the United Kingdom as well. "Both people in America and people in Europe should reflect on what will be the major power in the decades to come, which will be China," Tony Blair said at a press conference as he prepared to give up the reins as prime minister. "For America and Europe, that basically share the same value system, to stick together is in my view vital."

It is unlikely that a Chinese global narrative will ever win over the hearts and minds of Americans and Europeans. But this is not a fatal blow to a Chinese Century. The peoples of North America and Europe, with Russia thrown in, add up to about 2.4 billion. The beauty of the Chinese narrative, in any case, is that it is not designed to appeal to the rich peoples of the North; it is tailored to the poorer and more plentiful peoples of the South—to the hopes and also to the accumulated resentments of the region where Henry Kissinger once famously said nothing much happens. "History has never been produced in the South," Kissinger lectured Chile's foreign minister in 1969. "The axis of history starts in Moscow, goes to Bonn, crosses over to Washington, and then goes to Tokyo. What happens in the South is of no importance." Like the American narrative, the story of how a people cast off the yoke of British oppression and came into their own, the Chinese narrative also has an anti-imperial theme. This is the tale of how a once-great civilization became weak and was dismembered by the rich and arrogant powers of the nineteenth century. But the civilization kept its pride and sense of itself and eventually drove the oppressors from its lands. And then the people set out on a course of economic development, carefully directed by the state, which began to earn for China wealth and the respect of those who once scorned it.

This is not a flawless narrative. It is immediately called into question by

Beijing's bullying behavior toward Tibet. But the American narrative was not flawless, either. America became the world's most compelling story of the late nineteenth and early twentieth centuries despite the slaughter of women and children of the Lakota Sioux tribe at Wounded Knee Creek in South Dakota in 1890—a notorious event that the commanding U.S. general later described as a "massacre." The America of this age exploited child labor and maintained "Jim Crow" laws that discriminated against blacks. The ripe question is whether the Chinese narrative is better than what anyone else has to offer—at this moment.

This is a comparative exercise—and a highly practical one. One of the things it comes down to is whether the Chinese have something to offer the Southern hemisphere that Americans and Europeans do not. Westerners need to be careful as they ponder this question. Consider the case of Africa. Since the Second World War, a guilt-prone West has treated a decolonized Africa like a charity ward in need of economic and humanitarian aid, dispensed by large international and governmental agencies based in America and Europe. The presumption, a deeply patronizing one, is that the West is in possession of formulas to help "underdeveloped" societies, whatever that means. While the Chinese also are building village schools and anti-malaria clinics, the core of their approach is a cold-eyed business one. They are in Africa not to do philanthropy or to act as substitute parents but to extract resources to grow their economy back home. That may sound horribly mercantile—or even neocolonial—but the bottom line is billions of dollars of investments in places like the Democratic Republic of Congo and a burgeoning China-Africa trade that has climbed to $55 billion from less than $5 billion in 1998. And while the Chinese can be faulted for supplying arms to the government of oil-rich Sudan, which is a party to the genocide of the people of Darfur, Africans can also look back to the days when European imperialists came to the "dark continent" to capture slaves to work the plantations of the New World in the Americas. Africans may be less prone to condemn the Chinese as predators than Westerners are. Among sub-Saharan African nations, while public opinion of America's influence is generally positive, "China's influence is almost universally viewed as having a more beneficial impact on African countries than does that of the United States," the Pew Research Center found in a survey published at the end of 2007. Even China's "growing military influence" was seen as a "good thing" by majorities in countries like Ivory Coast, Kenya, and Nigeria.

Nor should Westerners take refuge in the notion that there is a historical destiny to their greatest creation, the liberal civilization, as a winning brand for the world. No civilization is better at protecting the rights of the individual human being, but the best does not always win. And a debate, in any case, is under way on whether the Western model is, for all others, the best. Daniel A. Bell is a professor of political philosophy and ethics at Tsinghua University in Beijing. In his 2006 book, *Beyond Liberal Democracy*, he argues that "there are morally legitimate alternatives to Western-style liberal democracy in the East Asian region. What is right for East Asians does not simply involve implementing Western-style political practices when the opportunity presents itself; it involves drawing upon East Asian political realities and cultural traditions that are defensible to contemporary East Asians." Bell's argument can be broadly extended to the Southern hemisphere, which has a mix of political, economic, and cultural traditions, some of which may well be more compatible with a Chinese-style example than a Western-style one.

Latin America, for example, is interested in the Chinese political-economic development model not simply because Latinos resent their overbearing neighbor to the north, but because the region's political and economic elite believe that the model may be of more service to them than the American one. Mexico, for one, is generally dissatisfied with the American approach and is flirting with the Chinese example. In 2006, one of Latin America's largest universities, Universidad Nacional Autónoma de México, known as UNAM, established a Center for Chinese-Mexican Studies in a joint initiative with the Chinese, "to improve and deepen the knowledge of Chinese society and its economy" in Mexico. The principal founder, the economics professor Enrique Dussel Peters, actively encourages Mexican undergraduates to learn Chinese, not English. What's striking to Mexicans and Latin Americans generally, Peters told me, is that China has "done everything wrong" according to the standard Western liberal model of development—he cited its state subsidies and nontransparent property conditions and laws, for example—"and still has the highest growth. . . . Of course Mexico can learn a lot [from] China."

If China can become a "soft power" superpower, as America once was, then there may be no stopping a Chinese Century. This remains very much an "if." Surveys of global attitudes suggest that most publics around the world are still making up their minds about the Chinese—just as the Chileans are. Unfavorable opinions are strongest, and probably least changeable, in Japan and continental Europe. Strong concerns about China's growing military power are evident in South Korea, Russia, India, and Japan. At the same time, America has a decidedly less favorable image around the world than China does. But these are just snapshots. It could be a long time, at least another decade, before the planet decides in a more definitive way whether it can accept the Chinese as the new leader of the world. If the Chinese economy stops growing, if China's one-party system of government implodes, then the Chinese will themselves destroy the opportunity they have to be globally preeminent. If political stability holds and the economy continues its spectacular performance and becomes an ever-greater share of the wealth of the world, then the Chinese, whatever their faults, probably can expect a warm embrace, much as America received as it rose to global heights in the nineteenth century.

What would it be like to live in a Chinese Century? A dark view of that possibility has to be taken seriously, if only because there is always a temptation for a newly dominant power, once the summit is reached, to settle scores. Nationalism is a live current in China, and for today's China, the "history we shall never forget," as a Chinese Web site says, is most grievously, in living memory, the history of Japanese war crimes committed on Chinese soil in the 1930s. The Rape of Nanking went on for six weeks and is still a raw wound; survivors, to this day, say things like "I really, really hate the Japanese. I was raped when I was eleven years old. I tried to commit suicide three times afterward." Others bore witness to victims being burned alive. China has published an eight-volume catalogue of victims of the atrocities that lists how the victims were killed and the Japanese army units responsible for the crimes. China and Japan, it should be noted, have improved relations in recent years, with better will extending even to the military realm—in the fall of 2007, a Chinese warship, *Shenzhen*, set sail for Japan for a four-day visit, at the invitation of the Japanese navy, to take part in joint military ceremonies between the two nations. Still, if there is anyone who needs to be worried about a Chinese Century, surely it is the Japanese, especially if a weakened America is in no position to protect them.

Those making the dark case for a Chinese Century might also argue that an imperial China is bound to treat the world just as it now treats its own peoples—with routine brutality, as in the case of Tibet. But this is not a good test. As a global empire, America on the whole has treated the world much more kindly than it treated, before it became the world's dominant power, its Native American and African-American minorities.

Does a Chinese Century mean doom and gloom for America? This is a widespread anxiety among Americans, but the case can be made that a Chinese ascension could be a useful spur to America. If America were to wake up one day and find that it was no longer number one, that the Chinese were now on top, then Americans might finally feel compelled to undertake the necessary changes that the country has so long resisted, like genuine improvements to its education and social-policy systems. It is all a question of how America adapts to the situation. Unless China's leaders decide to reverse the tack of their economic policy and shut the door on trade with the outside world, then there is nothing in the logic of China being the number-one economy that suggests that the American economy cannot continue to grow at a healthy pace, too. A richer China is a stronger bidder for the world's goods and services. America's Pacific Coast–based businesses, already profiting from the rise of China, might do especially well.

The critical assumption is that, in a transition from Washington to Beijing, a capitalism-friendly trading and monetary regime is maintained. But this is an assumption that even China's biggest critics in the West are generally willing to make. For America, there is one special hitch: In a Chinese Century, the Chinese currency, the yuan, would presumably supplant the dollar as the world's reserve currency, just as the dollar supplanted the British pound when America became the world's biggest economy. America would lose the benefit that any reserve-currency country has—the advantage, namely, of being able to borrow money relatively cheaply because of the world's preference for conducting its transactions in the reserve currency. In simplest terms, there has been a greater foreign demand for U.S. Treasury bonds than there otherwise would have been, and this demand drove down the interest rates that the Treasury was forced to pay the bondholders. Between 1980 and 2005, the United States was able to borrow money from the world at a discount of nearly 1.5 percentage points, the president of the U.S. Federal Reserve Bank of Cleveland has estimated. (Foreigners who owned U.S. assets accepted a yield on average of 4.9 percent; Americans who owned foreign assets got 6.3 percent on average.) This "liquidity premium," as the official called it, is not a small thing. But as things are now going, America is already losing its dollar hegemony in the world of the euro and other widely circulating currencies.

The optimistic view of a Chinese Century also rests on the proposition that the Chinese are largely indifferent to the cultural and religious practices of others, as the Chinese ambassador also made a point of saying in our meeting in Santiago. If China's basic economic and security interests are satisfied, its inclination may be to follow a "leave them alone" style of rule. The good news for America on this front is that Beijing presumably would let America govern itself as it wanted, leaving the country with its homegrown political institutions. The Chinese are unlikely to be a twenty-first-century version of the Spanish Inquisitors, forcing subjects to recite the teachings of Confucius at the point of a spear. Nobody would be made to eat with chopsticks; the decadent, yet quite popular, aspects of Western culture, like the availability of pornography 24/7 on the Internet, would remain untrammeled, as they would not be if, say, an Islamic Century and global Shariah law came to pass. An American family on an extended stay in Shanghai or Beijing, or even Nanjing or Hangzhou, might live comfortably in the Western-style suburban neighborhoods now cropping up for China's growing middle classes. A lover of the classical music of Europe's greatest composers, from Bach to Beethoven, might be in for an aural feast, because the Chinese are doing as much as any people anywhere in the world to keep alive this fragile musical tradition, which the regime in Beijing has decreed part of the "advanced culture" that a new China must build. The American style is famously a pastiche, but the modern Chinese style could turn out to be something of a hodgepodge, too.

Of course, there would be inconveniences. Americans involved in business dealings with China would have to make a time-zone adjustment. In the American Century, the world's traders set their clocks by Wall Street time. In a Chinese Century, Americans (and others) will get to know China's clock. A person on the East Coast of the United States will have to wait until eight p.m. his time to reach someone on the phone in Hong Kong at nine a.m. the following morning. A shift to a China-anchored global economy could give birth to a new generation of American night owls. Global maps might be changed. Instead of keeping China in the bottom right-hand corner of the map, mapmakers might shift to an Asian-centered image that would put China in the middle, flanked by Europe and Africa to the left and North America to the right.

While this may sound blithe, the point I am trying to nail home is a serious and underappreciated one: A Chinese Century is not an obvious loser for the world, nor even for America. The conviction that a Chinese Century will be a bad thing rests on the shaky premise that the Chinese will act counter to their own economic and political self-interest—which would be to ensure orderly conditions in which their own prosperity could continue. The wound to America, if it loses its hegemonic grip to China, may be more to the mind than to the pocketbook. But in *all* After America possibilities, Americans will have to make huge mental adjustments. In the case of a Chinese Century, one of the adjustments—an especially awkward one, which folks will find hard to talk about—will be a recognition that the leadership of the modern world has been won by a nonwhite group of people who come from a place remote from the origins of American civilization in the bosom of Europe. That realization alone could nourish a toxic brew of anxiety and racial prejudice and spur unhelpful inquiries along the lines of "Are they smarter than we are?" A Chinese Century, in this sense, could be the ultimate test of America's multicultural tolerance. It is easy to preach the virtues of global diversity when you occupy the world's tallest pulpit.

The arrival of a Chinese Century would not be an easy matter to spin for the history textbooks of the American schoolchild. It would represent the ascension of a civilization that embraced an extreme and brutal form of communism while Henry Luce's America was sermonizing on the virtues of the free market and popular democracy. At the same time, a burden would slip from America's shoulders—the burden of being number one. To the extent that America is disliked in the world, the sentiment has less to do with the personality qualities of "the American" than with the envies and animosities that naturally gravitate toward the leader, any leader, of the pack. Those attitudes would be directed away from Washington to Beijing, which would learn anew the eternal lesson that it is cold and very lonely on the mountaintop.

Chapter Ten

City-States

The city should produce good men, the villa good beasts.

Franco Sacchetti, fourteenth-century Florentine raconteur

Ludwig Engel is slim and elegant, with long wavy brown hair that tends to fall over his eyes. He likes to wear leather bracelets, and is the lead singer in a rock band, Eddie. He is also an analyst for DaimlerChrysler's Society and Technology Research Group—a global team of consultants, with offices in Berlin, Palo Alto, and Kyoto, whose job is to think about the future. He works alongside historians, physicists, and other specialists in a suite of glass-paneled penthouse offices on the River Spree. "We do prognosis" and have "all the freedom we need," Ludwig explained to me over the course of a Sunday evening that began with drinks at an outdoor café near the Alexanderplatz and finished at a trendy bar, a kind of concrete cave with graffiti on the walls and trash-pop on the music system, off the Oranienburger. Ludwig, who gets around Berlin on a bicycle, had ended his previous night's partying at seven-thirty in the morning at a rave inside a warehouse.

Ludwig's father was an architect and his mother a teacher of French, English, and Italian. He grew up in West Berlin and was seven years old when the Berlin Wall came down in the autumn of 1989. He began learning Chinese at age twelve, and for DaimlerChrysler he has been living and working part of the time in Beijing and Shanghai, as part of a research project on emerging elites in China. But when I turned the discussion to After America possibilities, he brought up another of his projects, relating to the evolution of global cities.

How about, he said, a future of city-states, a modern version of the city-states of ancient and medieval times? These would be places distinguished by their cosmopolitan outlooks and their role as incubators of creative thinking. The emphasis in such places would be on freedom and stimulating surroundings—on the arts, music, and culture, on intellectual life. Most important, these would be cities in which global elites, who could live anywhere on the planet, would choose to live.

This is an intriguing concept. Too much of the discussion about city-states among professional expert types focuses on the emergence of "money centers" like London, New York, Frankfurt, and Hong Kong, as hubs in a vast system of global capitalism. The possibilities for the twenty-first-century city-state are much broader and more interesting than that. Commerce has always been integral to the city, which is the natural home of the marketplace, whether the medium of exchange is the hide, the coin, or the electronic currency unit; but the city also deserves to be considered as a political-social-cultural entity, a full-fledged organic creature, in its own right. While it is possible for the world to contain, at the same time, great empires, great nation-states, and globally oriented cities, in practice the distribution of power and influence among them tends to shift with the tides of history. "France would be much more powerful if Paris were annihilated," Jean-Jacques Rousseau acidly declared in 1762, observing, "It is the big cities which exhaust a state and cause its weaknesses." After the collapse of the Roman Empire, the chaos of the medieval European world yielded not, in the first instance, to the nation-state but to the smaller and more manageable unit of the city-state. The city, not the tribe, became the primary unit of allegiance, and some of these cities, like Florence and Venice, became spectacularly inventive centers of culture, their names renowned in ports all over the "discovered" world. In an After America world, this could happen all over again—only this time on a global scale, with every continent contributing its city-states. Perhaps the new city-states, like those of old, would even develop their own "foreign" policies and maintain, in effect, their own armies or militias (as the county of Los Angeles, for example, already does). In such a world, both nation-state and empire would be passé.

If all this sounds like an impossibly distant destination, consider the forces propelling the world in this direction. The most important has to do with a matter of cartography. When "economic geographers" create their maps showing concentrations of commercial, financial, and manufacturing activity, they draw boundary lines not around nation-states but around economic megaregions, anchored to one or more large metropolises. About two-thirds of the world's economic output can be credited to forty of these regions. Some cut across nation-state lines. One example, which I explore in part 4, in the chapter on After America California, is the "bi-national" megaregion encompassing San Diego and Baja. To the north, Seattle and Vancouver, 125 miles apart, are considered part of a single northwest Pacific megaregion, dubbed "Cascadia" by the mapmakers. The economic powerhouse of this region, Microsoft, shifts labor between the two cities as if they were part of the same economic territory. So when the company had trouble obtaining visas for computer scientists from abroad to work at the corporate headquarters campus in Seattle, the scientists were sent instead to a research facility in Vancouver.

Whatever the future of Cascadia turns out to be, it probably will have little to do with the destiny of the Miami city-state region, which is heavily tied into the Latin American economy. The idea of a unified "national economy," especially for a country as economically diverse as America, is a quasi fiction perpetuated by bureaucracies trained—indeed required by national legislatures—to churn out national economic data, which they no doubt will continue to do no matter how much the world changes. A more honest system of economic accounting would focus more sharply on the megaregions, anchored by global cities. "The nation-state as an economic actor is basically toast. It was an arbitrary economic unit," Richard Florida, the global-cities expert, told me.

We were chatting in Florida's office in Toronto, which is in its own right one of the more outstanding global-city success stories of the last forty years. Florida was born in Newark and lived a number of years in Pittsburgh. He moved to Toronto in 2007, embodying the trend he described in his book *The Flight of the Creative Class.* Just as global movements of capital and goods are poorly understood when viewed through a national prism, "international migration trends," as the bureaucratic bookkeepers still like to describe them, are better grasped as relocations from the globe's economic hinterland areas to up-and-coming global-city magnets. "The major international flows of people were once coordinated by states, but today are more likely to be comprised of immigrants, transnational professionals, and tourists moving along the different intercity geographies that crisscross the planet," a group of global-cities experts concluded for a 2007 report commissioned by MasterCard. Cities and towns, for the first time in recorded history, now contain more than half the world's population—and by 2030, the urban share of the planet's population may be as high as three-fifths, according to projections by the United Nations.

The opportunistic person who can't find a decent job in depressed Tashkent, in former Soviet Central Asia, does not head for just anywhere in Russia—he or she heads for the super-magnet of Moscow, which is emerging as one of the great city-state regions of Eurasia. (There are more people in Greater Moscow than in all of the Baltic countries combined.) Moscow has always had a pull on the Russian imagination and in imperial times attracted ambitious people from Odessa on the Black Sea to Bishkek on the border with China. But today's Moscow may be the most alluring ever. In American terms, Moscow is Washington, New York, Los Angeles, and Las Vegas all rolled into one—the nexus of power, money, media, fashion, and culture, as well as organized crime and entertainments on every point of the innocent-to-carnal spectrums. While much is made of its depravity, Moscow of the early twenty-first century has become a remarkably creative place, as seen in the revival of its film industry. The provinces count for nothing—all governors serve at the pleasure of the Kremlin. Meanwhile, Moscow's petro princes, like the rulers of fifteenth-century imperial Venice, barter money and power in a complex web of relationships stretching across the capitals of Europe and Asia. In wooded suburbs heavily patrolled by private security teams, the princes are building their dachas—the Italian classical style of the late nineteenth century is an especially popular model. If Russia's population continues to wither on the demographic vine, the country could take on a truncated (if rollicking) life as a twenty-first-century reincarnation of the Muscovy city-state of old.

Other twenty-first-century city-states could emerge from the wreckage of the clash of civilizations. Consider the trajectory of the Jewish state of Israel.

The modern Jewish resettlement of Israel began as a movement away from the city, away from the suffocating urban Jewish ghettoes of Europe and the Russian empire, and toward the land on which the Zionist pioneers sweated to establish collective farms and strengthen their lungs and muscles. But the kibbutz, as a cultural and political ideal and as a practical way of life, peaked decades ago. Modern Israel's most impressive achievement, as a social-economic project, turns out to be the building of one of the Mediterranean region's most modern, vibrant, and prosperous cities: Tel Aviv. Secular and cosmopolitan, it is home to one of the world's great concentrations of high-tech industry and brainpower outside California's Silicon Valley. The Jews who have made it big in today's Israel live not on the collective farm but in the posh Tel Aviv suburb of Savyon, which is lined with million-dollar homes and resembles an upscale Long Island neighborhood. Israel's outward-looking secular Jews dominate Tel Aviv while Jerusalem, the inland capital backing into the West Bank, remains a geographically divided and politically polarized city, uneasily shared by Arabs and by a Jewish community with many of its own sectarian religious and cultural fragments. With Israeli towns in the south under periodic rocket attack from Hamas in Gaza, and towns in the north from Hezbollah, and with the Arab population in greater Israel/Palestine growing at a more rapid rate than the Jewish one, a fortresslike Tel Aviv could turn out to be the future of the Jewish state. Even as things are now, three-quarters of Israel's population of 7 million is concentrated on a narrow strip of Mediterranean coastline extending some eighty miles from Ashkelon to Haifa with Tel Aviv at the midpoint.

The city-state can be a refuge, and it also may be a better solver of modern social problems than the nation-state or empire. In part, this is a question of scale. India's political elite, at times despairing of the possibility of ever bringing efficient governance to a nation-state of 1.2 billion, talk of the merits of chopping up the country into ten large city-states ruled by president-like figures with broad writs of autonomy from New Delhi. But this is not only a question of size: The manager of the global city, with its large numbers of cosmopolitan expatriate and creative/artistic types, tends to be more in touch with the modern—especially with the latest in communications and transport—than the custodian of the nation-state. "The most future-oriented country in the world," according to the Thunderbird School of Global Management, based in Arizona, is Singapore, which of course is a city-state republic, carved out in the mid-1960s by Lee Kuan Yew and ruled by him, sternly, for decades.

Cities also tend to be more willing to learn from one another than nation-states are. Michael Bloomberg of New York City, a practical-minded technocrat who projects an image as the mayor of a global city, not merely an American one, crafted a traffic-congestion pricing plan based on the systems that London, Stockholm, and Singapore have already adopted. He personally checked out London's system and visited the mayor of Milan to hear how that city was dealing with congestion. (The minders of New York state government in Albany have for the time being stymied Bloomberg's effort.) He crafted a proposal to equip New York's skyscrapers, bridges, and other structures with wind turbines after spotting windmills in the Irish Sea off the coast of Blackpool, England. He even invited thirty mayors from around the world to a summit in New York to address global climate change. "A new urban global community is emerging in which cities are collaborating with each other on common problems while simultaneously competing with each other in the global marketplace," Bloomberg has said. "The days of sitting back and waiting for national governments to act are becoming a memory."

Perhaps the future political power brokers of the world will be the mayors of the great cities—a "G-8" of the leaders of metropolises like New York, Los Angeles, London, Paris, Hong Kong, Shanghai, and Tokyo. Perhaps the players will be more numerous—there are dozens of second-tier global cities scattered around the continents. In such a world, "postnational" Europe stands to be a major player, more so than in a multipolar order of nation-states. There is a fresh enthusiasm for city-state building projects in Europe as there is not, for the most part, for nation-state building projects. Old industrial cities like Bilbao and Stuttgart are leaders in innovative recovery projects that have caught the eyes of American urban planners eager to reinvent U.S. cities of the Rust Belt.

Global cities, to be sure, are not likely to solve global warming, any more than nation-states have been able to. That particular problem is a good argument for global government, which will be explored in the next chapter. But if the great security threat of the twenty-first century proves to be not the belligerent nation-state or the conquest-seeking empire but the nonstate terrorist with a dirty bomb, then the city-state could emerge as the most important line of protection. New York City's globally oriented police department is a good example. The NYPD operates a CIA-like global counterterrorism program consisting of more than one thousand officers, some based in overseas locations like London, Lyons, Tel Aviv, and the Persian Gulf city-states. David Cohen, the department's deputy commissioner of intelligence, is a thirty-five-year veteran of the CIA, and the department has some 275 interpreters certified in forty-five foreign languages, including Urdu, Hindi, Pashto, and Arabic. After the 2004 Madrid train bombings by Islamic terrorists, "the NYPD guy was there before the FBI was," a Bloomberg aide boasted. "We're not going to wait for anyone to protect New York," he said.

Which globally oriented cities will reach the front rank? Among those interested in the answer to that question are investors with an eye toward the next spike in real estate values. I spoke with a private-funds manager based in Toronto, who told me that the global city could be an investment concept. He was especially bullish on Vienna as a place with a central location, in terms of East–West connections, first-rate communications, and "superb culture—like one hundred out of one hundred." My own feeling is that there are going to be some surprises. The past, for one thing, is probably not a good guide. In dozens of conversations I've had on this topic with well-traveled cosmopolitan types in Asia, Europe, America, and Latin America, no one has ever mentioned Cairo, that great cradle of urban civilization, as a contender for a top-rank global city of the twenty-first century. And this is no prejudice against the Islamic world, as Istanbul, Persian Gulf city-states like Dubai and Abu Dhabi, and even Kuala Lumpur are part of this conversation. Nor has anyone volunteered Buenos Aires, even though it ascended in the nineteenth century to become one of the world's wealthiest and most ethnically diverse metropolises. Today's Buenos Aires is more fun and has more charm than Santiago, a short plane flight away, but Santiago feels more outward-looking and purposeful.

Broadly speaking, two quite different types of city-states are competing for global preeminence in the twenty-first century. There is the familiar organic type, formed in layers over long periods of time in a mostly unplanned way, of which London is a classic example. And then there is the invented city, the time-compressed, piece-by-piece execution of a central grand vision, of which

Singapore and Dubai are contemporary examples. The invented city may lack charm, not to mention soul. But it allures its visionaries by offering something that the organic city cannot—a blank canvas—and as I saw on a visit to Dubai in February 2008, the invented-city project may be especially well equipped to thrive in a globalized environment in which virtually all of the necessary inputs are available for hire and readily transportable.

Near midnight on a Monday at Vu's, a glass-walled bar on the fifty-first floor of the Emirates Tower, Dubai shows off its globally eclectic character. A group of British-based consultants are sipping white wine while discussing a local bank merger on which they are advising Dubai officials. A pudgy, middle-aged Arab man, clad in a white robe and headdress, a thick cigar clamped between his teeth, is occupying a corner table with two fair-skinned young ladies in mini-skirts and tight blouses. The drinks are being poured by dark-skinned South Asians who speak English in a British accent. The manufactured wonders of Dubai twinkle in the darkness below: Burj Al Arab, the seven-star hotel that resembles a sail, built by the British architect Tom Wright on an island re-claimed from the sea; the Mall of the Emirates, with its famous indoor ski slope; and DP World, which includes the world's largest man-made port. Beyond the city lights is open desert—a template for the most ambitious under-taking of all: Dubailand. Plans call for a $70 billion development, including theme parks, sports stadiums, and a wellness resort, stretching over 3 billion square feet of land.

On the day after my visit to Vu's, I met with Soud Ba'alawy, a member of the inner circle of advisors around the ruler of Dubai, His Highness Sheikh Mo-hammed bin Rashid al-Maktoum. Sheikh Mo, as he has been nicknamed, lives in a palace in the center of town on wooded grounds stocked with well-fed pea-cocks. He succeeded his father on the throne and is the force behind Dubai's spectacular development over the past fifteen years. The kingdom has grown from a population of nearly 700,000 in 1995 to more than 1.4 million. Only 20 percent of those are citizens of the United Arab Emirates (UAE), of which Dubai is a part; the rest are foreign guest workers. Soud Ba'alawy made no apologies for the fact that Dubai is not a Western-style democracy or, for that matter, any kind of democracy at all, even though it is a good deal more easy-going than the neighboring theocratic kingdom of Saudi Arabia, whose women, clad in black burkas, frequent Dubai's glitzy shopping places. "With a monarchy and a meritocracy, you can achieve anything in the world," he told me. Our meeting was on the thirty-eighth floor of the Emirates Tower. He held white prayer beads in his left hand and at one point excused himself to retreat to his office for prayer. A former Citibank vice president, Ba'alawy helped oversee Dubai's investments in sectors including finance, health care, biotechnology, media, and real estate. Unlike Abu Dhabi, its fraternal UAE city-state, Dubai is no longer rich in oil. "We had to invent a purpose for living," Ba'alawy said when I prodded him on the motivation for Dubai. Why, I persisted, is the scale of everything done in Dubai, like the Dubailand project, so enormous? He answered that there is so much media noise generated by the political troubles of the Middle East that a project like the building of Dubai has to be done on a grand scale to register a global impact, to break through the image barrier of the region. And there is also, he allowed, a measure of Arab competitive pride. With Dubai, "we have led the Arab world in megaprojects," he told me.

The invented city is typically the creation of a monarch or some such person possessed of a grand vision and the land and labor to execute it. An early 1700s iteration of this model was created by Peter the Great of Russia. When Tsar Peter (not yet "the Great") first set foot on the soggy marshlands where the Neva River flows into the Baltic Sea, he had in mind a fortress to guard against the advance of the Swedish army into the Russian heartland. But the vision soon expanded into one of a commercial port with a capital city that would be a bridge to the modernizing Europe that Peter so much admired. An Italian architect, Domenico Trezzini, was brought in to supervise construction as the tsar's master of building, construction, and fortification. Unskilled peasants along with carpenters and stonecutters were conscripted as construction laborers from the distant reaches of the Russian empire, including Siberia, and they worked on a subsistence allowance for six-month stints, after which, if they were lucky enough to have survived, they could return home. "Workers lived on damp ground in rough, crowded, filthy huts. Scurvy, dysentery, malaria and other diseases scythed them down in droves," the historian Robert K. Massie recounted. (He pegged the death estimate at twenty-five or thirty thousand.

Whatever the precise figure, St. Petersburg well earned its reputation as a "city built on bones," Massie noted.) When the first phase of the building was completed, few among the Russian nobility wanted to give up the familiar comforts of Moscow for such a desolate spot. So Peter forced the nobles to move and even dictated the "English style" of their new houses on the left bank of the Neva. The new residents refused to be consoled, not even by the elegant flower beds laid out around the city by French gardeners. "Petersburg will not endure after our time. May it remain a desert," a Russian princess grumbled. As for a triumphant Peter, who viewed Moscow as fatally backward compared to the great cities of Europe, he believed he had found his "Eden." Time has vindicated his megalomania: Russians eventually took the city to heart, even if it was "the most abstract and contrived city on the entire earthly sphere," as Dostoevsky called it in the mid-nineteenth century. Foreign tourists invariably compare the place, with its Italian-style palaces and bridge-spanned canals, to Venice.

The Dubai invented-city formula offers some parallels, with adjustments made for the age of the jet plane. The pool of itinerant construction labor is drawn mostly from the poor villages and towns of the Indian subcontinent, with a growing contribution from the vast reservoirs of China. The workers, all men, who have left their families behind to earn money to send back home, live in camps on the outskirts of town, far removed from the beaches and tourist attractions. At dawn, small white buses take them to their jobs; in the evening, they are ferried back for dinner and rest. Early one evening I paid an unarranged visit to a large camp known as Sonapur. Foul-smelling water from an overflowed septic tank spilled across the road outside the concrete-block dormitories in which the workers lived. I walked around an open garbage Dumpster and into a courtyard strung with clotheslines for the men's laundry. I had been warned about aggressive bosses at the camps, on the watch for intruders, but no one tried to stop me. In one small dorm room, I found six men huddled on the floor, preparing their modest dinner on portable gas stoves. They slept on double bunk beds. This was a work crew from the northwest Indian state of Rajasthan. They spoke Hindi and some broken English. I had expected to find young men, up to the rigors of manual work in the open desert, where temperatures regularly reach above one hundred degrees Fahrenheit, but this group looked middle-aged. "Subash" told me that he was thirty-two, with a wife and two children, and had been living in the camps, off and on, over a period of eight years. An unskilled construction worker, he said, starts off at a salary of $250 per month.

Troubling stories are told about the camps and treatment of the workers. The bosses, I had heard, routinely confiscated the passports of arriving workers, and workers sometimes died of sunstroke in the glare of the desert sun. Subash insisted that conditions were improving as the Dubai government, faced with complaints from workers and outside human-rights groups, were riding herd on the contractors in charge of the camps. Salaries were being paid regularly, passports were returned on request, and there was even a toll-free Dubai government number to call to register complaints of abuse. This sounded heartening, but on the day after my visit to the Sonapur camp, I read a newspaper item about a labor protest staged by workers who lived farther out, in camps in the adjacent city-state of Sharjah, and were bused to work on projects in Dubai. The workers said they were starving, as their bosses had not paid them salaries for five months.

The foreign-worker ladder in Dubai scales all the way up to the suit-and-tie likes of David Knott, a friendly fifty-nine-year-old Australian recruited by the Sheikh Mo team to preside as the top regulator of Dubai's expanding financial-services industry. (Goldman Sachs, Morgan Stanley, and the Carlyle Group all have offices there.) Knott is a former chairman of the Australian Securities and Investment Commission. We chatted over coffee in his comfy and immaculate office suite. He told me that he was drawn to Dubai "by the ambition of this place" and the opportunity to draw up a new regulatory scheme on "a clean sheet of paper." (He chose a model based on the Financial Services Authority in London.) "I'm here essentially as a guest worker," he told me, with no expectation of ever becoming an Emirati citizen. But the trade-off, he added, is that he paid no income taxes, in either Australia or the UAE. No taxation, no representation.

Knott worked out of a complex designed to resemble Canary Wharf in London, the showy development that combines business offices and shopping and eating pleasures in one compound. This, too, is part of the Dubai formula. Large chunks of the city, which is divided into clusters, are imitations of what has been patterned elsewhere. It is this sort of imported artifice that makes Dubai the butt of scorn. Before I visited, I spoke with Samer Shehata, a native of Egypt who is a professor of Arab politics at Georgetown University in Washington, D.C. "Dubai is not a society," Shehata said. "A society is where people have connections to each other. Dubai is simply an amalgamation of individuals who are in a place for their short-term economic needs. You don't know you are even in an Arab country to some extent."

While it is true that Dubai does not feel like a traditional Arab milieu, Sheikh Mo is not trying to create (or simulate) that kind of environment, except in some of the theme-park exhibits planned for Dubailand, like "Sahara Kingdom," an "Arabian legend and folklore-themed development inspired by the tales of 1001 Nights." The point is to create a global place that will serve as a magnet for talented, ambitious, highly cosmopolitan people to engage in "wealth creation," Soud Ba'alawy explained to me. "We are talking about global citizens." On these terms, Dubai appears to be succeeding, and doing so at the expense of others. Houston's reputation as the preeminent global energy-services capital suffered when David Lesar, the chief executive officer of Halliburton, decided to move his headquarters to Dubai. Lesar, a native of Wisconsin, said that Dubai was better situated than Houston for the future of Halliburton's business, which was gravitating toward the Eastern Hemisphere. Months later, Houston-based Baker Hughes, Halliburton's competitor in the oil-services business, announced the opening of a twenty-five-acre manufacturing and operations center in Dubai, to serve as its "Middle East Asia Pacific" headquarters. Lesar, who worked out of the pink-tinged Al Moosa Tower on Sheikh Zayed Road, in the city center, declined to see me when I was in Dubai. However, I spied his photograph on the front page of the *Emirates Business 24/7* newspaper, for which he writes an "exclusive column."

A well-connected American expatriate businessman who lives in Dubai with his family told me that he has made his peace with the place, which he described as a more fun, looser version of Singapore. Dubai "looks like the West, smells like the West," but "don't forget, this is a dictatorship," where phones are routinely tapped, he pointed out. "I don't mind. My kids are safe. The trains run on time. They're not killing people." He listed other positives: His family is actively involved in a local Christian church; there is not much crime; the Sheikh Mo regime makes sure that prostitutes who enter the country are checked for AIDS; Jewish businessmen face no hassles. Al-Qaeda types were known to use Dubai as a convenient place to conference—"it's hard to meet people in Afghanistan"—but the plus side is that the terrorists may, if only for practical reasons, spare the city from attack: "You don't want to piss in the soup." Americans who believe that only a democracy can create a desirable place to live are "naïve," he told me. "Dubai is becoming a destination—this is becoming part of the real world."

Nor is Dubai only about conspicuous consumption. Another of Sheikh Mo's megaprojects is known as Dubai Healthcare City—envisioned as a cluster of hospitals, teaching institutes, wellness spas, and hotels (five star and three star) for "medical tourists," including the families of patients in town for treatment, along with a tax-free zone for pharmaceutical companies and medical-equipment firms. Patients are expected to come from all over the Middle East and possibly Eastern Europe. In this case, the brand of global excellence is Harvard Medical School, the anchor for the first phase of the project, which features a four-hundred-bed teaching hospital as well as a Harvard-operated institute for postgraduate training of physicians, nurses, and research scientists. Partners Harvard Medical International, a division of the medical school, is playing a leading role both as a consultant for the design of the hospital and as a screener of candidates to chair the medical departments. On my visit, the teaching hospital, scheduled to open in 2011, was in an early stage of construction. I later talked about the project over the telephone with Andrew A. Jeon, the CEO of Partners Harvard Medical International. Jeon is a certified pediatric anesthesiologist with an MBA from Harvard Business School. He is based in the Boston area, where he was born in 1951, but joked that for more than four years he has been commuting to Dubai as some in Boston do to Manhattan. As for the Dubai teaching hospital, he first told me that the model was Massachusetts General Hospital, the world-renowned Harvard-affiliated facility in Boston. Then he jettisoned that comparison: "We are not trying to replicate anything. This supersedes anything that I have seen in any hospital in the world." For example, a patient in intensive care at MGH has to be wheeled through four buildings in order to get an MRI or a CAT scan; the Dubai facility is set up to do the test at the patient's bedside or just down the hall.

In the same vein in which David Knott raved to me about the prospect of building from scratch a world-class financial regulatory system in Dubai, Jeon enthused about "the beauties of having a green field hospital like this." He recalled the nightmare of making improvements to Harvard's Brigham & Women Hospital in Boston, of which he used to be chief of operations. That hospital dates its origins back to 1832. I asked him whether Harvard had any qualms about taking the lead role on a project commissioned by a hereditary monarch. Sheikh Mo is "a change agent," Jeon replied. "There are certain advantages to working in a benign monarchy. It cuts a lot of the red tape out." I asked whether the construction workers from the labor camps would have access to the hospital that Harvard is designing. "The guiding philosophy of HMI," according to its mission statement, "is that every citizen of the world should have access in their own community to quality health care of a world standard." "They can certainly come in. I don't know if they can afford it," Joen replied. HMI, he noted, inspected the labor camps from which the hospital construction project was drawing its workers and determined that the camps passed muster. The nursing staff is likely to consist mostly of expats from the Philippines and India; some of the positions for doctors, he said, may be filled by Arab Americans eager to return to the region. "People from these cultures want to return home—the U.S. is not necessarily the most wonderful place to live if you are not a Caucasian, blue-eyed male," Jeon said.

The global economic crisis of 2008 did not spare Dubai or other city-states. At the end of the year, ten months after my visit, Dubai was suffering from ailments that included an imploded real estate development sector. Demand for imported labor had slacked off. Predictions of Dubai's utter demise, though, seem too dire. Although modern Dubai began as the ruling family's grand vision, the vision would not have worked had the city-state not found a niche in the regional economy of the Middle East and the broader global economy. Easily overlooked amid the steep decline in property prices, for example, are the trade and other practical ties that continue to bind Dubai to Iran, much as Hong Kong is bound to mainland China. With thousands of Iranian businesses established in Dubai, in part to evade sanctions on Iran from the United States, "the best place to do business in Iran," an Iranian businessman told a *New York Times* reporter, "is in Dubai."

The Dubai concept lends itself to replication. None of the essential ingredients on which it is based are in short supply: visionary (or egomaniacal) autocrats; world-class expatriate talent in search of new challenges and tax-sheltered income; world-class nonprofit institutions, like Harvard, eager to make a social-purpose imprint; vast pools of unskilled migrant laborers, for whom life in a grungy labor camp in a foreign country is still better than anything available back home. An exact copy, of course, is unlikely—for one thing, no dictator worth his name could bear being accused of plagiarizing the work of another. But the template could be transferred to other places for customized adjustments. There might be, indeed, a spirited competition among the new crop of invented cities to score the most amazing global "first." That rivalry is already under way between Dubai and Abu Dhabi, with Lord Norman Foster's commission to build Masdar City, the world's first all-green, renewable-energy city. Masdar City is an effort to create no less than an urban prototype for the twenty-first century, not simply a showcase for the ecologically state-of-the-art. "One day, all cities will be built like this," the planners say. Foster also has done eye-catching projects for the dictator Nursultan Nazarbayev's invented city of Astana, in Kazakhstan. Perhaps the invented city-state can succeed in the lands in which the modern nation-state largely has been a failure.

For the likes of David Knott and Andrew Jeon, the emerging global city-state, no matter what form it takes, is a boon. With their prestigious credentials and track records of success, they are exactly the kind of people who can find creative and well-paying work in just about any of these metropolises. A hard question is what happens to the poor in a new order defined by the global city. Dubai has been able to evade that question, with its tight controls on who gets to live and work there, but other cities will have to deal with it. As the planet becomes more urban, the population of the shantytowns keeps growing. By the count of UN-HABITAT, a United Nations agency, the total population of urban slums rose from 715 million in 1990 to approximately 1 billion in 2007 and may reach 1.4 billion by 2020. As dangerous and as unhealthy as conditions in these slums may be, they nevertheless tend to offer more economic opportunity, a better chance to escape from poverty, than life in the rural village. At the same time, many of these slums are located in image-conscious cities that aspire to be global powerhouses—and that do not necessarily welcome a reputation as havens for slum dwellers. A confrontation is brewing.

This is an age-old problem that the city, even at the height of its prestige and prosperity and creative powers, has never been able to solve. The urban poor, the *poveri*, were easily the largest social grouping in the city-states of fifteenth-century Renaissance Italy, and they were widely despised by their better-offs. "If the lowest orders of society earn enough food to keep them going from day to day, then they have enough," one contemporary said with typical hardness of heart. "Our main evidence about them," a historian has noted of the urban masses of city-states like Florence, "comes from court records: a stream of tales of violence and degradation, illiteracy, open and universally condoned exploitation, and a latent hatred which on rare occasions burst out in open revolt."

The question of whether the poor—the slum dweller—will fare any better in the global city of the twenty-first century will be answered in places like Bangalore. In America, Bangalore, also known in India as Bengaluru, evokes the image of the low-cost Indian call center. It is the symbol of an information-age disembodied place that seems to exist only as a voice, on the other end of a telephone connection, answering questions about your credit-card billing statement. Bangalore is also well known in the global high-tech community as an outsourcing center for multinationals like Microsoft, Cisco, and Germany's SAP Labs. But the city is not satisfied with this role as an appendage of the machine of global capitalism. Bangalore wants to be one of the engines: It aims to become one of the twenty-first century's preeminent global cities.

Bangalore, I found on a 2008 visit, has quite a long way to go before arriving at the destination of a cosmopolitan haven in which the twenty-first century's global citizens might consider making a home. Spectacular traffic jams, the equal of New Delhi's, clog its thoroughfares, where the traffic police wear air-filter masks to protect their lungs from the exhaust fumes of three-wheeled auto-rickshaws, mopeds, and sleek sedans. Pedestrians cross the street at great peril, and then take good care to avoid stepping into the craters along the sidewalks—or onto the homeless people and stray dogs stretched out on the filthy pavement. In an alley adjacent to a fancy coffee and pastry shop, street vendors prepare a tantalizing variety of local food specialties at a small fraction of the cost of the fare indoors, but Western stomachs, like my own, are well advised to stay away. At least a fifth of Bangalore's 8 million inhabitants lack proper homes; high-income residents of the Koramangala neighborhood live adjacent to one of the city's largest slums, an area of tin sheds and other makeshift homes illegally inhabited by squatters. No wall or fence demarcates the slum, a typical entry point for the poor migrant from the countryside needing some place to start a new life. The key to the slum dweller of an Indian city is a condition of poverty—the slum dweller is not, as might be thought, necessarily a member of a lower caste. Nor, for that matter, are the slums devoid of economic activity—the immense Dharavi slum of Mumbai, said to be Asia's largest, is well known for its "vibrant, informal economy" of shops and bakeries, amid the stench from open sewers.

Bangalore is the capital of the southwest Indian state of Karnataka. It is located on an inland plateau, favoring the city with a mild climate, and is several days' drive from the Arabian Sea. It was a provincial backwater during colonial times, featuring little more than a British army base and lacking the imperial prestige of Calcutta and Bombay. Even in the early decades after independence, Bangalore enjoyed a reputation mainly as a sleepy retirement town for Indian army officers. Nevertheless, there was, beneath this surface, a foundation for grander prospects. Bangalore had been part of the ancient kingdom of Mysore, which became a princely state under British rule, and the Mysore royal family were known in British times as responsible managers of the state, as "builders of colleges and hospitals and irrigation systems." Postindependence, India's new rulers in New Delhi made Bangalore the hub of India's nascent space-research program, and the city became a haven for the aircraft industry and the home of various scientific institutes. As India finally began to retreat from Fabian-style soft socialism and open itself to the cutthroat world of global capitalism, Bangalore, more than most other places in the country, had something to offer the Western-based multinationals in search of an educated labor force available for wages many times lower than those demanded by workers in Europe and America. By the mid-1990s, notwithstanding persistent power-grid failures, contaminated tap water, and a year's wait for a land phone line, Bangalore was already a software base for Motorola, AT&T, Oracle, and Hewlett-Packard. The American software consultant Robert Binder, after a visit to Bangalore in 1995, saluted the programmers at the Motorola facility for the "incredible performance" of designing software with a measured failure rate on the order of one per million lines of code.

The story of Bangalore is often taken in the West as a metaphor for the rising nation-state of India, but this may well be a mistake. Bangalore's rise does not necessarily foretell the rise of the rest of India, because the city has certain special qualities apart from the superb technical skills of its workers, which can be found in other Indian cities as well. Bangalore's most precious characteristic—instrumental to its global-city ambitions—is its cosmopolitanism. This is the trait that makes Bangalore as good a bet as any other metropolis in India, including the more obvious possibility of Mumbai, the home of Bollywood and the powerhouse in finance, to become a front-rank global city. Most Indian cities, in this linguistically divided nation, tend to be magnets for the people of their surrounding regions. Bangalore has taken a different turn, drawing a remarkable three-fifths of its residents from outside Karnataka. Not only Hindi and English but also languages like Kannada, Tamil, and Malayalam are spoken on the streets. Restaurants specialize in cuisines from Punjab, Gujarat, West Bengal, and Kerala, as well as a variety of international ones. Bangalore is gaining a reputation as an entrepreneurial, wide-open place in which ambitious and talented people from diverse backgrounds can have a future. Even talented Indians with the means and the opportunity to make it in places like America are drawn to Bangalore, where they are running their own companies, not working as managers for Western ones. One of the magnates of the Bangalore technology scene, Azim Premji, the force behind Wipro, was born in Mumbai to an Ismaili Muslim family and attended Stanford University as an undergraduate in electrical engineering. This shift in power—from Western-based multinationals to homegrown companies—is a critically important one, as it gives Bangalore a chance to exert more control over its destiny.

"Yes, we were at the low end of the tail in terms of IT services. But I think the tail is beginning to wag the dog," one of Bangalore's young civic leaders, Ramesh Ramanathan, told me in a conversation in his office in the city center. Handsome and energetic, with a Rolodex of contacts at universities and think tanks around the world, Ramanathan is the founder of the Janaagraha Centre for Citizenship and Democracy, a citizens' group that works in coalitions with business and political leaders to try to reach consensus on issues relating to Bangalore's long-term development. He is also a rarity in today's Bangalore—a native of the city, born there in 1963. "There is nothing to stop Bangalore from growing," he told me, noting projections that the population will triple, topping 25 million, within twenty years. With a few keystrokes on his laptop, he called up a chart estimating that Bangalore will hit 37 million air passengers in 2012, up from 11 million in 2008 and 5 million in 2005.

Bangalore is now making the decisions, on air and ground transportation and related infrastructure projects, that will guide its development for years to come. The temptation, Ramanathan said, will be to short-circuit the process, which ought to include the voices of both the poor and the business elite, with autocratic-like edicts. Splicing his conversation with references to global-cities experts like Saskia Sassen of Columbia University, he told me that he wants Bangalore to be a model for the kind of global city in which everyone is a participant in its making, not a place "engineered from the top down." His ideal of Bangalore would be a kind of anti-Shanghai. "You cannot talk about a global city without graffiti on the walls," he said. When he told me that he was studying lessons from the European and American experience of building great cities, I suggested he read *The Power Broker*, Robert Caro's monumental biography of Robert Moses, the builder of so many of New York City's parks and roads. While it is easy enough to criticize Moses as an autocrat, his detractors tend to skate over the awkward question of whether New York needed a Moses-type figure to execute a modern vision of the city.

As Bangalore develops, as land prices continue to appreciate, another temptation will be to raze the slums, especially those closest to the center, to make way for apartment buildings for the middle and upper classes and for corporate office parks, pricey restaurants, and shopping malls. Technically speaking, the slum dwellers have no legal standing to prevent this—they are, after all, occupiers of land to which they have no title. Some city planners, no doubt, will make an argument for such action, as has been taken in Mumbai. "The mantra" among all too many urban planners in India "is that there are no places for slums in a global city," Bharati Chaturvedi, a longtime activist on behalf of improving India's slums, told me. Proof that this is wrong, she said, is offered by New York City. Indian cities like Bangalore would be lucky to have slums on the level of those that can be found in Brooklyn: "A world-class city can have slums. It does not have to be shitty housing. They could just be places where poor people live." If the city-center slums are razed, she pointed out, the poor will rebuild their shantytowns farther on the outskirts—and be even farther away from their jobs. Her model solution for the slums of Bangalore is to improve them through public investments in sanitation facilities and other vital infrastructure, coupled with the award of long-term land rights to the squatters. "You don't have to spoon-feed the poor" of the slums—you need to give them an environment in which families can work and educate their children, she said. She's more hopeful of this kind of solution being achieved in Bangalore than in most other Indian cities, because of the ethos of "corporate social responsibility" among Bangalore's rising class of globally minded entrepreneurs. "Commerce is so politically correct," she said. But she recognizes that things could go the other way. To lay claim to their place in the new global cities, she said, the poor must "fight for their rights." As ever.

How might Americans—and the territory on which Americans live—fare in a world of global cities? The answer, on the whole, is a hopeful one. One of the myths of Western history is that the city is a quintessentially European creation. True enough, the story generally begins with Athens and moves its way up to fifteenth-century Renaissance Florence and late-sixteenth-century Elizabethan London. But when America enters the picture, it does so in a large way, at first in imitation of the European model, with cities like colonial Boston and Philadelphia, but later with its own highly original contributions, like Los Angeles, which today ranks with New York and Chicago as an America front-rank global city. These three are likely to do well no matter what shape an After America world takes—assuming that global warming does not put New York under water. In the second tier, San Francisco, Miami, and Atlanta face favorable prospects in a world defined by global cities. Less obviously, Las Vegas, that most invented of all American cities, may also have a good future in this kind of world. (It simplifies things, but not all that much, to say that Las Vegas was the invention of Bugsy Siegel and his fellow mobsters, as Hollywood told the story in *Bugsy*.) Although Las Vegas has been eclipsed by China's Macau region as the world's number-one gambling locale, today's Las Vegas is not only about gambling. Robert Lang, the codirector of the Metropolitan Institute at Virginia Tech University, shared with me his PowerPoint presentation called "Is Las Vegas a World City?" Yes, the paper argued, because "LV is the world's largest ad-hoc exchange for business information" as a result of its preeminent role as a meeting place for global conventioneers. The numbers are impressive: 150,000 folks attending the annual International Consumer Electronics Show, 85,000 the World of Concrete Exposition, 15,000 the International Wireless Communications Expo. Lang's conclusion is that Las Vegas can succeed as a "major world city" if it can address its "critical" land and water shortages.

Or perhaps some other place will make a global mark, as New Orleans did with jazz and Memphis with rhythm and blues music in the twentieth century. The end of the American era of global dominance need not be the end of the American flair for urban creativity. There is really only one overarching threat to the global city as a project constructed on American ground: the danger of mounting nativist sentiments. As the historian Peter Hall points out in his encyclopedic *Cities in Civilization*, the outsider—in today's term, the foreign immigrant—is essential to stir the pot for the creative success of a city. This has been true for millennia. Thus, the so-called *metoiki*, or resident aliens, of ancient Athens, who paid a special tax to live permanently in the city, were crucial to its financial, artistic, scientific, and economic vitality. "They played precisely the role that, much later, would be played so outstandingly by another group of Mediterranean migrants: the Jews in Vienna, London, New York, Los Angeles, and a score of other places," Hall observed. "People who are socially 'marginal'— either because they are still young, or because they are social outsiders—may prove more creative, because they do not fully subscribe to the dominant value system."

Americans generally are not in the habit of paying much attention to the goings-on in the land of their neighbor to the north, but if they cast an eye on Toronto, they would see how relevant Hall's insight is to the global city of today. Until the 1970s, Toronto was a dull, provincial town of a predominantly Anglo-European character. Since then, the city has been transformed by massive waves of immigration from Asia, Africa, and the Caribbean. By the mid-1990s, Toronto was a city of 4 million with a fair claim to being "the world's most multi-cultural city," as boosters advertised the place. Remarkably, no one ethnic group represented more than 20 percent of the population—Toronto combined large numbers of Chinese, Vietnamese, Indians, and Pakistanis from Asia, along with

Greeks, Hungarians, Italians, and Estonians from Europe; Somalis, Ethiopians, and others from Africa; and Trinidadians, Jamaicans, and others from the Caribbean. Toronto also laid claim to being North America's safest piece of multicultural urban real estate, and there was no reason to challenge that assertion, either. These days, a remarkable 49 percent of Toronto's population is foreign-born, compared to 35 percent for Greater Los Angeles and 27 percent for London.

Toronto's reputation as an "international microcosm," as the writer Robert J. Kasher put it, is essential to its global-city hopes. When I visited in a chilly week in January 2008, I toured the MaRS Centre, a modern new building in the heart of downtown, on the site of the old Toronto General Hospital. The center is the anchor for BioDiscovery Toronto, the city's initiative, assisted by federal funding from Ottawa, to become a world-class participant in biomedical research. The biomedical field is truly a global one, both a competitive and a collaborative effort playing out in a single, planetwide arena. The "winners" will be the particular places—not really the countries—establishing themselves as innovation hubs. Everything in this field depends on talent—and the search for talent, naturally, is a global one. So far, Toronto's recruiters have lured scientists from the United States as well as China, India, Korea, Japan, Great Britain, France, Germany, Spain, and Russia. One of the stars is Thomas James Hudson, the Canadian-born genome scientist who spent much of his career at the Massachusetts Institute of Technology. The recruiters are helped by the fact that virtually all of those lured to Toronto can find someone to speak about science in their native tongue.

Across Lake Ontario from Toronto is Detroit, which had a creative golden age a century ago but has never recovered from the race riots of the 1960s and from the failure of vision of the later-generation managers of its once-preeminent auto industry. Unless industrial-age cities like Detroit, Cleveland, Pittsburgh, and St. Louis can find new functions that connect them to the twenty-first-century global economy, they are likely to deteriorate even more. Such places may be destined to be America's "Midlands," as Rob Lang told me. Their most promising young people can be expected to move to America's rising global cities—or perhaps, with other talented Americans, to the global cities thriving outside the United States. On the principle that "anywhere is home in the twenty-first century," and with the likelihood that gifted young Americans, as they rise in their careers, "will be offered very attractive packages to relocate not just to another state, but to another country," the business consultants Edie Weiner and Arnold Brown have predicted that "it is quite possible that, for the first time, the U.S. will begin to see a significant proportion of its own leave the U.S. and emigrate elsewhere." The out-migration of Americans is especially likely to reach high numbers if English remains the lingua franca for the global elite, given the reluctance many Americans have to learn a second language.

A first thing to expect in a world of global cities is a shift in primary identity from the nation-state to the city-state. As it has been in earlier ages, city-statism would become the new nationalism, the masses' new flag of allegiance. This could make for some passionate rivalries, a political version of the (not always peaceful) competition between Boston Red Sox and New York Yankees baseball fans. (Full disclosure: I'm a lifelong Red Sox fan.) The city-state in history is not necessarily a serene creature, as the warring Italian city-states showed, but today's emerging city-states are not as freighted with considerations of "hard power" as modern nation-states are. An age of city-states, for this reason, has the potential of being a less violent one than the age of the nation-state and of the empire. It also might make for a more even distribution of power: It is much easier to imagine a world in which twenty-five city-states are all big players than a world in which twenty-five nations are roughly equal in clout.

It is possible that global city-states would all come to resemble one another, that there would be a bland shopping-mall-like homogeneity to this kind of era. But I suspect that things will turn out otherwise as city-states compete with one another for brand identification. This is already happening in Europe, with global-city competitors like Vienna, Barcelona, and Berlin carving out contrasting identities based on their distinctly different cultural styles and histories. In medieval times, the Italian city-states also developed sharply different styles of politics, architecture, and economic and cultural life—in part because the cities were hyperconscious of one another. They celebrated their differences, as might a twenty-first-century cadre of global city-states.

The grandest prize in this contest will be awarded to the city-state that can lay claim to the most prestige. There are any number of ways, from the crude to the subtle, to measure prestige—one being the place deemed most desirable by the world's superrich. The spirited competition between twenty-first-century London and New York is waged on this plane. "London has bypassed New York and has become the capital city maybe of the world in some respects," David Rubenstein, the managing director of the Carlyle Group, the private-equity firm based in Washington, D.C., told me as we chatted one afternoon in his Pennsylvania Avenue office. A Jewish-American native of Baltimore, he currently travels outside the United States about 125 days of the year, making business trips to the major cities of Europe as well as places like Hong Kong, Tokyo, Shanghai, Beijing, Singapore, and Dubai. London is ahead of New York, he explained, because the world's wealthiest people would prefer to own a home there—and that is mainly because the tax regime is less onerous. For one thing, tax authorities are less likely to inquire into the sources of a Londoner's wealth. "I don't know that we will get rid of nation-states and national pride," Rubenstein said, "but those people who can afford to be global citizens will be an important part of the global economy because they can move their assets so quickly. And a large part of this group lives in London."

History supports this correlation between a city's prestige and its hospitality to rich people. While the rich do not in themselves make a city interesting and innovative, it is difficult to think of a city that managed to be vibrant and cosmopolitan while at the same time being unwelcoming to the wealthy. Post-Soviet Moscow, with its streets crammed with Porsches, is a good deal more interesting than Soviet-era Moscow; the same can be said of Shanghai after the Chinese Communist Party's economic reforms of the 1970s and 1980s. Of course, geography also matters. Rubenstein pointed out that London is better situated than New York, time-zone-wise, for flying to the Middle East or Asia. And if the balance of economic activity continues to shift in the direction of Asia, then Hong Kong, which is already a global money center in the front rank, could emerge as *the* city, ahead of London and New York, for the world's superclass migrants.

In the late nineteenth century, a spirited competition between raw, fast-growing American cities like New York and Chicago, each with a nouveau riche population eager to prove its civic-mindedness, was an enormous boon to private philanthropy. The magnificent New York Public Library on Fifth Avenue in midtown Manhattan was launched with a bequest of the private fortune of the state's onetime governor Samuel J. Tilden—and the library's extensive branch system was paid for by the steel magnate Andrew Carnegie. The New York elite of that time was painfully conscious of New York's cultural deficits compared not only to older and more refined Boston, the original "Athens of America," but also to London and Paris across the Atlantic. Similar sentiments spurred the remarkable wave of civic projects—in this case, many of them involving cathedrals—mounted by the city-states of Renaissance Italy. This history suggests that a twenty-first-century competition between global cities for preeminence could be a fresh spur for philanthropy. The key, as ever, is the nouveau riche, the sharp-toothed strivers nowadays found in cities like Moscow, Shanghai, and Mumbai and also, less obviously, in cities like Saigon and Kiev. While the nouveau riche may start off as vulgar consumers of luxury products, from sports cars to caviar, that appeal to their senses and impress their peers, at some point it occurs to at least some among them that their wealth also creates the opportunity for a more enduring and ennobling contribution to humankind—and specifically to the cities in which they made their mark. The age of the city-state could reap a public harvest of the billions piled up in the quest for private gain.

City-states also will gain prestige to the degree that they can show themselves to be efficient models of governance—ideally scaled to the competitive rigors of the twenty-first century as not too small and not too big. A benchmark example is Greater Stuttgart, the Verband Stuttgart region created by a German federal law in 1994. The Stuttgart area has long been known globally as a center of automobile design and manufacturing; the shift to metro government is part of a plan to enable the region to become a twenty-first-century global haven for research, design, and production of clean-energy technologies. The law established a regional assembly of members elected by citizens—a kind of metropolitan authority—to take charge of planning for housing development, public transport, and major roads, parks, and even sites for wind-power plants. The region encompasses 179 municipalities and five counties and has a population exceeding 2.5 million. The Stuttgart model of the greater metropolis as the whole—erasing artificial boundaries between a city center and its suburbs and "edge" cities, on the frontier—offers a paradigm of practical use to American cities, which have been slow to reconfigure themselves in this manner, noted Bruce Katz, a cities expert at the Brookings Institution in Washington. The future of America, he likes to say, lies not in its small towns and not in its urban cores, but in its metro units. One leading-edge U.S. urban region that has grasped this principle is metropolitan Denver, which has undertaken regionally financed projects, including a light-rail system.

Political science suggests that public institutions like Greater Stuttgart's regional assembly will vie in a Darwinian way to prove their fitness by taking on additional responsibilities, thus expanding their power base. A sure sign that the city-state model is gaining momentum will be expansion of the city's portfolio, from tasks like infrastructure planning to other duties, like counterterrorism, typically lodged in the nation-state. For a true golden age of city-states to develop, they will have to articulate a vision that transcends competition between them, as healthy as that may be, and takes into account the need for mechanisms that promote cooperation. Small steps toward such a vision are starting to be taken—for example, with the establishment in 1999 of the Global Cities Dialogue, an initiative involving hundreds of mayors from around the world that is focused on building an "equal-opportunity Information Society" for all urban citizens. The promotion of democratic "electronic government" is one major aim. There is, at least not yet, no global-cities version of a United Nations, and perhaps there never will be. Still, one of the consequences of globalization is a greater consciousness among cities that they face common problems—housing, traffic congestion, security—and can benefit from sharing their experiences and cataloguing what works and what does not. Examples are piling up of city-states copying one another—and of nation-states taking their cues from what city-states do. Michael Bloomberg's New York City set a global marker with a law enacted in 2002 to prohibit smoking in public places—including bars and restaurants—and places of employment. New York's action boosted the drive for smoking bans in European nations, and six years later Mexico City, one of the world's largest cities, with a population approaching 20 million, passed a smoke-free law.

A new era of city-states would have many blemishes. The democratic-governance model exemplified by the Stuttgart region might not prevail—there is bound to be a tendency, in the interest of greater efficiency, to lodge city-state projects in the hands of autocrats. City-states also have a history of breeding oligarchies. This was the unfortunate path that the Italian city-states tended to follow. As noted by a historian, "The small ruling councils of Renaissance republics had remarkable discretionary powers, the sort that most Europeans today would think of as dictatorial. It is not merely that they could arrest, try, and even execute people at will; they could also suspend constitutional guarantees. They could bypass legislative councils, declare war, impose taxes, or simply silence the murmuring community by decree." In order to avoid this fate, the Italian Renaissance experience suggests, the global city-state of the twenty-first century will need to develop a large, self-assured bourgeoisie—a middle class confident of its position and its rights and willing to fend off challenges from a grasping elite.

Even if global cities do prosper, there remains a problem of justice implied by a new era of global city-states. They are not going to be able to accommodate everyone—what happens to those who live outside their borders? I have yet to hear a good answer to this question—and cannot come up with one myself. Consider Africa. Short of postapartheid Johannesburg, a financial-services hub and base for multinational corporations, with about 7 percent of South Africa's population, no other African city is at this moment contending for a spot as a top-rank global city. When I asked Richard Florida about how Africa would fit into a world defined by global city-states, he replied, "I think that as far as I know Africa, it's a big dead spot." The people living in dead spots presumably could become part of the global pools of migrant labor gravitating toward the world's next big urban project. But not everyone is going to want to make this choice, and at the low end, as seen in the labor camps on the outskirts of Dubai, membership in these pools is not the happiest of prospects. A world of unaddressed dead spots could stoke an angry rebellion sufficiently powerful to overturn a global political and economic structure based on city-states. Still, let's not forget that the age of nation-states and empires has been full of dead spots as well. And if the city is the natural home of the gangster and petty thief, it was not the city that produced the Holocaust or the slaughter at the Marne in the trenches of 1914 France. A city-centered world of the twenty-first century would likely give the lie, once again, to Rousseau's prejudice against the city as "the abyss of the human species."

Chapter Eleven

Universal Civilization

The universal civilization has been a long time in the making. It wasn't always universal; it wasn't always as attractive as it is today.

V. S. Naipaul, in a lecture at the Manhattan Institute
in New York City, October 1990

Henry Luce's fondest dream was that the American way of life would become the basis of a universal civilization in which all peoples of the world would live happily. This was what the idea of the American Century was all about—an omnipotent, omnipresent America as the inspiration and the enforcer of a universal democratic ideal, embodied by the peerless American republic of Jefferson and Franklin. But while that dream has evaporated, the idea of a universal civilization is very much alive. In fact, it has never been more alive—and never closer to becoming a reality—than it is today, in the globalizing world of the twenty-first century.

A universal civilization can be considered like any other civilization—as a distinctive mix of customs, habits, and beliefs, of amusements and ritual practices. A universal civilization, for it to deserve that name, must have global institutions, including a global media and global universities, which will observe the world with a global eye and apply global standards of judgment to the news and social trends. It must produce people who naturally think of themselves as belonging to this civilization. If the "global citizen" is ever to have a passport, that person first must think of his or her identity in those terms—and not simply, say, as a member of a global city-state. In these terms, a universal civilization suggests the grandest After America possibility of them all—the possibility of global government.

The chain of reasoning is straightforward enough. This is the sort of process that belongs to the paradigm of tipping points. Before America could become a republic, it had to feel keenly its sense of Americanness; and before Europe could become the European Union, it had to cross a certain threshold feeling of Europeanness. In both cases, these processes took a great length of time. More than a century and a half passed between John Smith's landing in Virginia, on behalf of the British Crown, and Jefferson's Declaration of Independence; and even with the passage of another seventy years, Emerson still found cause to lament the tendency of Americans to imitate Europe in styles of art and architecture. The same logic suggests that a universal civilization, over time, could—let's just stick with "could" for now—give rise to a universal government. The key is a critical mass of people and institutions with a sufficient sense of universalness.

The case for world government has tended to belong to the poets. If the globe had but one monarch, Dante mused in an unfinished treatise known as *Convivio*, "The Banquet," war and indeed the cause of war would be no more: "Because he possesses everything, the ruler would not desire to possess anything further, and thus, he would hold kings contentedly within the borders of their kingdoms, and keep peace among them." Dante began work on *Convivio*, which he wrote in Latin, at the dawn of the fourteenth century. His muse, Beatrice, had died some years earlier, and his native Italy, as ever, was embroiled in strife, a sequence of wars involving factions representing the papacy on one side and the Holy Roman Empire on the other. His yearning was understandable, but his timing could not have been worse. His world of city-states would in a few centuries give way to the even more cutthroat world of European nation-states.

But let's depart from the realm of poetry. The plausible path to global government is a prosaic one—a creepy-crawl of an organic kind. It's the sort of thing that, after it happens, everyone will look back in astonishment and say that they never quite realized that this is where things were headed all along. It's best to think not in terms of a Dante but, considerably less lyrically, of a Talcott Parsons, one of the more influential sociologists of the twentieth century. Although his writings are difficult to digest, Parsons, the Colorado-born son of a

Congregational minister, was an interesting and original thinker; and he can be broadly associated with those, like Tolstoy and Braudel, with a perspective on change as a bottom-up process. Parsons's key insight, as he began to develop it in the 1930s, was known as "structural functionalism." The basic idea is that social institutions adapt and evolve, of their own accord, to meet unmet needs—the institutions thus can be said to serve a rational, problem-solving role, in the interest of efficiency and productivity. In this way of thinking also can be seen shades of Darwin: Parsons studied both biology and the social sciences at Amherst College in the 1920s, and his career is defined by an effort to combine the two disciplines within a single theoretical model.

Parsons himself viewed America as the *summa* of modern, efficient social development, but in this he can be seen as a product of his times. His influence peaked in the 1950s, when the American Century was in its infancy and Europe was still a mess. Since his time, the European Union has evolved, to the point of a common currency, to make Europe more governable, and an alphabet soup of supranational institutions like the International Criminal Court have taken on problems, such as the pursuit of justice against war criminals, that tend to fall between the cracks of the nation-state system. And in our times, the twenty-first-century version of globalization—aided by the marvels of modern communication technologies that improve by the month—is promoting a feeling of universal oneness as never before. I have in mind, to start with, three examples, each of which can be seen as a path by which the universal civilization, and hence global government, can be constructed. The first and most progressive path is what might be called the commerce path, advanced by economic globalists—including multinational corporation executives, lawyers, and economists—who already view the world as one big market and are seeking, for the sake of efficiency, to work out common operating rules. The second path is the human-rights one, advanced by transnational groups like Amnesty International, seeking to replace the traditional law of the sovereign-state system with a universal regime of justice. The third path might be called the planetary-health one. In this path, common environmental challenges, such as global warming, are rallying activists, including many government leaders, to think and act globally. Although the three paths are distinct, they have some common features and could at some point converge, contributing to momentum for world government.

America is often seen as an opponent of the supranational impulse and supranational institutions—as in its refusal to be a signatory to the treaty creating the International Criminal Court. But how America acts as a nation-state needs to be separated from how Americans, and nongovernmental institutions, are acting on their own initiatives. Across the broad spectrum of society, and even within certain quarters of Washington, there are many Americans—judges, businessmen, educators, scientists, political activists, various other intellectual types—who are helping to build the global institutions that could produce global government. Although they may not see their work quite this way, they are helping to construct the conditions of an After America world.

A universal civilization needs a system of universal law, and that process is well under way, aided by the likes of Justice Stephen Breyer of the U.S. Supreme Court. Breyer is well-known in legal circles for his debates with Justice Antonin Scalia on the question of whether the Supreme Court should pay attention to the decisions of foreign judges in the process of making the law in the United States. For Scalia, the answer is a definite no. As he once put it, speaking of Americans, "We don't have the same moral and legal framework as the rest of the world, and never have. . . . I doubt whether anybody would say, 'Yes, we want to be governed by the views of foreigners.'" This is spoken like a good American Exceptionalist. Breyer, though, ardently believes that American courts can profit by keeping up with what is happening elsewhere on the legal front. His passion came across at a 2007 forum in Washington that the French-American Foundation organized to give him a chance to talk to a small group about his views on the law. When I asked him to elaborate on his perspective, he responded with a vivid metaphor. All those involved in making the law, all around the world, he said, are seated together at a loom, "knitting or weaving" a "carpet or fabric." And "that's what the world is like today."

I later met with Breyer in his chambers at the Supreme Court. A former law professor at Harvard, he was born in San Francisco in 1938 and was named by

Bill Clinton to the Supreme Court in 1994. He worked out of a corner office, on the first floor, previously occupied by Justice Harry Blackmun. He had removed the wall-to-wall carpet to expose the hardwood floors, changed the fluorescent lighting to natural settings, and put up on the walls oil paintings, selected from the U.S. government's vast art collection, by Gilbert Stuart and James Whistler. But the eye-catcher, for me, was a book prominently displayed on the coffee table, titled *Ciel! Blake!*, a *Dictionnaire Français-Anglais des expressions courantes*, by the French author Jean-Loup Chiflet. I knew that Breyer was fluent in French and liked to visit the country, but I had not really grasped the depth of his interest in French culture and history. He told me that he liked to keep up with news and trends in France by tapping into French sources on the Internet.

Breyer looked rather buttoned-down, in his business suit and dress shirt with cuff links, but his sentences had an animated crackle to them. To start things off, I asked him to elaborate on his image of the loom. Critics tend to caricature Breyer's views on the importance of foreign law. For one thing, he does not really have in mind hot-button social-policy issues like gay marriage—this is not about, as cultural conservatives worry, his desire to smuggle the law of the Netherlands into the United States. His main focus, as he told me, is global commerce—how a "tremendous knitting together" of the law is taking place in the global business and economic arena. He ticked off four examples. First, he said, the weaving is occurring at the very practical level of the international conferences that he regularly attends in Europe and elsewhere. One of his favorites is the annual economic forum every July, in Aix-en-Provence, organized by the French group Le Cercle des Économistes. The event is attended by a global elite crew of jurists, law professors, economists, and others and addresses the sorts of problems that need to be solved in order for globalization to advance. Thus at the 2005 conference, discussion revolved around the question "How to reconcile two legal systems, one stemming from the Anglo-Saxon law and the other, from the Roman law and Napoleonic Code?" Another typical conference topic is intellectual property rights. On that subject, Breyer explained to me, "everyone is interested in solutions" to a common problem. "They may arrive at different solutions, but inevitably that kind of discussion promotes tremendous similarity because people learn from each other" and because "the underlying principles are similar." And so "the discussion becomes universal and the law becomes universal."

Breyer's second example is the evolution of a global commercial code gradually being adopted in various countries, in the same way the Uniform Commercial Code came to be adopted in the United States. The UCC, as it is known, evolved as private organizations and individuals involved in commerce made recommendations that state legislatures adopted as laws that became, in turn, the basis for court decisions. Nowadays, Breyer said, American state legislatures are bound to pick up recommendations from foreign sources as commerce becomes increasingly global. His third example was the work of international trade institutions like the World Trade Organization, which are knitting together both "laws and practices," and his fourth example, coming from outside commerce, was the harmonization of global law-enforcement institutions as they addressed common problems like terrorism.

I asked Breyer if the evolution he was describing amounted to "modernity," to the next logical step for a modernizing world. "Yes, that's right. It's exactly what I'm talking about," he replied. He balked, though, at the suggestion that he was seeking to impose his values on the world, emphasizing that he was in the business, above all, of problem solving: "I'm looking for means, not ends." While I take his point, it still seems to me that his choice of means—his eagerness to partake in a global discussion on what the law should become—was in itself a reflection of a certain value. Breyer is an enthusiastic, unapologetic globalist, just as Scalia, a Reagan appointee, is an unapologetic American Exceptionalist.

Still, it is not as if Breyer, philosophically speaking, is occupying an isolated island. America's Founding Fathers readily looked to foreign examples, like the Swiss and German systems, in devising the U.S. Constitution. (Scalia concedes that point but argues that once the U.S. Constitution was settled, there was no need to keep looking beyond America's shores for legal guidance.) On the east pediment of the Supreme Court—at the rear of the building—is a sculpted trio of three great lawgivers: Moses, Solon of Athens, and Confucius. This grouping is the conception of the American artist Hermon Atkins MacNeil, who worked with the architect Cass Gilbert on the Supreme Court's construction in the early 1930s. "Law as an element of civilization was normally and naturally derived or inherited in this country from former civilizations," MacNeil explained to the committee formed to supervise construction of the Court. In other words, even the law of the United States is derived from a universal stream of law as old as human civilization itself.

If the law of commerce is becoming universal, it is not only because "the discussion," as Breyer puts it, is becoming universal; it is because, more fundamentally, the great institutions of modern capitalism—the corporation, the investment bank, the hedge fund—treat the world as one. In certain respects, this is not a new thing. In nineteenth-century London, and even earlier, business and finance operated on a global scale. Back then, though, there was intimate joining of money and imperial political power: The purpose of these enterprises based in London was to make the British Empire rich and powerful. In today's wave of "globalization," the globally minded corporation and financial house do not really have this type of bond—or, to put it another way, they are absent a national political loyalty. They are heartless creatures, faithless to their roots, as Halliburton was when its CEO, David Lesar, decided to move the company's global headquarters from Houston to Dubai. This was a cold-eyed business decision that angered the community leaders of Houston and some members of the U.S. Congress, who believed that Halliburton was seeking to evade the web of U.S. regulators, but what of it? There was nothing to stop Halliburton from leaving.

Were Theodore Dreiser alive today to write a new trilogy of novels on the rise of the modern business tycoon, surely his "Titan" would be not a baron of American capitalism but a prince of global capitalism—a financial predator-prince (and creative genius) of the planetary scale and ambition of a Rupert Murdoch. The story line would take us from the prince's middling origins in Australia to his ascension in the great global centers of popular media and commerce— Hollywood, London, New York—and his bid for the new markets of places like China. While Murdoch became a naturalized American citizen in 1985 in order to be legally eligible to purchase U.S.-based television stations, America is no more his home than Australia or the United Kingdom. The global tycoon, like his tamer counterpart, the global business manager, is a person without a country.

America's time of robber-baron capitalism, in the nineteenth century, eventually gave way to the Progressive Era, in which Washington sought to rein in the barons with regulatory institutions intended to protect the broad public interest. At the World Economic Forum's meeting in Davos early in 2008, George Soros argued that today's global economy needs a "global sheriff" to keep order. His proposal was greeted with skepticism, but Soros may be ahead of his time—he was, at the least, several months in front of the financial crisis that brought down some of Wall Street's biggest firms and knocked back on their heels bank regulators the world over. As markets in the United States, Europe, and Asia together melted down, British prime minister Gordon Brown called for a "global system of financial regulation" to replace the antiquated patchwork of national regulators. This is already happening in the area of corporate accounting principles as multinationals gravitate to a single standard as published by the International Accounting Standards Board, based in London. The U.S. Securities and Exchange Commission, in August of 2008, proposed a series of steps by which all major U.S. companies would switch away from U.S. Generally Accepted Accounting Principles, known as GAAP, to uniform international standards by 2014. Perhaps the next step will be a global currency, as proposed by an Italian count, Gasparo Scaruffi, in the sixteenth century. "A global economy requires global currency," Paul Volcker, the ex-chairman of the U.S. Federal Reserve, likes to say.

Might the global multinational company come to have an active preference for world government? I put that question to Richard Burt, who served as U.S. ambassador to Germany in the 1980s. Burt now works at Henry Kissinger's global consulting firm, which specializes in advising clients like the multinationals on relations with the various governmental regimes of the planet. We met at his office in Washington's Farragut Square on the eve of a visit to town by the German chancellor, Angela Merkel. He told me how eager Merkel was to engage Washington on the vexing issue of "regulatory harmonization"—how to bring about a synchronization of the rules governing business in Europe and America. Yes, Burt answered without hesitation, the multinationals would prefer world government to current arrangements. "It would be good for them, assuming they could lobby and influence the process," he told me.

If the commerce path toward a universal civilization is advancing according to the imperative of global money and a quest for economic and legal efficiency, the human-rights path is advancing according to a certain moral imperative—a demand for justice that the imperfect system of nation-states often fails to oblige. While in Santiago, I got a tutorial on this path from a man whose own life embodies the strides the global human-rights movement has made since the Second World War.

My teacher was José Zalaquett Daher, the head of Centro de Derechos Humanos, the Human Rights Center, at the University of Chile's law school. We met in his cramped office on the fourth floor of the law school and later followed up on the telephone. Our conversation began on the plane of high philosophy. Speaking in fluent English, he talked in sweeping terms about the role of the human-rights movement in history, shifting from Kant to Tocqueville in service of his points on the nature of humankind and the rhythms of civilizations. A tall, stout man with an impressive, fleshy nose—what the Chileans call a *nariz de papa*, a potato nose—he leaned back in his chair while listening to my part of the dialogue and leaned forward to stress his own.

Daher was born in Chile in 1942, the son of Arab Christians who had immigrated to the country from their native Lebanon. His father was a garment merchant. "I was raised with a sense of justice. I went to study law because I felt it was a continuum. I didn't learn that—it was in my bones," Daher told me. He attended law school at the University of Chile in the mid-1960s, when Latin America was in political turmoil, polarized between right and left factions. He identified with the left-oriented ethos of the sixties—with the idea that "you could effect a major revolutionary change that could lead to social justice"—and went to work in the legal department of Salvador Allende's government after Allende's election in 1970. Allende proved a weak leader, unable to temper the harder-line element of his constituency, which aimed to bring about a Castro-style Marxist revolution in Chile. Daher, a member of the moderate faction in Allende's camp, felt that things were getting "out of control" and left his job.

After the 1973 coup by Pinochet, many of Daher's friends and colleagues from the overthrown Allende regime were arrested and jailed or went missing altogether. The families turned to sympathetic lawyers like Daher for help. He began by forming an enterprise to deliver packages of food to the soccer stadium in which many of the detainees were being held. Then he became more of an activist, sending information about these people to journalists and human-rights groups like Amnesty International. He joined up with a committee formed by Catholic, Protestant, and Jewish leaders in Chile to coordinate the legal defense of the victims of Pinochet's regime. By the end of 1975, the regime had had enough and moved to disband the committee. There was a knock on the door of Daher's Santiago home at one a.m.—three men had come to arrest him. They had a car waiting to take him to the notorious Tres Alamos center, the prison camp in Santiago that had formerly belonged to a religious order and was being used as a successor to the soccer stadium as a jail for the detainees. "Of course you are frightened—you don't know what will happen to you," Daher told me. But lawyers like him were generally not tortured, as were other regime opponents, and he was never physically harmed. He was released after several months and picked up his activities where he had left off. The regime arrested him again—and this time forced him into exile.

First Daher lived in Paris, and later he moved to Washington, D.C. He broadened his activities in the human-rights movement, serving for several years as the head of the international executive committee of Amnesty International. Finally he returned to Chile in 1986, in the waning years of the Pinochet regime. After Pinochet left the presidency, in 1990, Daher served on the National Truth and Reconciliation Commission to investigate the human-rights crimes of the regime. Although he could have made his home elsewhere, in any of the big cities in America and Europe, Daher chose to stay in his native land. But Chile was just his base. He lived the life, in effect, of a certified member of the global human-rights community, a kind of personage who simply did not exist in earlier ages. UNESCO awarded him a prize for "human rights education"; he received honorary doctorates from Notre Dame and the City University of New York; he was a member of the Geneva-based International Commission of Jurists and a director of the International Center for Transnational Justice. In 2003, Chile awarded him a national prize for his "contribution to the protection of the rights of individuals and of ethics in politics." His life was one thread in a fabric woven over the last half century.

As Daher noted, the modern global human-rights movement has evolved in a series of waves—first in the sun and then in the shadow of the American Century. The first wave emerged from the debate over how to prosecute the Nazis for their war crimes. As World War II wound down, Winston Churchill

mocked the idea of a war crimes tribunal as "a farce" and favored summary execution of the "principal leaders" if apprehended alive. Stalin was agreeable, but
the Americans balked, and it was largely at Washington's impetus that the Allies agreed to launch the Nuremberg Trials of captured Nazi leaders, adminis-
tered by an International Military Tribunal. Indictments were prepared alleging
"crimes against humanity" in a process that critics, including jurists in the
West, said amounted to "victor's justice." No matter. The trials went ahead, and
Nuremberg became the seed for a much more ambitious effort, bound up in the
formation of the United Nations, to articulate a single global standard of human rights. The leader of this push was Eleanor Roosevelt, the widow of Franklin
Delano Roosevelt and a powerful force in her own right. The Universal Declaration of Human Rights, adopted by the UN in 1948, contained thirty articles,
beginning with "All human beings are born free and equal in dignity and rights"
and also including "Everyone has the right to education" and "Everyone has the
right to a standard of living adequate for the health and well-being of himself
and of his family." Eleanor Roosevelt allowed that "it is not a treaty," but still, it
"may well become the international Magna Carta."

This first wave of the human-rights movement ended with an understanding of norms but without practical mechanisms for enforcing them. Governmental regimes, including America's, the human-rights advocates grasped,
could not be relied on to make sure the norms were observed. Indeed, in their
eyes, America's own unpunished crimes, in places like Vietnam, showed how
weak the movement still was. Thus began, in the 1960s, the second wave, the
growth of a global network of citizen-action groups, known as nongovernmental organizations, or NGOs, operating as lobbyists on behalf of the human-
rights cause. The trailblazer was Amnesty International, created in 1961 by an
English lawyer, Peter Benenson, who was outraged by newspaper tales of "forgotten prisoners," like a pair of Portuguese students supposedly jailed for daring
to make a toast to "liberty" in a Lisbon café. Benenson, who himself came from
wealth and privilege (he had been privately tutored by W. H. Auden), hit upon
the strategy of mobilizing England's decent-hearted middle class to write protest letters on behalf of such prisoners, and within a year, similar Amnesty
groups were up and running in seven countries. The Amnesty logo was a visu-
ally evocative one—a lit candle wrapped in a strand of barbed wire. Rather than

accept honors from governments, Benenson never stopped reminding them of their various injustices. The NGOs fittingly have become known in some quarters as the Fifth Estate, as adept in the arts of attracting press notice as in the craft of international law.

The third wave, the "globalization of justice," in Daher's term, grew out of the Balkan wars of the 1990s and led to the establishment of the International Criminal Court in 2002 at The Hague, the first permanent tribunal with the power to issue its own arrest warrants to prosecute offenses like genocide and "crimes against humanity," as well as lesser war crimes. The ICC was created by a multilateral treaty to which more than one hundred nations, although not America, are signatories. As critics in America (and elsewhere) correctly say, the ICC, despite the word "international" in its title, is indeed better thought of as a supranational entity to which the nation-states have ceded some of their sovereignty. According to the rules by which it operates, the ICC must give the national courts of a country the "first opportunity" to investigate or prosecute an alleged crime, but if that country is either unable or unwilling to do so—if, for example, the country is shielding a perpetrator from prosecution—then the ICC has the authority to investigate and prosecute on its own.

At the heart of the thinking that led to the ICC is the notion known as "universal jurisdiction"—essentially an unbounded right to bring human-rights offenders to justice wherever they committed a crime and wherever they may reside. This is a radical, even a revolutionary, doctrine—a dagger that some states are pointing at the heart of the traditional system of state sovereignty. Belgium in the 1990s enacted a universal-jurisdiction law, which led to a procession of complaints filed against political leaders from Fidel Castro to Ariel Sharon. The Belgian law was widely seen, even in Europe, as a stretch—why should Belgium be the seat of universal-jurisdiction cases?—but the concept of universal jurisdiction has survived, much to the anxiety of traditional statesmen. In 1998, a British court agreed to the detention of Augusto Pinochet, then living in Britain, in response to an extradition request from a judge in Spain, who was overseeing a case involving possible crimes committed by Pinochet against Spanish citizens in Chile when Pinochet was leader of the country. The Pinochet case spurred Henry Kissinger to write an essay in *Foreign Affairs* on "the pitfalls of universal jurisdiction." Kissinger quite correctly argued that this "unprecedented movement," spreading with "extraordinary speed" around the planet, had developed well beyond the UN-adopted Universal Declaration of Human Rights of 1948. Eleanor Roosevelt, Kissinger noted, had referred to the declaration as a "common standard," which implied that she had in mind some "general principles" and not a new system of law outside the state system. Kissinger asked whether, in the future, "any leader of the United States" could be hauled before an international tribunal.

This is a ripe line of questioning as the After America world takes shape. International law is inevitably shaped by the prevailing distribution of power in the world. As the world becomes less U.S.-centric, less subject to American control, U.S. officials should expect to feel increasingly vulnerable to prosecution by some international court, or the court of another nation-state, on a claim of universal jurisdiction. The George W. Bush regime's approval of practices like waterboarding in interrogations of al-Qaeda prisoners may prove a test case. Bush, Dick Cheney, and other former administration officials may need to watch where they travel: "I expect that there will be people in other countries demanding the arrest of individuals associated with our torture program," Jonathan Turley, a constitutional scholar based in Washington, D.C., told me. Although Turley said he personally would support "any institution" investigating a war crime, national or international, such efforts tend to infuriate imperial Washington. There is a sense that the world asks America to play the global-policeman role and then turns around and punishes America after it agrees to undertake this always untidy job. But there is little sympathy for Washington's feelings in capitals around the world. Germany has enshrined universal jurisdiction as a central plank of its foreign policy. Aiming to bolster the prestige and clout of the ICC, German government officials have proposed a law that would make it a crime even to deny or minimize findings of genocide or other crimes by the ICC. The German justice minister has explained: "When an international court determines that such crimes have taken place, then you should no longer be able to say: 'You're making that all up.'"

Where does it stop? It doesn't have to stop at all. The idea of a transcendent system of justice draws on a powerful moral urge. As Daher told me in Santiago, hardly anyone would have predicted that the global human-rights movement would have come this far in only six decades. "People despair of not having a world government—it will come in time, perhaps," he said, likening this period to the age when Europe was assembling the nation-state out of the pieces of feudal estates. "We are in the middle of that messy process. We are halfway, maybe a quarter of the way, there."

The idea that "the Earth is one but the world is not" sounds like something that Dante might have written, but this particular line is of more recent vintage. It comes from the 1987 document known as the Brundtland Report, named at that time for the Norwegian prime minister, Gro Harlem Brundtland, who chaired a commission on global environmental challenges, which noted that "ecology and economy are becoming ever more interwoven locally, regionally, nationally, and globally into a seamless net of causes and effects." And yet, "traditional forms of national sovereignty raise particular problems in managing the 'global commons' and their shared ecosystems—the oceans, outer space, and Antarctica." Two years later, Brundtland met at The Hague with colleagues including Helmut Kohl of Germany and P. V. Narasimha Rao of India, and this crew of global leaders, numbering twenty-four altogether, signed off on a declaration, drawn up in French and English, calling for a new supranational authority to tackle environmental problems like global warming.

It is this impulse—the supranational impulse—that sets the environmental movement of the last half century apart from past efforts to protect the earth. The American conservation movement, typically, began as a patriotically inspired national one—with a consciousness, above all, of the role that Americans could and should play in protecting their lands from the abuses of modern, industrial civilization. This was viewed principally as a job for America's federal government in combination with individual states, localities, and private groups of American citizens. John Muir, the great American naturalist of the nineteenth and early twentieth centuries, teamed up with President Theodore Roosevelt to make conservation a banner public cause. Born in Scotland and raised in Wisconsin, Muir eventually settled in California. He was a founder, in 1892, of the Sierra Club, which devoted much of its energies to preserving wilderness areas like the Yosemite Valley. Roosevelt visited Muir there in 1903. Muir was certainly sensitive to the interconnectedness of the ecology of planet Earth.

"When we try to pick out anything by itself, we find it hitched to everything else in the Universe," he once wrote. But neither Muir nor Roosevelt, a zealous guardian of American sovereignty, was talking about a concerted global action, above the level of the nation-state, to protect the planet.

Ironically, one of the reasons that environmental consciousness went "global" in the 1960s was the American space program, which had been conceived in the 1950s in the cold war military competition with the Soviet Union. The Brundtland Report's "Call to Action" began with this insight:

> In the middle of the 20th century, we saw our planet from space for the first time. Historians may eventually find that this vision had a greater impact on thought than did the Copernican revolution of the 16th century, which upset the human self-image by revealing that the Earth is not the centre of the universe. From space, we see a small and fragile ball dominated not by human activity and edifice but by a pattern of clouds, oceans, greenery, and soils. Humanity's inability to fit its activities into that pattern is changing planetary systems, fundamentally. Many such changes are accompanied by life-threatening hazards. This new reality, from which there is no escape, must be recognized—and managed.

A global awareness of man-made threats to the global environment was also raised, several decades earlier, by America's dropping of the atomic bombs over Hiroshima and Nagasaki to speed Japan's defeat in the Second World War. Early in the 1970s, Greenpeace burst onto the global scene with worldwide media attention to its "David versus Goliath" efforts to disrupt American nuclear bomb tests in the Aleutian Islands off the coast of Alaska. Greenpeace was founded in Vancouver—a city that became during the 1960s a haven for political activists of all types, including American anti–Vietnam War protestors who were dodging the draft.

As the environmental movement evolved in America in the 1960s and 1970s, most of its energies were devoted to national-agenda issues like passing clean-water and clean-air legislation and creating a federal environmental protection agency. There was, among activists in the movement, an understanding of how global such issues were becoming, but in practical terms, Europe was the leader in cobbling together supranational solutions to planetwide environmental problems. There were two main reasons for this. First, America had a huge sovereign territory to address, while the European continent was already divided into relatively small nation-states, sharing mountains, rivers, and forests. Second, the great political experiment of the European Union was already under way, and this experiment, above all, was an exercise in the supposed advantages of pooled sovereignty, as the supranational approach was unthreateningly called. Environmental issues were an irresistible candidate for the project. Thus did Europe begin to build the political and regulatory institutions of a cross-border environmental-protection movement—and as this happened, it was natural for Europeans to become accustomed to thinking about ecological matters in supranational terms. The "green" parties that cropped up in Germany and elsewhere abetted such thinking by popularizing a kind of postnational politics. For the German federal elections of 1990, the Green Party came up with a memorable slogan: "Everyone is talking about Germany; we're talking about the weather!"

In recent years, America's government has been assailed, often in vitriolic terms, by critics around the world for failing to work in a more globally cooperative way on environmental challenges. This criticism, though, misses an important development. While Washington has been a laggard, a growing number of prominent Americans, acting in their roles as concerned global citizens, have joined up with the supranationalists. No one better illustrates this trend than Al Gore. The man who began his political career as a congressman from a tobacco-growing district in Tennessee, and who almost became president in 2000, is today a paramount example of the post-American. Gore's great cause is the health of planet Earth—and he does not hesitate to lecture anyone, including Washington, about what needs to be done. Like former president Jimmy Carter in the area of human rights, Gore has migrated to a platform larger than the American one. In his case, it was a globally marketed media product—the documentary *An Inconvenient Truth*, on the perils of climate change—that transformed him into a global personage. Spain, Scotland, and Norway all obtained the DVDs for instruction in public schools. Gore attended openings for the film in such cities as Helsinki, Brussels, Berlin, Hong Kong, and Tokyo, and he presented his slide show lecture on global warming to the National

Assembly in France and at the United Nations in New York. "What we are going to have to put in place is a combination of the Manhattan Project, the Apollo Project and the Marshall Plan, and scale it globally," Gore told *Fortune*, with the "we" referring to leaders of the planet.

Gore's warnings of the dire ecological threats to the planet go back at least as far as his 1992 book, *Earth in the Balance*. American conservatives had fun lampooning him as a Chicken Little type. But expert scientific opinion on climate change was on his side. As a political matter, the balance even in America seems likely to shift toward the side of the supranationalists demanding global action. Suppose that global warming causes, as some scientists speculate it might, a severe drought in the American Southeast, a drought that does not abate for decades and leaves huge metropolises like Atlanta parched for water. This is the heart of "red" Republican America, the region that has traditionally tended to side with business in an aversion to environmental regulation. But how long could such attitudes persist in the face of a clear ecological catastrophe? Already, "one world" rhetoric is finding expression deep in America's heartland. In 2007, Virginia DuPuy, the Republican mayor of Waco, Texas, had this to say to a reporter from National Public Radio on the subject of climate change: "I am realizing more and more that we don't live on an island, that whatever we do is going to have an impact on people not only in our state but apparently across the world. There's major impact from the overall carbon emissions. So we need to go ahead and look at this holistically." The crafters of the Brundtland Report could not have put it better themselves.

As the commerce, human-rights, and environmental paths all suggest, the natural builders of a universal civilization are those whose work requires or invites them to think globally. The roster includes not only multinational corporate executives like Halliburton CEO David Lesar, global financiers like David Rubenstein of the Carlyle Group, and global jurists like Stephen Breyer, but also global philanthropists like Bill and Melinda Gates, global architects like Norman Foster, and globally minded filmmakers like Alejandro González Iñárritu, the director of *Babel*. Such people constitute what is often called a "superclass."

The image suggested by the term is a small elite of highly talented, mostly wealthy people far removed from everyone else in society. But the superclass is representative of something much more basic in global society—its members are products of institutions that are molding a new generation of global citizens. The most powerful of these institutions is that ivory-tower edifice that can be called the global university. Because of its ability to reach a generation at a relatively tender age, and because it has a hand in such a broad range of disciplines, from law, science, and medicine to government and management, the global university has an enormous potential to shift vistas toward a global horizon. This is already happening in fast-growing academic fields like public health. Students "intuitively realize that the world is their community," a health-policy teacher at the University of Virginia has observed. In 2006, the school began offering a minor in global public health, and students on their own have established a Global Public Health Society to promote awareness of these issues.

America is a trendsetter in the evolution of the global university, as best illustrated by the example of Harvard, the most prestigious university in America and probably the world. Over the last several decades, Harvard has exchanged a national identity for a global one. To the extent that this trend has gained attention, it has generally been characterized as an ideological one—the migration of the Harvards of the American educational elite away from the political mainstream and toward the (unpatriotic) Left. In 2007, the Harvard professor Stephen P. Rosen chastised the university's president for not attending the commissioning ceremony honoring the seniors who were leaving Harvard to enter the active forces of the U.S. military. "Harvard honors public service, but is uneasy with national military service, because it is uneasy with war, and with warriors, and it is no longer comfortable with the idea of Harvard as an American university, as opposed to an international university," Rosen said.

In response to Rosen's criticism, it might be pointed out that a global identity is truer than a national one to the raison d'être of a great university. Harvard was founded in 1636, about a century and a half before the creation of the American republic. It was based on the Oxford-Cambridge model of the university—and that model drew inspiration from, above all, Aristotle of ancient Athens. If the core premise of the university is the Aristotelian notion that "all knowledge is a whole," as John Henry Newman wrote in his 1853 classic, *The Idea of a University*, then Harvard, in denationalizing itself, is relocating on the most solid philosophical ground of all. Harvard's shift in perspective from national to global is driven not by ideology but by a functional adjustment to a changing world. There is no better illustration of Harvard's changing orientation than the Harvard Business School, a citadel of capitalist thinking, whose graduates are famous for their interest in making money, not in tilting the world to the Left. The B-School, as it is known, was founded in 1908 to train American students to be managers of American industry, and for a number of decades, until well after World War II, it served just that function. Not anymore. Over the last twenty years, the business school has remade itself into an institution that serves the global community, with a faculty and a student body drawn from all over the world, with research centers in places like Mumbai and Hong Kong, and with a curriculum made up of case studies increasingly based on non-American examples.

The trend can be seen in the evolution of the flagship monthly the *Harvard Business Review*, founded in the 1920s. As late as the mid-1960s, the *Review* was publishing J. Edgar Hoover on the topic of how American businessmen, when traveling abroad, needed to be on the lookout for Soviet spies. These days, the *Review* is making a strenuous effort to de-Americanize the magazine, to the point that baseball metaphors are considered verboten. "We are not an American publication," an editor told me. With domestic circulation flat, the *Review* is seeking to increase non-American readership, to publish more non-American authors, and to promote foreign-language editions in Mandarin Chinese, Taiwanese, Japanese, Polish, Russian, Hungarian, Italian, German, Hebrew, Spanish, and Portuguese.

American nationalists may decry Harvard's shift to a global platform, but this transition is exactly what a Parsonian functionalist of a Darwinian bent would predict. As the global community grows, so does demand for globally oriented knowledge. Educational institutions must evolve to meet that demand; and if they do not, they might die. Justice Breyer told me that what people like him—members of the global community—could really use is a set of reliable "editors" and "evaluators" who could make sense of global trends and sift the wheat from the chaff. The global university can play that role.

So, too, as the example of the *Harvard Business Review* suggests, can the emerging global media. Like the university, the media have a broad reach—in fact, even broader. And the media are thinking more globally than ever. In the next chapter, on After America California, I explore how Hollywood is becoming a maker of the universal civilization. This trend is also apparent in the media that cover scientific enterprise. This is to be expected, because the leading-edge scientist of the twenty-first century, like the leading-edge businessman, is a transitional operator, a member of a global community, not a national one.

Founded in 1845 in New York, *Scientific American* was a bible for the American industrial revolution of the nineteenth and early twentieth centuries. The magazine, whose focus during this time was more on practical innovations than on scientific research, counted among its friends the likes of Thomas Edison and Orville and Wilbur Wright. After the Second World War, as American science blossomed, *Scientific American* became a megaphone for explaining America's scientific discoveries not only to a readership in America but also to the world beyond. This wheel started to turn in the late 1960s and 1970s with the publication of foreign-language editions, increasingly made up of foreign content. The rest of the scientific world was starting to catch up to America. These days, *Scientific American* publishes nineteen foreign editions, operating largely independently of one another, and the English-language edition, intended principally for Americans, gets about a quarter of its content from authors doing research outside North America. The magazine's owner, a German publishing house based in Stuttgart, also publishes, for an American readership, *Scientific American Mind*, a monthly focused on trends in psychology and modeled on the German original, *Gehirn & Geist* ("Brain & Mind"). The *Scientific American* empire is an American one in name only.

A global media, detached from particular national concerns, are taking longer to develop in the coverage of politics. Matters of politics, especially those involving war, are more sensitive, more culturally loaded, than matters of science or business, and American-based news media outlets that aim to cover the world in a dispassionate fashion, like the *New York Times*, battle criticism on their home turf that they are insufficiently attentive to the national security interests of the United States. Still, the first shoots of a politics-oriented global media are taking root. The borderless Internet, not surprisingly, is in the advance guard, offering sources like the Globalist, which calls itself "the daily online magazine on the global economy, politics and culture." The founder, publisher, and editor in chief is Stephan Richter, a native of Germany who grew up in Frankfurt in the 1960s and relocated to Washington in 1980. "I'm postnational," he told me, describing the mission of the Globalist, launched in 2000, as an effort "to figure out the biggest journey of our lifetime," the voyage known as globalization. Noting that too much of the discussion about globalization has been confined to the "ghetto" of superclass confabs like Davos, he said he was preparing a version of the Globalist for high school students in countries including Sweden, Turkey, and Romania. In the meantime, he's peddling some of his content to mainstream American news organizations, including the *Boston Globe*.

Dipping a toe into these waters, washingtonpost.com, the Web news product of the *Washington Post*, in 2006 launched PostGlobal, a self-described "experiment in global, collaborative journalism," with discussion on the grand issues of war and peace and the global economy moderated by a crew of editors and writers based all over the world. The intriguing thing is that the premise is implicitly postnational—it is not "We're all Americans" but "We're all global citizens." When moderators invited commentary on the question "Do you see China as a threat?" they left it to the commentators to identify the possible object of the threat—whether to Western values generally or to global stability, for example. PostGlobal is the brainchild of David Ignatius, a *Washington Post* columnist who pushed for a similar approach while he was based in Paris as editor of the *International Herald Tribune* from 2000 to 2003.

It remains difficult, though, for the titans of the American media to embrace postnational styles of coverage and analysis. This kind of thinking is more easily pursued in global capitals outside the American homeland, which is no doubt why the pioneer among English-language daily newspapers is the London-based *Financial Times*. The salmon-colored *FT*, as it is known, was founded in the late nineteenth century as the *London Financial Guide*, and it was just that, a sheet narrowly targeted at readers in the City of London, the mightiest financial community of its day. But the disappearance of the British Empire, coupled with the emergence of the global business class, has given the *FT* a new lease on life. Now, especially with its weekend lifestyle supplement, it provides a cosmopolitan diet of the latest in books, film, music, wine, and food. The *FT* has transcended its roots in London in a way that neither the *New York Times* nor the *Wall Street Journal* has with respect to New York or the *Washington Post* with respect to Washington. It has become the paper of the global citizen.

Ultimately a universal civilization will be defined by its values. So far I have been describing the building blocks of a liberal universal civilization—a civilization hospitable to markets, democracy, and freedom of expression. But there are other possible variants of a universal civilization. Communism made a strong bid to become a universal civilization starting in the nineteenth century, and not until well into the twentieth century did it become apparent that this effort would fail; even today, the flames of Maoism and related peasant-based movements flicker from the Indian subcontinent to Latin America. As of now, the main competitor to the liberal civilization as a universal standard is the Islamic caliphate, which deserves to be treated in this regard because it aspires to cover everyone on the planet, with a comprehensive set of rules and system of justice—a world government of a kind. As Baitullah Mehsud, the leader of the Pakistani Taliban, has said, "Islam does not recognize boundaries."

The Islamic caliphate has to be taken seriously, if only because a fair number of people appear willing to kill others and become martyrs for this endeavor— and also because there is the historical precedent of the jihad that came to large portions of Europe and Asia in medieval times. Philosophically speaking, the modern-day effort to establish a caliphate by violent means can be thought of as a branch of the totalitarian thinking that made its own bid for control of Europe and Asia in the early twentieth century. Washington's intelligence analysts take the prospect seriously: The National Intelligence Council's *Mapping the Global Future* report, published in 2004, imagined a scenario in which a new caliphate is proclaimed "and manages to advance a powerful counter ideology that has widespread appeal." A fictional grandson of Osama bin Laden writes a letter to a family relative in 2020, boasting that "an almost forgotten word reentered the Western lexicon and histories of early Caliphs suddenly rose to be bestsellers on Amazon. . . . The Europeans thought they could dodge a clash of civilizations, but they now see that growing numbers of Muslims in their midst are turning to the Caliph." At this point, though, the idea of a new caliphate is a profoundly controversial and divisive one within the Muslim world itself; as the example of Turkish society illustrates, questions of how far to proceed with Islamic law and identity are as likely to provoke as to unify Muslims. The caliphate has no prospect of becoming a universal standard until Muslims themselves claim this banner as their own, and there is a better than even chance that they will not.

As for a universal liberal civilization, its sources are various. Although America is not going to be *the* source, as Henry Luce hoped, it is certainly one source. A small example is the American style of casualness in business dress and manners, which has infiltrated itself into modern business life just about all over the planet. Another source, perhaps a more important one, is Europe. In my earlier discussion of the prospects of a multipolar world, I suggested that postnational Europe lacked the will to power necessary to reconstitute itself as a great power. But this is not the same as saying that European civilization is moribund. As seen in its efforts to transcend the traditional nation-state—in its reach for a European Union and its contributions to a global environmental and human-rights movement—Europe is making its own bid to define the landscape of a universal civilization. The universalist impulse is especially powerful in northern Europe and in particular in Germany. Historian Isaiah Berlin called the Germans "the first true nationalists," and now they may be the world's most ardent postnationalists. This is not surprising. Notwithstanding the German embrace of Nazism, German philosophy has long had a powerful current of universalist thinking, as seen for example in Kant's efforts to articulate a universal standard of enlightenment.

In these terms, the ongoing two-steps-forward, one-back effort to achieve a united Europe can be seen as a proxy for an effort to achieve a universal civilization. Sometimes the European Union is portrayed as a United States of Europe. But the EU and the USA embrace distinctly different formulas for unification. American civilization was all about forging "a new race of men," as Hector St. John de Crèvecoeur, the mid-eighteenth-century immigrant from France, defined the melting pot. The European vision of unity is a multicultural one, with much wider scope for ethnic and linguistic diversity. Justice Breyer suggested that I watch a film called *L'auberge espagnole*, "The Spanish Apartment," to get the flavor of how Europe is trying to come together. The movie, made in 2002 by the French director Cedric Klapisch, is about a French economics graduate student, Xavier, who leaves his native Paris to study in Barcelona on an EU-sponsored program known as Erasmus. He moves into an apartment occupied by other students in the program, from such places as Belgium, England, and Denmark. His real education takes place in the apartment and in the streets of Barcelona, and while his Spanish improves, he is baffled by a teacher who insists on speaking in Catalan. At the end of the film, we find a somewhat disoriented Xavier, back in Paris to work at the plum business job his studies have earned him but no longer quite at home there. His experience in Barcelona has left him with an identity crisis. He is sitting shirtless in the room in which he grew up, with snapshots of his ex–apartment mates scattered on the floor. "I'm French, Spanish, English, Danish," he says. "I'm not one, but many. I'm like Europe. I'm all that. I'm a mess."

That parting image, "a mess," is meant sardonically; the movie's message is more along the lines that Europe is an uneven work in progress—confusing and at times dispiriting, but moving along nevertheless. One does not imagine Xavier becoming a French nationalist any more than one imagines him giving up his precious new friendships—his European identity is something to wrestle with, not discard. Sometimes messy arrangements prove more enduring than tidy ones. "Europeanism," with its acceptance of multiculturalism, is less of a forced conversion than traditional Americanism, with its fundamentalist insistence on the melting pot. The European multicultural union is not unlike the union that keeps ethnically and linguistically divided India together, and as I explore in the following chapter, multiculturalism is also making powerful inroads in parts of twenty-first-century America.

There is also a contribution to the universal civilization that can come from the East. The twenty-first century may be shaping up as the century of resource constraints. It could be a new age of limits—not least, on consumption. Although all religions, including the Judeo-Christian variants, emphasize the need to moderate one's material wants, this tradition is especially well grounded in Eastern religions like Buddhism. Global warming and the exhaustion of hydrocarbon reserves could turn a growing number of Western minds (and souls) to Eastern sources of spiritual wisdom. The East may also prove a growing influence on global medical practices as the limits of the traditional Western model, with its tendency to divide body from spirit, become increasingly apparent. For the better part of five hundred years, the West has dominated the East. Perhaps what comes next is not the return of serve, the Eastern domination of the West, but the universal civilization that marries strands of both.

Let's suppose the liberal universal civilization continues to gather force. It is then, and surely only then, that big pieces, like a meaningful global-security force and a global taxation authority, with maybe a global parliament to boot, would come into play. A truly horrific cataclysm—like the incineration of parts of the Middle East from a nuclear exchange between Israel and an enemy like Iran—might hasten this process, as the vast destructiveness of the Second World War sped the creation of the European community; but as things are proceeding, an apocalypse is not essential to world government. For all the scorn heaped on the United Nations for its bureaucratic and dithering ways, the remarkable thing is that so many people, if not their national leaders, continue to believe in the supranational ideals that led to the creation of the UN in the first place. One survey of publics representing more than half of the world's population (including China, India, and the United States) found large majorities in favor of strengthened powers for the UN, including having a standing peacekeeping force "selected, trained and commanded by the United Nations." And an impressive 46 percent said they favored "giving the UN the power to fund its international activities by imposing a small tax on such things as the international sale of arms or oil"—against 37 percent opposed. Among leaders on the world stage, UN secretary-general Ban Ki-moon was the only one to receive "largely positive ratings" in a poll taken in 2008 of peoples in nations comprising 60 percent of the world's population. Such surveys may say less about the global public's faith in the UN than about its lack of faith in the traditional system of nation-states, but it is precisely when a long-standing order becomes discredited that a new way of doing things becomes possible.

What might it be like to live in an era of world government? Critics have long feared that global government would be an invitation for utopian thinkers to impose all sorts of misguided plans on an unwilling planet. There undoubtedly would be that invitation. And at the beginning of the experiment, the utopians would undoubtedly have the upper hand, because they would be the ones with the most enthusiasm for the idea. But things may not work out as utopians hope, because the global community of the twenty-first century is a diverse one of contrasting ideologies. There might be two main parties—a party of the grand planners, but also a party of the libertarians. This reflects the division that already exists among globalists. In one camp are folks like Jeffrey Sachs, who believe that with enough money and sufficient central initiative, stubborn problems like global poverty can be overcome. But in the opposite camp are folks like William Easterly, the former World Bank economist who has come to believe in the timeless virtues of bottom-up "homegrown development." Easterly is as much a globally minded thinker as Sachs is—both stake their cases on the travels they have made all over the world, buttressed by their research. I asked Easterly to play the role of chief economic advisor to a world-government party of the libertarians. He resisted the exercise, as would any libertarian, but finally said, "The main task would be to convince those parts of the world that have severe restrictions on economic freedoms to get rid of them." And just as every nation-state is now, in effect, a free-trade zone within its borders, he added, "maybe the whole world could become a global free-trade zone." As Easterly's answer suggests, a world government might project onto a larger stage the policy debates already happening in political capitals all over the world on questions like trade, taxes, and health care.

Democratic accountability would be essential to the success of a world government project. But unless humankind's DNA changes, there is no particular reason to believe that world government would fulfill Dante's ultimate hope of an everlasting peace. Instead of wars between nation-states, there would be only "civil wars," but the bullets are all the same. Henry Kissinger is quite right to worry about the possibility of a "judicial tyranny" in such a world; a "dictatorship of the virtuous," as he calls it, has always been the risk of liberal Enlightenment projects, as illustrated by the excesses of the French Revolution. World government, in short, would no doubt be quite untidy. It would not be a variation of an "end of history," as claimed by Francis Fukuyama on the eve of America's triumph in the cold war, because there is, to say it once again, no end to history. It would be, rather, a new phase of history, as indeterminate, no doubt, as its precursors. The universal civilization can rise—and it can also crumble.

PART FOUR

America, After America

T he After America world is coming into focus. One way to think about this world is as a set of images superimposed on one another, like a cubist painting. Chaos, a multipolar order, a Chinese Century, a world of global cities, the universal civilization—all are represented. If I were to dip into my travel bag, the images might consist of a bearded hatemonger invoking Allah in a speech at a jihadist war rally in Anatolia; a slate-gray destroyer at dock in the blue waters of the Indian naval base at Karwar on the Arabian Sea; the Chinese footprint in the copper fields of the Atacama Desert in northern Chile; the glitzy shopping malls and grim labor camps of Dubai; and, closer to home, Justice Breyer, the global jurist in cuff links, expounding in his chambers inside the Vermont-marble U.S. Supreme Court building in Washington.

All this may seem strange and somewhat alien to an American eye. But the After America world is not just about the trajectory of the world beyond America's borders—about the resurgence of China and Russia, the growing clout of India and Brazil, and the dynamism of new global cities like Bangalore and old ones like London. America is part of this landscape—America is going to be transformed by whatever path the After America world takes. To put this in a different way, globalization, whatever form it takes, is not an exotic movie that Americans will watch; it is more like an unscripted play in which they are one of a number of actors.

At some point, America will become an After America place—with a culture, an economy, and a politics that reflect the basic outlines of America's readjusted place in the global cosmos. As chapter 12 illustrates, California,

America's most future-oriented (and most successful) place, is already acquiring an After America sort of character. That may sound scary; and as the conclusion explores, there are indeed dark possibilities for America in an After America world. But this world does not have to be dark—there are bright possibilities as well. It is even possible to glimpse that the After America world may prove liberating, rather than imprisoning, for Americans of the twenty-first century.

Chapter Twelve

After America California

We are a nation-state. . . . We're acting as a new country.

California governor Arnold Schwarzenegger, April 2007

On a 2007 visit to Los Angeles with my six-year-old son, we stayed in a modest bungalow motel in Santa Monica, a two-minute walk from the original Muscle Beach and the next-door amusement pier, with a Ferris wheel affording spectacular views up and down the Pacific coastline. Muscle Beach, "the birthplace of the physical fitness boom of the twentieth century," according to a plaque at the site, had its first run from the 1930s to the late 1950s, at which point the city shuttered it after an alleged rape. The current version was introduced in the 1980s. My son and I watched young men lifting barbells while others practiced martial-art routines. The most captivating spot of all was an imaginatively constructed playground in which toddlers scampered barefoot over smooth, egg-shaped stones that resembled Henry Moore sculptures. The language environment, as in so much of the Greater Los Angeles area, was a remarkably varied one—amid the chattering of mothers and nannies, the kids kicking around a soccer ball on the beach sand, the young couples holding hands on the pier, and the older men seated at chess tables, my ear picked up a good deal of Spanish, a smattering of Asian languages, including Korean, and some English. Santa Monica, circa the first decade of the twenty-first century, had come a long way from its mythical namesake origins some 250 years earlier, at the start of the Caucasian chapter of its history, as the site of a spring said to drip the tears of

Saint Monica of Hippo, the weeping mother of Saint Augustine, distraught over the conduct of her hedonistic son before he saw the light.

The American Century was in many respects the California Century. No place did more to define the American Dream; no place did more to contribute to the global perception of America as tomorrowland, the place where the future happens first. These days, California is still the pacesetter, but in a different way: as the trailblazer of America's migration to the After America world. It is no longer the engine that it once was for spreading the seeds of a distinctive American civilization around the planet. Instead, it has become the most After America part of the country. California is not so much remaking the world as the world is remaking California.

Ever plastic, ever promiscuous, California is pregnant with all the After America possibilities. Its critics tend to make much of its potential for a dark chaos, as imagined in iconic movies like *Blade Runner*. But California also has a potential for a happy chaos. It is the most modern, the most playfully libertarian (think San Francisco), and the most technologically sophisticated patch of ground in America—an experimental model of an anti–Big Brother, personal-choice-oriented, Kantian-enlightenment society. Alternatively, the notion of "nation-state" California suggests a role in a multipolar global order. Then, too, California could come to be defined by its ties to the emerging Chinese titan across the Pacific, by its global cities, or by the threads binding it to the universal civilization in the making. In one form or another, the emblem of the American Century stands to become the defining symbol of After America America.

After America California is the third great phase of California's history, starting from the time of American settlement. The first phase might be called Frontier California. This was the California of the gold rush of the mid-nineteenth century; it was all about the exploitation of nature's treasures in the pursuit of profit—and it was unapologetically racialist in the rights and privileges awarded to the settlers above all others. California's admission into the union as a state in 1850 was accompanied by laws and court rulings that had the effect of depriving "foreigners"—a category that included some Hispanic natives of the land—of property rights and even the right to pursue stakes in the gold mines. Frontier California was an imperial possession of the United States, seized during the Mexican-American War in a sideshow sparked by an impetuous army captain, the Savannah-born John Charles Frémont, who quite likely was acting without orders. Frémont was the son-in-law of Thomas Hart Benton, the senator from Missouri who was second to no one in America in his crusading on behalf of Manifest Destiny. For Benton, the conquest of California represented the fulfillment of a racialist prophecy. "It would seem that the White race alone received the divine command, to subdue and replenish the earth," he said in 1846. For a long time afterward, California's development remained lodged in this original spirit of martial adventure and sharp-edged nationalistic passion.

The second, postconquest phase of California's history might be called American Century California. This was a tamer, if by no means tamed, California, defining the essence of a new American aesthetic in fashion, dining, and other forms of popular culture. American Century California represents an American apotheosis—a remarkable distillation of American values, American dreams, and the American way of life. This is the California that pioneered fast food—the McDonald's chain has its roots in a hamburger joint founded by brothers Dick and Mac McDonald in San Bernardino in 1940—and spawned wave after wave of green-lawn, middle-class suburban development from the Bay Area, around San Francisco, all the way down to the San Diego region, near the border with Mexico. It is the California that, in its overwhelming Americanness, featured what the great California historian Kevin Starr called "a certain egalitarianism" in its hospitality to men and women from all social classes. San Francisco, Los Angeles, and San Diego all featured a brassy, American-style honky-tonk culture, evident in their bars, movie houses, and tattoo parlors, which appealed to off-duty sailors and soldiers and many others of no great wealth. It is the California of the Hells Angels motorcycle club, founded in Fontana in 1948, a noisy fulfillment on wheels of Woody Guthrie's exhortation, in "This Land Is Your Land" (written in 1940), to travel that "ribbon of highway" in an America of an "endless skyway."

The melting pot was a signature feature of American Century California. If Frontier California was about exclusion, to the point of elimination, of the "foreign" element, now the Anglos were in the majority and the expectation was one of assimilation. California became a powerful enactor of Theodore Roosevelt's dictum at the dawn of the twentieth century: "We have but one flag," and "we must also have but one language, and that language is English."

Arnold Schwarzenegger is an embodiment of the American Century phase of California history. In 1968, at the age of twenty-one, he left his native Austria for a new life in Southern California. He was on his own and able to speak little English. But from the moment he arrived in America, as he likes to tell the story, he "very rarely spoke German to anyone." He lived in Santa Monica, and when he wasn't pumping iron at Gold's Gym on Second Street, he attended classes at Santa Monica College. His teachers there told him to "read the *L.A. Times*, even though you don't understand it. . . . Look at books that are English, look at comic books that are English, watch television, listen to radio that is English." Schwarzenegger took that advice to heart, and within two years he was able to make his way through the paper and in other small but practical ways navigate his way through his adopted language environment. It was an impressive feat, requiring the same high level of discipline it took for him to become a champion bodybuilder.

That California is now more or less dead. After America California, the third phase of California's history, can be seen first of all in the attenuation of the melting pot and the shift to a multicultural society not so much typically American as typical of what can be found in the rest of the world. The main idea of multiculturalism is that a society can comprise many cultures, with no one culture necessarily superior to any other. Cultural diversity is prized for its own sake. Multiculturalism gained popularity in Europe, Canada, and Australia, as well as 1960s and 1970s America, as part of a larger backlash against Western colonial rule—the rule of the white man—and the Western tradition itself. Nowadays, multiculturalism draws on a certain consumer- or service-oriented appeal. The California Department of Motor Vehicles, in what might be seen as a prudent accommodation of street-level realities, offers its driver's handbook in nine languages, including Vietnamese, Russian, and Punjabi.

"That's an older-generation model" of assimilation, Eric Garcetti, the president of the Los Angeles City Council, told me when I brought up the Schwarzenegger example. We were chatting over breakfast at Alexander's Brite Spot, a diner on West Sunset Boulevard in the Echo Park neighborhood, the heart of his district. Garcetti, who was born in 1971, is an up-and-coming smart young Democrat, a Rhodes Scholar, and son of Gil Garcetti, the former Los Angeles County district attorney. His mother is Jewish, his father from Mexican-American stock. His district is a reflection of LA's Hispanic-leaning multicultural profile: The population is roughly 60 percent Latino (about half with roots in Mexico, the other half in Central America) and 20 percent Asian, with the rest a mix of African Americans, Armenians, and others. The public schools in his district are attended overwhelmingly by Latino students, but the talk on the streets is not only in Spanish and English but also in Mandarin Chinese, Tagalog, and Khmer.

Multicultural California is a work in progress, but it feels not like a temporary phenomenon but like part of an emerging political and cultural mainstream. Decades into the future, American Century California, with its insistence on a homogenous American cultural confection, will stand out as an ephemeral moment. That version of California denied, not least, its geography—namely, its territorial contiguity with Mexico. In After America California, Hispanic culture, in particular, is part of the mainstream—in fact, it helps to define the mainstream. Garcetti, who speaks fluent Spanish, told me that "California's success will be its geography, its linguistic fluency, and its creativity. Knowing Spanish is good for all three." I mentioned to him that, by my count on a car radio, ten of the twenty-one radio stations on the AM dial in the LA area, and ten of the thirty-nine stations on the FM dial, were broadcasting in Spanish. In ten years' time, I asked, would this likely still be the case? No doubt it will be, he responded.

After America California is also postimperial—it has lost its will to impose a dominant culture on the outside world. Consider the evolution of California's politicians over the centuries. California's original conqueror, John Charles Frémont, also served as one of its first U.S. senators. In the twentieth century, the state nurtured a pair of the American Century's most prominent anti-communist warriors, Richard Nixon and Ronald Reagan. But these days, California is best known for exporting to the nation's capital some of America's most liberal antiwar figures, like Democratic senator Barbara Boxer and Speaker of the House Nancy Pelosi. Boxer occupies the onetime Nixon seat; in 2004, she was reelected to her third term by a margin of 20 percentage points. The last time that California elected a Republican to the Senate was 1988 (Pete Wilson), and in every presidential election of the post–cold war era, starting in 1992, California has voted Democratic. In 2004, John Kerry beat George W. Bush by 10 percentage points in the state's vote. In 2008, forty-seven-year-old Barack Obama, a former community organizer who leans to the postimperial in his politics of engagement and empathy, beat seventy-two-year-old John McCain, a former jet fighter pilot who is emblematically out of the American Century in his politics of honor and national supremacy, by 24 percentage points in California. Obama's margin in California even exceeded Lyndon Johnson's eighteen-point victory over Barry Goldwater in 1964.

A postimperial political class is presiding over a postimperial economy. In the first decades of the American Century, California was the biggest single cog in America's military-industrial complex. Washington drove the California economy with enormous defense contracts for companies like Hughes, Lockheed, Northrop, and TRW. At its peak, in the late 1960s, Pentagon defense spending accounted for nearly 14 percent of the California economy. Even as late as 1990, California's economy depended more on the defense sector than did New York's on Wall Street. Things began to shift with the end of the cold war and accelerated with the collapse of the Soviet Union, as Washington declared a "peace dividend." From 1989 to 1994, California suffered the closure of twenty-one military bases, including the Presidio, containing eighty-two thousand military and civilian personnel. By comparison, the rest of the nation lost bases accounting for a total of thirty-seven thousand personnel. At the same time, the Pentagon funding spigot dried up. From 1990 to 1994, California lost 146,000 jobs in the defense aerospace sector, a decline of 45 percent.

California's twenty-first-century economy, weaned away from dependence on military spending, in some ways resembles the postimperial European economy of the present age. And as is the case with modern Europe, the loss of the imperial reflex is not necessarily a loss of dynamism. This can be seen in the example of Silicon Valley. After the Second World War, the Pentagon supplied a crucial stimulus to the region's development—Defense Department purchases accounted for some 40 percent of Silicon Valley's output of semiconductors, its signature product. But by the 1980s, the Pentagon's share was down to only 8 percent. The Valley's legendary venture-capital firms still finance local start-ups, but they also scour the globe for promising opportunities in Asia and elsewhere. The economist Steve Levy has been following the Valley for years as director of the Center for Continuing Study of the California Economy, based in Palo Alto. The time when the Valley was oriented to the imperatives of the U.S. economy is long gone, he told me: "We serve global markets." In that sense, today's Silicon Valley can be thought of not as an American institution but as a global one. The Valley has become an expression of California's After America–ness.

These, then, are the principal character features of After America California—the growth of multiculturalism, the transition to a postimperial politics and economy, and the immersion in a globalized world. These traits underscore California's exit from the American Century, but they do not point in any one direction. At this early, indeterminate stage, After America California engages all of the narratives explored in part 3 of this book.

Consider, first of all, the possibility of a dark chaos. This is a familiar trope for California portrayals—part of a literature of disenchantment in paradise, at least as old as Nathanael West's 1939 novel, *The Day of the Locust*, which ends with the torching of Los Angeles. The cliché, though, cannot be dismissed, for in After America California, there undoubtedly will be added social stress, especially if the current global economic downturn continues to add to its unemployment roll. Multicultural California, with its intense varieties of identity politics, broaches the specter of all multicultural societies—of a dreaded "balkanization" as the mosaic becomes unglued.

As things are, it is not hard to find examples of a fractured California. Among the most worrisome is a wave of Latino gang violence in Los Angeles directed at black residents—a string of attacks that frightened members of besieged black communities have likened to a campaign of "ethnic cleansing." In early 2008, I spent a Sunday afternoon in Jefferson Park, a once predominantly black neighborhood in South Central Los Angeles that is becoming Latino. A few months before, a fifty-three-year-old black man had been killed in a drive-by shooting while walking on the sidewalk; the murder was presumably the work of Latino gangbangers. I chatted with Rodney Blackmon, an African American who worked as the groundskeeper at a Baptist church in Jefferson

Park and who had spent his life, all forty-six years, in this part of LA. When I asked whether the African-American community in Jefferson Park was feeling "squeezed" by the Latino community, he gave me a sharp look and replied, "Squeezed ain't the word." The message from the Latinos to the blacks, he said, is more along the lines of "Get your little black ass out of here." The atmosphere is "really ugly—it really is," he continued, likening the climate to the jousting on the West Bank between Israelis and Palestinians.

Encounters like this one may seem to confirm long-standing anxieties about the dangers of multiculturalism. In the early 1990s, Arthur M. Schlesinger, Jr., the historian and liberal wise man who had been an advisor to President Kennedy thirty years earlier, wrote an impassioned bestseller called *The Disuniting of America: Reflections on a Multicultural Society*. In it, he warned that the "ethnic upsurge" had become "a cult" and preached against bilingualism as a recipe for racial antagonism. He held out the prospect of a multicultural America succumbing to the disease of tribalism and following in the bloody trail of Lebanon or Somalia. California was a prime target of his criticism; he tartly noted that "no history curriculum in the country is more carefully wrought and better balanced in its cultural pluralism than California's."

But for all its strains, multicultural California is not looking, on the whole, like a social disaster. After all, the "virus" of multiculturalism has been in circulation, in various forms, including in school curriculums at all levels, for decades, and California has not become a new Lebanon. In fact, that image of sectarian warfare is not a good fit even for Los Angeles, where the murder rate steadily declined from 2003 to 2007, resulting in fewer homicides in 2007, a total of 392, than in any other year since 1970. (Although the "ethnic cleansing" story draws the headlines, black-on-black and Latino-on-Latino violence is much more common in LA than black-Latino violence.) And the California economy has adjusted, notwithstanding the fact that better than 40 percent of all Californians, amid a tidal wave of immigration, speak a language other than English at home. Reflecting, perhaps, the eternal optimism of youth, 78 percent of Californians in the sixteen-to-twenty-two age cohort said, in a 2006 poll, that they expected life in the next ten years to be "better than it is now."

California's ability, at least so far, to weather the breakdown of the American Century phase of its history raises the intriguing possibility that its After

America future could be more like a happy chaos. Indeed, California is probably as ripe a ground as anywhere in the world for this prospect. American Century California of the 1950s, like America as a whole, was a portrait of corporate paternalism. This was the age when megacorporations in the great manufacturing industries, from automobiles to airplanes, dominated the U.S. economy and defined a bland, bureaucratic, conformist culture. As John Kenneth Galbraith would later write, post–World War II America had become a "new industrial state," a "technocracy" ruled from above by committees. But in the 1960s, the youth-led counterrevolution shattered that paternalistic compact—and no place in America played a more creatively destructive role than California, especially the Bay Area, with its embrace, in music and drug culture, of a spirit of radical freedom and a disdain for authority. While the revolt against the establishment had plenty of awful moments—elements of a dark chaos—it also helped transform California's staid business culture into a freewheeling entrepreneurial dynamo. Silicon Valley's Apple Computer is a direct organic by-product of the California counterculture. Founder Steve Jobs has described the *Whole Earth Catalog* as "one of the bibles of my generation" growing up in 1960s Northern California—"sort of like Google in paperback form, 35 years before Google came along: It was idealistic, and overflowing with neat tools and great notions."

As I discussed in part 3's chapter on chaos, happy chaos is saved from being a utopian impossibility only by the prospect of the new technologies of personal empowerment. This is a postnational strand of modernity—California is joined in its search for happy chaos in the most modern, technophilic patches of Europe and Asia. An apt experiment in a postpaternal global happy chaos is craigslist, founded in 1995 by Craig Newmark, who was working as an analyst for Charles Schwab in San Francisco. As an online global bulletin board, craigslist is not about advancing the American way of life, in the tradition of American Century California; it is about facilitating "billions of human interactions" in the global marketplace, including hastily arranged sexual encounters between partners meeting in person for the first time. In a section on safety tips— "tell a friend or family member where you are going"—craigslist insists that "the overwhelming majority of craigslist users are trustworthy and well-intentioned" and "the incidence of violent crime has been extremely low." Skeptics can raise an eyebrow, but craigslist is still going strong nearly fifteen years after its creation, with a network of users dispersed around more than fifty countries. Immanuel Kant would no doubt be horrified by some of the goings-on made possible by craigslist—he believed in the possibilities of the Enlightenment libertarian society, not in new forms of catering to the desires of libertines. But he would doubtless recognize that inventions like craigslist make more realizable his ideal of a society in which people are their own governors.

Another variant for an After America California is its possibilities as a "nation-state"—that is, California as a player in its own right in a multipolar world. This construct begins with some statistical muscle. On its own, California, with economic output of about $1.8 trillion, is the world's eighth largest economy measured by GDP, just behind Italy and ahead of Spain, Canada, Brazil, South Korea, and India. No other U.S. state is in California's economic league—Texas, second to California, has only 60 percent of California's output. With a population of some 38 million (projected to reach 50 million in two decades), California has more people than Canada and nearly as many as Spain. "California has more Nobel Laureates, more scientists, more engineers, more researchers, more high-tech companies than any other state," Schwarzenegger has said, backing up his claim on behalf of California as a nation-state.

Impressive as the numbers are, the key question is whether California has the *consciousness* of a nation-state, thinking of itself as an independent entity— or at least the seeds of that mind-set. In certain respects, the answer is yes, as best illustrated by California's independent action on global warming while America dithers. Much to the consternation of federal officials in Washington, California is starting to act as if it is a sovereign in the domain of regulation of greenhouse gas emissions. Thus, this rather startling headline from the BBC in the summer of 2006, following a meeting in California between Governor Schwarzenegger and UK prime minister Tony Blair: "California and UK in Climate Pact: The UK and California Are to Work Together on Reducing Greenhouse Gases and Promoting Low-Carbon Technologies."

An After America California that feels sovereign will inevitably act sovereign. This is not just whimsy—California's sense of separateness is fed in part by the sheer bigness of America, the problem that so worried George Kennan in his later years. Picking up on Kennan's concerns, the political economist Gar Alperovitz noted in 2007 that "if the scale of a country renders it unmanageable, there are two possible responses. One is a breakup of the nation; the other is a radical decentralization of power. More than half of the world's 200 nations formed as breakaways after 1946." In Western Europe, this trend is evident today in Spain, with Catalonia insisting on its separateness, and likewise in the UK, in the case of Scotland. In America, Alperovitz observed, "regional devolution would most likely be initiated by a very large state with a distinct sense of itself and aspirations greater than Washington could handle. The obvious candidate is California."

California is indeed the obvious candidate, and that in itself represents a large turn of the wheel of American history. The original separatist bastion of America was the Old South, which in the twenty-first century is probably more intense than any other part of America in its fusion of God and country, in its identification with traditional American Exceptionalism, and in its commitment, in blood and treasure, to America's global empire. And now it is California, the Manifest Destiny prize that came to symbolize an American essence, that is the most resonant example of an After America separateness.

Perhaps, though, even the "nation-state" of California is sized too big—just consider the troubles that perennially afflict the state as it tries to agree on its budget. It might be that California would fit even better into a world of global city-states. A ranking by the global-cities experts Peter Taylor and Rob Lang of the top twenty "globally connected" U.S. metropolitan areas includes a quartet of California cities: Los Angeles, San Francisco, San Diego, and San Jose. No other state, except for Texas, with Dallas and Houston, could claim more than one global city in the ranking.

Consider the city-state prospects of Greater San Diego. During the American Century, San Diego was a sleepy military outpost of the U.S. Navy. Pressed by cutbacks in military spending at the end of the cold war, San Diego has reinvented itself as a global force in the life-sciences industry; it is now home to the Salk Institute for Biological Studies and more than five hundred biotech companies, with a $9 billion impact on the local economy. At the same time, the economy and to a certain extent the culture of the San Diego area began to merge with Northern Baja, the adjacent California peninsular territory across the border in Mexico. Recognizing these organic realities, San Diego's leaders are starting to think of the future in transnational, megaregional terms. In 2008, the San Diego Regional Economic Development Corporation, a nonprofit funded by large businesses, including the Sony Corp., with activities on both sides of the border, launched an initiative aiming to market and develop the megaregion in the global economy as a single bi-national economic unit. The idea is to combine San Diego County's strengths in research and high-tech industries with next-door Imperial County's abundance of inexpensive land and water rights and Northern Baja's manufacturing base, relatively low labor costs, and ability to supply the San Diego area with electricity during peak-use times.

The project is overseen by Christina Luhn, a historian who worked as a staffer on the National Security Council in Ronald Reagan's White House in the 1980s. She spends much of her time fleshing out the concept in meetings with folks in the San Diego area and in Northern Baja. "We need to think mega-regionally," Luhn told me. "It is not just nation-states competing against nation-states anymore." The goal of the project goes beyond mundane aims like reducing the time of border crossings; officials are also taking a regionwide per-spective on matters like improving the quality of education in K–12 public schools. The megaregion can also be a framework in which homeland security issues are addressed, Luhn said. And no doubt, she added, this will be a bilin-gual region, with an imperative for educated workers and managers to be profi-cient in Spanish as well as English. In a PowerPoint presentation, she defined "success," medium term, as a "globally identified brand," and long term, over a quarter-century horizon, as a "Southwest equivalent of Hong Kong–Shenzhen Corridor." The U.S. Department of Commerce is backing the project, as a global-competitiveness initiative, with a $225,000 grant. While things are in an early stage, there is probably no more visionary effort in "city-state building" under way in America.

A Chinese Century might seem a less auspicious time for California. It would certainly be a role reversal. It was an impoverished China, carved up by the European powers, that exported manual laborers to mid-nineteenth-century California to build the railroads that were essential to making an industrializ-ing America a preeminent economic power. Railroad magnates welcomed the

Chinese workers as "quiet, peaceful, industrious, economical"—and easily re-
placeable in case of death or injury on the job. Threatened white American
wage earners had a less favorable view. A female labor organizer of the period
declared: "It was a mob that fought the battle of Lexington, and a mob that
threw the tea overboard in Boston harbor.... I want to see every Chinaman—
white or yellow—thrown out of this state." In 1854, California Supreme Court
chief justice J. Murray ruled that Chinese people, like "everyone who is not of
white blood," could not testify as witnesses in legal actions involving a white
person.

The Chinese undoubtedly have not forgotten these humiliations—what
people possibly could? Still, it was another age. In my earlier chapter on the
possibility of a Chinese Century, I suggested that it might not go nearly as badly
for America as popularly feared. Surely if there is any place where it might go
well, that place would be California. While the growth of China's manufacturing sector contributes to the loss of factory jobs in California, as in other states,
the overall rise of the Chinese economy is creating bountiful opportunities for
California's exporters. From 2004 to 2007, California's exports to mainland
China jumped from $6.8 billion to $10.6 billion. Even though China is destined
to supplant America as the world's biggest economic power, economist Albert
Keidel told me, China can be expected to maintain an enormous appetite for
the kinds of high-value technology products—in areas like biotech, nanotech,
and computer-chip design—in which California specializes. A more environ-
mentally conscious China, in decades to come, could be a major purchaser of
the clean-fuels technologies that California's entrepreneurs are seeking to develop.

There is a potential for a cultural backlash in twenty-first-century California against an encroaching Chinese presence. In the Silicon Valley town of
Cupertino, home to Apple and with a nearly half-Asian population, some residents have complained about merchants posting their business signs exclusively
in Chinese. "We don't want Cupertino to become another Chinatown," one
resident explained. These anxieties may intensify as China's economy gets
closer to surpassing America's. California is home to some 40 percent of America's total Chinese-American population—in over 1 million people, about twice
as many as New York State, with 520,000, according to 2006 U.S. Census

estimates. (There are nearly 400,000 Chinese Americans in Los Angeles County alone, followed by some 150,000 in San Francisco County and 140,000 in Santa Clara County.) Still, in an After America world defined by a Chinese Century, California's Chinese-American community is likely to prove an advantage, as a cultural resource as well as an economic one. After all, if China is going to be the global hegemon, like it or not, then it would help to understand the new giant. California's diverse immigrant populations, from Asia and elsewhere, sharpen its global vision. As America can attest from its various imperial misadventures, from Vietnam to Iraq, cultural myopia can be enormously costly.

Most intriguing of all are the ties binding an After America California to the emerging universal civilization. A transnational Silicon Valley, as mentioned earlier, is one example. Another is Stanford University, founded in the late nineteenth century by Leland Stanford, a railroad magnate who had been a governor of the state. Like Harvard in the East, Stanford has become a preeminent global university. Stanford of the twenty-first century is not about addressing the particular challenges facing California or America—it is more ambitiously about solving the problems of the planet, for "we live in an increasingly interconnected world that faces complex problems on a global scale," as the university's mission statement attests, citing the environment, health, and security threats as examples. The Stanford graduate is best thought of as a member of a global elite, not the U.S. elite.

The best example of California's links to the universal civilization is Hollywood. The story of how Hollywood has arrived at this point, as a preeminent After America institution in its own right, is a remarkable one that merits a close look as an illustration of the powerful forces—economic and cultural—that are pulling California away from the world of the American Century into the vortex of the After America world.

In the beginning, Hollywood was the creation of Jewish immigrants from Eastern Europe keen to assimilate into America. The studio bosses were eager to make movies that embodied their patriotic sentiments and extolled the American way of life, so different from the lands of their birth. Sensitive to anti-

Semitism, they wanted to make clear that they were, above all, American citizens, not beholden to their religion. The story is well told by Neal Gabler in *An Empire of Their Own: How the Jews Invented Hollywood.* During World War II, Gabler notes, "the Hollywood Jews were deliriously patriotic, turning out film after film about the Nazis' cruelty, the sedition of Nazi sympathizers here, the bravery of our soldiers, the steadfastness of our people, and the rightness of our mission, and they were no less zealous against the Japanese." The studio mogul Jack Warner told a columnist, "I want all our films to sell America 'long' not short," and Paramount's president, Barney Balaban, asserted, "We, the industry, recognize the need for informing people in foreign lands about the things that have made America a great country." Most of the overtly anti-Nazi films made during the war were forgettable; not so, of course, *Casablanca*, a Warner Bros. film that premiered in the fall of 1942 in sync with the Allied invasion of North Africa. *Variety* called the movie "splendid anti-Axis propaganda," and it won the award for best picture at the Oscars in 1944.

Shortly after the 9/11 attacks, George W. Bush sent Karl Rove, his top political advisor, to Hollywood. Rove was looking for moviemakers to respond to the new war on Islamic terrorism as it had once before responded to the war on Japanese-German fascism. He might as well have stayed home. The Hollywood of the 1940s, aligned with Washington as part of an ascending America's cultural-political hegemony, had long ago ceased to exist. "We're not in lockstep anymore," Michael Lynton, the chairman and CEO of Sony Pictures Entertainment, told me in a talk in his office suite in Culver City. Hollywood turned out a few pictures of a muscular-patriotism sort—notably *United 93*, the story of the doomed 9/11 flight kept from completing its suicide-terrorist mission by a heroic band of passengers who forced a crash landing, and met their own deaths, in a Pennsylvania field. Britain's Paul Greengrass wrote and directed the film, which was distributed by Universal Pictures. But mostly Hollywood ignored the war on terrorism. In March 2008, on the weekend following the fifth anniversary of the invasion of Iraq, the top-grossing film was *Horton Hears a Who!*, followed by *Meet the Browns* and *Shutter*, a remake of a 2004 Thai horror film.

As America's cultural conservatives tell the tale, the story of a "lost Hollywood" revolves around the capture of the film industry by a countercultural liberal-Democratic crowd who are out of touch with mainstream American political values and indeed actively hostile to them. But while it is certainly true that Hollywood is a liberal community, politically and socially speaking, its break with the American Century is driven by commercial rather than ideological imperatives. Above all, Hollywood's transformation is a thread in the larger After America narrative of economic globalization. The culprit is transnational capitalism, a much weightier planetary force than sixties-style liberalism.

The evolution of Sony Pictures Entertainment, from its early days as Columbia Pictures to its current status as a cog in a global conglomerate, illustrates Hollywood's identity makeover and suggests where things are headed. Columbia was founded in the 1920s by the legendary Cohn brothers, Jack and Harry, the high school dropout sons of a German Jewish tailor. Its logo was a lady holding a torch—an image suggestive of the Statue of Liberty—and at first the lady was draped in an American flag. Columbia's great early talent was the director Frank Capra, the Sicilian immigrant who made a remarkable string of pictures showcasing "ordinary" Americans and their heartfelt struggles and exploits, including the Jimmy Stewart classics *Mr. Smith Goes to Washington* (1939) and *It's a Wonderful Life* (1946). Capra's films, which sentimentalized small-town America, not only won Oscars but also were box-office successes.

In the decades following World War II, Columbia became, like other big Hollywood studios, a conglomerate, producing formula-driven entertainment "product" for diverse segments of the marketplace. Coca-Cola bought Columbia in 1982 and, after seven years of mixed success, sold out to Sony in 1989. Sony Pictures Entertainment's "world headquarters" in Culver City is enclosed by high walls with ancient Greek-style columns. I arrived early for my appointment with Lynton, and after the valet had taken my Hertz rental off my hands, I wandered around the lot, taking care not to stray into the path reserved for golf carts.

My talk with Lynton began with geopolitics—the status of superpower America. The day before, he told me, he had been discussing this topic with the head of RAND, the Santa Monica–headquartered think tank. "It's happening much more quickly than I expected," he said, referring to how "the conversation," among financial and other types, had shifted from America's preeminence to what it might be like to enter an era in which the United States is no longer able to call the shots. That era, he agreed, is already here.

In traditional Hollywood terms, Lynton is a mogul—the head of a major motion-picture studio. But "mogul" is not really the right description of his role. Although he is the top man of Sony Pictures, the studio is only one of the profit centers of the Sony Corp., and not the most important one. And his bosses are based in distant Tokyo. Lynton is better thought of as a top-echelon corporate executive, with precisely the right upbringing and experience for a job for which multicultural and multinational fluency is essential. Born in London in 1960 to native-German parents, he was raised in the Netherlands, outside The Hague. He graduated from Harvard College and Harvard Business School before proceeding to a series of senior executive postings at media-entertainment companies, including chairman and CEO of Pearson's Penguin Group. He is fluent in Dutch, German, and French. His portfolio includes the business and creative domains of Sony Pictures' movie, television, and digital-entertainment divisions.

Lynton became the head of Sony Pictures in 2004, and in 2007 signed on for a second five-year contract. During his watch, the studio has scored a number of profitable movie successes, including the *Spider-Man* series, *The Da Vinci Code*, and *Casino Royale*, the James Bond sequel. In Hollywood parlance, these are known as "tent pole" movies—blockbusters, with tie-in possibilities and the potential to open simultaneously in theaters all over the world. The offshore dollar is increasingly important to the success of these and other Sony Pictures products. Ten years ago, Sony Pictures derived about 25 percent of its revenues outside America; these days it derives about 50 percent; in another ten years, Lynton told me, the number could reach 60 or even 70 percent. As a practical matter, he explained, the big-budget movie has to have multicultural appeal—it has to feature, as in the love interests of James Bond, "a real mélange." This is even the case with a *Pink Panther* movie, he added. And what, I asked, about the future of the "American element" in Sony Pictures films? "It is still very present in our movies," he said, pointing to the Will Smith vehicle *The Pursuit of Happyness* (2006). At the same time, he continued, "it sounds a little hollow. It travels less abroad. There was a time when people saw the U.S. as the only place to achieve their dream. That's no longer the case."

The future of Hollywood is not only about the generic tent-pole movie, stripped of any revenue-draining nationalistic content. It is also about making entertainment product tailored to compete with the fare produced in growing markets like India. This effort—also dictated by commercial imperative—moves Hollywood even further away from the old model of producing entertainment loaded (deliberately or not) with American cultural values. Lynton is a big believer in the proposition that local markets are interested in local content—he doesn't think the future of the movie is *only* about the cross-cultural blockbuster. He is mindful of Bollywood, the Mumbai-based Indian film industry, which is why Sony Pictures is a leader among Hollywood studios in producing Indian-style pictures in Bollywood itself, starting with *Saawariya* (2007). The film is a song-and-dance extravaganza loosely based on "White Nights," the Dostoevsky short story about a young woman who pines for her absent older lover to return to her town to take her hand in marriage. By investing in Bollywood, Sony Pictures has a hand in an industry whose products sell well not only in the huge Indian market but also in the Middle East and former Soviet Central Asia.

Hollywood's twenty-first-century success rests, in part, on its ability to surmount the challenge, an ever more vigorous one, presented by "indigenous" entertainment studios, as they are called in Los Angeles. I replayed for Lynton an earlier conversation I had had on this topic with Strauss Zelnick, a former CEO of BMG Entertainment, the music and entertainment conglomerate, and a former president of 20th Century Fox. Because "culture wants to be local," Zelnick told me, indigenous cultural product will trump more general fare so long as the quality of production is top-notch. This is already happening in the music business, Zelnick said, because the costs of production, compared to the film business, are relatively low. Lynton agrees with this analysis. "The music industry is in front of us," he told me. "Film will come later, but it will come."

The television division of Sony Pictures likewise is intensifying its efforts to develop indigenous product. The international TV guru at Sony Pictures is Steve Kent, a senior executive vice president for programming at Sony Pictures/ Television. He is also responsible for American soaps. He greeted me in Hollywood producer uniform—a black polo shirt, blue denim Levi's, and new-looking white leather sneakers. Kent, who was born in 1954, grew up outside New York City near the town of Bedford in Westchester County. In explaining to me why the local model made sense for a global company like Sony Pictures, he said that sometimes as a teenager he would prefer to listen to music on a small local radio station rather than on one of the megastations broadcasting out of Manhattan, simply because the station was local. His instinct about local television is much the same—the French and the Italian viewer don't necessarily want the same thing. He described his awareness of the importance of the local as largely an accidental thing, born of his travels in places like India, China, and Europe. He lived in Milan for six months and also helped launch a Hindi television channel in India.

We talked at length about Sony Pictures' efforts in the fast-growing Russian market. Russian authorities permitted Kent's team to use the Winter Palace in St. Petersburg for filming of *Bednaya Nastaya* ("Poor Anastasya"), a television soap drama of forbidden love involving a beautiful young serf and a nobleman. Sony also has done a Russian-language adaptation of the *Married with Children* series, which is playing on Russian TV. I asked Kent whether Sony Pictures is seeking to export American-style values to Russia. "We have no interest in doing that," he said. "We want to entertain people—make them laugh, make them cry." So what, precisely, is Sony Pictures exporting when it hires or collaborates with foreign producers, writers, and others on productions like a Russian version of *Married with Children*? "It's technology," he first answered, but then stopped himself and said that was not quite right. After a pause, he said: "We are not exporting American story content. What we are exporting is mechanisms, technique"—a "structure" for "managing the creative process" essential to the success of a television series, which is not just about one strong episode, a relatively easy feat for a production team, but an extended sequence. What Hollywood is bringing to the table, he summarized, is nearly a century of experience in the craft of a certain type of storytelling. But, I interrupted, isn't Sony Pictures, as in Russia, training the people who will eat its lunch? "We are," Kent agreed, which was why the company had already purchased a majority interest in a Moscow-based Russian television company. Sony will "fade more and more out of the mainstream" as its local television company takes on more responsibilities, Kent said. "The Americanization of the world isn't going to happen"—at least not as a trend driven by twenty-first-century Hollywood, he told me.

Might it now be possible to glimpse the future of California somewhere else? In the American Century, this question had no standing. California was not only the future of America; it was also a future, if not *the* future, for the world. But an After America California, by definition, will be a less distinctive society— more in the grip of trends starting somewhere else. So it pays to search the globe for harbingers.

In this regard, the most intriguing reference point is Australia—another Pacific coastal, affluent, market-based, immigrant-rich society (including a large Chinese immigrant population) with cultural roots in Anglo civilization. The comparison is of course not a perfect one. Australia is an island continent with a predominantly resource-based economy and has been able to keep a tighter control over immigration flows. Still, Australia is notably ahead of California in one of the most important trends at work in After America California: the embrace of the multicultural society. If only for this reason, Californians may well want to look to Australia for what might lie ahead for them.

In the 1970s, Australia jettisoned a de facto whites-only policy for one that welcomed immigrants from predominantly Muslim lands like Indonesia and the Arab Middle East as well as from China, Thailand, and India. "Multiculturalism for All Australians" was in turn adopted as a kind of state ideology. "Multiculturalism should not just mean majority group assistance for minority cultural groups, but rather should be a way of perceiving Australian society as a whole. Thus, all Australians would accept and appreciate diversity as a normal fact of communal life and, within the necessity to maintain social cohesion, all people would be free to express their cultural identities," an Australian government panel concluded in the early 1980s. An editorial of the time, in the Melbourne *Age*, said that multiculturalism "is not a dangerous new 'ism' to be foisted on an unsuspecting nation. It is not a radical plot to change the nature of Australian society. It is not a devious attempt to open the immigration floodgates. . . . It is essentially a recognition of reality and an enlightened attempt to respond positively to changes in a growing community."

In today's Australia, just as in California, about a quarter of the population is foreign-born. While Governor Schwarzenegger of California bemoans the lost ethos of total immersion in English, Prime Minister Kevin Rudd of Australia shows off his abilities as a fluent speaker of Mandarin Chinese. And the Australian Department of Health and Ageing outdoes the California Department of Motor Vehicles in its receptiveness to foreign-language speakers by offering an explainer of its hearing-service program in no fewer than thirty-three languages, ranging from Albanian and Amharic to Turkish and Ukrainian. An annual highlight in Canberra, the national capital, is the National Multicultural Festival, which in 2008 featured attractions like "Show Us Your Roots," a "tongue-in-cheek look at what it's like growing up in multicultural Australia, through the eyes of ethnic Australians." The show had already played to sold-out houses in Sydney and Melbourne.

Multicultural Australia is not a paradise. In the summer of 2005, Sydney, which makes everyone's list of the top twenty global cities of the twenty-first century, had a race riot—not a big one, by the American standard of a 1960s Watts or Detroit, but still a shocking event, at least for the city's elite, with its apparent faith that an investment in multiculturalism would bear the dividend of peace on its crowded streets and beaches. The trouble started after several thousand drunken white youths gathered to retaliate for an attack on two lifeguards—rumored to be the work of Australians of Lebanese descent. The white mob fought with police and went after anyone who looked like an Arab. "We grew here, you flew here," the mob chanted.

On balance, though, Australia's experiment with multiculturalism as a way of building an immigrant society has worked well. Australia has earned a global reputation as a welcoming place: A U.S.-based pollster found that, in a global opinion survey in fifteen countries in Asia, the Middle East, and Europe, Australia and similarly multicultural Canada were the top choices of where people would advise a young person to go to lead "a good life." It helps that Australia is in the midst of a historic economic boom stretching back a quarter century, nourished in part by exports to the growing Chinese market. If Australia is a portent of California's After America future, then Californians can sleep easier.

While it is fashionable in American political circles to view twenty-first-century California as out of step with the mainstream of the country, it could also be the case that California, as ever, is simply far ahead—in a place that the rest of the country eventually will reach. There is no reason to think that California's role in contemporary American civilization as a living laboratory—the first to encounter the social and cultural trends that the rest of the country will confront sooner or later—is over. Today's California is an exhibit of how the country can adjust to an After America world. It is from this work in progress that Americans might glean some useful lessons.

Conclusion

Life After the American Century

But what else is life but endless lending and borrowing, give and take?
Kurt Vonnegut, *A Man Without a Country*, 2005

Who lost America? As the American moment recedes, the visceral impulse is to point a finger of blame. How did this happen? Who lost the America that was the sun of the global solar system? There is no shortage of available culprits across the political, economic, and cultural spectrums, and passions are already welling up in the always heated blogosphere and talk radio and television forums. Maybe it was George W. Bush and his Iraq obsession. Maybe it was the Washington lobbyist, putting the interests of his foreign client ahead of America's. Maybe it was the (now busted up) Wall Street investment houses, selling America short and investing in more promising overseas economies. Maybe it was postnational Harvard, Hollywood, and Halliburton, migrating from an American identity to a global one. Maybe it was the Latino immigrants, failing to learn America's tongue. Could it be the upper crust of a selfish, callow baby boomer generation, who left the fighting of America's wars to others? Or the political consultants, who sliced and diced the country into ever tinier demographic fragments and played the bits off one another? "There is no One America anymore," Mark Penn, guru for the likes of Hillary Clinton, wrote in his book *Microtrends*.

"America is facing an identity crisis," the Bradley Foundation, a well-respected U.S. philanthropy, declared at the outset of *E Pluribus Unum*, a report released in June 2008. "One of the challenges we face is that the idea of national citizenship is weakening," the authors said, reporting on a Harris survey showing that only 38 percent of Americans responded "yes, definitely" to the question of whether Americans "share a unique national identity based on a shared set of beliefs, values, and culture." At the same time, "phrases such as 'global citizenship' and 'citizens of the world' are more commonplace in educational discussions today than 'patriotism' and 'national unity.'"

There are two paths for America and its people in the After America world—a dark path and a bright one. I will start with a description of the dark one, not because I believe in it but because it has to be considered a plausible possibility. In the dark path, the disorientation occasioned by the identity crisis generates frustration and anger, and these raw sentiments connect to a more tender but no less toxic feeling of nostalgia for a lost America. In the grip of nostalgia, the "great nation of futurity," as John O'Sullivan called America in the mid-nineteenth century, becomes entranced by a past that seems to have been a better time than the present—and better than anything likely to come next. In his song "What Happened?" Merle Haggard asks:

> *Where did America go?*
> *How did we ever go so wrong?*
>
> *... I miss America.*

Nostalgia is a form of homesickness, always better expressed as art than as politics. It seeks an idealized past, not the past as it truly was. Nostalgia yearns for the homemade chicken soup that was on the table, not remembering that the soup often came from a can. Nostalgia cuddles up with an illusion. It is a seductive siren but a false one, because you can't really go home again.

In the dark path, nostalgia seeps into the political arena as a polarizing agent, composed of both illusion and resentment. A harbinger came at the tail end of John McCain's losing 2008 presidential campaign, when his running mate, Alaska governor Sarah Palin, offered a paean at campaign rallies to a forgotten small-town America, to the "pro-America areas of this great nation." The dark path may take America further down the road of military misadventures, perhaps a fracas in Iran as a sequel to the melee in neighboring Iraq, as an aggravated America refuses to admit any limitations to its hard powers. This would be the Accidental Empire at its most reckless. It is often the case that empires are most dangerous to themselves, and to the world, in their twilight moments, as illustrated by the Suez Crisis in the 1950s, in which Britain's and France's desperate effort to reassert an imperial hand in the Middle East threatened to spark a global conflagration. The more America's actual power declines, the greater the impulse, perhaps, to throw around its remaining weight.

And the sentiment that could lead to misadventures abroad might produce a Fortress America strategy at home. New trade barriers might be erected in an effort to protect American industry from the currents of economic globalization—but these efforts, which may have served America well in the nineteenth century, when its output was a relatively small share of the global economy, would merely encourage other countries to adopt protectionist policies and thus likely impede, not spur, America's economic growth. America's southern border with Mexico might become a quasi-military zone as a permanent wall along the border is strengthened and extended to try to stop the tide of illegal immigration. An obsession with national identity might be married to information-age technologies to provide for a 24/7 Big Brother surveillance of the entire population. Some airports are already moving to a video form of body strip searches, thus bringing the facilities in line with state-of-the-art practices at U.S. penitentiaries.

As America's economic position continues to slip relative to the rising Indias and Chinas of the world, foreigners might no longer be willing to finance America's debts. Lacking funds to meet legally mandated obligations on entitlement programs like Social Security and Medicare, Washington would have to slash benefits. Class-based resentments would sharpen between haves and have-nots. Congress might raise tax rates on the rich, but in response the wealthy could merely shift their assets abroad—a growing number leaving the sinking country for one of the ascending global cities in Europe or Asia.

There are all sorts of dark scenarios for America in an After America world. All are manifestations of the same pathology: a failure to come to grips with present realities. At the start of this book, I mentioned that James Schlesinger, the former U.S. secretary of defense and energy and former director of the CIA, offered me Thomas Mann's story of the generational decline of the Buddenbrooks family of northern Germany as a metaphor for the "mental illness" that comes from an inability to recognize that things have changed from the past. There also is an example of this disease from America's own experience: the decline and fall of the Old South. For a long time after the Civil War, there was a blind refusal to accept the passing of antebellum civilization, accompanied by a nostalgic sweetening of the way life actually had been. In the 1930s, while Margaret Mitchell was writing *Gone With the Wind*, political reactionaries were still preaching the virtues of segregation and the pastoral life. In *I'll Take My Stand*, a manifesto published in 1930 by a group of Southern writers, the "fugitive poet" John Crowe Ransom called for the reconstitution of the Democratic Party along "agrarian, conservative, anti-industrial" principles. His peer Donald Davidson believed that "in its very backwardness the South had clung to some secret which embodied, it seemed, the elements out of which its own reconstruction—and possibly even the reconstruction of America—might be achieved." There was, thankfully, a limited constituency for this message, and America moved on to the future.

If twenty-first-century America tries to cling to the America that once was, then the prospect is for pain and misery. Fortunately, there is an alternative. Politics in a democracy, Emerson once said, is a contest between memory and hope. A hopeful, forward-looking narrative can also be found for an After America world. In this narrative, the "Who lost America?" debate ends, however it might have started, not on notes of bitterness and division, but on a recognition that America is living in a new age and has to start making some rather large cognitive adjustments. This America becomes, as it must, post-arrogant, leaving behind the ethos of hyperhubris ingrained in Henry Luce's vision of America as teacher and preacher to the world.

The adjustments must start with a new vocabulary—a new way of talking about America's twenty-first-century place in the world. During its global ascendancy, culminating in the American Century, America was a giver to the rest of the world. America offered a model of democratic politics and a vital cultural style evident in distinctive architecture, music, literature, and even philosophy. And these were not loans, on which interest was charged, but gifts. There was no charge to a society that sought to emulate the American way, in the belief that this was indeed the best way.

The American ascendancy found sustenance in Emerson's dictum "Never imitate." This was necessary advice to a youthful civilization still in thrall to European ways. But that America no longer exists. In an After America world, Americans can profit by being takers as much as givers. Americans have the opportunity to receive the gifts of others, just as others once relied on the gifts of Americans. I am not saying that America should become a nation of imitators, in a reversal of Emerson's imperative—I am saying that America could benefit from an infusion of fresh ideas. An analogy from an earlier era in American history is instructive. Back in the 1930s, Supreme Court Justice Louis Brandeis envisioned state governments as "laboratories" for policy experimentation. As the country was shrinking, as the road system and telephone exchanges were patching communities together, Brandeis felt hopeful about the possibilities for states to learn from one another and for Washington, in turn, to learn from the states. This kind of thinking can inform life in an After America world and help make a bright path for America a reality. Only, in this case, the laboratories are not limited to the states of America—they include other nation-states, global cities, and global businesses.

One reason California remains so successful in the twenty-first century—its current fiscal ailments notwithstanding—is that it already thinks and behaves this way, as a shameless borrower and mixer of multicultural styles and habits. Americans everywhere need to take a cue from this and open their eyes to see how others are doing certain things better than they are. The world abounds in such examples, like the French health care system, the regional government city-state model of Stuttgart, flex-fuel cars in Brazil, and the wireless wonders of South Korea. If Americans continue to dismiss such examples, they are really only damaging their own prospects. Americans will have won this mental struggle when they come to accept that Henry Luce and others of his view, in tying America's progress and happiness as a civilization to the condition of America's global dominance, were profoundly wrong.

That is the beginning of After America enlightenment. The adjustment that

America must make to fare well in an After America world is a societywide one—there is no part of American life that can escape this world. That may sound daunting, but the process of adjustment can start with individuals, with families, with communities. Consider the issue of language, perhaps the most organic of all of humankind's creations. Americans tend to take it for granted that English is and always will be the lingua franca of the world. This is dangerous thinking. First of all, English's roots as a global language are not in the American Century but in the British one—the British Empire was the great fountainhead for the spread of English around the world; America was a free-rider beneficiary of the work that British educators did in places like India. Second, the lingua franca over the centuries has always been a reflection of the political, cultural, and economic powers that be—from the widespread use of Greek and Latin in ancient times to the use of Italian in European courts during the Renaissance, Spanish in the sixteenth and seventeenth centuries, and then French. With the collapse of the Soviet Union, use of the Russian language is waning in former imperial borderlands. English at first dominated the Internet, an invention hatched by American national-defense planners, but the traffic in non-English languages has now surpassed that in English. "English can hardly expect that its linguistic vogue will continue forever," the language historian Nicholas Ostler observed in *Empires of the Word*, his fascinating exploration of the rise and fall of languages over the millennia. Not even in America, he noted, can the dominance of English be assured, for "no law and no decree anywhere has ever yet stemmed the ebbing of a language tide." Nor is America immune from global trends changing the way in which English is spoken: In Singapore, for example, a hodgepodge known as Singlish, consisting of elements of English, Malay, and certain Chinese dialects, is emerging in the streets and popular culture. Such forms of "Asian English" inevitably will visit themselves on America as part of the rising global influence of Asian societies.

The good news is that learning a second language is the sort of thing that Americans, the younger the better, can do in their schools, even on their computers. Nobody has to wait for Washington to act. This can be thought of as risk insurance. Even those Americans who recoil from the very idea of an After America world are apt to entertain the possibility that this is the way things are going. It may be that the After America moment, the moment when it becomes undeniable that America is no longer number one, happens not in five or ten or fifteen years' time but in twenty-five years. A quarter century may seem like a long way away, but some important things in life are premised on that time horizon. "If I had a recommendation," Justice Breyer told me, "it would be that everybody in the United States learns one other language."

Some communities, concerned about the future well-being of their children, are taking matters into hand. The Wolftrap Elementary School lies in a verdant patch of Northern Virginia suburbia. On a rainy Tuesday afternoon, a classroom of first-graders greeted me with a bow. I was there to observe their Chinese-language class. The instructor, Bibi Kearney, a Taiwan native who came to America thirty years ago, told them the Chinese year of the pig was about to become the year of the rat. The students practiced the word for "rat"— *lao shu*—and distinguished it in tone from the word for "teacher"—*lao shi*. Then they practiced making firecracker sounds with their hands while singing *gong xi*—congratulations—to the tune of "Frère Jacques." For each grade at the school, this is the program: lessons twice a week, an hour for each lesson. It's not a lot, but it is a start. "China is quickly becoming a dominant player in the world economy, and I want my child prepared for that," one of the mothers told a *Washington Post* reporter.

Like language, personal finance is another controllable domain for After America adjustments. Professional money managers the world over think in an After America fashion, so why shouldn't young, middle-class folks who are at the early stages of assembling a portfolio in the stock market? "One of the concepts that we've had in our country for so long is that you should invest in this country," the Carlyle Group's David Rubenstein told me in our talk in his Washington office. "But if you want to make money, you probably ought to invest outside the country to some extent." Rubenstein, a Democrat who once worked in Jimmy Carter's White House, pointed, for example, to opportunities in Asian markets. In America, he noted, 93 percent of people over the age of twenty-one have life insurance, while in China the figure is a mere 8 percent. "As China gets wealthier, life insurance is going to boom." This is not a strategy of selling America short, as some hyperpatriots might say—it is a strategy of accepting the world as it is, a strategy of financial realism. One of the smartest money managers I know is an American expatriate, living in London, who made a fortune for himself and for his wealthy clients by investing early in post-Soviet Russia. Several years ago, he told me that he was opening up a new investment front in Brazil. Only rich people are eligible to invest in his particular funds, but small-fry investors can profit from opportunities in places like Brazil through retail mutual funds with relatively low initial-investment thresholds. Wage earners can lobby their benefits departments to broaden the menu of their 401(k) retirement plan choices to include a wider variety of international choices, beyond the usual fare of U.S.-oriented funds. If Brazil and China are viewed as too risky, then employees might be given a chance to invest in neighboring Canada, whose banking system is among the soundest in the world. The same thinking applies to the dollar. The dollar may not be fated to lose value relative to the euro and other major currencies, as it has been doing over the last few years, but even so, how much sense does it make to keep all of one's assets in one currency? In the After America world, savvy Americans will become smart hedgers of financial risk.

In other respects, adjustment to the After America world means not overreacting to changes that may feel more threatening than they actually are. The shift away from the traditional ethos of the melting pot toward a more multicultural world—the transition already so evident in California—is in this category. Surely there is no going back from an age in which an American can sit at home and watch satellite television programming from just about every metropolis on the planet. I grew up with the melting pot mind-set, and like many native-born Americans of my generation, I sometimes feel disoriented by its demise. Still, the multicultural society brings its rewards. I like being in American cities and suburbs where different languages are spoken on the street, even if I only understand fragments; I like the Southern California experience of dinner and a margarita or two in a Mexican restaurant, followed by a drive with the car radio set to a Spanish-language music station. I understand that this is a matter of personal taste, but even those more anxious than I am about the coming of multicultural America might reflect that the dire consequences predicted by so many analysts and politicians have yet to come to pass. While multiculturalism might make America more like Western Europe, Canada, and Australia, the After America version of the multicultural society will no doubt be distinctive.

One reason I expect a bright version of an After America world to win out is that Americans tend to be a practical-minded people. While they may linger in an illusory shadowland of power and prestige, eventually they will move on. Americans are not especially neurotic; they are not a nation of idle dreamers. American romanticism has never, blessedly, approached the level of European romanticism, which spilled over into fascism, the political embodiment of nostalgia at its most rancid. America has made strategic mistakes during its century, but it has never been suicidal, as Europe was in the first half of the twentieth century. And even though an imperial mentality has become more entrenched since the 9/11 attacks on the country, that mentality continues to reside mostly in the Washington political class and not among the people at large.

That said, the adjustment to the After America world is going to be tougher for some parts of America than for others. In general, young people, less set in their ways, should have an easier time than older folks. The cosmopolitan regions along the Pacific and Atlantic coasts may have an easier adjustment than the less globally aware American heartland (with an exception for the Chicago metropolis). Some institutions—political, economic, cultural—will feel more threatened than others, a point that is illustrated by the likely impact of After America trends on Red and Blue America, the large voting blocs claimed by the Republican and Democratic parties, respectively.

The After America world is most threatening to the Republican Party, because it is this party, the party of Red America, that is most deeply invested in the myth of American Exceptionalism. The party's most inspiring modern figure remains, by far, Ronald Reagan, who ascended to the presidency by embodying this myth, by declaring, as he did in a speech in Washington in the mid-1970s, to an audience of conservative political activists: "You can call it mysticism if you want to, but I have always believed that there was some divine plan that placed this great continent between two oceans to be sought out by those who were possessed of an abiding love of freedom and a special kind of courage." It followed directly from Reagan's presentation that it really could be, after all the centuries, "morning again" in America, that America was as young and pure as it ever was. Thus, one of the Reagan coalition's stalwart components is the Christian evangelical voter. That voter fits into a certain stream of the American narrative. She, let's say, has fused her religious and national identities. America, she believes, is a Christian nation, uniquely blessed by God. The song "God Bless America" is not only a prayer for the Almighty to look after the nation. It is a statement of faith that God *does* bless America, which is the reason why America, as a chosen country, a new Jerusalem, became as successful and powerful as it did. This set of beliefs is severely strained by the ebbing of American dominance. In the face of unimpeachable evidence of national decline, when a stubborn posture of denial is no longer possible, what can this person say to herself? Perhaps she will retain her religious faith, as the deepest part of her being, but reevaluate her belief in a political party that has not allowed for the possibility of America being anything other than number one. Perhaps she will retreat from politics altogether—there has always been a strand of Christian evangelical thinking that regarded politics as a tainted arena, best avoided by those who devote their lives to Christ. The prospect, in any case, is that the Republican Party could lose support from a crucial bloc.

The After America world also could present a crisis of faith for segments of the Republican Party's elite. What story do the neocons—the neo–Henry Luceans—tell themselves as Washington finds it ever more difficult to boss around lesser powers and manage America's "democratic empire"? At this point, they are deeply in denial, believing against all evidence that the planet is as enthralled with the American way of life as it has ever been. Like the Churchill wing of the British Conservative Party, the neocons could fade into oblivion, perhaps going out with more of a bang than a whimper, but going out anyway.

I don't mean to present the Republican Party as a doomed entity. In the short term, it stands to be the main beneficiary of any nostalgia boom that attends anxieties about America's ebbing global power. A Sarah Palin could have a future in that party, and the party's sympathetic organs in the media, like the hypernational Fox News channel, can be expected to promote such a boom for all it's worth. In the long term, it is conceivable that the wiser and cooler heads in the conservative movement, the ones who understand that America does not have a monopoly on all of the world's good ideas, could make their influence more deeply felt. David Brooks, the conservative-leaning op-ed columnist for the *New York Times*, has sensibly counseled conservatives in the United States to study the current example of British conservatives in building "a new global movement, with rising center-right parties" in Sweden, Canada, Australia, France, Germany, and the Czech Republic. "American conservatives won't simply import this model. But there's a lot to learn from it," Brooks suggested in a column, "The Conservative Revival." America's corporate boardrooms and investment banks contain Republicans with an appreciation of the After America world because they grasp that their businesses could die unless adjustments are made. The party's brain trust straddles the neocons and the opposing camp of the so-called realists—the foreign policy equivalent of the realists from the business world. Realists understand that the American Century was a product not only of certain qualities of American character but also of certain contingent circumstances in history, like the frailty of Europe. This camp readily accepts limitations on America's global capabilities; it does not believe, as Robert Kagan argues in his neocon interpretation of American history, that America has always been, and by implication always should be, a "dangerous nation," a force for intervening in global affairs on the side of liberal democratic values. George H. W. Bush's national security advisor, Brent Scowcroft, reflected the realist perspective in his futile advice to George W. Bush not to invade Saddam's Iraq. Foreign policy realism, a bipartisan tradition with philosophical roots in Old Europe, seldom held sway during the American Century, as Walter Lippmann often found to his frustration. As long as America was so clearly ahead of everyone else, the price of ignoring the realists, of acting as if America would be omnipotent for all time, was not an especially high one. But this will not be true of the After America world. For the Republican Party to stay relevant in this world, it will have to pay heed to its realists.

The Democratic Party ought to have an easier time of adjustment to the After America world. "Blue America" is much further along than "Red America" in its adaptation to America's waning global clout. There is already a cosmopolitan, secular stamp to the party elite and to the wealthier, better-educated Democratic voters in the cities and suburbs of Blue State America, from Boston to Seattle. A certain type of Democratic voter—the environmentalist, pro-choice, pro–gay rights, UN-embracing type of voter—has counterparts across the Atlantic on the European continent and in the British Isles, as well as in Canada, South Africa, and Australia. The party's traditional sources of progressive ideas are happily casting their eyes overseas for good policy solutions. The *New Republic* magazine was founded in 1914 by Herbert Croly, the Progressive Age author of *The Promise of American Life*, with a mission to provide readers "with an intelligent, stimulating and rigorous examination of American politics, foreign policy and culture." And for nearly a century, it has been doing just that, with the occasional embrace of neocon-like imperial ideas in the foreign policy arena. But these days, the magazine realizes, the American progressive cause might benefit from imported examples. In a 2007 article, "Great Danes," senior editor Jonathan Cohn touted Denmark's centrist welfare-state policies as a model for America. "Scandinavia's success has particular relevance today, when the Democratic Party suddenly finds itself with real political power again—and a mandate to address the rising economic insecurity that many American workers feel," Cohn noted. Likewise, at the *American Prospect*, a magazine founded in 1990 by leading progressive thinkers to offer a dose of "liberal intelligence," associate editor Ezra Klein advised Barack Obama, in the 2008 campaign season, that the "next time McCain goes off on the horrors of national health care," Obama should respond with a litany of the advantages of the French or the German health care systems over the current American one—systems with "lower infant mortality, high life expectancy, shorter wait times, the promise that no one will ever, ever, ever become uninsured," and all for less money.

Leading Democratic politicians, likewise, are more apt than Republican officials to acknowledge that lessons can be learned abroad. Hillary Clinton talks about what the Europeans do better on health care. New York senator Charles Schumer suggests that America's securities markets would be much better served by the London "single regulator" model of unified regulation than the Washington arrangement in which multiple regulators oversee different pieces of the markets. "To Save New York, Learn from London" was the headline for a column written by Schumer with New York City mayor Michael Bloomberg, a lifelong Democrat who switched parties when he ran for office and has since become an independent. Al Gore, as noted, has become a quintessential global person of the universal-civilization-in-the-making—a frequent scold to Washington on the environment, as is Jimmy Carter on human rights. As these examples suggest, the Democratic Party seems more likely to hatch global cosmopolitans who look beyond the problems of America to the problems of the planet as a whole. A future Bill Clinton, instead of dreaming of the day he would become the president of America, might instead imagine becoming president of the world.

At the same time, the After America world can be expected to nourish a new breed of voter—the postimperial voter—with a natural leaning toward the Democratic Party (and possibly also the Libertarian Party, which is seeking to siphon voters in favor of limited government away from the Republican Party by offering a platform vowing that there will be no more Iraq-like invasions to try to plant the flag of liberty in foreign soil). "I personally wouldn't mind being the second or third dog in the world," one such voter—a well-educated white woman who has lived in Southeast Asia and currently works for an educational institute in Santa Fe—told me, because then there would be less need to spend money on national defense and more money available for domestic programs.

President Obama, who emerged from the globally oriented, cosmopolitan wing of the Democratic Party, embodies certain After America themes. One is his call on Americans to follow Europeans and Indians in becoming bilingual or even trilingual as an imperative in a globalized world. "It's embarrassing when Europeans come over here, they all speak English, they speak French, they speak German," he said in a campaign appearance in Georgia in July 2008. "We should have every child speaking more than one language." On a conservative Web site, National Review Online, a critic correctly noted that "this is a very dramatic change from the position of American leaders for most of our history." There is a duality in Obama; he is capable of seeing the world with a global eye, not only an American national one. Certainly no American president, with the possible exception of Thomas Jefferson, who spent six years in Paris as ambassador to the France he so admired, has better credentials as a global citizen. Born in Hawaii to a white mother from Kansas and a black, Muslim father from Kenya, Obama spent part of his childhood in Indonesia and still speaks some "rusty" Indonesian. In his 2006 bestseller, *The Audacity of Hope*, Obama used U.S. policy toward Indonesia, which has included interventions in that country's internal affairs by CIA operatives, as an example of America's cultural blindness to the wider world. He is mindful of America's failure to match the rest of the postindustrial world in action to combat global warming. His foreign policy vision, while still evolving, appears to be a postimperial, multipolar one.

This can be seen in his pledge to withdraw American troops from Iraq and thus reduce the size of the American military footprint in the volatile Persian Gulf region. Obama also appears to be more accepting than are most Republican leaders of a role for Iran as a power broker in the Middle East. Nor does he seem as apt to confront the shift toward authoritarianism in Putin's Russia. With his apparent willingness to accept certain unpleasant but probably unalterable realities, Obama could prove the ideal president to help America make a graceful passage into a world that no longer lends itself to American domination.

His election, in any case, suggested a strengthening of the cosmopolitan segment of the Democratic Party—a segment that may be ripe for a boom. Consider, for example, how Democrats may be helped by an After America world defined by globally oriented cities. The analyst Rob Lang notes that of America's top twenty globally connected metropolitan areas—the regions, including the urban core and surrounding cities, most tied into the global economy—fifteen are Democratic voting strongholds, led by the top five: New York, Chicago, Los Angeles, San Francisco, and Miami. The Republican-leaning global cities are Atlanta, Dallas, Houston, San Diego, and Phoenix. Global cities, particularly in the British Isles, Northern Europe, North America, and Australia, tend to stress tolerance—for example, toward the gay community—and in America that ethos is stronger in the Democratic Party than in the Republican one. Meanwhile, metropolitan America continues to grow at the expense of more Republican rural America. In 1950, less than 50 percent of the country's population lived in major metropolitan areas; today, more than 80 percent live in them.

I don't mean to exaggerate the ease of Democratic adaptation to an After America planet. Democrats also face a challenge in adapting their party's policies and message to the economic realities of this world. The traditional blue-collar manufacturing worker—the kind of worker who helped Democrats put together their electoral majorities during the American Century—is a dying breed. The problem is not that the American manufacturing sector is globally uncompetitive but that manufacturers have had to shed workers to produce more widgets with less labor. Capital-intensive automated production processes drive this shift. It is the same inexorable trend that steadily reduced the share of farmworkers in the U.S. economy in the nineteenth century. And yet, Democratic political leaders have not leveled with base voters in Rust Belt areas like

Ohio, Pennsylvania, and Michigan on this unavoidable economic truth. Instead, politicians have blamed the decline in manufacturing's share of the workforce on phony issues like the North American Free Trade Agreement. The Democrats are playing to a nostalgic image of American industrial greatness, and if they take this play too far, they risk the fate of the British Labour Party, which nearly went to its grave in the decades after World War II by tying its political fortunes to the faded industrial glory of the Midlands.

Should either of the two major parties fail to adapt to the After America landscape, the opportunity will arise for a new party to take its place. Such events are rare in American political history—the last time a major new party was born was in the crisis atmosphere before the Civil War, when the antislavery, pro-tariff Republican Party of Lincoln was created from the ashes of the Whig Party. But the end of the American global ascendancy is a big enough event, with enough potential for crisis, to produce political change on this scale. The challenge for any party braving the currents of the twenty-first century is to replace the old myths of the American mission with a new myth that is faithful to the realities of the After America world while offering hope for America and Americans to prosper. The After America world awaits not a Merle Haggard, lamenting what used to be, but a twenty-first-century Walt Whitman, celebrating what can be.

As the challenges facing the political parties suggest, the institutions most likely to fare well in an After America world are those not held hostage to the mythology of American Exceptionalism and the fate of the American imperium. These institutions include not only Hollywood and Harvard but also Wall Street, the multinational corporation, and Silicon Valley. The British parallel is again instructive: The British Empire collapsed sixty years ago, but Oxford and Cambridge and the City of London, the capital's financial quarter, survived to become global institutions. So, too, America's centers of culture, education, and finance have the potential to thrive in the After America world, whether the future is a multipolar system of nation-states, a world of global city-states, a global government, or even a Chinese Century.

The toughest adjustments will be for the institutions of American empire. It will be hard on the army, marines, navy, and air force. And yet even within the military there have always been skeptics of the "only America" proposition—the idea that the world implodes into a dark chaos without an American Goliath to enforce the peace. "We have to step back from that world-policeman-type mentality," Col. Kenneth Stefanek, the vice commander of U.S forces at Incirlik Air Base in Turkey, told me. "There's too much blowback." The American armed forces have less of an investment in an imperial mission than did the soldiers of the British Empire. That should ease the pain of accommodation to an After America world, especially if the future is a multipolar world made up of rising powers like Brazil and India, which show an interest in working cooperatively with American forces even though they do not see themselves functioning as junior partners.

The most difficult accommodation of all will be for those at the nerve center of American empire, in Washington, D.C. Nearly seventy years have passed since Washington became "the capital of a World in the Making," as the publishing magnate W. M. Kiplinger called the city in the early 1940s. Whenever I am in New York or Los Angeles, I am reminded of how much less global Washington feels, notwithstanding its center-of-the-world pretensions. Still, the American Century has been good to Washington—so good that Washington doesn't really want to think about what comes next. The American Century has allowed research fellows at think tanks like the American Enterprise Institute to have a hand in world-altering events, like the war in Iraq. It has allowed senior civil servants at the Pentagon and the State Department to shape decisions on weapons systems and aid programs affecting every major continent on earth. It provided the dramatic material that the *Washington Post*, once a daily as sleepy and provincial as Washington was, used to turn itself into a world-class newspaper. It has helped make millionaires of the top lawyers, lobbyists, and public relations executives representing regimes from around the world, from Saudi Arabia to South Korea, for which good relations with the White House and the U.S. Congress are vital. And it was the American Century that made Washington the natural home for the World Bank and the International Monetary Fund and gave prestige to neighborhoods like Georgetown and Kalorama, favorite haunts of the diplomats and other foreigners who have flocked to Washington over the last six decades.

Given the scale of Washington's psychological and material investment in the American Century, a funk is unavoidable in the transition to the After America world. Sooner or later, Washington will have an "After Washington" moment—an unhappy flash of understanding that its global centrality is a thing of the past. New York and Los Angeles may escape that kind of "after" moment, with their vibrant roles in global commerce and culture, but Washington cannot because of how tightly its identity is bound to the image of superpower America. The institution of the presidency will suffer most. The imperial president is already, in some ways, an archaic figure. The "red phone" that the president is famously supposed to use in times of global crises is a relic of the cold war and no longer exists. The notion of the president as "leader of the free world" is a source of puzzlement in a place like India, the world's largest democracy, a nuclear power that regards itself, not America, as the guardian of its freedom. These clichés are staples of Washington's political class. Official Washington has attached itself to the fantasy that the president can make all the difference in history. Once it becomes clear—unmistakably clear—that the time of American hegemony is over, the mood inevitably will take a turn for the bleak at 1600 Pennsylvania Avenue and for all those invested in the power of that particular address.

The After America presidency will become a less glamorous institution, and the After America president, painfully aware of how the world looked to Harry S Truman for leadership at the dawn of the American Century, will be an especially ripe candidate for nostalgia. But there will be a historic opportunity, too, for this president to brave the political waters by telling the people some awkward but necessary truths. There seems to be an unspoken rule that no sitting American president can address the prospect of the United States no longer being number one in the world. Bill Clinton has addressed this possibility, but only after leaving office. In 2003, in a speech at the Yale Center for the Study of Globalization, Clinton talked about the need for creating "a world with rules and partnerships and habits of behavior that we would like to live in when we are no longer the only military, economic, and political superpower in the world." The historian Paul Kennedy was in the audience, and he later told me that he nearly fell off his chair at such a bald acknowledgment of America's prospects. One day, perhaps, a sitting president—Barack Obama?—will try to convey the dimensions of this change to the American people. There might be nothing in such a speech that the people will not have already sensed, but it would still be useful for them to hear the message from the nation's highest quarter. The speechwriters might suggest something like this:

My fellow Americans,

The history of America has sometimes seemed like one unbroken stride, from the first steps of the Pilgrims in the New World to the giant leap of Neil Armstrong when he became the first person to walk on the moon.

One of the lessons that history teaches, though, is that nothing is forever. What some call the American Century began in the ashes of the Second World War. With Europe on its knees, with Joseph Stalin's Communism a menace to the world, America filled a breach. Our economy, our culture, our military, all became dominant, our global influence reaching a peak with our victory in the Cold War.

Now history is entering a new phase. A wheel is turning. The era of American dominance is ending as the gap narrows between America and the rest of the world. This is not the fault of any one person, party, or faction in America; indeed, Americans can take pride in having helped to create the conditions by which the rest of humankind became more prosperous and better able to defend itself.

After all, it was never our mission to remain strong by keeping all others weak. Our experiment began as a city on a hill. We offered the world our example, which many chose to emulate. Others, though, have chosen to go their own way, and it is not our task to stop them. America was never meant to be the policeman of the world or the arbiter of all that is best in the world.

We do not know what will come after the American Century. Sometimes history pauses before forming a new order of things. It does seem certain, though, that the rising civilizations of the East, in places like China and India, which together comprise one-third of the world's population, are going to matter more than ever before in modern times. Our good friends in Europe also are adjusting themselves to this reality.

America has freely given much to the world. The world of the twenty-

first century has much to offer America. Our job now is not to look back,
because there is no profit in dwelling on what once was, but to cast our
eyes forward. We can learn from others, as others have learned from us.
Our best course for the future is an openness of mind, an openness of
spirit, and a curiosity about the great wide world beyond our borders.

Washington's dejected mood need not abide. Indeed, for some in the capital, the transition to the After America world could be a liberating one. The think tanks, which house an impressive amount of intellectual capital, could take on a more global orientation, as postimperial London's have done. So could the Washington fourth estate, also following the London example of devoting greater attention to the broader concerns of global journalism. And the American prospect, a staple concern of the Washington journalist, could be better understood for what it already is, a subset of the global prospect.

Congress might find a new lease on life. It wasn't the intention of Henry Luce to diminish the role of the legislative branch of government in the American Century, but that was the inevitable result of the rise of the Accidental Empire, with its emphasis on state secrecy and an all-powerful commander in chief, expected even by legislators to respond to national security crises with dispatch—with or without their approval. As America's global-policeman role fades, and especially if the After America world takes the form of a multipolar order of nation-states, Congress will have an opportunity to become a weightier actor in the political system—returning to the coequal role in government that the Founding Fathers intended for the legislative branch. Congress will be particularly relevant if postimperial America directs its energies away from foreign nation-building projects to domestically oriented ones, like reforming the nation's health care system; repairing the worn physical infrastructure of roads, bridges, and schools; and bringing the digital infrastructure up to global standards. After all, legislators feel more assured about addressing the needs of Appalachia than those of distant provinces of the Middle East.

Unlike London, Washington has never been a center of finance or a breeding ground for painters, novelists, and others in the arts. In that sense, postimperial

Washington will have fewer resources to draw upon than London did after the British Empire. Still, an After America Washington can be a draw for the global tourist, just as postimperial London and Vienna are to this day. After all, Washington's great memorials, like those commemorating Jefferson and Lincoln, are timeless marvels belonging to the world.

The world at the close of the first decade of the twenty-first century exists in a suspended state of in-betweenness. This quality of indeterminateness extends across several dimensions. One is geography: Is the planet in the process of shifting the main axis of influence toward Asia and away from both Europe and America? Another is a matter of political architecture: Is the nation-state, after a good long run, an exhausted form? Still another relates to ideology and social norms: Is the era of individualism, the Enlightenment goal of "the pursuit of happiness" as a supreme right of every human being, giving way to a revived ethos of communitarianism as a chastened planet recognizes its resource limits? Might it be that neither an enlightened form of individualism nor a sense of community-spiritedness will prevail, but rather a time of survivalism, defined by base animal energies?

The striking thing is how unresolved such questions remain. But these moments do not last forever. At some point—and it could be a while—one of the narratives for what might come next will take hold and begin to define at least the first phase of the After America world. Which narrative takes over is a matter of probabilities, the lifeblood of the betting man, and that is not a bad way to think about things.

Conventional wisdom suggests that, at least in the short term, the likeliest possibilities for the After America world involve a mixture of patches of dark chaos and the gradual transition to a multipolar world featuring rising powers like China, India, and (so long as oil prices don't collapse entirely) Russia, alongside America. In this standard appraisal of the future, the big question mark is Europe—whether a major economic power that hesitates to become a big military power can still be a top-rank geopolitical player in the world. Conventional wisdom is often right. Certain recent events seem to validate predictions of the coming of the multipolar world, such as Russia's effort to reestablish a traditional sphere of interest along its southern underbelly in the South Caucasus and Central Asia. My best guess is that Russia's actions will determine whether a multipolar world can take shape, in the near term, because it is the Kremlin more than any other ruling power that sees this kind of world as an urgent geopolitical priority for which it is willing to fight. In Washington, the Obama administration must make a strategic decision as to whether to accede to Moscow's pressure to withdraw U.S. troops from areas on the Russian periphery, like Kyrgyzstan in Central Asia. Should the global economic crisis severely weaken Russia, however, then the Kremlin's bid to make the world a more multipolar one is likely to be ruined as well.

Standard geopolitical thinking also leads naturally to the notion of a Chinese Century as a plausible replacement for the American one. The Chinese Century looks like an especially good bet if there should be a steeper-than-expected decline in America's global influence—the sort of vacuum that led Washington to take over for London after World War II. The point is not that the Chinese are a "master race" with a six-step plan for world domination, as suggested by fearmongers in Europe and North America. The case for the Chinese Century rests on the proposition that an After America multipolar world will prove to be an unstable formula for global order. The job of alpha dog would fall to the Chinese because no one else appears to be a plausible candidate. For all of India's economic and cultural dynamism and its determination to assert its military influence in the Indian Ocean region, Indians do not seem to conceive of themselves in this role; the prevailing attitude in India is of an anti-imperial kind. While Americans are also fond of regarding themselves as an anti-imperial people, America, as exemplified by the advocates of Manifest Destiny in the nineteenth century and kindred spirits like Henry Luce and the neoconservatives in the twentieth, has a crusading spirit that postcolonial India seems to lack. In contrast to India, Russia is by tradition comfortable with a role as a dominating great power, but there is only the slimmest of chances that Russia can become the global hegemon of the twenty-first century. Compared to China and India, Russia is an economic lightweight, and Russia tends to inspire fear more than fascination in the world. So if there is to be an After America global hegemon, surely it will be China.

The conventional thinking on the possibilities of the After America world has its limits. Its main limit has to do with what Thomas Kuhn described as the nature of paradigms in his landmark 1962 book, *The Structure of Scientific Revolutions*. In a critique of the scientific method, he described how scientists tend to become captive to a shared "constellation of beliefs" that at first yield significant insights but in time become shopworn. At some point, the prevailing paradigm is toppled by a fresh set of beliefs—and thus does science, in a distinctly nonlinear fashion, make progress. Kuhn's model relates to thinking about global affairs in the sense that such thinking is still profoundly shaped by a paradigm that places the system of nation-states at the center of things, with the allowance that a particularly powerful nation-state can become a global hegemon. This paradigm is a legacy of the creation of the nation-state system in the mid-seventeenth century. Much of what we think of as standard geopolitical thinking—of a world in which national armies, national economies, and national narratives compete for advantage—is derived from this paradigm. And this mind-set has had a powerful influence not only on analysts of global affairs but also on generations of practitioners.

The paradigm, at long last, is starting to splinter. "The age of nonpolarity" will follow U.S. dominance, Richard N. Haass, the president of the Council on Foreign Relations and a strategist for George W. Bush's State Department, strikingly wrote in the spring of 2008 in *Foreign Affairs*, the council's venerable flagship publication. By "nonpolarity" Haass does not mean a dark chaos. He means "a world dominated not by one or two or even several states but rather by dozens of actors"—nation-states but also global and regional organizations, big cities, militias, NGOs, religious institutions, multinational corporations, and others—"possessing and exercising various kinds of power." His essay represents the search for a new prism for understanding global affairs—a search that is helpfully if belatedly gathering momentum in the U.S. foreign policy establishment.

At the outset of this book, I suggested that an organic conception of history offered the most useful way of exploring the possibilities of an After America world. In this framework, the American ascendancy needed to be grasped not as the rise of a new democratic republic or even of a global empire but as something more encompassing and more elemental than either of these constructs: the rise of a civilization with a distinctive set of habits and beliefs. The end of the American ascendancy, as I argued in part 2, needs to be grasped in the same terms, as an ebbing of the American model as an ordering principle in global life. This is a multifaceted, long-term trend, and not a matter of a straight-line, across-the-board descent. Barack Obama's election in 2008 revived foreign regard for America as a land of democratic promise. It is doubtful, though, that the "Obama effect" will long endure. The political, economic, and cultural forces that have eroded America's primacy and given rise to middling America—from the country's severe indebtedness to its failure to keep pace with Europe in digital infrastructure and the development of the green society—reflect attributes of contemporary American civilization that cannot be easily changed, even by a charismatic leader who bids to become a transformative figure. As impressive as Obama's victory was, it came with only modest coattails in Congress and fell well short of the electoral landslides achieved in the twentieth century by Ronald Reagan, Lyndon Johnson, and Franklin Roosevelt. His triumph does not necessarily herald a new popular consensus on behalf of the governing philosophy of his party, the Democrats; there remain the sharp partisan political divisions that have long stymied substantial reforms in areas like health care. No president possesses the godlike power to reverse the currents of globalization that enable capital and labor to flow so easily around the world and help depress the wages of American factory workers. As for America's Accidental Empire, even a well-managed retreat from Iraq will still leave America with vulnerable imperial frontiers. Despite the efforts that Obama—Barack Hussein Obama—will make to improve relations between America and the Muslim world, he will still be captive, as are all American leaders, to the popular perception of America's being foremost a protector of the Jewish State of Israel.

As for what might come next, the organic perspective offers a useful way of orienting the After America conversation—useful, not least, because it throws into relief possibilities that barely get a passing mention if the framework is the traditional geopolitical mind-set on world affairs. In these terms, a happy chaos is worth taking seriously because it seems to be emerging in an unplanned way from the fruits of technological innovations that no one besides science-fiction writers thought could arrive with such a rush. Although I continue to be a skeptic, I must at the same time confess astonishment at how thoroughly the digital technologies of personal empowerment, like YouTube, have already upended establishment practices in areas like American politics. Modern society appears to be at the beginning, certainly nowhere near the end, of a revolution that, if things motor along, will destroy paternal institutions long thought necessary to keep a check on the human beast. A new flowering of the libertarian spirit, in the best sense, of each person as his or her responsible governor, might force biologists and anthropologists to rewrite what we think we know about human nature.

As I began gathering materials for this book, the idea that city-states could become the main organizing feature of an After America world was not on my horizon. My thinking was along more conventional geopolitical lines. But it didn't take long for me to become focused on city-states. No traveler in the twenty-first century can fail to notice the dynamism of today's global cities. While so many nation-states seem stuck in familiar, hidebound patterns, cities from Toronto to Dubai have turned themselves into global actors in a matter of decades. Modern energies seem concentrated in city-building projects in a way that they do not in nation-building or empire-building projects, with the major exception of China. Big cities are attracting a growing share of the world's population, in one of those long-wave trends that so interested organically focused historians like Braudel; and there is an intensifying competition among the cities for wealth and prestige. As cities devote more attention and resources to protecting their populations from terrorism and other scourges, they inevitably become more statelike in their character. City-states are being hurt by the global economic downturn, but no more so than are nation-states. City-states, I have come to think, are one of the great bets of the twenty-first century.

And so, too, is the universal civilization. "Hardheaded" geopolitical types tend to dismiss the notion of a universal civilization as a romantic ideal, but modern nationalism is no less of a romantic ideal, with its sentiment-laden celebration (literally lending itself to opera) of mythical bonds of blood and community. What is impressive is how far the universal civilization has evolved over the last half century or so. An embryonic, postnational civilization that can be said to include giant investment banks, major motion-picture studios, world-class universities, and preeminent nongovernmental institutions in pursuit of human rights and environmental action clearly is tapping some vital energies. While the possibility of a universal civilization generates considerable skepticism in America, which is still accustomed to thinking of its way of life as the model for emulation, this prospect is taken more seriously in Europe and

India. It is conceivable that the growth of transnational institutions that deepen linkages between city-states will, in the end, provide further impetus for the universal civilization by helping to foster a "global citizen" consciousness among the elites of the city-states. Like the narrative of ascendant city-states, the narrative of the rising universal civilization compels because it has the feel of a response to threats and opportunities posed by globalization—the single most powerful force of our time. Whereas nationalism often takes the form of a response to hold back the flood tides of globalization, the universal civilization seems more like an effort to accommodate and productively channel them. In this sense, the universal civilization may be rather well aligned with the currents of modernity.

The organic perspective suggests a certain fated quality to things—it may seem to allow too little scope for human actors to determine their futures. But while history is generally not made by the "great man," it is powerfully shaped by elites and by the collective impact of the choices made by masses of ordinary individuals. One important determinant of the answer for "what's next," after the American moment, will be the planet's young people. The vexing question of identity most urgently addresses those who are coming of age. Will their primary loyalty rest with the tribe, the nation, the city-state, some transnational group? Will many choose to become, with the aid of personal-empowerment technology, global nomads? Never before has the menu of possibilities been so rich.

As of this writing, at the start of 2009, the global economic crisis continues to rage. It is an unnerving event, inevitably fostering various predictions of "the end." The crisis, some say, heralds the end of American-style capitalism, the end of the Chinese miracle, the end of invented places like Dubai—even the end of globalization, as battered nation-states, city-states, big businesses, and other institutions retreat to their shores. My guess is that the crisis will not in itself usher in a new era of world history but rather hasten and in some cases retard certain trends already long in the making. In exposing frailties in the American model of lightly regulated capitalism, the crisis can be expected to speed the planet's passage into an After America world. The chaos narrative is already getting a boost from the political stress the crisis is placing on governments in Asia and Europe. While China's struggles to contain economic unrest at home may suggest that any Chinese Century will happen later rather than sooner, it also bears noting that China is using its massive cash reserves to replenish its stock of global commodities at bargain-basement prices. In the short run, the crisis may improve prospects for a multipolar world by stoking a sense of nationalism, or at least a sense of economic nationalism, as afflicted countries attempt to save their key industrial sectors with subsidies and trade protections. India, so far holding up fairly well, may emerge with an improved geopolitical position. But in the long run, the crisis seems more likely to demonstrate the principle that the twenty-first-century world is so helplessly interconnected that institutions of global governance are more vital than ever. The crisis suggests not a failure of globalization per se but a profound failure by the world to manage globalization. In that sense, the economic ashes may prove most nourishing of all for the future of the universal civilization.

Who wins and who loses in the After America world? In this chapter, I have wrestled with that question in terms of American society. It deserves to be addressed from a global perspective as well. In a dark chaos, the answer is not, as might be thought, losers everywhere on the planet. The winners, or at least the beneficiaries, will be the vultures of the world—in the financial area, for example, the short sellers, the hopers for the worst, who profit *only* when prices plummet. In a dark chaos, there will be many corpses to pick clean. The growing numbers of people around the world who already think in brute survivalist terms—who have stockpiled their supplies of canned food, bottled water, and antibiotics and dug their shelters—will be winners in the sense of having prepared for times that most others ridiculed them for predicting. Gold hoarders may feel smug. A happy chaos by contrast will reward those who are able to unbutton their collars and find their innermost Merry Prankster. Victory goes to those who can think and act laterally, defeat to those who can operate only in a world of hierarchies. Perhaps the patches of the planet that in the past have spawned interludes or at least ideologies of happy chaos—like Dada Zurich and Berlin after the First World War and Grateful Dead California of the 1960s— will prove especially fertile ground for a twenty-first-century variation of this type. Perhaps a happy chaos will flourish in Eastern societies, like India, with an ingrained skepticism of a world defined by power relations. More than anything else, winning in happy chaos will require a certain philosophical pre paredness.

In a multipolar world of nation-states, the biggest winners will be those states that can succeed in establishing regional hegemonies in their neighborhoods. The world's regional policemen might include the United States in North America; Brazil in South America; India and China in Asia; Russia in its "near-abroad"; possibly Iran in the Middle East (with Israel fending for itself); and South Africa in sub-Saharan Africa. Europe can be a winner if it finds the will to assert itself in this order. If not, Europe can expect to find itself increasingly encroached upon by other powers, like Russia. The losers will include weak small states—the Georgias of the world—that bank on protection against the local neighborhood bully—in Georgia's case, Russia—from an America no longer up to the task. The grimmest fate will await those peoples who feel themselves as a nation but are bereft a viable state. These are the Palestinians of the world, the many millions who live in what seem to be permanently failed states—states in name only. The multipolar world will likely be democratic in some regions and autocratic in others, according to the traditions of the neighborhoods—and in that sense, this world will represent a defeat for champions of liberal Western values as a universal standard. The multipolar world will be peaceful to the degree that the big players can arrive at satisfactory terms for coexistence.

China wins in a Chinese Century, but who else? Asian societies with a history of tense relations with the Chinese, including the Japanese and the Vietnamese, may be losers. India fears being a loser but may not be, given the protection afforded by its sheer size and the ways in which its economy complements China's. Distance may prove a blessing for the economies that succeed in developing profitable trade relationships with China—from the Pacific Coast of America to continental Europe. For resource-rich lands that China aims to exploit, like Chile with its copper treasure, much depends on whether China is disposed to be a benign or a cruel imperial ruler.

An age of global city-states as well as a universal civilization offers a chance for Europe to matter again, in a large way, because Europe is a font of the cosmopolitan values that would be ascendant in these worlds. But North Americans,

South Americans, and Asians are by no means dealt out. There would be tremendous opportunities for global elites—for architects, artists, business executives, university presidents, political leaders, global health specialists, and others who tend to live in big cities and who already are starting to think of themselves as a superclass. The multilingual person stands to do better than the monolingual one. Woe to those in the provinces, on the margin of things, and unable to think or operate in a global way.

As the After America world starts to take definition, the planet naturally will become less America-focused. For some, America's descent from the heavens will be cause for what the Germans call Schadenfreude, pleasure taken in another's pain. But as the world becomes accustomed to a new order of things, I suspect the enduring sentiment will be more like indifference. Our species tends to be heartless that way. I have in mind W. H. Auden's poem "Musée des Beaux Arts," a commentary on Pieter Breughel's sixteenth-century painting of the fall of Icarus. The usual lesson of this tale as one of youthful hubris, of the boy who ignored his father's warning not to fly too close to the sun on wings of feathers and wax, is not what interests the painter or the poet. In Breughel's canvas, the tragedy is presented as a scene from everyday life in which bystanders pay no heed to the suffering of Icarus, who is depicted flailing in the waters, in a bottom corner of the canvas. Auden picks up on this theme:

> . . . how everything turns away
> Quite leisurely from the disaster; the ploughman may
> Have heard the splash, the forsaken cry,
> But for him it was not an important failure; the sun shone
> As it had to on the white legs disappearing into the green
> Water; and the expensive delicate ship that must have seen
> Something amazing, a boy falling out of the sky,
> Had somewhere to get to and sailed calmly on.

Empires come and go; in time the world will sail "calmly on," indifferent to the fact that once upon a time there was an American epoch in global history. It is up to Americans to figure out how they can fit into a new phase of history. This is a huge task, full of pitfalls, and it is easy to see ways in which the job might be botched. The good news is that it is also possible to see ways in which Americans can make a graceful accommodation to an After America world—to see how we might move on, after the splash.

Acknowledgments

Time spent outside one's native land can be usefully jarring to the mind. From 1999 to 2003 I was based in Moscow as the bureau chief for *Business Week*; thanks to my editors over those years—Bob Dowling, Chris Powers, Patty Kranz, and Rose Brady—for allowing me to roam outside the usual confines of business coverage. This project took a more definite shape on my return to Washington, D.C., to write for *National Journal* and *Atlantic Monthly* magazines, which are part of the Atlantic Media family of publications. David Bradley, Atlantic Media's chairman and owner, supported my request for a leave of absence to write the book—and graciously provided me with an office at the Watergate. Thanks, too, to my editors—Charlie Green and Patrick Pexton at *National Journal* and James Bennet, Scott Stossel, James Gibney, and Don Peck at the *Atlantic*—for their support and encouragement. Cullen Murphy, formerly an editor of the *Atlantic*, backed my reporting on Russia in 2005. Atlantic Media invites efforts to think beyond the fury of the moment; there is no place in American journalism more welcoming of long-form writing on ideas and issues. The book proposal was based, in part, on a five-thousand-word essay, "Beyond Hegemony," I wrote for *National Journal* at the end of 2006.

My agent, Andrew Stuart, has the gift of an editor's eye and ear—and was always available for a friendly word of advice. My editor at Viking Penguin, Paul Slovak, offered many wise suggestions for improving the manuscript and displayed a gentle and patient hand in steering the project to its end. Sharon Gonzalez did a wonderful job of production editing. Shelley Sperry fact-checked the manuscript—I am responsible for any mistakes, I hasten to add—and Shelley and Teri Sperry helped compile the end notes.

A number of people assisted me in my travels. In Washington, thanks to Rahul Chhabra at the Indian embassy, Nan Li at the Chinese embassy, and Soner Cagaptay at the Washington Institute for Near East Policy. Thanks to Matthias Penzel and Constanze Stelzmueller in Berlin; Ludmila Mekertycheva and Catherine Belton in Moscow; Monica Tyszka and Steve Reifenberg in Santiago; Sabrina Tavernise, Sebnem Arsu, Rusen Cakir, Mahmut Kaya, and Capt. Rose Richeson, U.S. Air Force, in Turkey; Patricia McGourty Palmer in Dubai; and Vinay Diddee in India. Thanks to Marisa Katz for research in Israel and to Christian Caryl in Tokyo for help directing me to sources in Japan. Tarun Khanna at the Harvard Business School guided me to sources in India.

Thanks are due to friends and colleagues, including Peter Baker, Rich Cohen, Françoise Djerejian, Sydney Freedberg, Shane Harris, Corine Hegland, Margie Kriz, John Moore, Julia Nanay, Glenn Oeland, Alyssa Rosenberg, Burt Solomon, Bruce Stokes, Peter Stone, Jim Thomas, and Kirk Victor.

The Starobin clan wins gratitude for helping one of their own make it through the more stressful passages of his book-writing journey. My sister, Leslie, got into the creative spirit of the project and was ever willing to listen to my assorted peeves. Eran Segev cheerfully volunteered to read every page of a first draft—and he sent back the chapters with a raft of corrections, insightful comments, and suggestions for further research. At home, Nargiza, Samuel, Deora, and Babula held me together; I am lucky to have you. Cookie helped clear my head on our walks in Temple Park. Bob Dylan often kept me company in the car. "I'll know my song well before I start singin'," a line from his early work, felt like good advice for this first-time author.

Notes

Epigraph

vii *"And indeed there is a serious criticism here":* G. K. Chesterton, *What I Saw in America* (New York: Dodd, Mead and Company, 1922), p. 85.

Prologue

1 *The crowd flooded:* Oksana Yablokova, "Bringing Down the Glory of the KGB," *Moscow Times*, August 22, 2001.

1 *"The twilight descended":* "The Grand Opening of the Monument to F. E. Dzerzhinsky in Moscow," *Pravda*, December 21, 1958.

2 *desire to "shatter totalitarianism":* Gavriil Popov, *Again in Opposition* (Moscow: Galaxy Publishing House, 1994), p. 229.

2 *As legend has it:* Although Popov, Moscow's mayor in August 1991, helped to perpetuate this legend in *Again in Opposition*, he recently acknowledged in an interview that he was only on the scene briefly and "later I was told that the crane was brought from the U.S. embassy." Deputy Mayor Sergei Stankevich, who managed events at the square, said in an interview that he secured the cranes from an Austrian businessman. In an e-mail, James F. Collins, second in command at the U.S. embassy in Moscow at the time, said that he had reviewed matters and "I have now established that none of the top three people at the Embassy," himself included, had authorized the use of a crane to remove Iron Felix.

3 *"I am a World War Two veteran":* Deborah Seward, "Statue of Soviet Intelligence Chief Pulled Down," Associated Press, August 22, 1991.

3 *"to be part of":* John Lloyd, "The New Statesman Profile—Vladimir Putin," *New Statesman*, July 31, 2000.

3 *"We're only toddlers":* Boris Yeltsin appearance at National Press Club, Washington, D.C., June 20, 1991.

4   *"Should the United States want":* Aftab Iqbal, *Seatbelt* (Lahore: Pakistan Books, 1990), pp. 11–103.

4   *11:28 p.m. Moscow time:* Seward, "Statue of Soviet Intelligence Chief."

Introduction

5   *"Ours is the power":* Robert Edwin Herzstein, *Henry R. Luce: A Political Portrait of the Man Who Created the American Century* (New York: Scribner's, 1994), p. 178.

5   *a still-famous five-page editorial:* Henry R. Luce, "The American Century," *Life* 17 (February 1941), pp. 61–65.

5   *"equated a happy future with American hegemony":* Herzstein, *Henry R. Luce,* p. 24.

5   *"the powerhouse from which the ideals spread":* Luce's article is available in full in Michael Hogan, *The Ambiguous Legacy: U.S. Foreign Relations in the "American Century"* (New York: Cambridge University Press, 1999), pp. 11–29.

6   *In an essay published in the summer of 1989:* Francis Fukuyama, "The End of History?" *National Interest* 16 (Summer 1989), pp. 3–18.

6   *"the idea that the United States":* Chicago Council on Global Affairs 2007 poll at www.thechicagocouncil.org/media_press_room_detail.php?press_release_id=62.

7   *"is losing the central role":* "U.S. Court, a Longtime Beacon," *New York Times,* Sept. 18, 2008, p. 1.

9   *"more and more subject to uncanny delusions":* Thomas Mann, *Buddenbrooks,* trans. Helen Tracy Lowe-Porter (New York: A. A. Knopf, 1938), p. 561.

13 *Hence the bookstores:* A typical example is Jean Edward Smith's highly readable and impeccably researched *FDR* (New York: Random House, 1998). Smith begins the book by asserting: "Three Presidents dominate American history: George Washington, who founded the country; Abraham Lincoln, who preserved it; and Franklin Delano Roosevelt, who rescued it from economic collapse and then led it to victory in the greatest war of all time." The strongest claim is on behalf of Lincoln, all of whose presidency was consumed by crisis management of the gravest magnitude; he may be the rare exception of the indispensable man. As for Washington, he is best understood as part of an elite of Wise Men who helped found and maintain the Republic in its early days. FDR, for all his exceptional leadership skills, did not single-handedly rescue the country during the Great Depression, which ended only when America stoked up the economy to fight World War II. Nor is there any particular reason to believe that the United States, as the greatest industrial power on earth, would have lost the war without FDR's leadership. The Great Man rendering of history invariably becomes a form of hero worship.

14 *"the enormous mass of history"*: Fernand Braudel, *Capitalism and Material Life*, trans. Miriam Kochan (New York: Harper & Row, 1973), p. ix.

14 *He described history as an "ocean"*: Leo Tolstoy, *War and Peace: A Novel*, trans. Constance Garnett (New York: McClure, Phillips & Co, 1904), epilogue and p. 389.

14 *"When in doubt, my dear fellow"*: Leo Tolstoy, *War and Peace: A Novel*, trans. Ann Dunnigan and John Bayley (New York: Penguin, 1991), p. 896.

Part 1

19 *While the British monarchs had an interest:* Fernand Braudel and Richard Mayne, *A History of Civilizations* (New York: Penguin, 1995), p. 461.

19 *"feared that France might be depopulated"*: Ibid.

19 *"Just as England during the revolution"*: James M. McPherson, *Battle Cry of Freedom: The Civil War Years* (New York: Oxford University Press, 2003), p. 336.

Chapter 1

21 *"Dog's flesh is a dainty dish"*: Letter written in 1623 from Lincolnshire, England, quoted in Peter Bowden, ed., *Chapters from the Agrarian History of England and Wales, 1500–1750*, Vol. 1 (Cambridge: Cambridge University Press, 1990), p. 52.

21 *"This England grows weary"*: Quoted in Francis J. Bremer, *John Winthrop: America's Forgotten Founding Father* (New York: Oxford University Press, 2003), p. 158.

21 *"I wish oft God"*: John Winthrop, *The History of New England from 1630 to 1649* (Boston: Phelps and Farnham, 1825), p. 341.

22 *"at some future date"*: John F. Kennedy, speech, January 1961 (transcript available at www.jfklibrary.org/Historical+Resources/Archives/Reference+Desk/Speeches/JFK).

22 *"open to anyone with the will and the heart to get here"*: Ronald Reagan, speech, January 1989 (transcript available at www.reaganlibrary.com/reagan/speeches/farewell.asp).

23 *"Every civilization imports and exports"*: Braudel and Mayne, *A History of Civilizations*, p. 14.

23 *"rather like a railway goods yard"*: Ibid., p. 29.

24 *famous 1996 treatise:* Samuel P. Huntington, *The Clash of Civilizations and the Remaking of World Order* (New York: Simon & Schuster, 1996).

24 *"matter of willpower"*: Braudel and Mayne, *A History of Civilizations*, p. 458.

24 *"My means here are so shortened"*: Quoted in Alden T. Vaughan, *The Puritan Tradition in America, 1620–1730* (Hanover, N.H.: University Press of New England, 1997), p. 33.

24 *not only a religious proposition but also a business one:* David Underdown, *Fire from Heaven: Life in an English Town in the Seventeenth Century* (New Haven: Yale University Press, 1992).

26 *"melted into a new race of men":* J. Hector St. John de Crèvecoeur, *Letters from an American Farmer* (1782; reprint, New York: Fox, Duffield & Company, 1904), p. 55.

26 *"promiscuous breed":* Ibid., p. 51.

27 *"Africans and Europeans came here":* Transcript of Rice news conference with *Washington Times* editorial board, March 28, 2008.

27 *comically imitative:* W. J. Cash, *The Mind of the South* (New York: Knopf, 1974). Cash is described and his book excerpted in Edward L. Ayers and Bradley C. Mittendorf, *The Oxford Book of the American South: Testimony, Memory, and Fiction* (Oxford: Oxford University Press, 1997), pp. 75–86.

27 *"modern and economically successful system":* "Unchained by Idealism," *Washington Post*, June 20, 2007.

28 *commander of a militia regiment:* Bremer, *John Winthrop*, p. 261.

28 *including women, children, and the elderly:* Ibid., pp. 271–72.

28 *savagery of such events:* Ibid., p. 272.

28 *"He saw, and made people see":* Quoted in Peter Gay, *Voltaire's Politics: The Poet as Realist* (Princeton, N.J.: Princeton University Press, 1959), p. 26.

28 *Franklin was enormously proud:* Benjamin Franklin, *The Autobiography of Benjamin Franklin*, ed. Kenneth Silverman (New York: Henry Holt and Company, 1916), pp. 289, 296.

29 *"Thank heaven the American mind":* Letter to William Green Munford, June 18, 1799, in Jean M. Yarbrough, ed., *The Essential Jefferson* (Indianapolis: Hackett Publishing, 2006), pp. 193–95.

30 *"a barbarian":* John Quincy Adams, *Memoirs of John Quincy Adams* (Philadelphia: J. B. Lippincott, 1876), p. 546.

30 *"general equality of conditions":* Alexis de Tocqueville, *Democracy in America*, Vol. 1 (New York: Vintage, 1990), p. 3.

31 *"top 1 percent":* Edward Pessen, *Jacksonian America: Society, Personality, and Politics* (1969; rev. ed., Urbana: University of Illinois Press, 1985), p. 81.

31 *"the civilization of the future":* Ibid., p. 8.

32 *"Insist on yourself":* Ralph Waldo Emerson, *Essays, Lectures, and Orations* (London: William S. Orr and Co., 1848), pp. 45–46.

32 *"Where is the master":* Ibid., p. 45.

32 *"Doric or Gothic model":* Ibid.

32 *"ample geography dazzles the imagination":* Ralph Waldo Emerson, "The Poet," in *Essays and Lectures* (New York: Library of America, 1983), p. 465.

33 *"We have it in our power":* The *Thomas Paine Reader* (London: Penguin Classics, 1987), p. 109.

33   *"destined to be* the great nation *of futurity"*: John O'Sullivan, *Democratic Review* 6 (1839), p. 426 (italics in original).

34   *"God has predestinated"*: Herman Melville, *White-Jacket; or, The World in a Man-of-War* (1850; reprint, New York: G. P. Putnam's Sons, 1893), p. 144.

Chapter 2

36   *"Chicago, when it finally dawned on him"*: Theodore Dreiser, *The Titan* (New York: John Lane, 1914), p. 4.

36   *"French civilization is so above"*: Quoted in John Graham Brooks, *As Others See Us: A Study of Progress in the United States* (New York: Macmillan, 1908), p. 63.

37   *In 1840, the U.S. economy . . . and by 1905:* All statistics in this paragraph appear in Angus Maddison, *The World Economy: Historical Statistics* (Paris: Organisation for Economic Co-operation and Development, 2003), p. 47.

38   *"perhaps more responsible"*: Harry J. Carman and Harold C. Syrett, *A History of the American People* (New York: Knopf, 1960), p. 75.

38   *"a host of other questionable devices"*: Ibid, p. 94.

38   *"malpractices" that "have been carried on for a series of years"*: Quoted in ibid., p. 94.

38   *Wall Street grew to become second only to London:* John Steele Gordon, *An Empire of Wealth: The Epic History of American Economic Power* (New York: HarperCollins, 2004), p. 199.

38   *"New York never exhibited such wide-spread evidences of prosperity"*: Ibid., pp. 199–200.

39   *the Civil War "transformed Washington"*: Willard Monroe Kiplinger, *Washington Is Like That* (New York: Harper and Brothers, 1942), p. 123.

39   *"There were no weaklings in this selected company"*: Dreiser, *The Titan*, p. 10.

39   *"To a man with great social and financial imagination"*: Theodore Dreiser, *The Financier* (New York: A. L. Burt Company, 1912), p. 155.

40   *"He was the stuff great war heroes are made of"*: Chicago Rapid Transit System history at www.chicago-l.org/figures/yerkes.

40   *"Abandonment of the protective policy"*: Abraham Lincoln, *Speeches and Writings, 1832–1858* (New York: Library of America, 1989), p. 158.

41   *From 1870 to 1880 . . . from 1900 to 1913:* Maddison, *The World Economy*, p. 260.

41   *"One of the prime dangers of civilization"*: Theodore Roosevelt, "The World Movement," speech delivered at the University of Berlin, May 12, 1910.

42   *"Thank God I am not a free-trader"*: Theodore Roosevelt and Henry Cabot Lodge, *Selections from the Correspondence of Theodore Roosevelt and Henry Cabot Lodge, 1884–1914* (New York: Scribner's, 1925), p. 204.

42   *"These forty-odd years"*: Theodore Roosevelt, *The Roosevelt Policy* (New York: Kessinger Publishing, 2004), p. 216.

42   *took issue with virtually every aspect of the American "persona":* Anthony Trollope, *North America* (Philadelphia: J. B. Lippincott & Co., 1862), p. 24.

43   *"not a technical matter":* William James, *Pragmatism: A New Name for Some Old Ways of Thinking* (New York: Longmans, Green and Co., 1908), p. 4.

45   *"America will begin":* D. H. Lawrence, *Studies in Classic American Literature* (New York: Penguin, 1991), p. 14.

45   *"more than a religion; it was a summons to social activism":* Herzstein, *Henry R. Luce*, p. 26.

46   *"help ease China's passage into the modern world":* Ibid.

46   *"native Lucepower":* Ibid.

46   *"overpaid their coolies":* Ibid., p. 33.

46   *"smelly old prison":* James L. Baughman, *Henry R. Luce and the Rise of the American News Media* (1987; rev. ed., Baltimore: Johns Hopkins University Press, 2001), p. 13.

46   *"dressed in imperial white pith helmets":* Ibid.

46   *predicting "America's leadership of the world at the close of the European war":* Ibid.

47   *"the lame, the halt and the blind among nations":* Ibid.

47   *"If America were to accept the mandate":* Andrew Mango, *Atatürk: The Biography of the Founder of Modern Turkey* (New York: Overlook Press, 2002), p. 245.

48   *"Whereas their nation became in the 20th Century the most powerful":* Michael J. Hogan, *The Ambiguous Legacy: U.S. Foreign Relations in the "American Century"* (Cambridge: Cambridge University Press, 1999), p. 20.

48   *"If any permanent closer association":* Ibid., p. 18.

49   *"We need most of all":* Ibid., p. 26.

49   *"engineers, scientists, doctors":* Ibid., p. 27.

49   *"the nail on the head":* Herzstein, *Henry R. Luce*, p. 181.

50   *"the main premises of Western Art":* Quoted in Serge Guilbaut and Arthur Goldhammer, *How New York Stole the Idea of Modern Art* (Chicago: University of Chicago Press), p. 172.

50   *"America is one of those places":* Quoted in Braudel and Mayne, *A History of Civilizations*, p. 506.

50   *Was there no one willing:* Lippmann's perspective as a critic of the American Century gospel is explored by John B. Judis in *Grand Illusion: Critics and Champions of the American Century* (New York: Farrar, Straus & Giroux, 1992), pp. 76–88.

51   *"Great as it is, American power is limited":* Ronald Steel, *Walter Lippmann and the American Century* (Piscataway, N.J.: Transaction Books, 1999), p. 425.

52   *"You must realize we were not a worldly people":* Studs Terkel, *The Good War: An Oral History of World War Two* (New York: Pantheon, 1984), p. 250.

52 *"tore the guts out of the German army"*: Quoted in David Mayers, *The Ambassadors and America's Soviet Policy* (New York: Oxford University Press, 1995), p. 138.

Chapter 3

53 *"The principal imperialism"*: Max Lerner, *America as a Civilization: Life and Thought in the United States Today* (New York: Simon & Schuster, 1957), p. 208.

53 *"I can't believe that we can fight a war against fascist slavery"*: Quoted in Jesaiah Ben-Aharon, *America's Global Responsibility: Individuation, Initiation and Threefolding* (Great Barrington, Mass.: Lindisfarne Books, 2004), pp. 15–16.

53 *"no tampering with the Empire's economic agreements"*: Elliott Roosevelt, *As He Saw It* (Westport, Conn.: Greenwood Press, 1974), p. 37.

54 *"The plains of North America and Russia are our corn-fields"*: W. Stanley Jevons, *The Coal Question* (1865; reprint, New York: Macmillan Company, 1906), p. 411.

54 *"the Americans constructed a new kind of empire"*: John Lewis Gaddis, *We Now Know: Rethinking Cold War History* (New York: Oxford University Press, 1998), p. 289.

56 *"There are four hundred thousand Jews and forty million Arabs"*: Quoted in Walter Isaacson and Evan Thomas, *The Wise Men: Six Friends and the World They Made* (New York: Simon & Schuster, 1986), p. 452.

56 *"You win"*: Quoted in David McCullough, *Truman* (New York: Simon & Schuster, 2003), p. 607.

56 *"What do you mean 'helped create'?"*: Quoted in Michael T. Benson, *Harry S. Truman and the Founding of Israel* (Westport, Conn.: Greenwood Publishing Group, 1997), p. 189.

57 *"If a burglar breaks into your house"*: Robert Beisner, *Dean Acheson: A Life in the Cold War* (New York: Oxford, 2006), p. 348.

58 *"we are insulated by water against effective attack"*: Quoted in Manfred Jonas, *Isolationism in America, 1935–1941* (Ithaca: Cornell University Press, 1969), p. 70.

58 *"not an aberration but a culmination"*: Arthur M. Schlesinger, Jr., *The Imperial Presidency* (New York: Houghton Mifflin, 1973), p. 417.

59 *"What should we do about the Italian elections?"*: Quoted in Evan Thomas, *The Very Best Men: Four Who Dared: The Early Years of the CIA* (New York: Simon & Schuster, 1995), p. 11.

59 *"We are in a position in the world today"*: Schlesinger, *The Imperial Presidency*, p. 138.

60 *"severely crossed eyes"*: Richard Mervin Bissell, Jonathan E. Lewis, and Frances T. Pudlo, *Reflections of a Cold Warrior: From Yalta to the Bay of Pigs* (New Haven: Yale University Press, 1996), pp. 2–3.

61 *even though Bissell found Peabody to be something of a bully:* Ibid., pp. 4–6.

62 *Bissell worked as a consultant for the CIA:* Ibid., pp. 80–91.

62 *"I was not competent to handle relations with the Mafia":* Ibid., p. 157.

62 *Bissell was an architect of the anti-Castro Bay of Pigs invasion:* Ibid., pp. 59–63.

62 *"the end justified the means":* Ibid., p. 157.

63 *a supporter of Charles Lindbergh's prewar America First Committee:* Ibid., pp. 13–14.

63 *"publicity is the enemy of intellectual honesty, objectivity and decisiveness":* Ibid., p. 206.

65 *"The situation is being cured":* David Wise and Thomas B. Ross, *The Invisible Government* (New York: Random House, 1964), p.356.

65 *"The American people are entitled":* Ibid.

66 *"to get some of the people in these down-trodden countries to like us":* Quoted in Stephen Kinzer, *All the Shah's Men: An American Coup and the Roots of Middle East Terror* (New York: John Wiley and Sons, 2007), p. 158.

68 *"Throughout the world there is a fear":* Max Lerner, *America as a Civilization* (New York: Simon & Schuster, 1963), p. 61.

68 *"most of the world consented to the rise of American hegemony":* Emmanuel Todd and C. Jon Delogu, *After the Empire: The Breakdown of the American Order* (New York: Columbia University Press, 2003), p. 14.

70 *"I don't know him":* Quoted in Frank A. Ninkovich, *Modernity and Power: A History of the Domino Theory in the Twentieth Century* (Chicago: University of Chicago Press, 1994), p. 403, n. 57.

70 *"carrying out a routine mission":* Encyclopedia Britannica at www.nationmaster.com/encyclopedia/Gulf-of-Tonkin-Resolution.

70 *"how wisely, how gracefully, how skillfully":* Steel, *Walter Lippmann and the American Century*, p. 582.

71 *"I would thumb my nose":* Quoted in Stanley I. Kutler, *The Wars of Watergate: The Last Crisis of Richard Nixon* (New York: Norton, 1992), p. 603.

71 *"elaborate abstraction of ideas":* Quoted in Robert L. Hutchings, *At the End of the American Century* (Baltimore: Johns Hopkins University Press, 1998), p. 3.

72 *"Chinese competitiveness and expansionism":* Reprinted in Gearóid Ó Tuathail, Simon Dalby, and Paul Routledge, *The Geopolitics Reader* (New York: Routledge, 2006), p. 123.

72 *"we have become an imperial nation":* Irving Kristol, "The Emerging American Imperium," *Wall Street Journal*, August 18, 1997.

Part 2

76 *a British journalist posed the question:* J. L. Garvin, "The Maintenance of Empire: A Study in the Economics of Power," in Charles Sydney Goldman and Rudyard Kipling, *The Empire and the Century* (London: John Murray, 1905), p. 69.

Chapter 4

77 *"It isn't supreme"*: Henry James, *The Novels and Tales of Henry James*, Vol. 18 (New York: Charles Scribner's Sons, 1909), p. 119.

77 *"I met black people"*: Fernand Braudel, *The Identity of France* (New York: Harper-Perennial, 1992), p. 203.

77 *"America, still so young"*: Braudel and Mayne, *A History of Civilizations*, p. 459.

77 *"But let us not forget"*: Ibid., p. 505.

78 *"the powerhouse from which the ideals spread throughout the world"*: Luce in Hogan, *The Ambiguous Legacy*, p. 28.

79 *questions that "go to the heart of our identity as a nation"*: Katherine Bradbury and Jane Katz, "Are Lifetime Incomes Growing More Unequal?" *Regional Review* (September 2002), pp. 3–5.

79 *A 2007 study by the Pew Charitable Trusts:* Julia Isaacs, Isabel Sawhill, and Ron Haskins, *Getting Ahead or Losing Ground: Economic Mobility in America* (Washington, D.C.: Pew Charitable Trusts, 2007).

81 *"an apostle of Americanism"*: Ilya Ehrenburg, *Memoirs: 1921–1941* (Cleveland: World Publishing Company, 1964), p. 167.

81 *"a conspicuously distinctive American gift to the world"*: Felipe Fernández-Armesto, *Civilizations: Culture, Ambition, and the Transformation of Nature* (New York: Simon & Schuster, 2001), p. 438.

82 *"The best new airports in the world"*: Paul Goldberger, "Situation Terminal," *New Yorker*, April 21, 2008.

83 *"We can imagine a very young person forgetting"*: Chesterton, *What I Saw in America*, p. 183.

83 *"the American fountain pen has hardly got a start in Europe"*: Mark Twain, "Some National Stupidities," in Charles Neider, ed., *The Complete Essays of Mark Twain* (New York: Da Capo Press, 2000), pp. 660–61.

83 *"always alive, alert, up early in the morning"*: Ibid., p. 664.

84 *"cell phones can be used to pay for parking or lunch"*: Joshua Davis, "Hackers Take Down the Most Wired Country in Europe," *Wired*, August 21, 2007.

84 *"Happily for Western Europe"*: Nicholas Eberstadt and Hans Groth, *Europe's Coming Demographic Challenge* (Washington, D.C.: AEI Press, 2007), p. 21.

85 *examined conditions for which hospitalization is avoidable:* Michael K. Gusmano, Victor G. Rodwin, and Daniel Weisz, "A New Way to Compare Health Systems: Avoidable Hospital Conditions in Manhattan and Paris," *Health Affairs* 25 (2006), pp. 510–20.

86 *"Although it is now commonplace to bemoan Europe's demographic handicaps"*: Eberstadt and Groth, *Europe's Coming Demographic Challenge*, pp. 24–25, 35.

88 *the robot will be as central to digital life:* Bill Gates, "A Robot in Every Home," *Scientific American*, December 2006.

88 *a cultural love affair:* Timothy N. Hornyak characterized Japanese attitudes

toward the robot in an e-mail with the author and in his book, *Loving the Machine: The Art and Science of Japanese Robots* (Tokyo: Kodansha International, 2006).

91 *"the frontier has gone":* Frederick Jackson Turner, "The Significance of the Frontier in American History," address delivered at the American Historical Society in Chicago, July 12, 1893.

93 *"Tag may look OK":* Quoted in David Harsanyi, *Nanny State* (New York: Broadway Books, 2007), p. 153.

93 *"Is There a Place":* Quoted in ibid., p. 151.

93 *"even if the university wanted to honor recent graduate-veterans":* Richard Miller, "Why Don't Harvard Graduates Join the Military Anymore?" History News Network, October 24, 2005 (available at http://hnn.us/articles/16884.html).

95 *"the past is beginning to weigh on its shoulders":* Braudel and Mayne, *A History of Civilizations*, p. 459.

Chapter 5

96 *"One takes what one can get":* F. Scott Fitzgerald, "The Bridal Party," reprinted in Matthew J. Bruccoli, *The Romantic Egoists* (Columbia: University of South Carolina Press, 2003), p. 175.

96 *He began with the rise of the Western world:* Paul Kennedy, *The Rise and Fall of the Great Powers* (New York: Random House, 1987).

96 *"decision-makers in Washington":* Ibid., p. 515.

97 *"the age-old dilemmas of rise and fall":* Ibid., p. 540.

97 *"These are not developments":* Ibid.

97 *The Great Powers travel "on the stream of Time":* Ibid.

97 *"will see its relative power position ended":* Mapping the Global Future: Report of the National Intelligence Council's 2020 Project (Washington, D.C.: Government Printing Office, 2004), p. 15.

97 *"The likely emergence of China and India":* Ibid., p. 13.

97 *"In the same way that commentators":* Ibid.

98 *"at an accelerating pace":* "Reduced Dominance Is Predicted," *Washington Post*, Sept. 10, 2008.

98 *Paul Kennedy cast this predicament:* Kennedy, *Rise and Fall*, p. 515.

100 *"frontiers of insecurity":* Christopher Layne, *The Peace of Illusions: American Grand Strategy from 1940 to the Present* (Ithaca: Cornell University Press, 2006), p. 128.

101 *providing necessary "public goods":* Michael Mandelbaum, *The Case for Goliath: How America Acts as the World's Government in the Twenty-first Century* (New York: Public Affairs, 2005), p. 3.

101 *"The owner of a large, expensive":* Ibid., pp. 8–9.

101 *In a poll published in the spring of 2007:* World Public Opinion, 2007 (Chicago: Chicago Council on Global Affairs and WorldPublicOpinion.org, 2007), p. 30.

104 *"the indispensable power":* Madeleine Albright, interview by Ted Koppel, *Nightline,* ABC News, February 18, 1998.

104 *"moderation in war is imbecility":* Victor Davis Hanson, "What Are We Made Of?" *National Review Online,* September 11, 2001.

105 *"If you did anything":* Bernard Lewis, "Was Osama Right?" *Wall Street Journal,* May 16, 2007.

105 *"Thus I have had many 'Defense World' conversations":* Michael Vlahos, "The Fall of Modernity," *American Conservative,* February 26, 2007.

105 *"unlike the prestige of Rome":* Hogan, *The Ambiguous Legacy,* p. 53.

106 *"Those who argue the United States has no empire":* Juan A. Alsace, "In Search of Monsters to Destroy: American Empire in the New Millennium," *Parameters* (Autumn 2003), pp. 122–29.

106 *"His skin was the color of clay":* Robert Kaplan, *Imperial Grunts: The American Military on the Ground* (New York: Random House, 2005), p. 3.

109 *"Yes, I am quite certain that Italy will survive this war":* Joseph Heller, *Catch-22: A Novel* (1961; reprint, New York: Simon & Schuster, 1999), p. 229.

Chapter 6

111 *"The Russians have a disturbing effect on the peoples of the West":* Nicolas Berdyaev, *The Russian Idea* (Boston: Beacon Press, 1962), p. 2.

111 *It is "last bell" day:* The author visited the Aksaisky Military School in May 2006; this section and several other portions of this chapter are drawn from Paul Starobin, "Putin's Russia," *National Journal,* July 8, 2006.

114 *America's "imperialism of attraction":* Max Lerner, *America as a Civilization* (New York: Simon & Schuster, 1957), p. 61.

114 *"I was stunned":* George Bush, with Victor Gold, *Looking Forward* (New York: Doubleday, 1987), p. 233n.

116 *"being treated like laboratory rats":* Quoted in Janine R. Wedel, *Collision and Collusion: The Strange Case of Western Aid to Eastern Europe* (New York: Macmillan, 2001), p. 171.

117 *As Russians recovered:* Post-Soviet Russia's search for ideas and traditions from tsarist times is explored in Fiona Hill, "In Search of Great Russia: Elites, Ideas, Power, the State, and the Pre-Revolutionary Past in the New Russia, 1991–1996," doctoral dissertation, Harvard University, March 1998.

117 *"we are restoring the pillars":* Konstantin Azadovskii, "Russia's Silver Age: Yesterday and Today: Questions in the Void," in Heyward Isham, *Remaking Russia: Voices from Within* (Armonk, N.Y.: M. E. Sharpe, 1995), p. 89.

118 *"morality triumphing":* Paul Starobin, "Putin's Russia," *National Journal*, July 8, 2006, p. 24.

119 *"be of at least some small help":* Quoted in Christopher B. Daly, "Solzhenitsyn Ends Exile in Vermont," *Washington Post*, May 26, 1994.

119 *He praised the foreign policy of Vladimir Putin:* Adrian Blomfield, "Solzhenitsyn Accuses the West of Plotting to Surround and Undermine Russia," *Washington Post*, April 29, 2006.

120 *I once had the chance to talk:* The author's conversation with Father Tikhon, in Paul Starobin, "The Accidental Autocrat," *Atlantic Monthly*, March 2005.

122 *On a visit to Moscow:* The author's interview with Dmitri Medvedev in the Kremlin on May 31, 2007.

123 *"I hope that now the West learns a lesson":* Quoted in Anne Barnard, "Russians Confident That Nation Is Back," *New York Times*, August 15, 2008.

124 *"the Russian feeling for freedom":* Berdyaev, *The Russian Idea*, p. 144.

125 *"The people live":* Leo Tolstoy, *The Cossacks*, trans. Louise and Aylmer Maude for the University of Adelaide Library Electronic Texts Collection (available at http://etext.library.adelaide.edu.au/t/tolstoy/leo/t65co/chapter26 .html).

Part 3

129 *"We are on the extreme promontory of the centuries!":* F. T. Marinetti, "The Futurist Manifesto," *Figaro*, February 20, 1909 (available at www.cscs.umich.edu/ ~crshalizi/T4PM/futurist-manifesto.html).

130 *"doctrine of inevitability":* Quoted in Richard E. Beringer, Herman Hattaway, Archer Jones, and William N. Still, Jr., *Why the South Lost the Civil War* (Athens, Ga.: University of Georgia Press, 1986), p. ix.

Chapter 7

133 *"The only thing standing between order and chaos is us":* Trey Parker, Matt Stone, and Pam Brady, *Team America: World Police* (2004).

135 *Experts on nuclear proliferation assess:* Graham T. Allison, "How Likely Is a Nuclear Terrorist Attack on the United States?" Council on Foreign Relations online debate, April 20, 2007, at www.cfr.org/publication/13097/how_likely_is _a_nuclear_terrorist_attack_on_the_united_states.html.

135 *According to one such scenario:* Sydney J. Freedberg, Jr., "Surviving a Nuclear Attack on Washington, D.C.," Global Security Newswire, June 24, 2005 (available at www.nti.org/d_newswire/issues/2005_6_24.html#A0F258F9).

135 *"a permanent climate of fear in the West":* Jeffrey Goldberg, "On Nov. 4, Remember 9/11," *New York Times* (op-ed), September 9, 2008.

136 *"Think Swiss Family Robinson":* Barton Biggs, *Wealth, War and Wisdom* (New York: John Wiley & Sons, 2008), p. 333.

137 *"in this large workshop called the New World":* Quoted in Oscar and Lilian Handlin, *From the Outer World* (Cambridge, Mass.: Harvard University Press, 1997), p. 6.

139 *The American military arrived:* The author visited Turkey in October 2007 to gather material for this book; all interviews with sources in Turkey are from this period. The U.S. Air Force granted permission to visit the Incirlik Air Base and provided the author with a tour and briefings.

141 *each as much as ten times more powerful:* Eben Harrell, "Are US Nukes in Europe Secure?" *Time,* June 19, 2008.

142 *"We will become civilized":* Quoted in Mango, *Atatürk,* p. 434.

143 *Public opinion surveys indicate that a sense of religious identification:* "Muslims in Europe," *Pew Global Attitudes Project,* July 2006 (available at http://pew global.org/reports/display.php?ReportID=254).

143 *The surveys also suggest:* Brian J. Grim and Richard Wike, "Turkey and Its (Many) Discontents," *Pew Global Attitudes Project,* October 25, 2007 (available at http://pewresearch.org/pubs/623/turkey).

147 *"The Jews, once settled in their own State":* Theodor Herzl and Jacob de Haas, *A Jewish State: An Attempt at a Modern Solution of the Jewish Question* (New York: Maccabaean Publishing Co., 1904), p. 98.

147 *"history shows both big and little decadences":* Jacques Barzun, "Toward the Twenty-First Century," *The Culture We Deserve: A Critique of Disenlightenment* (Middletown, Conn.: Wesleyan University Press, 1989), p. 163.

148 *"the last best hope of earth":* Abraham Lincoln, "Annual Message to Congress," December 1, 1862, in *Speeches, Letters, Miscellaneous Writings, Presidential Messages and Proclamations* (New York: Library of America, 1989), p. 415.

148 *"The end of an empire is messy at best":* Randy Newman, "A Few Words in Defense of Our Country," *Harps and Angels* (2008).

148 *"When we go under, Western civilization goes under":* Tom Tancredo, in the Republican Primary Debate, Columbia, South Carolina, May 15, 2007.

149 *the Antichrist is head of the European Union:* John Hagee, *Jerusalem Countdown* (Lake Mary, Fla.: Strang Company, 2006), p. 151.

149 *"Critics of U.S. global dominance should pause":* Niall Ferguson, "A World Without Power," *Foreign Policy* (July/August 2004).

149 *"violent, tormented, bewildered, suffering and disintegrating age":* Barbara W. Tuchman, *A Distant Mirror: The Calamitous 14th Century* (New York: Knopf, 1978), foreword.

150 *"They had lost their fortunes, their savings":* Quoted in George J. W. Goodman, "The German Hyperinflation, 1923," *Commanding Heights,* PBS (available at

www.pbs.org/wgbh/commandingheights/shared/minitext/ess_german hyperinflation.html).

150 *India would "fall back quite rapidly"*: Winston S. Churchill, "Our Duty in India," speech at Albert Hall, London, March 18, 1931. In *His Complete Speeches, 1897–1963*, p. 5007, from The Churchill Centre online: www.winstonchurchill .org/i4a/pages/index.cfm?pageid=1191.

150 *"I think it's so groovy now"*: Quoted in David J. Fekete, *A Rhapsody of Love and Spirituality* (New York: Algora Publishing, 2004), p. 284.

152 *"Now they are putting up barriers"*: Reported in Randal C. Archibold, "Far from Home, Mexicans Sing Age-Old Ballads of a New Life," *New York Times*, July 6, 2007.

153 *Chaos was an integral part of the formula:* Thomas K. McCraw, *Prophet of Innovation* (Cambridge, Mass.: Harvard University Press, 2007), prologue.

154 *"a monster country"*: George F. Kennan, *Around the Cragged Hill: A Personal and Political Philosophy* (New York: W. W. Norton, 1994), p. 143.

154 *"there is a real question"*: Ibid., pp. 149–50.

154 *"There can be no doubt of the closeness"*: Quoted in Thomas Naylor, Vermont Commons Web site, www.vtcommons.org/journal/2005/08/thmas-naylor-george-f-kennan-godfather-vermont-independence-movement.

154 *"wherever something is wrong, something is too big"*: Leopold Kohr, *The Breakdown of Nations* (New York: Routledge, 1986), p. xxiii.

155 *the year "2020 is filled with nomadic people in a constant flow"*: See Marcel Bullinga, Futurecheck blog, http://futurecheck.blogspot.com, May 4, 2006.

155 *"In a solar future, your mode of transportation"*: U.S. Department of Energy, "Solar History Timeline: The Future" (available at www1.eere.energy.gov/solar/solar_time_future.html).

156 *"who is himself enlightened and has no dread of shadows"*: Quoted in David Wootten, *Modern Political Thought: Readings from Machiavelli to Nietzsche* (Indianapolis, Ind.: Hackett Publishing, 1996), p. 576.

156 *"Immaturity is the inability to use one's understanding"*: Quoted in ibid., p. 573.

Chapter 8

158 *"The world must be multipolar; domination is unacceptable"*: Dmitri Medvedev, address on Russian television networks, August 31, 2008.

161 *"I wish to make a plea to the people and government of India"*: Martin Luther King, Jr., *The Autobiography of Martin Luther King, Jr.* (New York: IPM/Warner Books, 2001), chap. 13 (available at www.stanford.edu/group/King/publica tions/autobiography/chp_13.htm).

162 *"the spirit of this country is totally adverse to a large military force"*: Thomas Jefferson, letter to Chandler Price, Feb. 28, 1807, in *The Writings of Thomas Jeffer-*

son, Vol. 11 (Washington, D.C.: Thomas Jefferson Association of the United States, 1905), p. 160.

162 *"such a humiliating defeat":* Rohinton Mistry, *Such a Long Journey* (New York: Vintage Books, 1992), p. 9.

164 *"By all means":* Vice Admiral K. K. Nayyar, ed., *Maritime India* (New Delhi: National Maritime Foundation, 2005), p. 2.

165 *"string of pearls" strategy:* Christopher J. Peterson, *String of Pearls: Meeting the Challenge of China's Rising Power* (Carlisle, Penn.: Strategic Studies Institute, 2006).

166 *"I have a theory":* Nayyar, *Maritime India*, p. 19.

167 *"a treacherous and slippery people":* Quoted in Louis J. Smith and Edward C. Kefer, eds., Foreign Relations of the United States, 1969–1976, Vol. 11, *South Asia Crisis, 1971* (Washington, D.C.: Bureau of Public Affairs, 2005), p. 265.

167 *"a mass famine":* "Indians 'Bastards,' Indira 'Old Witch,'" *Tribune* (Chandigarh, India), online edition, June 30, 2005, www.tribuneindia.com/2005/20050630/world.htm#1.

172 *"Our choice of materials is poor":* Nayyar, ed., *Maritime India*, p. 238.

172 *"a tree hollowed by termites":* Arun Shourie, *Will the Iron Fence Save a Tree Hollowed by Termites?* (New Delhi: ASA Publications, 2005).

174 *"I don't really care about Gandhi":* Quoted in Edward Luce, *In Spite of the Gods* (New York: Doubleday, 2007), p. 33.

174 *"conceptual products":* Alan Greenspan, address at the Stanford Institute for Economic Policy Research Economic Summit, Stanford, California, February 27, 2004 (available at www.federalreserve.gov/Boarddocs/Speeches/2004/200402272/default.htm).

176 *Franklin Roosevelt, who during World War II courted:* Correspondence in Susan Butler, ed., *My Dear Mr. Stalin: The Complete Correspondence of Franklin D. Roosevelt and Joseph V. Stalin* (New Haven, Conn.: Yale University Press, 2005).

176 *"The French are enamored with the notion":* Hubert Védrine, "Recasting Sovereignty: France in a Globalized World," Brookings Institution, Center on the United States and Europe, 4th Annual Raymond Aron Lecture, November 15, 2007.

177 *"hooded hordes swarming":* T. S. Eliot, *The Waste Land and Other Poems* (New York: Harcourt, 1962), p. 43.

177 *"Aspiring sincerely to an international peace":* The Constitution of Japan (available at the Solon Law Archive: www.solon.org/Constitutions/Japan/English/english-Constitution.html).

180 *a great power of "global ambition":* Michael Rubin, "Iran's Global Ambition," *Middle Eastern Outlook*, American Enterprise Institute Online, March 17, 2008, www.aei.org/publications/pubID.27658/pub_detail.asp.

182 *"popular nationalism, which grew from the grass roots":* Norman Davies, *Europe: A History* (New York: Oxford University Press, 1996), p. 814.

182 *"It would not, I think, be an exaggeration"*: Quoted in Athena S. Leoussi, ed., *Encyclopedia of Nationalism* (Edison, N.J.: Transaction Publishers, 2001), p. 18.

Chapter 9

187 *"The leader of the pack"*: Vicky De Gruy, "Who's in Charge Here?" Chow Chow Welfare Society Web site, www.chowwelfare.com/cciw/alpha.htm.

188 *"Art's New Superpower"*: Barbara Pollack, "Art's New Superpower," *Vanity Fair,* December 2007.

192 *Chile is, by far:* Data on the Chilean copper industry drawn principally from the 2007 *Chilean Mining Compendium,* published for *Minería Chilena* magazine (Santiago). Translation from Spanish for the author by Monica Tyszka. According to the report, "Chile has the largest mineable copper reserves in the world, with more than 250 million tons of fine copper representing 38 percent of the world's total mineable copper. The United States has the second biggest reserves, with about 77 million tons."

193 *"faithful dog of the Yankee bosses"*: Ernesto Guevara, *Motorcycle Diaries: Notes on a Latin American Journey* (New York: Ocean Press, 2004), p. 79.

194 *In 1970, direct private investment: Covert Action in Chile, 1963–1973,* 94th Congress, Staff Report of the Select Committee to Study Governmental Operations with Respect to Intelligence Activities, December 18, 1975 (available at http://foia.state.gov/Reports/ChurchReport.asp).

200 *"the oceans are our lifelines"*: Gordon Fairclough, "Warship-Buying Spree Prompts New Worry in Washington, Tokyo," *Wall Street Journal,* July 16, 2007.

201 *As commander in chief of the Chilean army:* Lois Hecht Oppenheim, *Politics in Chile: Socialism, Authoritarianism, and Market Democracy* (New York: Basic Books, 2007), p. 242.

202 *In one survey taken in 2007 by an American polling firm:* Pew Global Attitudes Project, *2007 Survey,* June 27, 2007 (available at http://pewglobal.org/reports/display.php?ReportID=256).

207 *"Both people in America and people in Europe"*: Tony Blair, April Monthly Press Conference, April 17, 2007 (available at www.number10.gov.uk/Page11484).

207 *"History has never been produced in the South"*: Henry Kissinger to Gabriel Valdés, quoted in Jussi Hanhimäki, *The Flawed Architect: Henry Kissinger and American Foreign Policy* (New York: Oxford University Press, 2004), p. 101.

208 *"China's influence is almost universally viewed"*: Andrew Kohut, "How the World Sees China," Pew Global Attitudes Project, December 11, 2007 (available at http://pewresearch.org/pubs/656/how-the-world-sees-china).

209 *"there are morally legitimate alternatives"*: Daniel A. Bell, *Beyond Liberal Democracy: Political Thinking for an East Asian Context* (Princeton, N.J.: Princeton University Press, 2006), p. 8.

210 *"history we shall never forget":* Japanese War Crimes Web site: http://century
china.com/wiihist.

210 *"I really, really hate the Japanese":* Quoted in "The Scars of Nanking: Memories
of a Japanese Outrage," *Independent,* December 13, 2007 (available at www
.independent.co.uk/news/world/asia/the-scars-of-nanking-memories-of-a-
japanese-outrage-764827.html).

Chapter 10

215 *"The city should produce good men":* Quoted in Lauro Martines, *Power and
Imagination: City-States in Renaissance Italy* (New York: Taylor & Francis,
1988), p. 65.

216 *"France would be much more powerful":* Jean-Jacques Rousseau, *Émile; or, On
Education* (New York: Basic Books, 1979), p. 469.

217 *embodying the trend he described:* Richard Florida, *The Flight of the Creative
Class: Why America Is Losing the Competition for Talent—and What We Can
Do to Win Prosperity Back* (New York: HarperCollins, 2005).

218 *"The major international flows of people":* Yuwa Hedrick-Wong, ed., "The Dy-
namics of Global Cities and Global Commerce," *MasterCard Worldwide Centers of Commerce Insights,* 2nd quarter 2007 (corporate report), p. 3 (available at
www.mastercard.com/us/company/en/wcoc/pdf/insights_Q2_2007.pdf).

219 *"The most future-oriented country in the world":* Quoted in Mansour Javidan,
"Forward-Thinking Cultures," *Harvard Business Review* (July–August 2007).

220 *"A new urban global community is emerging":* Michael Bloomberg, "The City
Club," *The Economist, The World in 2008* (available at www.economist.com/
theworldin/unitedstates/displayStory.cfm?story_id=10093999&d=2008).

223 *"Workers lived on damp ground in rough, crowded, filthy huts":* Robert K. Massie,
Peter the Great (New York: Ballantine Books, 1986), p. 360.

224 *"city built on bones":* Ibid., p. 361.

224 *"Petersburg will not endure":* Quoted in ibid., p. 364.

228 *"The guiding philosophy of HMI":* "Our Origin and History," Partners Harvard
Medical International Web site, www.hmi.hms.harvard.edu/about_us/over
view/index.php.

229 *"One day, all cities will be built like this":* Quoted in "Lord Norman Foster to
Speak at World Future Energy Summit," Maktoob Business Web site, July 31,
2007, http://business.maktoob.com/NewsDetails-20070423117295-Lord_Nor
man_Foster_to_speak_at_World_Future_Energy_Summit.htm.

230 *"If the lowest orders of society earn enough food":* Quoted in John Arthur Gar-
raty and Peter Gay, *The Columbia History of the World* (New York: Columbia
University Press, 1972), pp. 496–97.

235 *"LV is the world's largest ad-hoc exchange":* Robert F. Lang, "Is Las Vegas a

World City?" Presentation at the Urban Land Institute meeting, October 26, 2007 (available at www.mi.vt.edu/web/page/957/sectionid/569/pagelevel/2/interior.asp).

235 *"They played precisely the role that"*: Peter Hall, *Cities in Civilization* (London: Phoenix Giant, 1998), p. 61.

235 *"People who are socially 'marginal'"*: Ibid., p. 17.

236 *On the principle that "anywhere is home"*: Weiner, Edrich, Brown, Inc., Issues Analysis, Working Paper, Distribution—March 2000.

241 *"The small ruling councils"*: Martines, *Power and Imagination*, p. 60.

241 *"the abyss of the human species"*: Rousseau, *Émile*, p. 59.

Chapter 11

242 *"The universal civilization has been a long time in the making"*: V. S. Naipaul, "Our Universal Civilization," *New York Times*, November 5, 1990.

243 *"Because he possesses everything"*: Quoted in Catherine Lu, "World Government," *The Stanford Encyclopedia of Philosophy*, Fall 2008 edition (available at http://plato.stanford.edu/entries/world-government).

245 *"We don't have the same moral and legal framework as the rest of the world"*: Debate between Antonin Scalia and Stephen Breyer, U.S. Association of Constitutional Law, American University, January 13, 2005 (full transcript online at www.freerepublic.com/focus/f-news/1352357/posts).

245 *I later met with Breyer*: The author interviewed Justice Breyer in his Supreme Court chambers on June 14, 2007.

249 *Brown called for a "global system of financial regulation"*: Quoted in "Gordon Brown to Set Out Regulation Plan at UN Assembly," *Irish Times*, September 22, 2008.

251 *Winston Churchill mocked the idea of a war crimes tribunal*: Reported in "Churchill: Execute Hitler Without Trial," *Sunday Times*, January 1, 2006.

252 *The Universal Declaration of Human Rights*: Eleanor Roosevelt, "Adoption of the Declaration of Human Rights" (1949), available on the Franklin and Eleanor Roosevelt Institute Universal Declaration of Human Rights Web site at www.udhr.org.

253 *According to the rules by which it operates*: International Criminal Court Web site at www.icc-cpi.int/about.html.

253 *The Pinochet case spurred Henry Kissinger to write an essay*: Henry Kissinger, "The Pitfalls of Universal Jurisdiction: Risking Judicial Tyranny," *Foreign Affairs* (July/August 2001) (available at www.globalpolicy.org/intljustice/general/2001/07kiss.htm).

254 *"When an international court determines"*: Quoted in Clare Murphy, "Banning the Freedom to Deny," BBC News Web site, February 7, 2007, http://news.bbc.co.uk/2/hi/europe/6336513.stm.

255 *"ecology and economy are becoming ever more interwoven"*: Gro Harlem Brundtland, chair, *Our Common Future: Report of the World Commission on Environment and Development* (New York: U.N. General Assembly, 1987) (available at
http://habitat.igc.org/open-gates/wced-ocf.htm).

256 *"When we try to pick out anything by itself"*: John Muir, *My First Summer in the
Sierra* (1911), reprinted in *The Eight Wilderness Discovery Books* (London: Dia-
dem Books, 1992), p. 248.

256 *"In the middle of the 20th century"*: Brundtland, *Our Common Future.*

258 *"What we are going to have to put in place"*: Quoted in Marc Gunther and Adam
Lashinsky, "Al Gore's Next Act: Planet-Saving VC," *Fortune*, February 12, 2008.

258 *"I am realizing more and more that we don't live on an island"*: John Burnett,
"Mayors Take Action as Texas Slacks on Climate," *All Things Considered*, November 26, 2007.

259 Students *"intuitively realize that the world"*: Ruth Gaare Bernheim, quoted in
David Brown, "For a Global Generation, Public Health Is a Hot Field," *Washington Post*, September 19, 2008.

259 *"Harvard honors public service"*: Quoted in "Commencement Confetti," *Harvard Magazine* (July 2007).

259 *"all knowledge is a whole"*: John Henry Newman, *The Idea of a University Defined and Illustrated* (London: Longmans, Green, and Co., 1905), p. 99.

260 *As late as the mid-1960s:* J. Edgar Hoover, "The U.S. Business Man Faces the
Soviet Spy," *Harvard Business Review* (January/February 1964).

263 *"Islam does not recognize boundaries"*: Quoted in Jane Perlez, "Taliban Leader
Flaunts Power Inside Pakistan," *New York Times*, June 2, 2008.

263 *"and manages to advance a powerful counter ideology"*: National Intelligence
Council, *Mapping the Global Future* (Washington, D.C.: Government Printing Office, 2004); also available at www.dni.gov/nic/NIC_globaltrend2020.
html.

264 *"a new race of men"*: Crèvecoeur, *Letters from an American Farmer*, p. 55.

266 *"selected, trained and commanded"*: "World Politics Favor New Powers for the
UN," May 9, 2007, at www.worldpublicopinion.org.

266 *"giving the UN the power"*: "World Poll Finds Global Leadership Vacuum," June
16, 2008, at www.worldpublicopinion.org.

Part 4

Chapter 12

273 *"We are a nation-state"*: Quoted in Karen Breslau, "We Are a Nation-State,"
Newsweek online (2007), www.newsweek.com/id/35586.

275 *"It would seem that the White race alone"*: Quoted in Sarah Mytton Maury,
The Statesmen of America in 1846 (New York: Cary and Hart, 1847), p. 64.

275 *"a certain egalitarianism":* Kevin Starr, *California: A History* (New York: Random House, 2007), p. 226.

276 *"We have but one flag":* Quoted in Richard M. Hogg and David Denison, *A History of the English Language* (New York: Cambridge University Press, 2006), p. 417.

276 *"very rarely spoke German to anyone":* Reported in "Hispanic Leaders Blast Schwarzenegger's Advice to Turn Off Spanish TV," Fox News online, June 15, 2007, www.foxnews.com/story/0,2933,283099,00.html.

276 *"read the L.A. Times, even though you don't understand it":* Reported in John Wildermuth, "Latinos Reject Governor's English-Immersion Advice," SFGate (*San Francisco Chronicle* Web site), June 16, 2007, www.sfgate.com/cgi-bin/article.cgi?f=/c/a/2007/06/16/BAGG3QGLFN1.DTL.

280 *he warned that the "ethnic upsurge" had become "a cult":* Arthur M. Schlesinger, Jr., *The Disuniting of America: Reflections on a Multicultural Society* (New York: W. W. Norton, 1998), p. 49.

280 *California was a prime target:* Ibid., p. 74.

280 *"no history curriculum in the country":* Ibid., p. 101.

280 *78 percent of Californians:* "California Dreamers: A Public Opinion Portrait of the Most Diverse Generation the Nation Has Known," *New America Media* (April 2007), http://media.newamericamedia.org/images/polls/youth/ca_youth_poll_presentation.pdf.

281 *As John Kenneth Galbraith would later write:* John Kenneth Galbraith, *The New Industrial State* (1967; reprint, Princeton, N.J.: Princeton University Press, 2007).

281 *"one of the bibles of my generation":* Steve Jobs, Commencement Address, Stanford University, June 15, 2005 (transcript available at http://news-service.stanford.edu/news/2005/june15/jobs-061505.html).

282 *"California has more Nobel Laureates":* Arnold Schwarzenegger, State of the State Address, Sacramento, California, January 9, 2007 (transcript available at http://gov.ca.gov/press-release/5089).

283 *"if the scale of a country renders it unmanageable":* Gar Alperovitz, "California Split," *New York Times*, February 10, 2007.

283 *A ranking by the global-cities experts:* Peter J. Taylor and Robert E. Lang, *U.S. Cities in the World City Network* (Washington, D.C.: Brookings Institution, 2005).

285 *"quiet, peaceful, industrious, economical":* Quoted in Ronald Takaki, *Iron Cages: Race and Culture in Nineteenth-Century America* (New York: Knopf, 1979), p. 219.

285 *"It was a mob that fought the battle of Lexington":* Mrs. Ana Smith, quoted in Patricia Nelson Limerick, *The Legacy of Conquest: The Unbroken Past of the American West* (New York: W. W. Norton, 1988), p. 264.

285 *"everyone who is not of white blood":* Ibid., p. 261.

286 *"we live in an increasingly interconnected world":* The Stanford mission statement can be found online at http://giving.stanford.edu/get/layout/tsc/The StanfordChallenge.

287 *"the Hollywood Jews were deliriously patriotic":* Neal Gabler, *An Empire of Their Own: How the Jews Invented Hollywood* (New York: Doubleday, 1989), p. 372.

292 *"Multiculturalism should not just mean":* Department of Immigration and Ethnic Affairs, *National Consultations on Multiculturalism and Citizenship* (Canberra: Australian Government Publishing Office, 1982), p. 1.

292 *An editorial of the time:* Quoted in ibid., p. 4.

293 *A U.S.-based pollster found:* "U.S. Image Up Slightly, but Still Negative," Pew Global Attitudes Project survey, June 23, 2005 (available at http://pewglobal .org/reports/display.php?PageID=801).

Conclusion

295 *"But what else is life but endless lending and borrowing, give and take?":* Kurt Vonnegut with Daniel Simon, *A Man Without a Country* (New York: Seven Stories Press, 2005), p. 35.

295 *"There is no One America anymore":* Mark Penn with E. Kinney Zelesne, *Microtrends: The Small Forces Behind Tomorrow's Big Changes* (New York: Hachette Book Group, 2007).

295 *"America is facing an identity crisis":* E Pluribus Unum: The Bradley Project on America's National Identity (June 2008), pp. 42 and 8 (available at www .bradleyproject.org/bradleyprojectreport.html).

296 *"great nation of futurity":* John L. O'Sullivan, "The Great Nation of Futurity," *Democratic Review* (1839).

296 *"Where did America go?":* Merle Haggard, "What Happened?" *The Bluegrass Sessions* (2007).

298 *"agrarian, conservative, anti-industrial":* John Crowe Ransom, "Reconstructed but Unregenerate," in *I'll Take My Stand: The South and the Agrarian Tradition* (New York: Harper & Brothers, 1930), pp. 26–27.

298 *Politics in a democracy, Emerson once said:* Ralph Waldo Emerson, "The Conservative," lecture delivered in Boston, December 9, 1841.

300 *"English can hardly expect":* Nicholas Ostler, *Empires of the Word: A Language History of the World* (New York: HarperCollins, 2005), p. 549.

303 *"You can call it mysticism if you want to":* Ronald Reagan, speech at the Conservative Political Action Conference, Washington, D.C., January 25, 1974.

305 *"a new global movement":* David Brooks, "The Conservative Revival," *New York Times*, May 9, 2008.

305 *as Robert Kagan argues:* Robert Kagan, *Dangerous Nation: America's Place in the World, from Its Earliest Days to the Dawn of the 20th Century* (New York: Knopf, 2006).

305 *George H. W. Bush's national security advisor:* Brent Scowcroft, "Don't Attack Saddam," *Wall Street Journal*, August 15, 2002.

306 *"Scandinavia's success has particular relevance today":* Jonathan Cohn, "Great Danes," *New Republic*, January 15, 2007.

306 *"next time McCain goes off on the horrors of national health care":* Ezra Klein, "What Clinton Should Demand," *American Prospect* blog, May 8, 2008, www .prospect.org/csnc/blogs/ezraklein_archive?month=05&year=2008&base_ name=thought_of_the_day_3.

306 *"To Save New York, Learn from London":* Wall Street Journal, Nov. 1, 2006.

322 *"how everything turns away":* W. H. Auden, "Musée des Beaux Arts," in Edward Mendelson, ed., *W. H. Auden: Collected Poems* (New York: Random House, 1976), p. 147.

Index

Abu Dhabi, 90, 221, 223, 229
Acheson, Dean, 55, 59–61, 63, 65
Adams, Carl, 51–52
Adams, John, 29, 30
Adams, John Quincy, 30, 106
Afghanistan, 6, 93, 100, 107, 109, 138, 139, 141, 158–59, 176, 177, 227
   Soviet invasion of, 58, 64, 71, 75
Africa, 53, 89, 98, 134, 182, 208, 241, 321
After America era, 7, 9–15, 127–323
Ahmadinejad, Mahmoud, 147
airports, 82, 297
Akgun, Eylem, 143
Aksaisky Military School, 111–12, 119
Albright, Madeleine, 104
Alexy II, Patriarch, 119
Allende, Salvador, 194, 199, 202, 250
Alperovitz, Gar, 283
al-Qaeda, 107, 137, 138, 141, 144, 183, 226, 254
Alsace, Juan, 105–6
Alsop, Susan Mary, 59
America:
   Accidental Empire of, 10, 53–72, 136, 297, 313, 317
   in After America era, 295–322
   ascendancy of, 5–7, 10, 13, 17–72, 298
   character traits of, 21–35
   cultural myopia of, 99–100, 166
   economic preeminence of, 36–42
   economy of, 7, 79–80, 98–99, 135, 203–5, 211, 217, 297
   end of ascendancy of, 6–10, 12, 13, 7–125, 316
   as global policeman, 100–104, 156, 183, 254, 310, 313

   Imperial Presidency in, 57–59, 64, 66, 69, 70, 71, 311
   middling status of, 77–95, 317
   military of, 78, 93, 100–101, 108, 109, 134, 135, 259, 278, 310
   missionary purpose of, 22, 35
   South in, 298
America as a Civilization (Lerner), 53, 68
America I Have Seen, The (Qutb), 137
American Century, 5, 8–9, 11, 37, 45–52, 57–59, 63, 65, 66, 69, 71, 76, 78, 97, 114, 134, 136, 206, 242, 278, 298, 305, 310, 311, 313
   California and, 274–81, 288, 292
"American Century, The" (Luce), 5, 48–49, 51–52, 105
American colonies, 19, 21–22, 24–30, 37, 175
American Dilemma, An (Myrdal), 68
American Exceptionalism, 19, 31–35, 36, 49, 78, 245, 247, 283, 303–4, 309
American Prospect, 306
Amnesty International, 244, 251, 252–53
Apple Computer, 281, 285
Arbenz Guzmán, Jacobo, 62, 65
architecture, 43, 81–82, 243, 298, 321
Argentina, 188–89
Around the Cragged Hill (Kennan), 154
art, 32, 34, 50, 188, 243, 313, 321
Astana, 229
Atatürk, Mustafa Kemal, 142–45
Atlanta Journal-Constitution, 3
Auberge Espagnole, L', 264–65
Auden, W. H., 322
Australia, 6, 86, 101, 185, 292–94, 305, 308
automobiles, 80, 83, 90, 91, 192
Awati, M. P., 166